*The publisher and the University of California Press
Foundation gratefully acknowledge the generous support
of the Constance and William Withey Endowment
Fund in History and Music.*

Imperial Wine

Imperial Wine

HOW THE BRITISH EMPIRE MADE
WINE'S NEW WORLD

Jennifer Regan-Lefebvre

UNIVERSITY OF CALIFORNIA PRESS

University of California Press
Oakland, California

© 2022 by Jennifer Regan-Lefebvre

Library of Congress Cataloging-in-Publication Data

Names: Regan-Lefebvre, Jennifer, author.
Title: Imperial wine : how the British empire made wine's new world /
    Jennifer Regan-Lefebvre.
Description: Oakland, California : University of California Press, [2022] |
    Includes bibliographical references and index.
Identifiers: LCCN 2021028951 (print) | LCCN 2021028952 (ebook) |
    ISBN 9780520343689 (hardback) | ISBN 9780520975088 (ebook)
Subjects: LCSH: Wine and wine making—Colonies—Great Britain. |
    Viticulture—Colonies—Great Britain. | Wine and wine making—
    Australia. | Wine and wine making—New Zealand. | Wine and wine
    making—South Africa. | Wine industry—History.
Classification: LCC HD9381.5 .R34 2022 (print) | LCC HD9381.5 (ebook) |
    DDC 634.80941—dc23
LC record available at https://lccn.loc.gov/2021028951
LC ebook record available at https://lccn.loc.gov/2021028952

Manufactured in the United States of America

28 27 26 25 24 23 22
10 9 8 7 6 5 4 3 2 1

Dedicated with love to Judith Murray Regan and
Richard M. Regan, Jr.

CONTENTS

ILLUSTRATIONS

MAPS

FIGURES

ACKNOWLEDGMENTS

Qui Transtulit Sustinet is the motto of the state of Connecticut: he who transplanted still sustains. The accompanying state shield, designed in the 1930s, shows three grape vines laden with heavy fruit. This emblem is illustrative of the main argument of this book, that British settler colonialism looked to viticulture to demonstrate civilizational progress. It is also apt to the book itself: when I began researching this topic in Cambridge in 2011, I did not imagine that the book and I would be transplanted multiple times. She who transplanted, sustained, and finally finished.

When extroverts write long, interdisciplinary books, there are many people to thank. My first debts are to Peter Mandler and Hugh Johnson. Peter encouraged me to throw aside the predictable (and ponderous) book I had been researching, and to write this one instead. *Placet,* Peter. Hugh Johnson asked me to do a bit of historical research for him in 2012. This was not a fair transaction: I learned an enormous amount from Hugh's generous mind, and I think he learned very little from me. For this, and for warmly encouraging me to write a history of London as the center of the global wine trade, I thank him.

In Cambridge, I am thankful to Peter de Bolla, with whose blessings I joined the King's College Wine Committee, which was an extraordinary education. For collegiality, friendship, and encouragement at King's, I thank all the fellows and staff, and especially Rowan Rose Boyson, Daniel Wilson, Victoria Harris, Brian Sloan, Tim Flack, David Good, Nicholas Marston, Robin Osborne, Megan Vaughan, Mark Smith, Peter Young, Richard Lloyd Morgan, and Tom Cumming. In the Faculty of History, I am thankful for stimulating discussion with Eugenio Biagini, Lucy Delap, Ben Griffin, Tim Harper, Renaud Morieux, Richard Serjeantson, Sujit Sivasundaram, and Emma Spary. Very special thanks to Alex Walsham, for her kindness and friendship, and to Jon Lawrence, who has great taste in wine. I am grateful to the Huntington Library Trinity Hall Fellowship, which allowed me to spend a month at Trinity Hall in 2017. I am particularly thankful to Jeremy Morris, Clare Jackson, Alexander Marr, Michael Hobson, William O'Reilly, and Colm McGrath, who made me so welcome.

In Paris, I thank Kerstin Carlson and Cary Hollinshead-Strick, for many laughs and for solidarity in scholarship. I thank fellow writers Olivier Magny for getting me into wine, and Frédéric Vigroux for teaching me to wield a sabre. For further wine-related chats, I thank Marissa Ocasio and my WSET tasting team, Kristin Cook Tarbell and Erin O'Reilly.

In Hartford, at Trinity College, I thank my colleagues in the Department of History, past and current: Clark Alejandrino, Zayde Antrim, Jeff Bayliss, Sean Cocco, Jonathan Elukin, Dario Euraque, Luis Figueroa, Scott Gac, Cheryl Greenberg, Joan Hedrick, Sam Kassow, Kathleen Kete, Michael Lestz, Seth Markle, Gary Reger, Allison Rodriguez, and Tom Wickman. Special thanks to modern superhero Gigi St. Peter. In the Dean of Faculty's office, I have been grateful for the unwavering support of Sonia Cardenas, Anne Lambright, Melanie Stein, Mitch Polin, Taku Miyazaki, and Tim Cresswell. Joanne Berger-Sweeney frequently encouraged me to write this book—by which I mean, finish this book. It paid off! I raise a glass of Ruinart to Cornie Thornburgh, for encouragement. Ben Carbonetti and Kristin Miller hosted my most productive writer's retreat, and chapter 10 is thanks to them.

Trinity College's Faculty Research Committee and Institute of Interdisciplinary Study awarded me multiple travel and manuscript grants, without which I could not have written this book.

Teaching at a small liberal arts college, I have been grateful to students in my British and wine history classes, who have been great sports about reading my work in progress. For their insightful comments, I particularly thank Matthew Benedict, Ansel Burn, Brendan Clark, Claudia Deeley, Kit Epstein, Tate Given, Macy Handy, Kip Lynch, Maia Madison, Tess Meagher, Daniel Mittelman, Gillian Reinhard, and Anthony Sasser. I also am grateful for the Public Humanities Collaborative and the Faculty Research Committee for funding undergraduate research assistants to work with me in the summers. Jaymie Bianca, Masho Strogoff, Doris Wang, and Kyrè William-Smith all read drafts of the book and offered me their honest feedback; thanks to Rich Malley and Cynthia Riccio for partnering with me on this summer project. Tanuja Budraj and Federico Cedolini helped me to organize thousands of archival photos. The brilliant Haley Dougherty spent hours poring over

South African trade data with me and entering it into Excel. A glutton for punishment, she gave up a day at the beach to help me work through archives in South Australia.

Librarians and archivists are wonderful, and I am grateful to all who have helped me track down material, in person and online. A few deserve special mention: Yannick and Steve in Microfilms at Archives Canada, and Agneiszka Ochal and Sam Percival for their assistance (and for giving me a bouquet of flowers!) at Murray Edwards College. At Trinity, huge thanks to Rick Ring, Erin Valentino, Peter Rawson, Sally Dickinson, Sue Denning, Jason Jones, Christina Bleyer, Angie Wolf, Cait Kennedy, and Mary Mahoney. Cheryl Cape is in a class of her own, for so much help over the years, and for creating the maps in this book using ArcGIS.

Material in this book was shared at many conferences and seminars and I thank both convenors and participants for their helpful feedback: at Yale, thanks to Tim Barringer, Becky Conekin, and Paul Freedman; at the Northeast Conference of British Studies meetings, particular thanks to Lucy Curzon, Paul Deslandes, Caroline Shaw, Lacey Sparks, and Brian Lewis; at the University of Sheffield, thanks to Phil Withington; at Queen's University Belfast, thanks to Daniel Roberts, Peter Gray, Maeve McCusker, and of course, Sean Connolly; at the University of Adelaide, thanks to Kym Anderson, Mariah Ehmke, Florine Livat, Vincent Pinilla; at the University of Wollongong, thanks to Clare Anderson, Rosalind Carr, Jessica Hinchy, Ruth Morgan, and Frances Steel; in Bordeaux, thanks to Julie McIntyre, Corinne Marache, Stéphanie Lachaud, Mikaël Pierre, Jennifer Smith-Maguire, Kathleen Brosnan, and Steve Charters.

I thank those who gave me feedback on chapters and early drafts: Rachel Black, Renée Dumouchel, Isaac Kamola, Caroline Keller, Reo Matsuzaki, Garth Myers, Dario del Puppo, Ethan Rutherford, Emiliano Villanueva, and Nicholas Woolley. Special thanks are reserved for those who read the full draft: Sarah Bilston, Elizabeth Elbourne, Seth Markle, Beth Notar, Judith Murray Regan, Stephen Bittner, and Dane Kennedy. Their generous and incisive comments improved the text. Naturally, I take responsibility for any errors that may remain.

My editor, Kate Marshall, has been a stalwart. Her insight and understanding have been invaluable. I also thank Enrique Ochoa-Kaup, for his unflappable professionalism.

Some friends and colleagues defy easy categorization. Richard Toye, Tim McMahon, James Golden, Graham Harding, Jacqueline Dutton, Chelsea

Davis, Chad Ludington, Michael Ledger Lomas, Christopher Hager, Hillary Wyss, Beth Casserly, Michelle Kovarik, Serena Laws, Michael Grubb, Jack Gieseking, and Ann Mah have all assisted on multiple occasions. The wonderful staff at TC4 have given me the peace of mind to work: special thanks to Tonee Corlette, for always asking me about the progress of my book. Thanks to my dear friends (and frequent research trip hosts) Caoimhe Nic Dháibhéid and Colin Reid, Justin and Aleks Jones, Joanna Brennan and Simon Rawlings, Tom and Rachael Davis, and Fionnuala and James Lodder.

Many have suggested that my research for this book involved drinking lots of wine. If only! I began working on this project in 2011 and welcomed Fiona in 2013, Felix in 2016, and Loïck in 2020. In hindsight, it was an audacious idea to write a history of wine that requires international travel whilst raising three tiny children. I also had not planned on a global pandemic, and it is my great regret that I was not able to travel to South Africa due to family circumstances and then travel restrictions. What I was able to do, was because of my loving family. I thank my sisters, Deirdre Lockard and Colleen Regan, my children, and above all, my husband, Thomas, who took on heroic stretches of single-parenting so that I could travel and write. Finally, my parents, Judi and Dick Regan. They have always supported my research career, but they have really come into their own as grandparents. This book is dedicated to them.

Introduction

ON A LATE SUMMER'S DAY in 1886, grape pickers at Dalwood Vineyards in Australia's Hunter Valley paused to be photographed. The men wore slouch hats, waistcoats, and cotton shirts with the sleeves rolled up, the women heavy skirts and cotton bonnets to shield their faces and necks from the searing sun. They picked together, collecting the grapes in gallon buckets, which were emptied into a wooden barrel on a cart drawn by a single pack horse. The grapes—black verdot, golden shiraz, and black hermitage—were grown head-high, espaliered in neat rows. The vineyard's soil is pale and dusty in the sepia photographs and only a few towering date palm trees break up the monotony of the vines. The surrounding land is scrubby and bland, with no concessions to ornamental gardening: this is a commercial operation, not a tourist attraction (see fig. 1). John Wyndham, the vineyard's owner, boasted that at seventy-eight acres and growing, through "judicious and intelligent expenditure of capital," the vineyard could support his large family comfortably and also employ dozens of families in seasonal work.[1] The Wyndhams and their workers were British settlers whose families had made the three-month ocean journey to the Antipodes in search of a better life. John Wyndham now had one of the largest wineries in the Australian colonies and was rich and respectable. He valued his estate at £20,000 and his wine stock at ten thousand,[2] and he was proud of what his family had achieved.

The main Dalwood House, built by John's father, George Wyndham, in the 1820s, sits on a rolling hill overlooking the vineyards. A single-story stone house, it is large but not majestic, despite the Greek Revival columns supporting the porch. The columns seem out of place in the commercial vineyard, a fanciful detail in an otherwise austere landscape. George Wyndham had been raised in Wiltshire, in southern England, and had emigrated to

FIGURE 1. Grape pickers at Dalwood Vineyards, 1886. H. Ballard, *Photographs of the Dalwood Vineyards, near Branxton, New South Wales, Australia, 1886*, plate 5. Used with permission from Cambridge University Library, Royal Commonwealth Society Papers GBR/0115/RCS/Y3086B.

Australia as a young man. The house's unusual architecture reflects his upbringing in a world that viewed classical Greece and Rome as paradigms of imperial valor and civilization. These ideas emigrated with Wyndham and shaped his business and, by extension, the character of his community. John Wyndham was proud of his success and wanted affirmation of that success back "home" in Britain; he undoubtedly also wanted British people to buy his Hunter Valley wine. The photographs he had commissioned were arranged in an elegant album and sent directly to the Royal Colonial Society in London, hand-inscribed with Wyndham's dedication. They now rest in the manuscripts library of the University of Cambridge, where I carefully turned the album's stiff pages.

The contemporary significance of this historical source was striking when I left Cambridge for nearby Stansted Airport. On a late summer's day in 2017, the terminal was crammed with travelers, lured by cheap airfares and the promise of sunshine in southern Europe. Millions of British people enjoy an annual holiday in a warm climate and consider it almost a birthright to escape the U.K.'s unpredictable weather to sip wine in the sun. At the Costa Coffee shop in the airport's arrivals hall, there are three wines available for those who want to get a head start on their holidays. All are Australian: Jacob's Creek Semillon Chardonnay, Jacob's Creek Shiraz Cabernet, and

Jacob's Creek Sparkling Rosé, at £4.25 for an 187.5ml glass.³ The Jacob's Creek brand has only been around since the 1970s, but it was built on a vineyard established in the mid-nineteenth century. It is a household name in the U.K., keenly priced and popularized through television advertisements featuring a welcoming winemaker in a slouch hat.⁴ Australian wines are affordable, approachable, and ubiquitous in British public spaces. Long associated with domestic beer and spirits, the U.K. has become a country of confirmed wine drinkers: on average a British adult now guzzles more than thirty bottles of wine each year, much of it produced by former British colonies Australia, South Africa, and New Zealand.⁵ The U.K. has been one of the world's largest import markets for wine for several hundred years. Britain's thirst for wine has a much longer history than most contemporary consumers recognize. Indeed, it is both the British demand for wine imports and British colonial expansion that have led to the creation of much of wine's "New World."

Why did British settlers in Australia, South Africa, and New Zealand decide to produce wine? How did the fledgling wine industries in British colonies grow to become the approachable New World wines of the twentieth century, and why has Britain remained such a vital market for the wines of its former colonies? How has wine become ubiquitous in modern Britain, which was traditionally a class-conscious country of beer drinkers who considered wine to be the stuff of snobs and elites? And was the wine any good? This book explores and answers those questions.

Weaving together economic, social, and cultural histories of wine production and consumption over the past three centuries, this book tells the story of how wine-growing and wine markets expanded through British imperialism. It documents and analyzes wine production from the eighteenth century up to the present day in former British colonies: primarily Australia and South Africa, but also Canada, Cyprus, Malta, New Zealand, and India. It tells the unlikely story of how British settlers with no winemaking experience crossed the globe and planted vineyards, believing that they were advancing the civilizing mission of the British Empire. In turn, I demonstrate how colonial wine producers saw the British import market as paramount, and I examine the efforts of colonial producers to sell their wine to the British public through networks of agents, shippers, importers, and retailers. My focus is mostly on the British market for these wines, and to a lesser degree the domestic markets of the producing countries. I show how governments and the British public sector also played a critical role in the pricing and marketing of colonial wines, and how frequently colonial wine-makers were frustrated with the indifference of London lawmakers. Ironically, wines from the Commonwealth did not enjoy their highest popularity in Britain during the heyday of British imperialism, but rather after the realization of decolonization in the 1980s.

One reason that the history of wine in the British Empire has not been written is because the amounts of wine produced, traded, and consumed appear small, both in terms of total agricultural production and as a percentage of total wine consumption. It is a mistake to conclude that because the industry was small, it was insignificant. What this book demonstrates is that those involved in the imperial wine industry bestowed upon it an ideological and sentimental value that vastly exceeded its worth in crude fiscal terms. Indeed, the very fact that the industry was established and persisted over long periods of limited commercial success testifies to the triumph of ideas over income.

Wine thus allows us to explore the contradictions of Britain's colonial empire. This is not a story of the glories of imperialism: impressive though the reach of British economic power was, wine actually offers a curious counterpoint to imperial hubris. Colonial commodity history is ripe with stories of entrepreneurship and pluckiness, but also with dispossession and pain. South African wine, for example, was originally created through the labor of enslaved people, and Indigenous Australian activists deny the legitimacy of colonial land claims. This book takes one step toward reintegrating the issues confronting postcolonial states like South Africa and Australia, with the long histories of European trade and consumption.[6]

Finally, I examine whether, why, and when British consumers drank colonial wines—either as opposed to a different beverage, or as opposed to European wines. Britain has long had a strong culture of drink, but consumer tastes have changed over time. Over the twentieth century, Britain transformed from a country where wine consumption was very low and socially restricted to elites, to one where wine consumption had become common and visible. Studying the consumption of colonial wine shows the British public in an unusually self-conscious pose. The story of broadening wine consumption in Britain is one of consumers needing to be taught, reassured, and made confident in their choices, and discussions of wine drinking often reveal deep cultural insecurities. Generally speaking, wine "democratized" over the twentieth century, becoming cheaper, more widely available, and more socially widespread. This was due in large part to the growth in availability of colonial wines. At once quotidian and exotic, wine allows us to follow deep social changes in Britain, from the fine wine imbibed at Victorian gentlemen's clubs to the plonk quaffed at drizzly barbecues in the early twenty-first century. Britain has also transformed from a country where the overwhelming amount of wine consumed was of European origin, to one where nearly half of the wine consumed is from outside Europe. How, why, and when these transitions took place is the focus of this book.

THE OUTLINE OF THIS BOOK

This is a transnational history covering wine production, trade, and consumption over three centuries. Although this book is chronological in structure, it is not intended to be a comprehensive history of wine production in the three main countries of study. There are two foundational concepts anchoring this broad-reaching approach: the first is the idea of a New World of wine and its relation to European imperialism, and the second is the idea of the "civilizing mission" driving British imperialism. These concepts are explained in two introductory chapters.

The historical narrative then opens with an empire under construction and in flux: the Cape Colony, and its Dutch-planted vines, becoming British through the Napoleonic Wars, and Australia and New Zealand being settled with a mishmash of British rejects. Part 1 explains the origins of the imperial wine industry, lays out the main characters in establishing wine industries, and documents the first decades of their labor. These characters include James Busby, who taught winemaking in Australia before being appointed the first British representative to New Zealand, where he brokered the Treaty of Waitangi. These chapters also engage directly with the issue of labor in the wine industry, and the devastating effect European agriculture had on native inhabitants.

Part 2 navigates the cool reception these early colonial wines received back in Britain, sketching the journey of colonial wine from the colony to the British table. While the second half of the nineteenth century was a period of growth for Australia and New Zealand, in South Africa, on the other hand, there was already crisis and talk of an industry in decline. British support for viticulture in the colonies was offset by tariff regimes that frustrated colonial winemakers.

I demonstrate, using a range of textual and pictorial sources, the cultural dreams vignerons pinned on wine as a "civilizing" force in a new society.

Lobbying for Britons to consume Australian wine, winemaker Hubert de Castella argued that "pride and interest, two powerful agents, keep the mother country and Australia bound together."[7] I explore the challenges colonial winemakers and their importers faced in marketing and selling their wine in Britain from 1860 up to the First World War, as they tried to market their wine as a distinctly imperial choice of beverage.

The First World War was cataclysmic for both British and colonial societies and it also dramatically reordered the international wine market. Part 3 examines how colonial wine producers responded. There were dramatic changes in British wine consumption in the interwar period. European wine competitors were ravaged by wars and colonial wines offered an alternative, and an expanding consumer society also saw wine being promoted to a broadening socioeconomic group as an accessible and approachable alternative to European wines. Moreover, Britain's colonies of white settlement had now become self-governing dominions, and they were asserting themselves as trading partners in the interwar period.

A "doodle bug" destroyed wine cellars during the Second World War, which, like the previous one, had a cataclysmic effect on society in Britain, its colonies, and the dominions. It also was a boon to colonial wine producers, who filled the market gap left by France. As with the First World War, one unexpected outcome was the travel and exposure it afforded to many British people. Part 4 brings our narrative full circle: if the eighteenth and nineteenth century had been about European "conquest," in the second half of the twentieth century the excolonial producers would conquer the British wine market. In 1977 British comedy ensemble Monty Python spoofed Australian table wines, inventing vintages and descriptions, such as "Melbourne Old-and-Yellow," a "good fighting wine... which is particularly heavy, and should be used only for hand-to-hand combat."[8] A decade later, Australia emerged from under this poor reputation. Starting in the 1970s, colonial wines began receiving major critical attention from international wine writers, and in the late 1980s they flooded the British market, which we might consider the final "democratization" of wine consumption post-1970. The availability of inexpensive New World wine imports in turn is a driving factor in changing British consumer preferences: drinking New World wine has become a commonly recognizable British leisure activity, associated and advertised with a modern outdoorsy lifestyle (of South African and Australian rugby players manning barbecues). We return to ethical discussions of wine production and consumption, both in terms of apartheid South

African wines (which were subject to some boycott through 1991) and environmental concerns in wine production and shipping.

Empire was a critical stimulus for wine production in colonies of white settlement, chiefly Australia and South Africa. This was not because there was enormous market demand in Britain (until the 1970s there was not), nor even that there were consistently favorable trade terms for colonial producers (for most of the period they enjoyed no special protection and sometimes they were categorically worse-off than European competitors). Rather, empire provided a coherent belief system that wine could be a stabilizing and civilizing tool in a new society. Empire provided an obvious export market to cultivate and established routes for long-distance trade, and gave hope to winemakers that if British consumers would only try colonial wines, they would appreciate them, at the very least as a comestible symbol of imperial unity. Britain was slowly shaped into a wine-drinking society thanks to its colonies, because over time these colonies provided affordable, accessible wines that were not intimidating and that seemed consistent with popular patriotism. This history of wine in the New World also uses wine as a barometer of profound social change in Britain over the nineteenth and twentieth centuries.

A NOTE ABOUT SOURCES

Per capita consumption is a very rough measure, and we should not assume that people in the past consumed wine in the same manner as we do today. We also should not let our assumptions about class, ethnicity, or gender close our eyes to potentially rich sources. Wine history often focuses on the obvious sources left by European male politicians, importers, and consumers; this is logical, as these sources are the plentiful. However, the absence of a historical source does not mean the absence of a historical experience. Some of the sources historians would love to read are just not available: illiterate, abused workers on eighteenth-century South African plantations have left few firsthand accounts of their experiences. However, we can be creative with sources to build a broader picture. If we look, for example, at publications written by and for British women, we get a different impression of wine consumption. Nineteenth-century household manuals, which were aimed at women, demonstrate that wine was not only drunk straight, but was very popular in wine punches (which would go out of fashion after World War I but return in the 1950s), in which wine was mixed with fruit juices, spices, and liqueurs, and served either warm or over ice. An 1887 recipe advised how even the cheapest wine from Germany or eastern France could be extended and prepared for a party: "May Drink.—Put into a large glass mug or china bowl about 2 doz. black-currant leaves, a small handful of woodruff,[9] and a quantity, according to taste, of pounded lump sugar and lemon juice; pour in 2 bot. hock or Moselle, never mind how common. Stir the whole occasionally for 1/2 hour, and serve."[10] Many more people might have been drinking wine than the per capita figures suggest, if wine was stretched and served in such concoctions. Historians are generally comfortable extrapolating that if a "May Drink" recipe was included in a household manual, then it was probably prepared by some readers and there was probably a culture of preparing wine punches. Strictly speaking, though, we only have proof that the recipe was published. This is a recurring methodological issue in the study of consumption. We have very few records or sources that document what most consumers bought. Wine retailers recorded numbers of sales in their business records, but rarely left descriptors or statistics of the types of clients they served. Shifts in overall wine consumption levels often leave us guessing: if more wine was consumed, did a broader range of people drink wine, or did the same people drink more wine? We make our best guess using the broadest range of sources available. I draw on a vast range of sources in this book to build the fullest picture of wine in the empire: its production, trade, and consumption. These include official government documents; records of wine producers; the correspondence of agents, importers, and journalists; advertisements; wine lists and menus; recorded interviews; and literature and popular culture. Some of these sources provide hard data and allow me to undertake quantitative analysis; some of them, whether texts or images, allow me to extract deep cultural assumptions through patient reading and careful probing.

PART ONE

———

Origins

C. 1650–1830

ONE

Writing about Wine

THIS BOOK TAKES A NEW APPROACH to the global history of wine. To begin, it redefines one of the main concepts of wine writing, which is the distinction between the "Old" and "New" worlds of wine. These terms are used widely and loosely in journalism, hospitality services, and historical writing. The "Old World" generally refers to wine-making countries of western, continental Europe, which have been consistently producing wine for thousands of years. The major wine-producing and exporting countries of Europe—France, Italy, Spain, Portugal, and Germany—are indisputably Old World. In contrast, Australia, South Africa, New Zealand, Chile, Argentina, and the United States are usually described as New World producers, a term that became popular in the second half of the twentieth century. The idea of two worlds is useful, but as it is currently defined it ignores the major historical divergence between the two.

New World is such a prevalent and loaded term that it is useful to explore its common usages and history. In the second half of the twentieth century there was a major shift in the distribution of wine production and export levels across the globe, and particularly in the Southern Hemisphere. As a result, the term New World usually refers to the wine-producing countries that challenged the market dominance of these European producers in the second half of the twentieth century, mentioned above.[1] In 2001 the Australia, South Africa, the United States and Argentina had become both top-ten global producers and exporters.[2] But in 1961 only the United States and Argentina had been top-ten producers (at fourth and eighth, respectively, and lagging far behind France, Italy and Spain), and they hardly exported any of their wine. However, two other major wine producers of the early 1960s had also disappeared from the rankings in this time period:

Algeria, which had been a French territory, and the Soviet Union, which split. It was a time of both emerging and disappearing global producers.

These market shifts were tied to other social and economic changes, and the six New World challengers shared some other features in terms of how and what kind of wine they produced. Wine experts therefore also make distinctions between the Old and New Worlds in terms of production methods, corporate models, classification systems, and ultimately wine styles. Technological improvements in the 1960s, 1970s, and 1980s enabled many New World producers to produce large amounts of reliable, undistinguished, but inexpensive wine. Whereas old European vineyards tended to be small, family-owned affairs, the New World became relatively dominated by international brands. The New World has also favored market concentration and larger producers, which tended to have lower marginal costs of production and greater economies of scale. This means that the New World became associated with large-scale production of cheaper wines. Furthermore, European producers (particularly France) pioneered place-based quality controls, which define wine quality through *terroir,* or the expression of a precise parcel of land in wine. Under France's protected appellation system, which evolved in the early twentieth century, winemakers also set strict rules regarding the grape varietals and production methods that can be used in their wines. The New World is comparatively relaxed.

These looser regulations, the proud promotion of affordable wines, and a hot climate mean that the New World is associated with bold, fruity, and often high-alcohol wines—as compared to the more refined and discrete wines for which the best northern European producers are famous. For some critics the New World was brash, inauthentic, and anonymous;[3] for others it was adventurous and refreshing. British wine critics embraced discussion of these differences. Oz Clarke, who helped popularize New World wines in Britain as a resident wine critic on the long-running BBC television show *Food and Drink,* gushed that "New World is not just where you're situated—it's how you think, it's what your ambitions are, it's what your dreams are," arguing in 1994 that Hungary and Moldova met this definition.[4] In a 2003 interview, Hazel Murphy of Wine Australia agreed: "New World is a state of mind, and you can have as many New World people in Burgundy as you can in Australia."[5]

More recently, wine connoisseurs have quibbled over whether countries like Greece or Georgia are "Old" producers, because they have undoubtedly produced wine for millennia, but have had little global export success in the past five centuries. With the emergence of even newer wine-producing countries, like India and China, "new" can no longer be synonymous with "non-European," and inevitably these nonaligned producers have been dubbed the "Third World" of wine. In an influential 2010 article, two scholars named Glenn Banks and John Overton analyzed the Old and New World dichotomy and found it "flawed" and overly simplistic, and accordingly rejected the Third World designation as unhelpful.[6] Banks and Overton's understanding of this dichotomy is based on "a number of putative differences to be found in the nature of wine production,"[7] such as artisanal methods versus mechanization, attitudes toward innovation, and regulation. They argue that there is a range of production models and methods within each world, which renders the dichotomy false. Indeed, all these distinctions are based on generalizations. France also produces plenty of cheap fruity wine, just as Australia produces fine wines of distinction. However, that does not mean that we should completely reject the Old and New World labels, since there is one vital feature that unites all of the New World producers: they did not emerge to compete *with* Europe, they were created *by* Europe.

Australia, South Africa, New Zealand, Chile, Argentina, and the United States were all established as European settler colonies. They also all began producing wine almost immediately: by 1600 in the Spanish settlements of modern-day Argentina, Chile, and the western United States, in the 1660s by the Dutch in South Africa, in the 1790s by the British in Australia, and in the 1840s by the British in New Zealand. As we will see in the case of British colonies, winemaking was neither an accident nor a coincidence but a deliberate economic and cultural strategy. The New World of wine should therefore be understood as historically fixed: rather than a shorthand for particular production models, it refers to those wine-producing countries that were established between 1500 and 1850 as a project of European imperialism. The fact that these countries managed to penetrate and exploit global markets in the twentieth century is part of the story, but it is not their founding moment. This creates a slightly awkward periodization, where "New" is now of the past, but "nouvelle" cuisine and "modern" art have survived such ambiguity, and wine can, too.

Rather than understanding the New World as a wine-producing block that emerged in the second half of the twentieth century, I redefine it as a creation of European settler colonialism over the sixteenth through nineteenth centuries. New World wine production has been, thus, global from its inception, because it was part of burgeoning networks of European mercantile and cultural expansion. The six New World producers were the product of four different European empires; this book focuses on the three major British colonies, Australia, South Africa and New Zealand. While it appears that the major European empires all spread viticulture, Britain was unique among the four competing powers for the longevity of its power into the modern era (compared to the Dutch), combined with the fact that it was not a major wine producer itself (compared to the Spanish and French). Spain and France have been two of the world's top wine producers and exporters for at least the past four centuries. They had high levels of domestic wine consumption and wine was a staple good. Vines were planted in their colonies by colonists who regularly consumed wine, and metropolitan leaders even sometimes restricted colonial vine growing to protect the domestic industry.[8] It was the opposite in the case of Britain, which has always imported nearly all of its wine. Indeed, British demand for wine over the seventeenth and eighteenth centuries both drove the expansion of wine production in mythical places like Bordeaux and the Douro Valley, and resulted in international treaties where Britain sought favorable terms on importing wine.[9] Thus, from its inception, Britain's stake in colonial viticulture was trade-driven as well as nationalistic and sentimental. Even if winemakers were not initially very successful at selling their wine in the British market, they persisted.[10] That commercial tradition, built on complex networks of imperial traders, is the reason Britain remains one of the world's most important wine markets in the twenty-first century.

To understand the New World's connections to the British market in the late twentieth century, we must appreciate and acknowledge this colonial history. Though historians and economists have not done this for the most part, trade bodies, ironically, have. Wine Australia, the Australian authority responsible for the development and promotion of wine, works from the concept that Australia's imperial past still shapes its export aspirations: "Australian wine producers initiated and fostered a growing worldwide consumer market for wine in the 1980s and 1990s, particularly in the U.K. . . . To date, much of Australia's export success has occurred in English-speaking or former or current Commonwealth markets."[11] This is neither accidental nor coincidental. What matters is not simply the massive size of the U.K. wine market, but its entangled historical relationship with half of the New World producers.

More specifically, these New World producers were what historians call "colonies of white settlement." These colonies were established with settlers from a European imperial country, where the settlers' express intention was to establish permanent communities with close ties to the home country. Australia and New Zealand were claimed by Britain, South Africa by the Dutch and then by the British, and Chile and Argentina by what the historian James Belich has described as "Europe's other great overseas settling society, Spain."[12] The territories that would amalgamate as the United States included British, French, and Spanish settlers. This is a different model from one found in European colonies like India or Nigeria, where a relatively small population of British people managed (or ruled) an indigenous population, and there was little effort to settle large numbers of Europeans. There is considerable scholarly debate as to why European states created colonies, and there will never be a satisfactory monocausal explanation: trade, prestige, strategic considerations, and cultural imperialism all played a role in varying degrees. Likewise, there was a great deal of variation in the administration of colonies within empires. Historians now tend to see the British Empire less as an integrated, top-down, consistently-administered unit, and more as a patchwork of possessions with a wide variety of administrative arrangements in which British administrators were compelled to accommodate local elites and practices. What is undeniable is that the British Empire became extremely large over the course of the nineteenth century, until, at its greatest geographic size (just after World War I), the empire's formal reach covered around a quarter of the earth's surface and a quarter of its population.

Settlers often sought to replicate institutional structures that existed in the home countries but had been personally unavailable to them: for example, by establishing democratic governance, when the settlers themselves might not have been eligible to vote in the mother country. Colonies of white settlement were codified such that only the settler population had the full share of evolving legal rights. Colonization inevitably meant the cultivation of land, which normally had been inhabited (one might say "owned") by native populations. "Settler colonies were usually more dangerous for indigenous peoples than subject colonies," as James Belich puts it.[13] The establishment of colonial vineyards was thus inextricably part of the painful histories of the devastation of indigenous populations. This narrative, almost entirely absent from most wine history, is fundamental to understanding the establishment of viticulture in the New World. It is challenging to account for the impact of the wine industry (or colonialism in general) on indigenous populations, because the sources available to historians are so strongly skewed toward the colonizers. Still, we must try to build a fuller and more inclusive understanding of the past. We would be remiss not to acknowledge that wonderful wines have been produced on land that, for many, invokes pain and exploitation. Wine is a celebratory drink, and much wine writing, as discussed below, is celebratory, but as a global commodity wine reveals more complex historical narratives.

There are four colonies of white settlement discussed in this book, all of which transitioned from colonies in the British Empire to independent members of the Commonwealth of Nations (an ever-loosening cultural and trade consortium). Australia, first colonized by the British in 1788, evolved into six different colonies that joined to create the Commonwealth of Australia in 1901. The Cape Colony, which was colonized by the Dutch in 1652, became a British possession in 1814 and joined with neighboring territories to form a Union of South Africa in 1910. New Zealand, which was "explored" by Europeans in the seventeenth century, was claimed by the British in 1840 and became a self-governing dominion in 1907. Canada, which was colonized in patches by British and French settlers beginning in the sixteenth century, became a British possession in 1763 and an independent confederation (and loyal dominion) in 1867. Colonies of white settlement do reveal quite starkly the racial and ethnic divisions within the empire, since they received self-government decades before other colonies (most decolonization took place after World War II). Their federations guaranteed many democratic rights for their white subjects, and they continued to make proud professions of loyalty to Britain as they navigated their autonomy on the world stage. As discussed in part 4, South Africa's apartheid system, which effectively treated nonwhite citizens as a subclass, led some—but certainly not most—British consumers to voluntarily boycott South African wine. For the ease of the modern reader, I (somewhat anachronistically) refer to all four states by their postindependence names. I also refer to "colonial wine" throughout the book, even when the producers are no longer colonies.

I also do not discuss the United States much in this book, although it is a major New World producer and was a British colony of white settlement. There is no doubt that the earliest British and French settlers in North America embraced the possibilities of viticulture. Grape vines were planted at early settlements in Jamestown, Virginia, and along the bank of the St. Lawrence River near Montreal. In the late eighteenth century, just as British ships carrying vine cuttings were docking in Australia, Virginia colonist Thomas Jefferson was tending grapes vines at his estate in Monticello. These particular efforts were not successful in the long term and they did not herald the start of an unbroken tradition of American wine production. The earliest winemakers in British settlements in what became the United States shared the ethos and worldview of early winemakers in Australia or New Zealand: they saw wine production as potentially contributing to the greater good of empire, as a potentially lucrative commodity that signaled refinement and successful conquest. However, since the United States's evolution as a serious wine producer took place after its independence and outside the cultural jurisdiction of Britain,[14] it largely falls outside the scope of this book.

Not all of the wine producers in this book were colonies of white settlement. The other type of British colonies that produced wine were Malta, Cyprus, and the mandate of Palestine. Malta became a British colony in 1800 and an independent state in 1964; Cyprus had transferred from an Ottoman territory to a British one in 1878, and later a Crown Colony, obtaining independence in 1960; Palestine had also been an Ottoman territory and in the wake of World War I briefly became a British mandate, until Britain withdrew in 1947 over the fraught creation of the State of Israel. These three areas had long-established wine-making traditions and nearly all of their wine was consumed locally and immediately. They were small producers and they did not engage in a high volume of transnational trade. That, and the fact that they also had small populations and miniscule numbers of white settlers, meant that they largely flew under the proverbial radar of the Colonial Office.

The irony is that these three Mediterranean states were geographically much closer to Britain than the four colonies of white settlement, yet it was these four—and primarily Australia and South Africa—that became the most important colonial wine producers and suppliers of wine to Britain. The reason Britain did not meet its wine demands from conveniently located Cyprus or Malta is because there was actually not a need to fill. Britain imported millions of gallons of wine in the eighteenth and nineteenth centuries, but it had no difficulty meeting its needs from its European neighbors. The Australia and South African New Worlds were created out of a dream, not a demand: they were created because early elite settlers envisioned a world that they civilized (a process so strongly suggested in vine cultivation) and in which they contributed to colonial coffers through trade. They produced wine for an imperial market, so it makes sense to see them as part of an imperial economy and not simply as individual state producers. The New World of wine was itself a product of European settler colonialism, and this is the first study to explore those origins in former British colonies over the nineteenth and twentieth centuries.

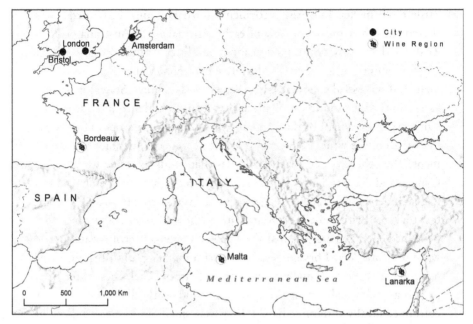

MAP 1. Europe. London, Amsterdam, and Bristol were ports in the wine trade. Lanarka, Cyprus, and Malta were British colonies but exported little wine, despite their relatively close proximity.

WRITING ABOUT WINE

This is not a biography of wine. Wine did not "make" the world, and it did not create or transform the British Empire, as other commodities—tea, cocoa, sugar, or coffee—might be claimed to have done.[15] But the British Empire was critical to the creation of wine industries and markets for wine in what would become the New World. This history of the growth of British colonial wine industries is a markedly different tale from, for example, the relatively quick explosion of the market for colonial sugar, documented by Sidney Mintz in his classic study *Sweetness and Power.*[16] Unlike other cult comestibles that were ravenously traded in the heyday of European empire, wine was a niche product with a small market in Britain until well into the twentieth century, and enthusiasm for British colonial wine was muted and limited for decades. Unlike many other colonial commodities wine was neither native to nor "discovered" in exotic lands, but purposefully introduced by Europeans as conscious acts of transplantation.

Wine does not happen by chance or by accident. Australia and South Africa possess climates that have proved fertile for wine, but their evolution into global producers was not geographically inevitable. Winemaking is a long, deliberate process that requires a significant investment of time and physical labor. For the purposes of this book, wine means a fermented product of the grape genus *vitis vinifera,* which may or may not be mixed or fortified with other ingredients. There are "wines" made from orchard fruits, barley, and other agricultural products, but they are not what are commonly known by consumers and retailers as wine and are not discussed here (one partial exception is my discussion of Canada, where until recently native *labrusca* varieties like Concord grapes were used, along with native-French hybrids). There is also a long tradition of what was known until recently as "English wines" in Britain, which are homemade fermented beverages, often made from soaking raisins or from wild plants like damsons, elderflowers, and cowslips.[17] Though these appear occasionally in British discussions of wine consumption, they not the concern of this book.

Wine begins in the vineyard. A site must be chosen, ideally taking into consideration soil type and quality and exposure to sunlight. And vines must be chosen, planted, carefully cultivated, and pruned. There are thousands of varietals of *vitis vinifera* and each might respond differently to a particular climate. Grapes must be harvested at the optimal time and gently handled; juice must extracted; and expertise must be applied in blending, fermenting, and aging. Eventually, the wine must be kept or transported to market for consumption, though even after wine arrives on the market it is never truly finished, as it will continue to evolve in barrel or bottle. Trial and error is unavoidable, and indeed the skill of the winemaker lies in the ability to respond to a changing, evolving agricultural project and to coax it into a stable comestible. Such challenges presented major obstacles to colonial winemakers, and there was much error in the early days of colonial vineyards. Until World War II most winemaking was done by hand.

Wine has been more useful in writing the history of settler societies, particularly in the trope of the enterprising winemaker. The difficulty that lies in creating good wines, particularly in a foreign environment, perhaps explains historians' emphasis on individuals who succeeded against the odds, of protagonists with vision and passion who were undeterred by enemies such as weather, phylloxera, and government regulation. This is particularly true of New World wine histories. In relation to "new" societies that promised unlimited social mobility in exchange for grit and initiative, bootstrapping winemakers who succeeded in producing a beverage that brought pleasure to many (not least the historian) of course are celebrated.[18] Thus for a product that is consumed socially, wine history shows winemaking to be curiously solitary and individual, with great focus on the winemakers and the purported secrets of their success. To the extent that there are revisionist approaches to wine history, they question whether the *right* people have been celebrated in the establishment of wine industries,[19] not whether we should look beyond the individual or the group to consider the system.

At times in the writing of wine history, wine itself has been treated as a historical actor. This is the case in many of the sweeping histories of wine, such as Hugh Johnson's original *Vintage: The Story of Wine*, Paul Lukacs's recent *Inventing Wine*, John Varriano's *Wine: A Cultural History*, or Marc Millon's *Wine: A Global History*.[20] These lucid and entertaining histories, written by great narrators with serious wine expertise, follow a similar narrative arc. Wine is the central protagonist, the potable Zelig, popping up in different historical moments in different parts of the world. The story begins in the Fertile Crescent, where Wine is born, or in the ancient Mediterranean, where Wine enters a boisterous adolescence in the symposia and bacchanalia of the ancient Greeks. The reader is invited to pause and appreciate the wine-themed mosaic and shards of amphorae. The story then skips a few centuries and a few hundred miles, to medieval Europe (we are left to wonder what Wine has done in between), where Wine joins forces with powerful and institutionalized Christianity and canny monks create a patchwork of orderly *clos* on the Côte d'Or: bless them! Wine remains in France, or perhaps summers in Germany, and Bordeaux emerges in the seventeenth century, eventually finding its way to Britain (we are treated to a Samuel Johnson quote, or Pepys). Port and sherry have their seafaring adventures. The nineteenth century opens with Champagne surviving war, producing widows and conquering Russian markets; France produces Pasteur, who produces better wine, a triumph of science and the Enlightenment; wine is enjoying its golden years. Then, three-quarters of the way through this drama, tragedy strikes, in the form of the vine disease phylloxera. Wine is dealt a staggering blow and its very survival is threatened. Fortunately, a new world of scientists, mavericks, and neoliberal entrepreneurs emerge: capital is found, the plucky New World steps in to help, and new vines are grafted. Wine is saved! This cannot be criticized as being a Eurocentric narrative, because the tale concludes in California, or Uruguay, or China. Undeniably, at the conclusion of this story there is incredible momentum and optimism. Global wine production is the highest it has ever been, consumption of wine is high, and wine is (relatively) cheap. Were he a wine historian, Francis Fukuyama would declare it the end of wine history.

This hagiography of Wine is a great read: a mouth-watering tale of high drama, blind monks, and supple tannins. And it is not necessarily *inaccurate*. But it is, on the other hand, what British historians have called a Whiggish narrative: one that presumes continual progress, culminating in the current era, which is assumed to be the best ever. This Whiggishness may overlook some of the current difficulties in the market, or shrug off past problems in the wine industry, since all ended well. Geographically and chronologically it is uneven, such that the producers studied here generally do not merit inclusion until they have become major global actors. This type of narrative structure is what gives the false impression that South Africa produced a great wine called Constantia in the eighteenth century, and then produced nothing again until 1994. The place of Wine as the embattled protagonist who overcomes many hardships (vine diseases, consumer apathy, high taxation) and emerges triumphant and affordable in the late twentieth century, is also what is known in Marxist terms as "commodity fetishism." As Bruce Robbins has argued, in the new commodity histories, "each commodity takes its turn as the star of capitalism."[21] The commodity itself, rather than the social and economic relationships that led to its production, becomes the driving force of the narrative.

Perhaps it is the passion that wine inspires in its connoisseurs that makes the writing of wine history so celebratory in tone. While there has been recent hand-wringing about the contemporary environmental impact of wine, particularly with regard to pesticide use, these ethical concerns have been not yet been absorbed into historical writing about wine. This stands in stark contrast to the writing of other global commodities, where there has been greater acknowledgment of the darker side of commodity chains, and the strong impact of European imperialism on the creation of those commodity chains.[22] Reviewing a history of tea in 2003, Jenny Diski matter-of-factly writes, "Consider only that tea is grown primarily in China, India and Sri Lanka and drunk in vast quantities in Britain and you can be sure that economic and political discrimination have been central to its production and consumption." The entrepreneurial exploits of British tea planters reveal "qualities of boldness, brutality and tragedy for all concerned central to the history of British colonialism."[23] For many wine historians, the sheer delight they take in wine itself can lead to a lack of historical and ethical perspective. Paul Lukacs, in his magisterial *Inventing Wine*, describes World War I as "a cataclysmic war fought in or near some of the world's greatest vineyards,"[24] which, even in a book about wine, is slightly jarring.

Our enjoyment of wine will withstand a critical reassessment of its history. I propose to integrate the history of wine in former British colonies with colonial history, and to balance the two extremes of local individualism on the one hand, and impersonal global systems on the other. There are tales of individual resourcefulness and initiative, and of business innovation, but they are enveloped in explanations of the larger systems at work. The major global system, which we will explore in the next chapter, is the cultural and economic organization of the British Empire.

TWO

———

Why Britain?

THIS BOOK FOCUSES ON THE CHANGING DYNAMICS of both the British Empire and the United Kingdom itself over the past three hundred years. Since the seventeenth century, Britain has been an ambitious maritime state that engaged in vigorous overseas trade for all sorts of goods. Because it has long had a healthy demand for wine, and meets virtually all that demand through import, Britain has been one of the world's largest markets for wine since the eighteenth century. Wine was traded, and imperialism broadened and strengthened trade routes.

One of the central ideas of scholarship in British imperialism is the concept of the "civilizing mission," a concept that has resonated greatly in the history of viticulture. Many historians acknowledge the idea of a civilizing mission as one potent reason for the expansion of European empires in the nineteenth and early-twentieth centuries. This was a belief held by some Europeans of the superiority of their own culture, and of the responsibility they had to introduce it to supposedly less civilized parts of the world. Christianity was the most obvious export, as Christianity is itself a missionary religion that compels its faithful to spread its message, and there is no doubt that Christian missionaries genuinely believed that their forays into colonial life, with their translated Bibles and makeshift Sunday schools, were saving souls.

The spread of British civilization would be measured not just in religious terms, but in economic terms, too. British imperialism was unambiguously capitalistic. The success of the empire was proclaimed in the wealth and advancement of its colonies, in the robust trade routes, and in colonists' standard of living. Winemakers and exporters who sought commercial success were not eschewing imperialism for profit: they were demonstrating

23

their commitment to that civilizing mission through trade. Prosperity itself would be evidence that civilizing was taking place in a new land.

But the civilizing mission could also be a mythical end that justified brutal means of colonization, and an empty rhetorical tool aimed primarily at galvanizing British supporters. Some scholars have argued that its cultural arrogance devalued the lives of indigenous people, inferring that they lacked any culture or sentience at all. A major critique of the civilizing mission, which falls into the broad area of studies known as postcolonialism, is that it still contributes to global inequality and rationalizes wars of aggression.[1] These are important critiques to bear in mind when considering the history of wine and its association with colonial projects.

If many British colonists were sympathetic to the idea of a Christian civilizing mission, then successful wine cultivation, with its biblical resonance, was a heady confirmation of their progress. The process of winemaking is intensive and sensitive enough that by engaging in it the winemaker can imagine himself or herself to be actively cultivating and civilizing. Tidy rows of vines, bearing fruit and creating wine—all out of what was previously imagined as *terra nullius*—were a potent achievement for colonizers. This attitude can be found well into the postcolonial era. As a South African wine-writer argued in 1961, "wine, and wine-drinking, is a basic part of the civilized life of man. In growing the wine, as [early Dutch colonists] Van Riebeeck and the Van der Stels knew well, men become a sturdy part of the land they live in. The wine-growers of the Cape have contributed through the centuries as much as any to the solidity of European civilization in what was an alien and most primitive land."[2] This statement might be expected from apartheid South Africa as a "wind of change" was supposedly blowing through the Continent, and native Africans were challenging the political supremacy of Europeans and their descendants, and assuming control over their own jurisdictions. But we find echoes of the civilizing trope well into the twentieth century, long after British rule had ended. "New Zealand is a freshly-packaged phenomenon," gushes the catalog for Oddbins, one of Britain's largest wine merchants, in 1999. Then it ratchets up the drama: "The pace of change— from primitive ancestral home of the Maori to the state-of-the-art, disarmingly progressive society of the nineties—has been alarming."[3] The history of New Zealand wines is not explained, but is invoked as a marketing tool designed to conjure up contrasting, vibrant images of New Zealand's past and present. The marketing department was apparently oblivious to the offense they could cause in inventing and romanticizing a "primitive" Maori past, but they must have believed that this description would resonate with the British public and, in turn, shift a lot of sauvignon blanc.

This is one example of how wine has played an important role in the construction and imagination of cultural and national identities. In the case of Britain, wine does not urgently plead for national identity: Britain has indeed been associated with beer and distilled beverages like gin and whiskey. Because wine is generally imported into Britain, wine consumption has at times even been deemed politically suspicious, such as during the eighteenth century, when Britain was frequently at war with France.[4] As explored in the following chapters, this presented a marketing challenging for imperialistic producers of colonial wines, who wanted their product to resonate with British consumers. But this problem was not unique to Britain: marketing was also critical in countries that we readily associate with wine. In France, winemaking has existed over millennia, large areas of the countryside have been delineated by specific vineyards, and superb wines are produced for a global market. Indeed, wine evokes Frenchness and can be used as a synecdochic image for France as a whole. But as Kolleen Guy has shown, even champagne's role in French national identity evolved through a deliberate process of construction, where champagne makers used marketing techniques to make consumers associate drinking champagne with being French.[5]

This exploration of the marketing of colonial wine in Britain dovetails with a major scholarly concerns over the past two decades. The investigation of how metropolitan Britain and British culture was shaped by the experience of having an empire is often known as the study of the "Empire at Home." This approach assumes that empire was not something that British people "did" to other people, but that it reflexively revealed and created British thought, habits, and culture. A broad literature has investigated the ravenous personal consumption of colonial goods in Great Britain and, to a lesser extent, Ireland. This includes tea, sugar, coffee, cocoa, calico, decorative objects and hardwoods, to say nothing of the raw materials consumed on an industrial level in the production of personal goods.[6] Much of this literature takes for granted that there was a demand for colonial and dominion goods in Great Britain: that foreign meant exotic, that exotic goods held an irresistible lure to Britons, that the marketing of such goods projected and reflected imperializing norms, and that the search for foreign goods was indeed a driving force of some imperial projects. (Indeed, there is even convincing evidence that the demand for foreign goods stimulated industrial innovation in Britain in a bid to substitute for imports.)[7] The assumption underpinning many of these discussions is also in itself a recurrent imperial trope: imperial cornucopia, colonies as abundant and fertile providers of foodstuffs.[8] More than chronicling simple resource extraction, historians have come to understand the importation, marketing, and consumption of imperial goods in Britain as a process laden with cultural meaning (even if the particular meaning, its intensity and its varied resonance across particular social groups, is highly disputed).[9] Wine, as we shall see, was also clothed in colorful layers of cultural meaning.

In the beginning of the nineteenth century, when vineyards were being planted in the young colony around Sydney, the United Kingdom of Great Britain and Ireland was a federation of two islands and four constituent countries. It was experiencing rapid population growth, with a total population of around sixteen million people (by 1900 it would be over forty million). Though the reasons for and the dating of an industrial revolution are contested, social and economic changes are starkly visible over the long term. In 1700 most of Britain had been agricultural and rural; by 1800 England, the most populous of the four states, was becoming profoundly urbanized and its economy oriented toward heavy industry, particularly in the Midlands and northern part of the country. Urbanization in itself requires economic shifts: urban dwellers are generally not self-sufficient, but are dependent on markets to obtain more ordinary consumer goods, especially food. A growing empire increasingly stepped in to supply these urban workers with clothing, food, and drink, and so the industrial revolution was inextricably entwined with a consumer revolution.

As a whole, nineteenth-century Britain had the dynamism we associate with modernity: industrialization, thriving cities, vigorous trade, a mobile population, and general freedom of communication and expression. Large parts of the U.K. were little touched by these changes, however; Ireland remained persistently agricultural and was not subject to the same intensity of industrial investment as England, Wales, or Scotland, the three countries that comprise the island of Great Britain. For this reason, and for other particularities of Ireland's social and economic development which I cannot responsibly condense to include here, I focus most of my discussion on affairs and markets in Great Britain, and not to those of Ireland or, after 1923, Northern Ireland. (I do use the term *British*, even though the U.K. includes millions who do not identify as British, because the English language does not have an adjective that corresponds to United Kingdom.) London-based businesses figure most prominently, as Britain has long been quite centralized in terms of national governance, trade and culture.[10] London was also the most important entry port for wine, because wine generally came from points south.

Nineteenth-century Britain had a growing economy and political leadership that valued economic growth. It also had a growing empire and political leadership, as well as perhaps a general public, that valued the mission of "civilizing" and of expanding Britain's prestige and might. There is considerable debate as to what extent free trade policies stimulated trade, particularly as regards the trade in foreign comestibles like wine.[11] There is also a strain of self-congratulatory thought in British history. Whereas most European states saw revolutions, regime changes, and upheaval in the nineteenth century, Britain was comparatively stable on the domestic front. It is unlikely that this was due to some special feature of the British character and it certainly was not because Britain was perfectly harmonious. Rather, Britain's trade-intensive, capitalist economy was built on a stratified system of social relations.

Britain's class structure was formally enshrined in its democratic system. Britain had evolved a bicameral parliamentary system over centuries, but up until 1928 it was only partially democratic. In 1800, when British convicts were being sent to Australia and British sailors were battling for South Africa, the British parliamentary system was considered thoroughly rotten. Votes were restricted to wealthy Anglican men who owned property. A major reform of the political system took place in 1832, expanding the franchise to a whopping 5 percent of adult men. Further reforms would gradually expand the electorate, lowering and then eventually abolishing the property qualifications until all men were given suffrage in 1918 and all women in 1928. Social class and gender determined political rights for most of the period under discussion in this book.

This is highly relevant to discussions of trade and wine consumption. Social and democratic restrictions were one of the "pull" factors that encouraged Britons to emigrate to new colonies like Australia, in the hopes that they could experience social mobility there. If Britain was peculiarly stable in the nineteenth and twentieth centuries, it was because its empire functioned as a very effective social safety valve. Not only did colonies provide Britain with vital resources to fuel its population and its industrial revolution, they also allowed undesirables to be placed at a healthy distance. Convicts, the poor, the frustrated, and the thwarted ambitious could take their discontent far, far away.

Social class is also a cultural construction, and wine has been a changing social marker. Historically, wine consumption in Britain has skewed toward the wealthier classes. This was true in the seventeenth century, when wine was a luxury for the upper-middle class and "a necessity" for the gentility, who bought it regardless of its price.[12] In nineteenth-century Britain most people did not drink much wine, many did not drink any at all, and wine was drunk overwhelmingly by a small, wealthy elite. In the first decades of the twentieth century, John Burnett has shown, per capita wine consumption increased by a factor of income, that is, that doubling one's salary also doubled one's average wine consumption.[13]

Many studies of consumption assume that people are naturally class aspirational and that they can express their aspiration in consumer goods. Tea is an example of another colonial beverage that began British life as an expensive elite beverage and trickled down over the course of the eighteenth century to become a staple of working-class life. But it is important to remember that working-class culture is a culture in its own right, and not a deviation from an elite norm. Furthermore, Charles Ludington has shown that in eighteenth-century Britain, elites sometimes imitated the wine-drinking habits of the middle classes, and not the other way round.[14] Class friction and interaction looms large in the histories of British drinking culture. Britain has a strong culture of drinking, in that consuming alcoholic beverages in a social setting has long been a socially acceptable leisure activity. Nor is there any expectation that alcohol must be consumed alongside food. The public house, or pub, is a recognized and accepted social hub. Its social role has widened over time, particularly as it has become more open to women after World War I.[15]

British wine consumption is thus a giant paradox. Even when Britain was the world's top wine importer, from at least the seventeenth century into the twentieth, per capita wine consumption in Britain was very low. Britain had an outsized role from the point of view of wine producers, but to a cultural observer within the country, wine played a marginal role for most people.

The story of wine in the British Empire is one of trade, prices, and customs duties, but it is more principally a story of ideas and how ideas become reality. This book explores the ideas that led people to dedicate their lives to a most unlikely crop, and the impacts, both good and bad, that their actions had on the global economy and on people's lives. There are an infinite number of stories that could be told in the history of colonialism and wine—indeed, the amount of material available to the historian is so staggering that I have omitted far more research material than I have included in this book. My story is not definitive, but it is accurate and true. It begins in the seventeenth century, in the shadow of majestic Table Mountain, on the Cape of Good Hope, where Dutch settlers arrived with visions of vineyards.

THREE

Dutch Courage

THE FIRST WINE AT THE CAPE

THEY ARRIVED THIRSTY.

In 1679 Simon van der Stel, recently appointed colonial governor by the Dutch East India Company, landed at the Cape of Good Hope, a southern tip of the African continent. Long home to the Khoikhoi people, the Cape had first been navigated by Europeans in the late fifteenth century, and it had now been conquered by the Dutch as a pivotal point in the web of European maritime trade. The Netherlands was a powerful country of keen traders, and Van der Stel had made his career as a bureaucrat in the Dutch East India Company, also known as the VOC. Nineteenth-century paintings imagine Dutch administrators standing imperious at the foot of Table Mountain, surveying the land and the native peoples they now presumed to control.[1] The Age of Exploration was an Age of Exploitation, too.

One of the only known portraits of Van der Stel, painted years before he was appointed governor, shows him clutching a ripe bunch of grapes. Back home in his village of Muiderberg, east of Amsterdam, he had maintained a small vineyard. And, while the VOC's Indian Ocean trade was devoted to spices, Van der Stel probably had some knowledge of the wine trade, for his father-in-law was a wine merchant.[2] In 1685, the governor was awarded land in the Cape by the VOC, in the outskirts of the port city of Cape Town. There, he planted what would become Africa's most famous vineyard, and began making wine. He named it Constantia: loyal, enduring, steadfast.

Van der Stel's plantings at the Cape have become the founding myth of South African wine. The basics of his story have been repeated so frequently as to take on a life of their own, regardless of whether they are accurate or not (and we have little way of verifying some of the details). The tale is usually

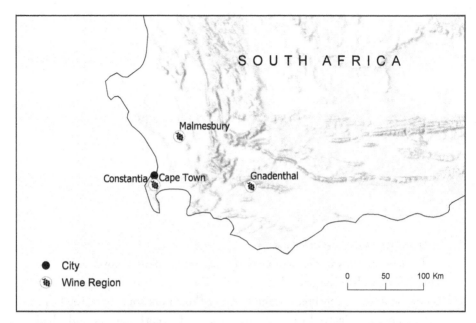

MAP 2. South Africa, showing places mentioned in the text. The longest-established vineyards are in Constantia, now a suburb of Cape Town. The planting of vineyards later spread north and east.

told as a celebration of one individual's foresight. However, Van der Stel was not acting in anticipation of a much later wine industry, but in response to the cultural and political conditions of his time. Wine was a staple to many well-off Europeans in the early modern period, and as European empires expanded they took vines with them. Spanish colonists had started making wine in modern-day Argentina, Chile, and California by around 1600. A few years later, British colonists in Virginia also experimented, with less success, with growing wine grapes. Wine production in colonies could foster economic self-sufficiency, by provisioning settlers and potentially providing a cash crop for export. Rather than an eccentric visionary, Van der Stel had typical interests for an early-modern imperialist.

Imperial rivalries and trade networks also molded the contemporary European wine and spirits trade. Bordeaux may be France's, if not the world's, most celebrated wine region, but the Dutch, British, and Irish bear much responsibility for transforming it from a wine-producing region to a wine-exporting behemoth over the seventeenth and eighteenth centuries. As Rod Phillips has shown, for most of the seventeenth century Dutch traders dominated Bordeaux's wine trade, exporting to England and the Netherlands and investing in the region to reclaim marshland and expand vineyards.[3] André Jullien, Frenchman and author of one of the first comprehensive wines guides in 1816, noted that while few vines grew in the Netherlands, Amsterdam had been one of the world's largest trading centers for fortified wines ("vins de liqueur de tous les pays").[4] Over the course of the eighteenth century, complicated geopolitics led to the French falling out of favor with the Dutch and the British, to the benefit of the Portuguese port-makers and traders. But Irish merchants, and later political exiles, flocked to France and gave their names to some of Bordeaux's top crus and cognacs: Kirwan, Barton, Lynch, and Hennessey. Thus, even the most iconic French wine region was profoundly shaped by foreign traders in the early modern period.

The Dutch put the same principles into practice in South Africa, hoping that wine would both wring profit from the soil and provision its merchant navy. They also experienced geopolitical upheavals with imperial rivals Britain and France. The eighteenth century closed with the Napoleonic Wars, from which the British navy eventually emerged triumphant. One of its spoils was the Cape of Good Hope. When Van der Stel arrived at the Cape it had been a strategic port at the nexus of maritime trade; when the British took formal possession of the Cape in 1814, it had become a permanent settlement with a notable wine industry.

TAVERN OF THE SEAS

The Dutch came ashore at Table Bay, Cape of Good Hope, in 1652, to establish a victualing, or refreshment station: a stop midway on the journey from the Netherlands to the Dutch colonies in modern-day India and Indonesia, where ships could restock with fresh water, produce, and meat. The VOC had modest ambitions for this site. A VOC administrator, Jan van Riebeeck, was appointed governor, and his mission was to provide foodstuffs for ships while minimizing either expenditure or friction with the native Khoikhoi, who were pastoralists and were willing to sell meat to the Dutch. After a few years van Riebeeck deemed it expedient to "grant" land to a few VOC employees, and to import west African and Angolan people to become enslaved workers on their farms.[5] These freeburghers, as the Dutch employees became known, would produce food for ships, and sell it exclusively to the VOC. They would enjoy a guaranteed market for their goods, although the prices were fixed low and they would be unlikely to become rich. The enslaved people would work, and die, and no doubt endure pain and humiliation, and the Khoikhoi would lose their meat market.

When Simon van der Stel was appointed governor twenty-seven years later, Cape Town was still a mere village, with frequent maritime traffic but a permanent population of just a few hundred people. Van der Stel was ambitious for his colony and for himself and his vision involved winemaking. But he was not the first to plant vines on the Cape, with which he is often credited. According to George McCall Theal, a pioneering historian and state archivist of the Cape, van Riebeeck had planted vines at Wynberg, outside Cape Town, by 1658. (The famous Franco-British wine expert André Simon dates the vine plantings even earlier, to 1653,[6] and the South African journalist Gordon Bagnall believes they were planted by 1655).[7] Van Riebeeck made southern Africa's first wine in February 1659, with his own hands, since he was "the only person in the settlement with any knowledge of the manner in which the work should be performed." Bagnall, an unabashed promoter of European imperialism, claims Van Riebeeck praised God for this first vintage. "Just as Roman civilization in ancient days took wine, and taught its use, to the barbaric lands of Europe and the islands [sic] of Britain off its shores," Bagnall wrote triumphantly in the 1960s, "so the Dutch brought wine, as one of the essentials of civilized life, to the rough land of South Africa where they were to build their European home."[8]

The reality was hardly so glorious. Theal describes Van Riebeeck's wine as made from "Muscadel and other round white grapes," possibly grown from root stocks imported from Spain.[9] Van Riebeeck apparently tried to encourage the burghers to plant vines, too, "but most of them satisfied themselves with planting a few cuttings round their houses." The burghers were not touched by the spirit of the educated European men of the day, who systematically repopulated plants throughout their empires in the hopes that experimentation would yield new cash crops. The burghers "preferred the fruit and grain of the Fatherland to such foreign plants as the vine and maize, of the manner of cultivating which they professed themselves absolutely ignorant."[10] Unlike Van der Stel, most Dutch people did not grow grapes. The burghers were also few in number, too, for the Dutch were not yet making a European home in South Africa, but were merely trying to run a cost-efficient refreshment station.

The early wines were disappointing but the experiments persisted. The VOC had begun purchasing Cape wine, but only for its ships' stores, since it was "not saleable in India, on account of its being of very inferior quality."[11]

In 1670 one of Van Riebeeck's successors, Jacob Borghorst, tried to incentivize the wine farmers to produce more wine, by offering an inexpensive licence to sell unlimited wine in Dutch Batavia (modern Indonesia). But this was unsuccessful, since the burghers "were too poor to wait a twelvemonth for the price of their produce. . . . their idea of a good market was a market where the price of everything was fixed, where a man could reckon to a stiver what his wine would bring before it left his farm. The freedom of the Indian market was thus no inducement to them to increase their vineyards."[12] Distillation, which was proving so profitable to the Dutch in Bordeaux, had an equally inauspicious start. In 1672 South Africa's first brandy was made by distilling some of this inferior wine, but "the quality of the brandy was however even less favourable [sic] than of the wine of which it was made."[13] South African wine was off to a rough start.

When Van der Stel arrived in South Africa, then, wine production was well established but the quality was consistently mediocre. As a colonial governor, Van der Stel focused on transforming the station into an actual colony of settlement, and that required boosting its population as well as improving its wine and other potential sources of revenue. He oversaw the arrival of new migrants, including a number of female European orphans, who were intended to marry with the single male burghers (so as well as slavery, the colony probably grew through sexual exploitation). The 1687 census of the Cape showed around six hundred Europeans and three hundred enslaved people. More significantly, as far as wine is concerned, the Cape welcomed a community of French Huguenots in 1688. These refugees were Protestants, fleeing France's Wars of Religion, seeking safe haven in the rival imperial power of the Netherlands. They populated the area that became known as Franschhoek (French corner). The ambitions of Dutch winemakers had already outstripped their expertise, and these new arrivals had expertise in winemaking and vine dressing (the art of pruning grape vines)—expertise which some scholars argue gave them a comparative advantage in winemaking for several generations.[14] There were by now a large number of grapes to tend: that same 1687 census had recorded 402,900 vines.[15] The amount of land these vines covered would have entirely depended on how they were spaced out, but using a traditional European measurement of ten thousand vines per hectare gives forty hectares, or about one hundred acres.[16] This is a very small parcel in modern agricultural terms, but an acre was meant to convey how much land a man and an ox could plough in one day, and in a colony with only a few hundred male workers, this was not insignificant.

Theal explains that the Huguenots were also cautioned that wine should not be made at the expense of grain production. While this might suggest suspicion about the potential for grapes, it more likely reflects the reality of a subsistence economy where bread is the staple food: even contemporary Burgundy had restrictions on vine planting in grain-producing areas.[17] Part of the appeal of wine grapes, to a subsistence farmer, is that they can sometimes flourish in poor soil that would be unsuitable for other crops.[18] Complementary, mixed agriculture was the goal.

Van der Stel's reputation as the father of South African wine is thanks to the vineyards he laid out in Constantia, now a southeastern suburb of Cape Town. A 1685 grant gave him 861 morgen,[19] approximately 737 hectares or 1,821 acres. His winery gave its name to the famous wine it produced, as well as to the surrounding lands. He and his son, Adriaan, who also succeeded him as a governor, encouraged improvements in agriculture among the burghers. When it came to wine, Simon experimented with grape varietals from France, Germany, Spain and Persia, both on his own farm and in gardens laid out by the VOC in Table Valley. Frustrated with the poor quality of the burghers' wine, he also forbade the pressing of grapes in the colony until he had personally verified their ripeness, on penalty of a stiff fine.[20] This micromanagement must not have endeared him to wine-producing burghers, and nor did his personal stake in the wine trade. By the early eighteenth century, the Van der Stel family had personally acquired the largest estates in the colony, producing grain as well as meat and wine. Their monopoly led to complaints and Adriaan's dismissal from the governorship in 1707.[21] While it is difficult to determine whether quality was significantly improving, the Van der Stels's wine operation was evidently becoming increasingly lucrative.

The Constantia vineyard was subdivided after Simon's death into three vineyards, Groot (great), Klein (small), and Bergvliet, and passed through the ownership of several different burgher families. By the first decades of the eighteenth century, other families, too, were becoming wealthy, creating a gap in the European population between a small number of rich families growing wine and wheat in the vicinity of Cape Town, and the poor burghers who began spreading into the hinterland, creating a frontier society. The wealthiest wine farmers, in Stellenbosch and Constantia, built Dutch gabled homes, many of which still stand, tall, proud, and white against their lush vineyards. The Cape's population was becoming more diverse, though it was still small. One of the wealthiest men in the Cape in the first half of the eighteenth century made his fortune from alcohol retailing, serving local wine and brandy, mostly to sailors passing through.[22] Sometimes several thousand sailors would come ashore for several weeks to frequent Cape Town's taverns,[23] so the population could expand quickly and temporarily.

The Constantia vineyards would become famous in Europe. It is difficult to put a precise date on when the Constantia estate began producing wines of distinct quality, but it was probably within Van der Stel's lifetime. Nor is it clear to what extent early references to good wines from the Cape referred specifically to Constantia or not, or at what point the terms ceased to be interchangeable, and in fact came to mean opposite things in terms of wine quality (Constantia good, Cape wine terrible). But because Cape Town was at such an important trade nexus, and administrators were anxious to promote a high-value product, it it not difficult to understand how a quality wine's reputation could spread quickly, even back to the wine-producing powers of Europe. Although the Dutch and the British were imperial rivals, they also traded with each other, and the strategic importance of the Cape on the European-Indian trade route exposed British traders to Cape wine. John Ovington, the English king's chaplain, who published an account of his 1689 voyage to India via the Cape, described the growth of the wine industry at this time. He said that they were "now able . . . to furnish the Indies with some quantity, where they sell it by the Bottle at a Roupie." This was a white wine in the style of German wines, probably sweet: "'Tis colour'd like Rhenish, and therefore they pass it under the specious Name in India, but the Taste of it is much harder and less palatable; its Operations are more searching, and the strength of it more intoxicating and offensive to the Brain."[24] This is one of the first of many documented examples of the New World styling and naming its wines after famous European wine styles, and even with the intent of misleading consumers: in this case, Cape wine being called Rhenish. Seventeenth- and eighteenth-century British people called most wines after places of origin, but in an informal way that bucked no legal definition.

It is also an early example of how the Cape—so much hotter and drier than the German Rheinhessen—probably produced wines that were higher in alcohol content than wines produced with the same grapes in northern Europe. Two English encyclopedists wrote in 1766 that when kept for two years, Cape wines "assume the taste of sack; and Cape wine that has been kept till six years old sparkles like old hock, and is as racy as the finest Canary."[25] Sack was a generic term for Spanish sherry, hock is a German-style white wine, and Canary refers to the sweet white wines of the Canary Islands, all of which were common in Britain. Sack and Canary were fortified wines, though, strengthened in both taste and alcoholic content by the addition of distilled spirits (which also decreased the risk of the wine spoiling, a good thing for export markets). In the case of the Cape wines, that strength presumably came, not from adding extra alcohol, but from the natural ripeness of the grapes. Hotter climates produce riper grapes, which in turn contain more sugar for conversion to alcohol. As we will see, in the late nineteenth century tariffs that were linked to alcohol levels became a nuisance for colonial wine importers. But for some wine lovers in the eighteenth-century British world, the potency of Cape wine was particularly appreciated. "The Cape wine is very rich and strong", the London *Gentleman's Magazine* wrote approvingly in 1738.[26] In a short 1734 poem, entitled "To Dr Mead, on His Cape Wine," the Irish poet Mary Barber celebrates that ripeness:

> Your Wine, by Southern Suns refin'd,
> Is a just Emblem of your Mind:
> Like You, the gen'rous Juice displays
> Its Influence a thousand Ways;
> Like You, it raises sinking Hearts,
> Inspiring, and rewarding Arts;
> Dispels the Spleen, and conquers Pain,
> Calls back departing Life again.[27]

Barber's poem, comparing the generosity and warmth of her friend Dr. Mead to that of a Cape wine, shows that in the mid-eighteenth-century Anglophone world, Cape wine was not seen as a vile imitation of a European wine, but a warming and pleasant beverage that owed its distinctive taste to its location. While Barber is taking artistic license in suggesting that this "gen'rous Juice" could save those on the brink of death, through the nineteenth century wine was commonly used for medicinal purposes,[28] and Cape wine was no exception. A 1753 London text shows a medical doctor specifying Cape wine to medicate a nobleman, without noting the vineyard or grape.[29] By the nineteenth century it was Constantia wine specifically, and not Cape wine in general, that apparently had such power. One of the most commonly cited appearances of Constantia in English is in Jane Austen's 1811 novel *Sense and Sensibility*, where it is invoked as a cure for both "colicky gout" and heartbreak.[30]

Cape wines were thus known and available in eighteenth-century Britain. These wines were evidently enjoyed or sought after by Britain's middling classes, whose low-staffed households were the intended audience for a very early English cookbook, Hannah Glasses' *The compleat confectioner: or, the whole art of confectionary made plain and easy*. This 1760 cookbook gives directions for creating imitation Cape wine at home by soaking "Belvedera raisins."[31] Cape wine must have had a distinctive taste well known to Glasse's readers, for she instructs how using other types of raisins could produce other styles of wine, such as either "Mallaga [*sic*]"-style wine (a sweet, fortified Spanish wine), or a "dry wine."[32]

At some point in the early eighteenth century, Constantia began developing an identity distinct from other Cape wines, and became established as a sweet dessert wine made from *muscat de frontignan* grapes. Part of the vast muscat grape family, *muscat de frontignan* is considered the "classic" muscat, and is known by a wide variety of other names, including *muscat blanc à petits grains,* muskadel, and muscadel. It has a close cousin, "generally considered inferior," called muscat of Alexandria, known in South Africa as *hanepoot*.[33] Both produce sweet white wines. André Simon wrote in the 1950s that the earliest grape varietals in South Africa were hanepoot, "a Muscat"; "*Steen* or *Stein,* a white *Sauvignon,* and the *Green-Grape,* a *Semillon*."[34] Steen was, and still is, the South African term for the chenin blanc varietal. Jancis Robinson writes confidently that semillon became the Cape's most important varietal, and that "In 1822 93 per cent of all South African vineyard was planted with this variety, imported from Bordeaux. So common was it then in fact that it was simply called Wyndruif, or 'wine grape.'"[35] Semillon is a white grape which is used for the famous French sweet wine Sauternes.

The Cape was certainly producing some red wines, too, and even Constantia came in both red and white varieties. We know this, for example, from mentions of Cape wine that appear in eighteenth-century British newspapers, such as a 1743 advertisement for "A Small Parcel of genuine red and white Constantia Cape Wine, very bright, and of a Fine Flavour, at 1 l. [pound] 1 s[hilling] per Gallon, including the Bottles."[36] A bankrupt London vintner auctioning his stock in that same year sold assorted hogshead barrels of French Burgundy and claret, Champagne, Frontignac, and Rhenish, as well as "twenty-two dozen and six Pint Bottles of fine red Cape Wine," plus a hogshead and some pint bottles of "white Cape Wine."[37]

Thomas Salmon's 1735 *Modern history; or, the present state of all nations,* referred to "the Cape Wine, of late so much admir'd in Europe," noting that "it was a great while, it seems, before they rais'd any Considerable vineyards," because of poor understanding of vine dressing. Now, however, "there is scarce a Cottage in the Cape Settlements, but has it Vineyard, which produces Wine enough for the Family, and some for Sale."[38] Johan Fourie has shown that Cape settler society, rather than being in an economic backwater, was becoming wealthier in the eighteenth century, and wine was an important commodity contributing to its wealth.[39]

None of this wine production could have happened without slave labor—indeed, part of the Cape's wealth was measured in the value that settlers placed on enslaved people.[40] Grape vines were vulnerable to the elements and winemaking was labor-intensive. Salmon noted that farmers had to deal with storm damage, mildew, locusts, and a "little black worm," which he specifies the enslaved people were tasked with removing from the vines every morning.[41] Van Riebeeck's original slave shipment was composed of people from West Africa and Angola, but increasingly enslaved people came from other Dutch territories, including Indonesia, Ceylon (Sri Lanka), and India. In 1717 the Council of Policy, a governing body in Cape Town, voted overwhelmingly that the colony should continue to rely on slave labor. Although the Cape colony never developed large slave plantations, as in the Caribbean or the southern United States, slavery was pervasive and essential, especially for wine as compared to other industries. Mary Rayner has found that at the end of the eighteenth century, while most slaveowners had fewer than eight enslaved people, wine farmers averaged sixteen enslaved people each.[42] In the second half of the eighteenth century, when a nascent campaign to abolish slavery emerged in Britain, it focused mostly on the use of slavery on British Caribbean sugar plantations. I have not found any particular condemnation of Cape wine in this movement's pronouncements, but of course British people consumed a tremendous amount of sugar, and a relatively small amount of Cape wine consumption. Wines that were shipped thousands of miles in ships' holds sometimes spoiled and evaporated; what also dissipated with distance was the consumers' sense of implication in the ethics of production.

There is frank racism to be found, instead, when white British wine drinkers were confronted by the physical intimacy of winemaking, by the Black and brown bodies that created the good that they ingested. During the first period of British occupation of the Cape, between 1796 and 1803, the wife of the secretary of the Cape Colony wrote of a visit to Cloete's Constantia estate: "Mynheer Cloete took us to the wine-press hall, where the whole of our party made wry faces at the idea of drinking wine that had been pressed by three pairs of black feet; but the certainty that the fermentation would carry off every polluted article settled that objection with me."[43] Slave labor was not made visible to the British consumer, but it was obvious to any visitor or settler at the Cape. European imperial projects were built on racial hierarchies and often counted on the forced labor of indigenous peoples, and wine was no different.

Wine shaped the Cape Colony over the course of the eighteenth century. It was critical to the creation of race and class distinctions that would hold steady in South African society for centuries. Wealthy whites were bound up in wine growing and retailing and concentrated in and near Cape Town; poorer whites spread out into the "frontier" of the Cape Colony; black and Asian enslaved people toiled in the vineyards; the native Khoi, weakened as a community by economic marginalization and a smallpox epidemic, were dispersed throughout and beyond. This was the small but increasingly diverse, even cosmopolitan, society that British troops first occupied in 1795: around twenty-five thousand enslaved people, twenty thousand white European colonists, fifteen thousand Khoikhoi, and a thousand free Blacks.[44]

The British occupation of the Cape, much like the Dutch occupation a century earlier, was strategic. In 1793 revolutionary France declared war on its European rival states, including Britain and the Dutch Republic, in what would turn into two decades of warfare. These were world wars, in that they involved colonies and their populations around the world: in India, in the Caribbean, and in South Africa. In 1795 the French overthrew the Dutch Republic and created the pro-French Batavian Republic in its place. Since French control of the Cape could have threatened British access to any colonies (and trade routes) in the Indian and Pacific Oceans, the British preemptively captured the Cape in 1795, and held it until 1803, when a European truce reinstated the Batavian Republic. When that truce failed in 1806, the British resumed control of the Cape. The Cape became an official British colony in 1814, as the Napoleonic Wars wound down, and remained a colony until it became a British dominion, as part of the Union of South Africa, in 1910. Napoleon's favorite wine, we are repeatedly told by wine historians, was Constantia, which he repeatedly requested in his final imprisonment on the island of St. Helena. Winemakers, shippers, sellers, and drinkers were nodes in the complex and entangled networks of European loyalties.

FOUR

First Fleet, First Flight

CREATING AUSTRALIAN VINEYARDS

SOMEWHERE, IN THE DANK HOLDS of the ships, there were grape vines, "of various sorts," purchased at the Cape of Good Hope.[1] Wine grapes cannot be reliably grown from seeds, so vine cuttings were carefully nestled in boxes and packed into the ships with other seeds, farming implements, small livestock, and reserves of food. These would be the materials that the fifteen hundred passengers on the First Fleet expected to need on arrival in Australia in 1788.

The passengers on the eleven-ship fleet were the first Europeans to establish a long-term settlement in Australia. Most were convicts, whose prison time had been commuted to banishment and indentured servitude across the world. The journey took over eight months; water and food ran low while vermin, disease, and stench proliferated. Yet the journey was aspirational, too: those plants in the hold were expected to transform both the convicts and the land into something better, more productive, and more civilized.

The colonization of Australia and New Zealand has two vital features in common with that of South Africa, as far as wine is concerned. First, all three were forcibly settled by Europeans as strategic territories in the zero-sum game of European imperial politics. Second, all three were immediately planted with wine grapes. In each colony, it took several decades of trial-and-error before satisfactory wine could be exported, but enthusiastic settlers persevered with viticulture as part of their civilizing mission.

Dutch ships had begun crossing the Indian Ocean in the late sixteenth century, and made first contact with western Australia in 1606. By the mid-seventeenth century, Europeans recognized the term "New Holland" as the Dutch claim to Australia, although the Dutch did not settle or establish a victualing station as they were doing in the Cape (and indeed, all Australian-

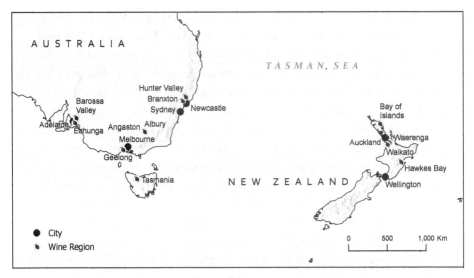

MAP 3. Australia and New Zealand, showing places mentioned in the text. Early winemaking was concentrated in eastern and then southern Australia, and in the North Island of New Zealand.

bound European ships would make great use of that station at Cape Town). Nor did the British or French explorers who wandered into Australian waters attempt to settle, much less conquer anything, until the 1770s. That change came about through a voyage led by British naval captain and cartographer, James Cook, who was accompanied by the botanists Joseph Banks and Daniel Solander. In an era of intense imperial rivalry, Cook was eager to stake a claim before the French could do so, and thus asserted that Botany Bay (the immense natural harbor around the modern city of Sydney) was British. The French were also "exploring" the South Pacific, so Britain's territorial claim would be strengthened by an actual settlement. It was thus decided in 1787 to send a fleet of ships—the "First Fleet," in Australian historical parlance—loaded with British criminals, and to use Botany Bay as a convict colony. Careful, recent research by Charles Tuckwell has shown that London lawmakers knew that transporting convicts to Australia made little economic sense—it would have been much cheaper and easier to build more domestic prisons—but that the British state was willing to spend deeply for strategic reasons.[2] The convicts were to be indentured for a period of time, then hopefully released as reformed members of society and eager workers. The First Fleet thus came equipped to set up an instant agricultural society, with seeds, plant cuttings, and tools for the convict workers.

Despite the intense scientific and botanical interest in Australia, British imperialists in the eighteenth century viewed Australia as *terra nullius*: land belonging to no one and on which nothing had been established. This emptiness was a mirage, a specter of willful nescience and imperial hubris. The modern state of Australia occupies a vast continent, spanning over two thousand miles from east to west. In the eighteenth century this enormous island was home to hundreds of Aboriginal nations, perhaps 750,000 people in total. There was great linguistic and cultural diversity across these first nations, but for the most part hunting and gathering were the mainstays of their economies, rather than pastoral agriculture, in part because Australia is so arid. Coastal communities traded with other peoples in the Pacific and Indian Oceans, though, and according to Maggie Brady, there is evidence that Aboriginal people on the northern coast were purchasing alcohol from Makassan traders (from modern-day Indonesia) in the 1720s.[3] They also brewed their own beverages, so Aboriginal peoples were not strangers to alcohol before European contact. Nor were they unsophisticated, by any measure: rather, they maintained a careful existence of harmony with the natural environment and with each other.

Nevertheless, British adventurers and government envoys alike saw Aboriginal presence on Australian land as a nuisance, and Aboriginal cultures as savage. The logic followed, then, that the land they inhabited was ripe for redevelopment. When an enterprising London publisher printed an account of British colonization of New South Wales in 1789, he prefaced it with a poem entreating the British to transform their conquered environment. In the poem, Botany Bay is personified as a voluptuous woman, opening her arms in welcome to the British ships, and urging those from "cultured" Europe to build, and plant, and expand:

> There shall broad streets their stately walls extend, . . .
> There, ray'd from cities o'er the cultur'd land,
> Shall bright canals, and solid roads expand.
> There the proud arch, Colossus-like, bestride
> Yon glittering streams, and bounded the chasing tide;
> Embellish'd villas crown the landscape-scene,
> Farms wave with gold, and orchards blush between.[4]

Lush vegetation and flourishing agriculture were absolutely central to the British imagination of colonization in the Pacific. So, too, were images of classical antiquity, and of Greek and Roman empires, to which Britons considered themselves the natural heirs: here, arches, villas, and colossal statuary are imagined rising triumphantly over the landscape. The author would have been proud to know that a few decades later, the Wyndham family would be constructing a colonnade on their villa overlooking vast vineyards, for grape vines and wine figured in the British imagination of their own civilizational accomplishments.

George Barrington, an administrator on the First Fleet, described the following transformation in his published memoirs of his first years in the new colony: "Considering the savage state from which he has so recently emerged, he may be deemed a polite man, as he performs the ceremonies of bowing, drinking healths, returning thanks, &c. with the most scrupulous exactness. He is very fond of wine."[5] Although this description perhaps could have been about one of the convicts in Barrington's charge, it actually described a man named Bennelong (or Banalong, in Barrington's text), a leader of the Eora people of eastern Australia. This brief passage reveals much about the architects of British settlement in Australia: their assumptions that indigenous people were uncivilized and inferior, their strict social codes that incorporated formal drinking rituals, and their commonplace consumption of wine.

The British envoys who amused themselves by sharing wine with Bennelong were of a high social status and were used to consuming wine (unlike most of the convicts, who were more accustomed to beer and spirits). On the First Fleet's voyage out, the social and meritorious distinction in wine consumption was clear in the ship's rations: "The allowance was, to the marines, a pound of bread, a pound of beef, and a pint of wine, *per* man, daily: the convicts had three quarters of beef, and of bread, but no wine."[6]

As well as a social marker, wine was widely used as medicine in the eighteenth century. It was certainly regarded as a critical medical and nutritional supplement on a long sea voyage, and not just by the British. Eighteenth-century Dutch shipwrecks off Australian coasts have yielded many fragments of ornate wine glasses.[7] The First Fleet ships departed England and replenished their supplies of food and Portuguese wine at both Teneriffe and then Rio de Janeiro, before crossing back across the Atlantic and rounding the Cape. Grape plants were purchased in both Rio and Cape Town, but the Rio purchases were probably of table grape vines, and only the Cape vines were for *vitis vinifera* wine grapes.[8] Despite having purchased fresh fruits and vegetables, as the journey continued the passengers began to show symptoms of scurvy, a debilitating and frequently fatal illness. Modern medical knowledge shows that scurvy is the result of a lack of vitamin C, a disease that Jonathan

Lamb and Killian Quigley have argued disproportionately affected Irish convicts.[9] When those on the ships began to show symptoms of scurvy, the captain distributed "porter, spruce-beer, and wine among the seamen"; when crew members became completely debilitated by the disease, "wine was daily served out to them."[10] Unfortunately for the sailors, fresh grapes do contain vitamin C but wine does not.[11] The wine might have alleviated their suffering, but it would not have cured their illness.

The presence of wine in late eighteenth-century British life—as the preferred daily beverage of those who could afford it, and as an occasional supplement or luxury for those who could not—meant that it was natural that the colony should try to produce its own. Liquids are heavy and space-consuming in a ship's hold, and the closest wine producer, the Cape, was two months' journey away. The progress of viticulture was slow, though, and hardly imperious. As in the Cape Colony, viticulture began as an imagined project of a small number of elite administrators. Whereas the Dutch Cape had been first settled by poor VOC employees, New South Wales was established as a penal colony for mostly working-class convicts from Britain and Ireland. Though established more than a century apart, the two settlements were similar in terms of demographics, for the settlers were mostly poor and male. Neither of these low-status populations was accustomed to much wine consumption back home in Europe, and they preferred distilled spirits and beer. They did not have firsthand experience in viticulture; in fact, many of them who were city dwellers had no work experience in agriculture at all. Furthermore, those convicts who were indentured to perform government labor or act as manservants for officials had little time to devote to experimental gardening in the early years of the colony. When William Bligh, an early British governor of New South Wales, testified before the House of Commons in 1812, he stated that "the encouragement of gardens was a thing I particularly attended to," but admitted that at best, the more industrious convicts grew "a few potatoes, or what they might find necessary."[12]

Still, a small vineyard was established at Governor Phillip's residence on Sydney Cove, and there the governor experimented with his vines, and possibly had made wine by 1792. Parramatta, a farming settlement established just west of Sydney, in 1791 boasted "nine hundred and twenty acres of land, thinned, cleared, and cultivated," of which four acres were dedicated to vines. (Most were devoted to maize, turnips, and enclosed pasture for animals).[13] Whether this is a large or a small number of acres is difficult to determine; the urgent priority for the colony was to supply subsistence food for people and livestock. Since vines took several years to yield grapes for wine, they could not be an immediate investment.

The governor also mobilized the nascent newspaper press to contribute to the cause. The very first issue of the *Sydney Gazette and New South Wales Advertiser,* an official government organ, on March 5, 1803, featured shipping news, death notices, and court reports, and a single feature article: "Method of Preparing a Piece of Land, for the Purpose of Preparing a Vineyard."[14] This anonymous article, "translated from the French," was serialized over several weeks and included brief instructions on preparing land, planting, vine dressing, and making wine itself.[15] The instructions were not, however, corrected to the Southern Hemisphere: they recommended pruning vines in January and February, which would be Australian summer, not winter.[16]

It does appear correct to write of a continuous wine-growing tradition in Australia that began in 1788, if we allow that the first thirty years saw sparse plantings and very limited production. The idea of Australian wine production and eventual export never seems to have disappeared from the recesses of the official mind, even if the results were slow to materialize. After all, as we have seen, Cape wine was established in the international markets in this period, and its production would be formally encouraged by British officials after 1814. But whereas the Cape had over a century of wine-growing experience, and had probably benefited from French Huguenot expertise in its early years, Australia was truly new at this wine game. Thus, from the 1820s Australian winemakers and elites desperately petitioned the government to allow a small number—first of German then of French—winemakers and vine dressers to enter the colony.[17] This was necessary because non-British migration to New South Wales was restricted, but none of the British migrants who entered either as convicts or, later, as assisted immigrants, had the necessary knowledge of winemaking and vine growing, though they may have had other kinds of farming experience.[18] These petitions were successful, probably because the winemakers (chiefly Edward Macarthur) argued that if they could bring in the requisite expertise to grow the fledgling wine industry, the industry could in turn attract migrants from Britain,[19] which would both ease population pressures in the imperial "motherland" and solve the general labor deficit in New South Wales. As a result, a small number of experts were imported in the 1820s and 1830s, although the impact was slow and halting.

Notwithstanding the slow progress of the colony, it is all too easy to mythologize the First Fleet. Because it introduced the first generation of

European settlers, the Fleet's arrival is now commemorated as the founding moment of the eventual state of Australia. But for Aboriginal Australians, and for kindred first-nation peoples in other parts of the world, the Fleet marked an entirely different kind of era: one of dispossession, death, and cultural loss. Colonialism is not simply about competition for resources, a fair fight of one group successfully wresting resources from another. It is ideological, and in the case of European colonialism in the New World, that ideology was based on the belief that Europeans were uniquely equipped to lead and prosper, and it was usually accompanied with scant regard for indigenous lives.

The emphasis that historians place on seafaring traditions can also leave a curious legacy. There is strong evidence that eighteenth-century British identity was imagined in relation to the oceans, and that British prestige was tied to naval prowess. British people living in port cities, especially, could imagine a wider world through the regular ship traffic that brought and sent people and goods across the seas. It is also clear, and is one of the main arguments of this book, that wine production was part and parcel of international maritime trade. Historians, myself included, rightly emphasize global trading networks to explain the connections between seemingly distant lands. But when historians make these arguments, we can unintentionally romanticize that trade. Jessica Moody, writing about commemoration and maritime museums in Liverpool, argues that the triangle trade works as a "displacement narrative," distancing the city of Liverpool from what actually was traded. "The use of the triangular device to describe the Atlantic routes of the slave trade," she writes, "keep [sic] human connections between Liverpool and slavery at bay, having ships leave and return with inanimate goods only, confining talk of slave bodies to the 'middle passage.'"[20] With regard to the First Fleet, it is easy to focus on the maritime journey itself, which is undoubtedly an epic story of human survival, of many individuals who were transported against their will. But recognition of this dramatic arrival should not prevent us from considering what happened once those settlers had installed themselves on Australian soil.

In the same vein, wine historians can stumble into mythologizing when documenting the first winemakers in Australia. It is, of course, intriguing to piece together the earliest years of vine cultivation in the fledging colony, and the historian's impulse is always to try to assemble a complete chronology. Julie McIntyre has documented these early wine promoters, and shown how the over the first few decades of this Australian settlement, administrators in

London and Sydney continued to support colonial wine production: allowing a handful of French and German settlers into the colony because of their wine expertise, writing back and forth with updates and questions about the progress of vines, encouraging the importation of vine cuttings.[21] "Without vineyards," McIntyre writes, "the imagined picture of the colony remained incomplete."[22] But these top-level interventions reveal not judicious support of a promising industry, but wistful desire to see grapes flourish. These early settlers were visionaries, not in the sense of being prophetic, but rather in having an idyllic vision of agricultural and economic prosperity. Thus, wine-growing was not a whimsical exercise, even if its profits appear insignificant in terms of the Australian (or imperial) macroeconomy. Wine became a serious undertaking, and one critical to the larger British imperial project.

FIVE

Astonished to See the Fruit

NEW ZEALAND'S FIRST GRAPES

IN THE EIGHTEENTH CENTURY it had become a rite of passage for wealthy British people—often young people—to conduct a "grand tour" of continental Europe, supplementing their formal education with visits to museums, historic sites, and ruins, and accumulating both knowledge and souvenirs along the way. This study-abroad experience would signal their sophistication and knowledge in polite society, and would open professional opportunities and contacts. A few ambitious Australian settlers undertook their own grand tours, but with a specific views toward learning about viticulture and wine production. John MacArthur, a merchant turned winemaker, conducted his own grand tour of Europe in 1815, visiting vineyards over several months to observe and learn about the winemaking process. But they were outdone by a young Scotsman on the make, James Busby, who envisioned his imperial career taking off through his wine expertise.

Part of the appeal of the empire to British people was that it promised career opportunity and wealth. Colonial service had the reputation of being more meritocratic than military or civil service in Britain. For middle-class British and Irish men, or for younger sons in wealthy families, frustrated with the opportunities available to them at home, working in the empire seemed an adventurous choice that might allow them to progress quickly and take on great responsibility. Many young men who worked for the East India Company and the Indian Civil Service, two of the largest employers, did not return, but succumbed to disease or violence. But others returned to Britain with wealth and prestige that they never could have earned at home, and their wealth was disbursed the full length of the U.K. Robert Clive, the notorious British commander in Calcutta in the 1780s, retired to Limerick, Ireland, and built himself a Palladian mansion among rolling grounds. He

48

named it Plassey House after his most famous battle. Indeed, much of the British landscape over the late eighteenth and nineteenth centuries was built and transformed through money from empire. Public and private buildings, infrastructure, and luxury purchases were financed by the proceeds of imperialism, through money that individuals had made and saved by working or trading overseas. More pointedly, a recent project at University College London has demonstrated how the state "compensation" offered to slaveholders after the abolition of slavery in 1833 was generally not invested in colonies, but was ploughed back into mainland investments. Monies awarded to slaveowners financed the construction of railroads, mines, country houses, and museums, and was invested through banks to capitalize many more projects unknown.[1] Labor had been extracted from colonies, and capital now was, too, to the detriment of these colonies' long-term economic development.

This ambitious imperialist career network was the milieu from which James Busby emerged, and this was the logic that propelled him into Australian wine. Busby is sometimes seen as a solitary visionary, a wine lover who serendipitously and generously brought his knowledge to Australia and New Zealand; a 1940 study by Eric Ramsden anointed him "James Busby, the Prophet of Australian Viticulture."[2] Busby's love of wine was probably genuine, but he made viticulture his specialty because he was a young man looking to advance as a career bureaucrat in the empire, and he saw wine as a niche area of expertise through which he could sell himself. He is an important personality in colonial wine history, but not for the reasons for which he has normally been credited.

Busby was born in Scotland in 1802 and emigrated to New South Wales with his parents in 1824; his father was a civil engineer recruited to undertake infrastructure projects in New South Wales, and James Busby was confidently educated. James Busby was granted two thousand acres in the Hunter Valley, where he could experiment with viticulture (to what ends, we cannot be certain), and he also briefly taught viticulture at a boys' school. But much more significantly to his rise to viticultural prominence, he published his first book in 1825, entitled *A Treatise on the Culture of the Vine and the Art of Making Wine,* a translation and compilation of Jean-Antoine Chaptal's writings from French, with Busby's own observations from his travels in France. Chaptal was an obvious and useful author to translate: a highly renowned French chemist, he had also served as French minister of the interior under Napoleon and was an energetic promoter of agriculture and manufactures.

Chaptal's name persists in oenology through the term *chaptalization,* which refers to the addition of sugar to grape must to boost fermentation.

Busby dedicated his *Treatise* to Major General Sir Thomas Brisbane, the governor of New South Wales, "being a humble attempt to promote the advancement of the interesting colonies under his command." The introduction to the book is not about wine, but reads like a cross between an undergraduate thesis and a policy brief, demonstrating Busby's command of basic ideas about imperial economics and advancing his argument as to why viticulture was a superior venture to wool or grain production. He began by proclaiming that New South Wales did not produce "any article of produce which might minister to the wants or comforts of Great Britain," was thus an expensive dependency Britain to maintain, and had not created "that regular and natural intercourse between a colony and its parent state, which consists in the exchange of the raw produce of the one, for the manufactured commodities of the other."[3] Given that wheat was amply produced by other countries, he saw little hope of Australia competing in the British market; he conceded that raising sheep was promising, but that the lack of infrastructure made it impossible to move large quantities of wool to market, without losing economies of scale. No, Busby argued, the future of New South Wales's prosperity lay elsewhere, in wine. He noted that the most famous wines of Europe were produced between the fiftieth and thirty-fifth parallels, and that New South Wales lay at the thirty-fifth parallel of the Southern Hemisphere—as does the Cape of Good Hope, which "possesses the vineyards of Constantia, than which, we need not go farther for proofs of the suitableness of the climate for the production of the finest wines."[4] This may be one of the first articulations of the "wine bands" around the globe, or the two latitudinal areas in which most wines are produced (although climate change and ingenuity are, in the twenty-first century, leading to "new latitude" wines).

Busby deduced that he could further impress his superiors by demonstrating skill and value to the colony, and so he set off on a professional development tour to learn about winemaking: a self-funded four months' journey through the vineyards of France and Spain, published as a book in Sydney in 1833: *Journal of a Tour through Some of the Vineyards of Spain and France.* The book, digitized and easily available today, describes in detail his tour through Xeres, Seville, Malaga, and Catalonia in Spain. He then crossed into France, progressing east through Perpignan, Montpellier, Nîmes, and Provence, and then north into Hermitage (the Rhône), Burgundy, Champagne, and finally Paris. The book is rich in detail but light in tone: it describes the soil at each destination, the winemaking processes used in different regions, and his interactions with winemakers and exporters.

The *Journal of a Tour* thus became Busby's calling card, his means of demonstrating his renown and expertise. In Sydney Busby would bring, quite literally, the fruits of his European tour to bear: 543 cuttings of European grape varieties, ready to be replanted in Australian soil. Some of these were obtained directly from the vineyards, including a "Ciras" or "Scyras . . . used in making the best red wines of Hermitage . . . originally brought from Shiraz, of Persia."[5] The rest were culled from the experimental botanic gardens of France, including the Luxembourg Gardens in Paris.

These cuttings were obtained through established protocols of botanic exchange. At the botanic garden in Montpellier, in southern France, Busby arrived without notice and introduced himself to Professor Delisle, the professor of botany and director of the garden, who warmly received him and offered a tour, pointing out Mediterranean plants that he thought would flourish in New South Wales. Delisle offered vine cuttings to Busby, and had seed packets prepared, and Busby, in return, "did not hesitate to pledge myself to make him whatever returns our Botanic Garden [in Sydney] could supply,"[6] for Montpellier already had a section devoted to Australian botany and was keen to expand it. Busby spent five days selecting, cutting, labeling, and packing hundreds of vines in Montpellier with the willing cooperation of the staff at the botanic garden. In Paris, he went to the "Royal Nursery of the Luxembourg," where he was able to obtain further vine cuttings "at a regulated price" of two and a half francs for one hundred vines.[7] These obtained, his journey was complete. He published a list of these vines, dedicated to the governor with a laudatory preface by five Sydney gentleman, with remarks on how they were faring in their new home in Sydney.[8] Some of the grape varietals are instantly recognizable to casual wine drinkers: pinot noir ("vigourous," but with "no fruit"), semillon ("no fruit, delicate"), grenache ("healthy"), and gamay ("Gamet, noire, Haute Saone, No fruit, Healthy"), and multiple varieties of muscat. Others will be more familiar to aficionados of southern French wines, such as cinsault, picpoul, marsan, and clairette. What appear to be missing from the list are most major grapes associated with twenty-first century wine production in Australia and New Zealand, namely, chardonnay, cabernet sauvignon, sauvignon blanc, and riesling.

Many wine lovers are familiar with Busby's exploits, but do not make the connection between this Busby and the colonial administrator. In fact, they are the same person, and the connection is causal rather than coincidental.

Busby's belief that wine knowledge would be a critical and unusual skill that would give him a leg up in gaining a colonial appointment, reflects the preeminence of agriculture in building British civilization in the Antipodes. For example in 1816, the *Hobart Town Gazette and South Reporter,* a newspaper of the young settlement in Tasmania, urged its residents to be proud of agriculture as part of the glory of being British colonizers: "Agriculture has been the basis of Empires.—Rome derived all her greatness, all her grandeur from her Agrarian Laws—the encouragement given to Agriculture by the equal division of her hands, on the foundation of the Colony, contributed more than any other cause to her advancement in the Scale of Nations—So proud an example ought to stimulate us to persevere in Agriculture, all is in our Favor, Climate, Soil, Manures, &c."[9]

In the history of Australian wine production, Busby has generally been given an exaggerated role.[10] He was not the father of Australian wine, and his physical residence in Australia was relatively brief. But from the point of view of imperial history, and in terms of explaining why and how viticulture spread through the British world, he is a critical figure, who demonstrates how imperial careering and economic vision coalesced. Busby's personality, talents, or interests are not the true explanatory factor; rather, the networks of migration and professional advancement and the ideology of imperial economics that he utilized are.

Busby's writings and lobbying paid off, and he was granted his long-sought professional opportunity in 1832, when he was appointed British resident to the islands known in English as New Zealand (so named by an early Dutch explorer, after his native Zeeland), and in Te Reo Māori as Aotearoa. Modern New Zealand is an island state, dominated by two major islands: North (now home to the capital of Auckland) and South. The initial British settlements were concentrated in the Bay of Islands, a beautiful and sheltered natural harbor on the eastern side of the North Island.

Early nineteenth-century Aotearoa New Zealand was already home to nearly a hundred thousand Maori people. The Maori themselves were Polynesian immigrants who had settled across New Zealand over the thirteenth through sixteenth centuries. Maori society was robust and adaptable, with a tribal structure presided over by hereditary chiefs, or *rangatira,* and a mixed economy that included settled horticulture. Unlike some Aboriginal peoples in Australia, alcohol researchers have noted that Maori were probably "one of the few indigenous populations worldwide that did not produce alcohol."[11] European explorers were thus probably entirely responsible for introducing alcohol into New Zealand. Although Maori people were initially nonplussed by this *waipiro* ("stinking water"), in the second half of the nineteenth century some would acquire a taste for alcohol, making it another European import that would bring pain and destruction to Maori society. The others were disease and weapons, both of which ultimately killed a significant portion of the population. Maori tribes had proud warrior traditions and intertribal conflict was not unusual, but the introduction of European firearms amplified the deadliness of such conflicts, resulting in a period known as the Musket Wars, between 1807 and 1845, when tens of thousands of Maori died in intertribal wars and raids.

Although Maori society was unquestionably weakened by disease and warfare, Maori were still at a complete advantage when British Christians began arriving in the 1810s with the intention of converting the population. These Christians were led by Samuel Marsden, an English Anglican priest and a chaplain based in New South Wales, and a leader of the London-based Church Mission Society. Marsden comes to our attention because he is generally credited with planting the first grapes in New Zealand, in 1819. He did not have an agricultural background before he arrived in Australia, but he adapted out of necessity: "I entered a country that was in a state of nature, and was obliged to plant or sow or starve. It was not from inclination that my colleague and I took the axe, the spade and the hoe."[12]

Marsden did not, however, attempt to make his own wine: perhaps he considered it too far beyond his skill set or available time. Rather, he believed in the potential of New Zealand to produce wine, and hoped to establish plantings so that later settlers could take up winemaking. "I have no doubt but New Zealand will be the finest country in the world for wine from what I saw. . . . If grape vines get into the island they will be ready for anyone who may come afterwards," he wrote, and he thus planted "a hundred grape vines of different kinds brought from Port Jackson,"[13] meaning the large natural harbor around Sydney. In the meantime, he believed that the grapes themselves served as a missionary tool that could facilitate Maori conversion. "The chief's sons who are with me visit our orchard and vineyards, and are much astonished to see the fruit," which were not native to the region. Marsden confidently concluded that Maori were in awe of British Christian life itself: "Various things here which they had never seen furnish us with much conversation about God. . . . They see such a difference between our civilized and their savage state."[14] For Marsden, it was not even the symbolism of grapes, perhaps in a biblical sense, but rather the demonstration that English settlers had a flourishing nonnative crop, that was living proof of their superior civilization. Whether the Maori visitors were genuinely in awe, politely feigning interest, or indeed poking fun at the earnest missionary, we may never know.

MARA WAINA

Marsden's ambitions were not realized in his lifetime. He died in 1838 in Australia, probably before the first New Zealand wine had been made. The CMS mission in New Zealand attracted few converts and was embarrassed by internal leadership feuds and scandals (one major figure, Thomas Kendall, married a Maori woman and effectively left the church). The mission closed in the 1850s. Enter James Busby, who would be marginally more successful in his chosen career than Marsden, and significantly more successful as a winemaker, in that he tried and succeeded to make wine from grapes he had grown himself. Busby's appointment as resident was something of a poisoned chalice. The resident was a sort of ambassador, to represent the British crown and look after the interests of the few thousand British settlers, but it carried little legal weight, and was dependent on the administration in New South Wales for its funding and any military support. This was problematic for Busby, whose independent spirit and ambition had chafed against the New South Wales establishment, and with whom he was not on the friendliest terms. Moreover, the task was large, with few resources: Busby was meant to mediate issues both within the British community and with the neighboring Maori.

Busby packed up and sailed to the Bay of Islands, where he set up his new home in Waitangi. One of his first endeavors, of course, was to plant a small vineyard around his home, taking a selection of cuttings from those he had installed in the botanic gardens in Sydney, adding another link to the international chain of botanical colonization. His wife, Agnes Dow Busby, joined him soon after, and it is likely that she assisted in labor around their home. We know little about her life at this point, but she may deserve as much credit as Busby himself for any wine that was made. We have thirdhand accounts of Busby's viticultural exploits in Waitangi. Keith Stewart cites a report from the French explorer Hubert Dumont D'Urville, who visited Busby's farm around 1840, and tasted his light white wine, declaring it to be "delicious" (though, as Stewart points out, after a lengthy ocean voyage, the Frenchman might have been delighted by any wine).[15] Stewart therefore declares 1840 to be the start of New Zealand winemaking, and this seem probable. We also have additional accounts of grape production in this early colonial period. Stewart writes of a William Powditch, a self-taught vigneron and ship captain who settled in the North Island in 1831, and endeavored to produce wine over the next two decades. Powditch's efforts were relatively short-lived, but Stewart claims he distributed vine cuttings among his neighbors, and may have encouraged others to grow grapes.[16] We do have record of a shipowner and settler named Lieutenant Thomas McDonnell, who was interviewed by a British parliamentary committee in 1844, and who claimed to have had four hundred varieties of grape flourishing on his property in Hokianga, in the North Island, although he admitted he had not made wine from them.[17] When William Williams, a CMS missionary and later Anglican bishop, published a Maori language guide for missionaries in 1852, he included the Maori words for vine (*waina*) and vineyard (*mara waina*), but not for wine itself.[18] This may have been for the purpose of reading the Bible as much as for describing local agricultural practices. On the other hand, Williams placed great emphasis on translating "colloquial sentences" so that missionaries could clearly instruct Maori to undertake labor for them ("Fence this piece of ground. Let it be firm, lest the cattle break it"),[19] so discussion of vines might have been useful in this context.

Busby's most significant, and controversial, undertaking as resident was not the production of wine, but the production of the Treaty of Waitangi, which was signed and ratified over the course of 1840. This was an agreement signed between the British, represented officially by the Lieutenant-Governor William Hobson, and over five hundred Maori rangatira. Although Busby had recognized New Zealand's independence in 1835, settler pressures and international competition pushed British officials to want to formally annex New Zealand. The treaty proposed that the British have full sovereignty over New Zealand and its people, and in return they would protect Maori and offer them British citizenship. The treaty was translated into Maori by British missionaries and was then circulated around the islands for signatures. Much was lost in translation, though: Maori had different concepts of sovereignty and land rights, and a traditional view is that they may have believed they were accepting temporary protection and governance, not signing over permanent power. The treaty is today a deeply controversial set of documents. From one Maori perspective, the treaty has been increasingly seen as a great dupe, in which thousands of Maori were inveigled into giving up their land and sovereignty to a foreign power. James Belich is one historian who has pushed back against this interpretation, arguing that it "portrays Maori as the pathetic victim of unrelieved tragedy," and not as the powerful actors that they were. Rather, he emphasizes that the British were in New Zealand with Maori consent, and that they willingly sold land to the newcomers.[20] Busby himself purchased land from Maori and then found himself unable to prove title to the Crown; he spent decades pursuing his case in vain and in bitter frustration. The Pakeha (or European settler) population in 1840 was a tiny fraction of the Maori population, but within two decades the Maori had lost nearly half their population and were outnumbered by Pakeha.[21] Land, the indispensable stuff of wine production, was increasingly transferred to Pakeha hands.

From a British imperial perspective, it was a *relatively* progressive venture, one that recognized the power of Maori and respected them as actual legal signatories (and, in the sense of Realpolitick, effectively conceded the weak position of the British). Such treaties were not offered to Australian Aboriginal peoples, to natives of India, or to other peoples colonized by the British. It demonstrates, in some perverse way, the relative esteem the British had for Maori people; as the *Botanical Magazine* in London described Maori, they "although savages, nay, even cannibals, possessed generous minds, and powerful intellectual faculties."[22] This cultural condescension would be no comfort to the Maori people who lost their land and their lives in contact with Europeans.

Indeed, Maori desire for protection—or, simply, relief from outside interference—reflects the fact that New Zealand was heating up on the European radar as an unattended site of potential colonization. The next major intervention in New Zealand winemaking came through French Catholic priests belonging to the Society of Mary, also known as Marists. The Catholic Church saw the Pacific as ripe for evangelization, a final frontier for missionary activity, and the Marists were assigned "western Oceania" as their responsibility in the 1836. This region included New Zealand, Fiji, and Samoa. In the late-1830s, a small contingent of Marist fathers began arriving in New Zealand and established themselves in the North Island. These fathers farmed where they settled, out of necessity and also as part of their spiritual commitment to humble and simple living. That included growing grapes and making wine, and thus the next major intervention in creating New Zealand wine came from a huddle of French priests.

Wine was an essential aspect of the culture of the French Marist fathers, to a degree that it was not among British Protestant missionaries. Moreover, wine production had an explicit religious imperative, for wine is used during mass in the Catholic rite of transubstantiation. Father Jérôme Grange, a Marist missionary who had continued on to attempt to Christianize Tonga, endeavored to grow his own grapes. He struggled, but eventually his plant bore a single grape, which he "solemnly picked, pressed in a very clean cloth, then after clarifying the juice, I used it to say mass on January 1, 1844."[23] Technically this was juice, not wine, but the intention was there. His colleague in New Caledonia, Monseigneur Douarre, also planted grape vines on his arrival, which he confidently told his superiors in France were bound to thrive, given the temperate climate.[24] The French were attentive to British grape growing, too. A young French priest arriving in (Australian) Perth for the first time, in 1846, wrote home to his mother that grapes vines grew "marvellously" there, and that they could even produce two harvests a year.[25]

In New Zealand, the Marists claim to have established the oldest continually producing winery, the appropriately named Mission Vineyard, in 1851. In fact, the modern vineyard is not situated at the original location in Hawkes Bay, but at a slightly larger one nearby, but the tradition of making wine was continuous. Indeed the Marists probably were making wine in New Zealand for a decade before 1851. The Mission site was chosen for its sandy soil, limestone deposits, and good drainage. The priests planted several grape varieties: black hamburg, both red and white sweetwater, chasselas, and alexandrian tardy.[26] Their need for wine was specific and constant and, although not all French people hail from winemaking districts, knowledge of viticulture was probably much higher among the Marists than in the general British population of the Antipodes. For Catholic missionaries, introducing Catholicism was about introducing civilization, and wine was central to the most essential Catholic sacrament.

It may seem contradictory that early inaugurators of civilizing vineyards in a British colony were, in fact, French. Several things should be borne in mind. First, the French government had its own interests in New Zealand, and prior to the signing of the Treaty of Waitangi, it did not seem impossible that the French would try to colonize the islands themselves. Second, Busby's own history demonstrates how, the rivalry between Britain and France notwithstanding, there was free and ample exchange between French and British people who worked in science and wine. Busby traveled freely in France, he translated referential French texts on winemaking, and he easily obtained vine cuttings from official French botanical gardens. Third, and finally, over the nineteenth century British colonies would acquire a reputation among many other Europeans as relatively open and relaxed societies that encouraged entrepreneurship and initiative. As we will see repeatedly, individuals from other parts of Europe happily settled in the British Antipodes and bought into the Anglo-Saxon vision of improvement through viticulture. In many cases, they were better equipped to bring this vision to fruition than their British neighbors.

By the 1850s, then, viticulture was firmly established in the Antipodes, with grapes having been grown in Australia for sixty years, and in New Zealand for about thirty. Just as at the Cape, grape growing was established immediately on European arrival, though these first decades showed more zeal than actual wine-making success. Early winemakers included a varied cast of characters, and a shared confidence that was often belied by the actual results of their labors. Busby's disputed land claims tied up his time and money in the post-Waitangi world, and as a result he was not able to sustain his viticultural projects, and instead branched into sheep ranching and running a sawmill[27]—an ignominious end to what had once appeared a promising career in wine.

One of the most important things historians can do in looking at the past is to clear their minds of hindsight, and to try to appreciate events through the perspective of actual people in the past. There is a tendency in wine-writing to feature early viticulturalists as prescient ancestors, who tilled and planted and begot and begot, and thus brought us directly to our present moment. In the strict chronological sense, that is true, but it tells us little about the context of early winemaking. In 1850, European settlers did not *know* that New Zealand would become resolutely British in the short term, and they certainly could not have foreseen that it would become an independent state with a celebrated wine industry. These were aspirations for the settler community, not known outcomes, and thus those early vineyards tell us about settlers' hopes, prejudices, and attitudes toward risk. What this chapter has shown is that colonial administrators in Australia and New Zealand had lofty visions of agricultural bounty and ripe vineyards from the beginning. The British settler who planted a vineyard in the North Island in the 1830s, though, had a precarious existence, and seen from this perspective, winemaking seems an almost absurd undertaking. How can such settler folly, or hubris, be explained? One explanation is cultural. Those vineyards indicate—and reinforced—the British view of their own cultural superiority over Aboriginal and Maori communities; planting a vineyard showed defiant commitment to a more permanent British presence, and it allowed settlers to convince themselves that they were building a civilized community in an alien place. The settlers' perspective is not the only one that matters. Settler colonialism, including the creation of these vineyards, was often experienced by native communities as violence and dispossession, and this is a social trauma that has repercussions to the present day.

A second explanation is economic. British settlers in the eighteenth and early nineteenth centuries had a global, networked view of economic relationships. They had themselves crossed oceans, had stopped at the Cape en route to the Antipodes, and had witnessed international trade. They understood that their precarious little communities in New Zealand were connected back to Britain through maritime trade, and even that a North Island settler could be asked to testify to Parliament in London about the health of his four hundred grape vines. An ambitious young man like Busby was willing to travel back to Europe from Australia—a journey that took months and was uncomfortable and physically risky—to visit vineyards, because he believed that wine expertise would give him a leg up in imperial administration. His tiny vineyard in Waitangi was, in his mind, connected to a global economy and a larger imperial purpose. The fact that Busby the winemaker also helped produce what is probably New Zealand's most significant historical document, is not coincidental, but emblematic of the larger British viticultural project. As we shall see in the next chapter, though, it did not take hold as readily with the British general public.

PART TWO

———

Growth

C. 1830–1910

SIX

Cheap and Wholesome

CAPE PRODUCERS AND BRITISH TARIFFS

Ye coop us up, and tax our bread,
And wonder why we pine;
But ye are fat, and round, and red,
And fill'ed with tax-bought wine.[1]

EBENEZER ELLIOTT,
Corn Law Rhymes (1831)

PRODUCING WINE IN BRITISH COLONIES was only half of the battle; selling it on global markets presented an entirely different set of hurdles. Winemakers and government officials alike believed that wine production was good for the development of the colonies themselves, but they also envisioned that wine would be exported, and that the proceeds from this trade would make the Cape, Australian colonies, and New Zealand prosperous and self-sufficient. They were particularly focused on selling colonial wine back to Britain, because it would bring revenue to the British customs and balance out colonial trade. The general vision shared by most British politicians and bureaucrats was that Britain would export manufactured goods to its colonies, and import raw materials and food stuffs from its colonies, and large-scale agriculture was encouraged in colonies as an efficient way to deliver these goods. (Busby, we have seen, was acutely attuned to this mode of thinking.) This project was simultaneously complex and simple: imperial trade was a dense web involving thousands of individuals around the world, although the idea of British capitalism's spread was based on the simple concept of colonies as unsophisticated providers to the "mother country."

One knotty complication for nineteenth-century winemakers, though, was the issue of British import tariffs. Tariffs were a surprisingly passion-provoking political issue in nineteenth-century Britain, and one that had a great impact on colonial wine. The early nineteenth century was a time of consumer revolution, when more and more commercial goods became available to ordinary people. With cities growing and the rural population dwindling, more and more British people were becoming shoppers. Increasingly, they purchased their basic items such as food and clothing, rather than producing them at home or bartering in a local economy. In principle this also meant that ordinary people had more choice in what they acquired, because urban markets drew from much wider sources. However, the ability to purchase goods did not actually mean that the standard of living rose for most people. For Britain's mid-nineteenth century urban working classes, it was not unusual for half of the household income to be spent on food.

Tariffs are taxes imposed on particular goods at the point of importation into a country, and they could significantly increase the ultimate price of consumer goods. (Wine could also be subject to duties—taxes paid by consumers on particular goods at the moment of sale, regardless of the goods' place of origin. Duties were levied on domestic beer and spirits, too, but because wine was virtually all imported, the terms *tariff* and *duty* were used flexibly in the Victorian press and Parliament when writing about wine.) Tariffs were levied on goods for a variety of reasons, such as to protect British industries from foreign competition or to punish foreign producers for unrelated political slights. One of the best-known examples in British wine history is the Methuen Treaty of 1703, which sealed a trade deal between Britain and Portugal, exchanging low tariffs on British wool for low tariffs on Portuguese wine—to the anger and exclusion of French wine producers, who suffered comparatively high tariffs. Charles Ludington has shown how as a result, political loyalties and cheap prices made port such a popular drink in eighteenth-century Britain, often at the direct expense of French claret. British tastes and consumer habits changed significantly as a result of a trade negotiation.

Wine featured frequently in media debates about trade and tariffs, since consumers were keenly aware that wine was not produced in Britain but imported. One antitariff pamphlet mocked Englishmen who were so obsessed with autarky that they would try "building hot-houses to make wine" in England, to avoid importing the Portuguese wine they so loved.[2] The author was not referring to actual attempts at English grape-production, but was using grapes as an absurd example of people expressing their passionate support for tariffs. These heated discussions about tariffs give more insight into why British settlers in the Cape and the Antipodes thought it was a good idea to start growing wine grapes: wine imports into Britain could be expensive and politically fraught, and didn't colonies exist to supply Britain with what couldn't be produced domestically?

The most heated tariff debate in nineteenth-century Britain concerned the Corn Laws, which were protective tariffs levied on imports of foreign grain. These tariffs were popular with British farmers, because they guaranteed that their grain prices would not be undercut by foreign suppliers. But they became notoriously unpopular with consumers in Britain's growing cities, since they kept the price of bread artificially high. Popular resentment of these tariffs led to the establishment of the Anti–Corn Law League, and eventually the repeal of the Corn Laws in 1846 by Robert Peel's Tory government. The Corn Laws had lasting significance in British politics, for they invigorated a radical wing of the Liberal Party and established free trade as a central part of that party's platform, and splintered the Tory Party, with the emergence of protectionism and landowners' interests as paramount to that party's platform. (These positions would shift significantly in the twentieth century.)

Bread was a British dietary staple; wine was not yet. Yet for both wine and imperial history, the Corn Laws demonstrate several important things. Tariffs, perhaps now considered an arcane and complex area of trade policy, were actually a political issue that British consumers understood, paid attention to, and cared passionately about in the nineteenth century. Furthermore, the question of whether it was appropriate to tax goods coming from British colonies became a fraught political issue, too. Many politicians and bureaucrats believed that colonies should supply Britain, but should tariffs be imposed on colonial goods? This was an uncomfortable debate that struck at the very concept of an empire: was empire meant to be a free-trade zone, a greater Britain, or was empire primarily at the service of metropolitan Britain, and intended to bring as much revenue to the exchequer as possible? A *Liverpool Mercury* editorial in favor of abolishing the Corn Laws in 1843 predicted that, even if Britain's markets were to be flooded with cheap grain from the United States and Poland, Britain had a massive economic advantage thanks to the production of its colonies: "In addition to her exports of cheap fabrics of cotton, wool, and flax, she [England] will, in all probability, soon have it in her power to export the raw material to her manufacturing rivals ... [and] the wool of Australia, the corn of Canada, the hemp, flax, and wine of New Zealand, and the cotton, coffee, indigo, and sugar of India."[3] For this journalist, wine production in colonies was integral to the vast British economic system and contributed to the greater strength and glory of the United Kingdom. The mention of New Zealand wine is particularly curious, because its production levels were miniscule at the time: and yet, the imperial dream of viticulture was present, even to a journalist in Liverpool.

Although he probably had no personal connection to New Zealand's fledgling vineyards, Liverpool was a thriving port city, and the mental distances to the farthest reaches of empire were shrunk in the minds of its residents by the frequency of ocean traffic.

One of the first major tests about tariffs and government investment in colonies was in the Cape Colony in the early nineteenth-century. The Cape Colony became a formal British possession in 1814 and its wines became a "British" product. This was a mixed blessing. On the one hand, Cape wines would now benefit from a lower import duty than European wines entering the British market: being a British colony, the Cape got a preferential rate, lower than the standard rate that was levied on wines from foreign countries. On the other hand, the trade that developed was unstable. Cape wine exports were already important to the colonial economy, but once the Cape was formally absorbed into the British system the trade became profoundly asymmetric: Cape wines made up a very small portion of British imports, but wine became one of the principal exports from the Cape and the British market was the main destination.[4] Rayner has shown that nearly all of the Cape import's came from Britain in the first two decades of British rule, and that the colony was running a serious trade deficit (meaning the Cape was not exporting enough goods to balance out its imports). Furthermore, the reliance on the British market meant that the Cape was exposed to British market fluctuations. While the end of the Napoleonic Wars meant that the Cape formally become a British colony, the end of the wartime economy led to dramatic oscillations in prices of British goods.[5] And yet the first few years of British rule looked promising for winegrowers. Wine sales to Britain skyrocketed to around 1,500 tuns in 1816, with an import value of £47,292, up from 341 tuns and £10,752 a year earlier. The wine imported in 1816 represented 64 percent of the value of imports from South Africa, and in 1817 it would climb to 87 percent.[6] Vine growing was immediately promoted under the new British regime as a means of raising revenue and improving the local economy. The new administrators may have been disappointed to realize that most Cape wines were not that sweet nectar known as Constantia, but much coarser wines. Still, the industry showed promise, and in the postwar period it was essential that the new colony bring in some income. Governor Sir John Cradock reestablished an office of wine taster, to ensure the quality (and, probably, the safety) of wines leaving the Cape colony. Arrangements were made to regulate wine sales (and probably ensure taxes could be accurately collected), with an 1823 decree from Governor Lord Charles Somerset that growers "shall not be allowed to retail their Wine or Brandy, on their respective Estates, by way of barter, or in any other manner whatsoever."[7] If wine were to be made, it would be taxed, too. Further, inns, taverns, and wine sellers were only allowed to sell alcoholic beverages between sunrise and 9pm, and were not allowed to harbor sailors, soldiers, or people of color in their premises outside of these opening hours. Subsequent decrees proclaimed that those selling wine would need licenses, that wine would be sold in standardized measures, and that overall the "numerous irregularities" of the trade would be straightened out.[8] Cape Town would be a productive, orderly, profitable, and civilized British port city, the decrees collectively announce.

For a few years, wine production thus became a promising and lucrative undertaking in the Cape, with the explicit encouragement of its British governors. There was a significant expansion of both the acreage under vine cultivation and the number of merchant houses engaging in the trade.[9] Keegan calculates that wine production increased 83 percent between 1809 and 1825.[10] By 1823 there were 376 "wine farms," using 5,930 enslaved people as laborers.[11] The East India Company joined in, too, advertising in Cape newspapers that it was accepting tenders to supply 150,000 gallons of Cape wine to the island of St. Helena, a garrison and home to Britain's most famous prisoner of war, Napoleon Bonaparte.[12] Cape newspapers show that wine was a vital part of commercial life in Cape Town and its surrounds in the early nineteenth century. Wine-related advertisements and features made hundreds (and later, thousands) of appearances in Cape newspapers. This included advertisements for wine importers, advertising their stock of Cape wines and imported foreign wines; estate sales, in which wines were specifically mentioned as items of value; bids for tenders to supply Cape wine to military and commercial ships; and notices of ships sailing, noting which ones had wine in their cargo. The formation of a Wine Trade Committee in the mid-1820s is reflected in the press, too, for the committee announced its meetings and posted its minutes and membership, in both English and Afrikaans, in Cape newspapers. This also demonstrates how individuals involved in the wine industry wanted their role to be publicly appreciated, and how the network of those involved in wine trade and production was large enough to require a printed announcement, and not simply notification by word of mouth.

Organization within the Cape wine industry became important because of several tariff debates that took place in the Westminster Parliament. As a colony, the Cape was run by a British governor, who ultimately answered to the Crown and Parliament in London; Cape residents did not elect members of Parliament, and if they wished to redirect imperial policy they lobbied—or "made representations"—to the governor and his team in Cape Town or to sympathetic British parliamentarians.

At the time the Cape became a British possession, Portuguese, Spanish, and French wines, which made up the bulk of British wine imports, had at the same time become subject to far higher tariffs—tariffs which had been carefully negotiated in the complex geopolitics of Napoleonic Europe. Charles Ludington has calculated many of these changes from parliamentary documents. In 1814 French wines were subject to a tariff of £144 per tun and Portuguese and Spanish to £96 per tun, whereas the Cape wine tariff was slashed to only £32 per tun, less than half of what it had been over the previous twenty years.[13] The result of this new tariff regime was that it had become more advantageous and lucrative for South African wine producers to export their wine to Britain. It is clear from the money and effort that South African governors were applying to viticulture, that they believed most Cape producers needed all the official help they could get.

But as part of the general and gradual swing toward trade liberalization in the 1820s, duties on European wines were more than halved in 1825. Cape wine duties were slightly lowered, from £32 to £25 per tun, but to the great chagrin of Cape winemakers, their relative advantage was also dramatically reduced. The reduction in tariffs for European countries meant that although Spanish wines were still taxed at £50 per tun, twice as much as Cape wines, they were much cheaper than they had been. European countries also enjoyed many advantages over the Cape, when it came to the British market: shorter transit routes, larger industries with longer expertise and probably better economies of scale, and overall more familiarity and better reputations among British consumers.[14] Although by the 1820s wine had been produced at the Cape and exported to Britain for nearly 150 years, the large number of new entrants in the early British colonial period still saw wine as an infant industry that needed imperial protection. When they first got wind of potential tariff changes in 1823, a lobby of Cape residents in the wine trade met and issued a proclamation that a hike in British tariffs would mean the "inevitable ruin" not of their personal businesses, but of the Cape colony itself.[15]

The election of a Whig government in 1830 ended twenty-three years of Tory rule, and introduced yet another new tariff regime. In 1831, the duty on Cape wines was slightly raised from £25 to £29 per gallon (or about 16 percent).[16] European duties went up slightly, too, from £50 to £58 per gallon, but given that Cape wine was a cheap product, the proposals drew vigorous protest that Cape wines would see a dramatic drop in demand. Cape wine growers and merchants sent petitions to Westminster, crying out against what they saw as a major pivot in colonial policy. For this Cape wine lobby, the 1831 customs duties would reverse the progress of a young colony that was impoverished, and that faced "great difficulty raising a Revenue sufficient to cover its unavoidable expenditure"; "should the cultivation of Wine be forsaken . . . the Revenues of the Colony will suffer most materially."[17] This would result, they claimed, in "irretrievable ruin" to "all those, who, upon the faith of *pledged support* from Government, have embarked their labour and means in the cultivation of the Vine, and in the treatment and manufacture of Wine, which the test of many years experience has proved to be better adapted to the soil and climate of any other article of colonial produce, and as such, must ever continue to be the staple of the Colony."[18] This was not simply an expression of anger at breach of promise; it also served as a statement of loyalty, and an affirmation of the industry and good will of South African settlers. Furthermore, the Cape lobby countered economic arguments with a subtle appeal to civilizational engineering. Cape wine, they argued, was "a cheap and wholesome beverage."[19] Wholesome, in this sense, means safe and free from dangerous additives. But it also means socially wholesome: as a middle-class beverage, wine consumption is a marker of respectability, and thus its consumption brings respectability to those who choose to consume it over, say, gin. Cape wine producers were positioning themselves as responsible citizens who had the capacity to improve white Cape society, which was largely poor and working class.

Cape producers and importers were also worried that raising the duty would put the price out of reach of poorer British consumers—a consumer base that they claimed to have created, since by providing a cheaper wine they had introduced new consumers to a product that had previously been out of reach.[20] One member of Parliament argued that less-wealthy consumers would be much worse hit by even a small rise in Cape wine tariffs: "There were many persons who were enabled to pay their 1s. 6d. or 2s. a bottle for Cape wine, who could not afford to drink more costly wines; and these individuals would be thus cut off from the indulgence of what to them was, probably, deemed a luxury."[21] A simple adjustment for inflation puts the 1s. 6d. bottle at around £100 in 2019 money,[22] but this might be misleading, because in the 1820s we are dealing with a society that expected food and drink to be one of their largest categories of household expenditure. We should put more emphasis on what lawmakers and wine merchants said about wine drinkers to get a sense of the value and cost of wine to consumers. Here, this debate clearly reveals that as early as the 1820s, the British wine market was socially segmented: although most regular wine drinkers were wealthy, there were people of more modest means who consumed wine, and they were able to do so because of colonial wine imports. Indeed, it can even be said that colonial wines *created* this commercial possibility, of middling classes being able to afford wine. We will see this repeated throughout the nineteenth and twentieth centuries.

As one parliamentarian countered, raising the tariff on Cape wine would indeed reduce demand, but if sufficient notice were given, "to the persons who had embarked their capital in this speculation, he could not conceive that any injury would be inflicted on them. They would then be able to withdraw their capital from a trade which was already declining, without the interference, or rather, under the fostering protection, of the Legislature. . . . He could not perceive that any injustice would be done to our *own* colonists."[23]—that is to say, British colonists, versus those of Dutch extraction. For the Cape wine industry, this was an alarming statement that metropolitan support was at risk of being withdrawn. It also affirmed that British official loyalty lay with settlers of British extraction first. Indeed, British commentators were quick to view success in wine growth with national character, to associate Britishness with rational, improving impulses and the Afrikaner population with backwardness and slovenly habits. Cyrus Redding, one of the most famous wine-writers in nineteenth-century Britain, wrote in 1836 about South Africa, that,

> In no wine country is there room for greater improvement, nor is there any in which care and science, properly directed, would earlier exhibit their effects. No method recommended by European science or experience prevails here. . . . Things are undoubtedly better now than they were twenty years ago, but amendment is very slow. The obstinacy of the Dutch character is proverbial. . . . The boors [*sic*] are a very ignorant race of people, and not at all of speculative habit.[24]

It is not clear that Redding visited most of the places he wrote about, and colonial historians note that feigning ignorance and refusing to cooperate may have been quotidian acts of resistance to imperial governance. There is no reason to take this statement at face value, but rather it demonstrates how the wine industry was summoned as evidence of Britain's superior civilizing ability. Many visitors to the Cape at the time mentioned, perhaps with some surprise, the wild and freeform nature of the vineyards. Christian Latrobe, who visited in 1815, noted that in Constantia itself, the vines "are without spaliers or poles, standing singly, like currant-bushes in a garden,"[25] and Campbell, traveling a few years earlier, echoed this: "The ground is uneven, and each vineyard being surrounded by tall oak trees, the place appeared like a wood."[26] The rustic Dutch interventions could no doubt be bettered by their British replacements, or so these British commentators presumed.

Ultimately, any sense of affection that British lawmakers felt toward the Cape's colonial wine industry was not sufficient to stop an adjustment of customs duties. Growing the South African wine industry was officially encouraged after British colonization but there was metropolitan reluctance to protect and prop up a poor-quality product; the needs of new South African winegrowers were, overall, a relatively low priority in late-Georgian Britain's foreign and trade policies. Wine, with other forms of alcohol, was an important good in the colonial imagination, but that did not make it a sure economic success in the imperial economy. In short, the geopolitics of the wine trade with France, Portugal and Spain were of much greater importance to British lawmakers, than that of the Cape colony. Ludington has argued that "wine was an instrument of both fiscal and foreign policy" for British lawmakers. He was referring to an earlier era, the Restoration period, but his argument holds true for the nineteenth century, too. What might surprise us, though, is that maintaining a peaceful foreign policy through trade agreements with Britain's close neighbors trumped protection of colonial infant industries. Producers hoped that the fact that they were producing a colonial product would be sufficient to protect them from unfavorable tariffs. It was not: their products weren't good enough, or the imperial feeling was not strong enough, or the size of the trade was just too small, compared to that of giants like Spain or France.

When these tariff debates were taking place in the 1820s and 1830s, they really only had a direct impact on Cape producers. Australia had only begun exporting a few sips of its wine to Britain, and New Zealand had barely begun producing wine, and certainly not enough to export on a commercial scale. But the issues raised in the tariff wars would resurface again and again—in the 1860s, the 1880s, the 1920s, and even the 1980s—when Australia, in particular, would be a more significant stakeholder. First, though, they had to make wine that people wanted to drink.

SEVEN

———

Echunga Hock

COLONIAL WINES OF THE NINETEENTH CENTURY

Mr Walter Duffield has lately sent, as a present to her Majesty
Queen Victoria, a dozen of his Echunga Hock. We had the
pleasure of tasting some of it; and if we may judge from our own
sensations, we can confidently state, not only that it does the
highest credit, both to the province and to the manufacturers,
but that it will give much satisfaction to her Majesty and to her
royal consort.[1]

"SOUTH AUSTRALIAN WINE,"
South Australian (March 4, 1845)

WHATEVER WAS ECHUNGA HOCK? And what, indeed, were the Cape
and Australia actually producing in the early and mid-nineteenth century?
Wine, that is certain, made from grapes, and probably both red and white,
but in many cases the precise wine style, grape varieties, color, and taste are
difficult or impossible to pinpoint. Perhaps surprisingly, there is no definitive
record that reveals the number of colonial wine farms and what they were
making. We can trace the shape of these colonial industries and fill in details
from a broad range of sources in both the colonies and Britain: customs
statements, news reporting, advertising, travelers' memoirs, the correspondence of importers and producers, and in rare cases the physical remains of
this world.

Another reason it is difficult to assess these wines is our own disconnect
from the language and aesthetics of nineteenth-century wine. Modern wine
values of terroir, authenticity, and traceability were not commonplace in
nineteenth-century Britain. Terroir is the idea that a foodstuff can have a
unique taste of its particular place of origin. But in the nineteenth century
terroir was in its infancy as a marketing tool, and reserved only for the finest
wines. The vast majority of wine sold by retail on the British market in the
nineteenth century could not be traced, by the consumer, to a precise and

limited place of origin, to a single vineyard or estate. This included many expensive wines, which would be identified by their general region of origin, but not necessarily their village, their winemaker, or their vintage, either: we see advertisements for "finest young Burgundy wine," for example, rather than Gevrey-Chambertin 1845. Constantia is the New World exception that proves the rule in this period. Touring the Cape in 1815, missionary John Campbell praised the "princely edifice" of Constantia and its "superb" wine, and wrote of enjoying "a glass of Constantia wine, on the farm where alone it is produced." He then made an argument for something approaching terroir: "Slips from the Constantia vine has [*sic*] been tried in various parts of the Cape colony; but away from their favourite native soil, they never produce grapes of the same flavour."[2] Another missionary, C. I. Latrobe, recounted a similar story in 1818, of viewing, on the Constantia estate, "a hedge, beyond which, all attempts to raise the same grape have failed."[3] Since both missionaries received guided tours at the vineyard, Constantia's owners may have been already trying to promote a distinct claim to Constantia's unique topography. However, as we have seen, even the term *constantia* was applied loosely to other Cape wines, and did not have a strict legal meaning in retail and marketing. A home-brewing guide published in Scotland in 1849 even offered a recipe for making "constantia" from rhubarb.[4]

Most of the wines produced in the British world in this period were made from blends of different types of grapes (and not rhubarb). This blending, in itself, is certainly not a sign of poor quality. Many of the major wines of France, then and now, are made from particular blends of grapes. The red wines of Bordeaux, for example, are usually principally based on merlot, cabernet sauvignon, and cabernet franc grapes. These wines of southern France directly inspired and even provided actual vines for the early wines of Australia.

However, the wines produced in British colonies and sold in Britain were also blended in a different sense. They were overwhelmingly exported as bulk wines, meaning they were shipped in large containers, rather than in individual bottles. These casks were wooden and came in different semistandardized imperial sizes, known as pipes, hogsheads, butts, and tuns. The wine that went into each cask might be a blend of different years or grapes, and that wine might be blended again by the wine importer or the wine merchant before it was sold to an individual.

Estate-bottling was relatively rare across the wine industry in the nineteenth century, even in continental European countries. Wine merchants in Britain would import, or purchase from an importer, wine in bulk. Records from a very expensive wine cellar in the 1930s show prestigious Bordeaux wines that had been bottled in Britain before the First World War: "16 bottles Château Lafite 1870, bottled in Scotland"; "18 bottles Château Mouton-Rothschild 1899, bottled by Page and Sandeman"; "12 bottles Château Margaux 1900, shipped by Eschenauer, bottled by Rigby, of Liverpool"; and so on.[5]

Clients with ample cellar space would purchase the wine in its barrels, and less wealthy clients or those in tighter urban quarters would have the merchant decant their wine into bottles or jugs. Taverns could also retail wine, which they would decant into bottles for customers, charging a small bottle deposit.[6] Glass bottles, which replaced earthenware or stoneware bottles or jugs, came into usage in the first half of the seventeenth century, but prebottling wine for sale requires not just glass bottles, but standardized bottles which can be produced on an industrial basis. This technology was developed and refined over the eighteenth century; before then, it was impractical, and even throughout the nineteenth century bottles were still not widely used by winemakers. An 1860 newspaper advertisement for James Denman, a London wine merchant who (dubiously) called himself the "Introducer of the South African Wines," offered to send his casks free to any railway station in Britain, with bottles included, and to provide free tastes of any wine by bottle, too.[7] The casks that were sent by rail might have been delivered to inns and wine shops as well as individuals, and the retailers could use the bottles to then portion off the wine for customers. As Troy Bickham has shown, from the eighteenth century onward Britain had "remarkably extensive" and efficient systems of moving imperial food imports from port, to wholesaler, to regional market, "ensuring that a miner's wife in Scotland had almost as much access to these imperial products as a nobleman living in London."[8]

The winemaker who chose to bottle his or her wine at the estate was showing strong confidence in that wine; by bottling, the winemaker insured against contamination or fraud, and exercised more control over how the wine would taste once the bottle was uncorked. But given that glass is heavy, fragile, and bulky, in the nineteenth century only a few wines were routinely estate-bottled: those that were from such prestigious vineyards that name recognition and quality control outweighed the inconvenience of shipping in glass; sparkling wines, because carbonation would be lost in casks; and small samples destined for the queen. The "twelve Echunga hock" surely referred to twelve bottles, and it is logical that an Australian winemaker proudly presenting his wine to his ruler would want to ensure its quality. What the queen thought of it, or if she ever tried it, we do not know.

Nor do we know what the "royal consort," the queen's husband, Albert, thought of the wine, although Duffield might have chosen a hock especially to appeal to the German-born prince. Hock is a generic term for a German-style white wine, and Echunga is a small town near Adelaide, South Australia. To the twenty-first century wine lover the name "Echunga hock" sounds almost oxymoronic, because it suggests a German wine that was not German, but this was a very common feature of wine in the British New World. (Besides, Germany was not yet Germany in 1845, but a collection of smaller states.) Most of the early wines from the Cape and Australia, from the earliest production up until the mid-twentieth century, were sold under the names of prominent European styles. The two most common in advertisements and auctions of the 1820s were Cape Hock and Cape Madeira (named after the sweet, fortified wine from that Portuguese island).[9] John Campbell, who visited the Cape in 1815 on behalf of the London Missionary Society, wrote that the area near Gnadenthal, which had some German farmers, produced "a wine resembling Rhenish."[10] Just as Huguenot settlers had been allowed into South Africa in the seventeenth century partly because of their useful agricultural skills, German farmers were allowed to migrate to both the British Cape and, later, to southern Australia, where they were involved in winemaking in the Barossa Valley.

On the one hand, there was nothing inappropriate about a New World winemaker taking inspiration from a European style of wine, particularly if the winemaker hailed from the inspirational region. There was no legal prohibition on using any of these names, and though the term *Cape Madeira* may have irked producers on the island of Madeira, the Cape winemakers were well within their rights to use this name. Naming their wines after popular European styles also made sense, because a unique name taken from the Cape or Australia might have confused British consumers. Appellations require geographic knowledge on the part of the consumer, which acts as a barrier to market entry: rather than chancing an unknown location on an expensive purchase, consumers are reassured by a familiar place name or style.

Naming colonial wines after European styles probably had more subtle marketing effects. First, it glossed over the less-savory elements of colonial production by distancing the wine from its place of origin, which was convenient in that Cape wine was produced through forced labor. Second, almost paradoxically, it Europeanized the place of origin, which reinforced the colonists' imagination of a civilizing net being thrown over the colony. Settlers were not only making wine in colonies: they were making *European* wine, not some bizarre colonial concoction. Or so they claimed.

On the other hand, the imitative nature of the Cape's winemaking also made sense in view of the often rudimentary skills and technology available to its winemakers. Another hint as to the quality of Cape wines comes from civic bodies with an interest in promoting robust colonial trade. The Society of Arts in London, for example, created a wine competition in 1822, "to foster the growth of the vine at the Cape," and not "for the sweet or Constantia wine, but to encourage the improvement of the vineyards more recently established." The winning wine, announced in 1827, was described as "far superior to the Cape wines in general. It is free from the unpleasant, earthy flavour by which such wines are usually characterised, and was considered to bear a near resemblance to that made at Teneriffe."[11] This prize reveals frank admission about the poor quality of most Cape wines exported, but also patient encouragement (and a sense of patrician responsibility) from a metropolitan source.

This same society also encouraged industry and quality among winemakers in Australia. The first well-documented export of Australian wine to Britain was in 1822, when Gregory Blaxland brought samples to present to the Society of Arts, earning a silver metal for its quality.[12] The society ran further competitions to encourage industry in British colonies and to substitute for imports from non-British sources. An 1824 competition included medals for wines from Australia, but also for olive oil, woolen cloth, substitutes for hemp, and, in a competition also open to the Cape of Good Hope and the British Caribbean, tea.[13]

Ersatz "Cape hock" or the more mysterious "Echunga hock" were probably seen by consumers for what they were: a cheap, inferior substitute for the original, though perhaps a curiously exotic one. The obscure and unverifiable composition of Cape and Australian wines, and probably some similarities in their style (strong and coarse, and relatively cheap), led to a catch-all term. Their wines became increasingly referred to as "colonial wine," which stressed its origins in the idea of empire, rather than the specificity of a colonial terroir. As the tariff debates demonstrate, producers could not hope to compete with continental European producers on taste, and they had to rely on arguing for the benefits they were providing for Empire and colony, rather than the quality of their products.

The actual quality of those products is, indeed, very difficult to determine: quality is not an absolute term, but is culturally specific and is understood relative to other goods. It is possible that the palates of British people in the nineteenth century were quite different from ours today, so what the historian is really investigating is what British people (in this case) thought about colonial wine in relation to other wines, or in relation to alternative beverages. We have seen that in the eighteenth century, the best Cape wines were compared to sweeter European wine styles, and were valued for their strength and body. In the nineteenth century, with the expansion of vineyards and trade, there does not seem to be a noticeable improvement in the quality of Cape wines, as far as the British were concerned. Some winemakers undoubtedly improved their wine with time and experience. But the expansion of vineyards, and the entrance of less-experienced winemakers into the field, may indeed have contributed to a decline in the overall quality of Cape wines. Given that many of the new market entrants were not wealthy, they often needed to sell their wine with an urgency that fought against the best winemaking practices. Grapes would be sold or crushed, whether it was an optimal harvest or not, and wine would not be allowed to linger in cellars when they could be bound for market.

The Cape did have a domestic market for its wines, too. The British Cape government inherited the VOC's right to buy a certain amount of Constantia, and thus "Constantia wine" was a regular line-item of modest expenditure on government balance sheets in first decade of British governance at the Cape.[14] In the 1820s a minister in Gnadenthal reported the sale of an "indifferent grazing farm, unfit for agriculture" for a staggering price, the reason being "a small vineyard, which yields a very inferior wine, unsaleable in the market, but which can with advantage by disposed of to the Hottentots and others in the neighbourhood."[15] To this minister the "market" refers to a specific site of regulated sale for white people. To the historian, on the other hand, this anecdote shows that native peoples were actors in economic exchanges, that they were involved in the market for wine. (Hottentot was a derogatory term used by Europeans for a San native of South Africa).

There was certainly a range of wines produced in the Cape. Cape wine sellers' own lists give an indication as to the perceived quality of the colony's wines. The Cape continued, through the nineteenth and twentieth centuries, to import European wines as well as to sell Cape wine for domestic consumption. This is evident in official trade statistics, but it is less clear in the ways these wines were marketed and sold. One advertisement from 1858 announced a merchant opening a bottle shop in Cape Town, meaning he would sell wine in bottles, both by the case of one dozen and by individual bottles. For a dozen bottles, the most expensive were "Best Paarl Sweet Wines, Burgundy, Port, [and] Lisbon," at 18s., followed by best-quality Madeira and sherry at 8s., ordinary sherry at 6s., "Aromatic Hock [and] Hanepoot" at 5s., and "Ordinary Table Wine" at just 4s. Despite their European names, all of these wines were produced at the Cape. None of them were listed according to a precise provenance or grape variety.[16] Competing retailers also offered, at similar prices, "Old Paarl Steen Wine" (chenin blanc from the Paarl district), Cape Madeira, Cape frontignac,[17] and Cape pontac.[18]

The challenges of knowing precisely which grapes were grown at the nineteenth-century Cape include a lack of comprehensive surveys, very little information communicated through wine advertising, and obscure or vague terminology. We know that both red and white varieties were grown, because we know that the Cape exported both red and white ones, through advertisements for such wines in Britain. One source for learning about the grape varieties grown in the Cape is land sales. An 1846 advertisement for 307 morgen of land included, among other plantings, twelve thousand "green grape plants" and three thousand hanepoot (muscat of Alexandria).[19] An 1850 advertisement for the sale of 13 to 14 morgen of land offered thirty thousand hanepoot vines.[20] Later advertisements include sales of "hermitage" and "red muscadell," although it is not clear if hermitage refers to the style of Rhône wine, or to the shiraz grape that dominates in Rhône blends.[21] Near the Moravian mission station of Gnadenthal, English missionary John Campbell enjoyed the hospitality of a German farmer and noted that "grapes in that part of Africa produce a wine resembling Rhenish." Rhenish refers to wines of the German Rhine region, the most prized of which are whites. Another missionary, C. I. Latrobe, wrote of visiting a woman farming near Constantia, and "tasting all the different wines made on her property. Among them were Hahnen Pootgen, white and red; Frontiniac; Klipp-wine, and another, of a rough taste." Hahnen Pootgen almost certainly refers to hanepoot, or muscat of Alexandria, which is normally white but also has a more unusual pink mutation,[22] and frontiniac is an alternative spelling of frontignac, or muscat blanc à petits grains. "Klipp-wine" is more mysterious: klipp means "stone" in Afrikaans, as does steen, and steen is a South African term for chenin blanc, a widely planted and "historic" variety at the Cape.[23] So klipp wine may have been chenin blanc, but it may have also been a misheard or misremembered term to this foreign missionary.

Wine writer Cyrus Redding, writing in 1836, bemoaned a lack of industry and expertise in the Cape, and concluded that the lack of knowledge about vine-dressing technique was responsible for the notorious "earthy" taste of its wines.[24] While this might be an accurate description of the Cape wines that were available in Britain, it is just as much an imperialistic dig at the skills of Afrikaans farmers. The term *earthy* does appear with frequency in British Victorian wine-writing. Robert Druitt, a medical doctor who penned a guide to wines as medication in 1865, was deeply critical of most Cape wine, and related this anecdote in his book: "I was at dinner one day, sitting next to the late Archdeacon ––, from the Cape. I asked him the reason of the earthy taste in Cape wine. He said, 'My dear sir, if you ever were at the Cape, and were to see the black fellows and their families in the vineyard at the vintage season, and how they make the wine, you would think *earthy* a very mild term indeed to be applied to it.'"[25] Like in earlier British accounts of Cape winemaking, this archdeacon's reference to the skin color of the wine laborers highlights the racial divides in the Cape industry and the pervasive racism of nineteenth-century colonial culture. This is not really a commentary on industrial hygiene or food safety (or even taste), but an ellipsis of Black bodies representing dirt and the earth, and tainting the wine itself. Cape newspapers from the early nineteenth century are a powerful reminder of the violence and indignities of slavery, and its central role in wine production. Court cases report torture of enslaved people, including one where a slaveowner beat his slave in his wine cellar.[26] Auctions and estate sales list enslaved people among property, such as an 1800 auction listing for "Bullocks, Waggons [*sic*], Wines of superior Quality, Excellent Casks, Good Slaves, Furniture of different kinds, etc etc."[27] Occasionally these enslaved people are named in cases where there is a specific property dispute, such as in Swellendam in 1828, where there were legal proceedings over "Oxen, Horses, an Ox Waggon [*sic*], a Horse ditto, empty Wine Casks, Brandy Still, etc, also, the Slaves *Carolus, Mentor, Diana,* and *Direada.*"[28] These names, fanciful classical ones no doubt chosen by the slaveowner, tell us nothing about the enslaved people as people.

Physical contact or touch, soil, body and terroir: these were fraught for British drinkers. Wine was obviously transformative in the body, through alcohol, which can alter human behavior, but far milder substances have also caused discomfort. Romita Ray notes that Britain-China tea trade in the eighteenth century was fraught: "Anxieties about tea cut deep in Britain because the commodity was ingestible and affected the body in ways that something like porcelain did not."[29] Dirt and soil were evocative for British commentators, too, in reinforcing their ideas of the social stratification of the Cape. Charles Bunbury, a well-connected gentleman botanist who toured the Cape in 1837 and published lengthy remarks a decade later,[30] applauded the "various arts of encroachment which European nations have so commonly practised [sic] against savages," and approved of early Dutch industry in civilizing through agriculture: "though the soil was not generally fertile, yet several tracts . . . were found to be adapted to the wheat and the wine."[31] The Cape Dutch farmers of the 1830s, though, he described as "dirty," and he condemned the condition of their homes; the "Hottentots" (indigenous Khoikhoi people), too, were "very filthy," but he conceded they were pastoral savages and generally a "mild, inoffensive, and unwarlike race."[32] Dirt was bad; agriculture, cultivation and the subordination of dirt was good, and indeed the ultimate sign of civilization. Another British traveler named Alfred Cole wrote in 1852 that the native "Hottentot" population was in steep decline, though "not by the cruelty of the colonists," but thanks to "[b]randy and disease."[33] He viewed this with indifference, because he believed the native man to be a "drunkard" and "the dirtiest fellow on earth." He shrugged: "Wherever the foot of civilization spreads, the native tribes melt away."[34] Cole was a zealous apologist for European colonialism, and like many of his contemporaries he judged people culturally inferior if they showed a dirty appearance and a fondness for strong liquor. (There is no reason to take his descriptions at face value: they reveal Cole's prejudices but tell very little about the San peoples of South Africa.)

Slavery was abolished across the British Empire in 1833, so at the time Druitt was writing, the "black fellows and their families" were technically free with their labor. However, the Cape passed a number of forms of legislation to restrict workers' mobility, including several masters and servants acts, which allowed employers to punish workers for breach of contract. Younger workers could be controlled in the guise of apprenticeships, and payment in kind (the dop system), where vineyard workers were paid in alcohol rather than cash, became common.

Druitt's contented ignorance about the labor that produced Cape wine was probably not unusual. In the late eighteenth century some small antislavery movements arose in Britain, lobbying Parliament to first abolish the trans-Atlantic slave trade, and then slavery itself in the British world. But these movements' efforts were primarily focused on the use of slavery in the West Indies, and on building consumers' awareness of the use of slavery to produce sugar. In the vast literature on British abolitionism, I have not found reference to Cape wine as a product of slavery or abolitionist petitions for its rejection. The British market for sugar was so much larger than that for Cape wine, and the abolitionist movement's focus on a single, ubiquitous commodity was ultimately effective. But this is one of many examples of how commodities from Britain's colonies were "pervasive and invisible" to British consumers, to use Joanna de Groot's phrasing.[35] This means that goods from the empire became staples in British diets, but that the origin of those goods was often obscure to consumers. Consumers either did not know, or did not care, how their foods were produced thousands of miles away.

Ironically, winemakers and governors continued to push a narrative that wine was beneficial, and potentially transformative, for the colonies that produced it. Often in imperial history, the civilizing mission of imperialists is treated as a separate issue from their capitalist ambitions. With wine, we see that they were one and the same. Busby, for example, argued that in New South Wales, "many situations may be chosen capable of yielding wines fitted for the British market."[36] But just as importantly, he believed that in Australia itself wine would prove "a healthy and exhilarating beverage, such as almost every farm will produce, and to which habit is sure to give a relish,"[37] to the improvement of the local population. Busby was concerned with the use of hard liquors like rum and whiskey, known as "ardent spirits," among the settler population. He connected this to the popular nineteenth-century belief that diet should be suited to climate, lest people become too excitable in the heat. "By those who have been accustomed to the use of spirits in a colder climate, some stimulant is undoubtedly required," he conceded, continuing, "but the great majority of the colonists have yet to learn that the free use of a light unadulterated wine, will not only strengthen their bodies and clear their minds, but weaken or destroy the relish for those stronger stimulants which are now poisoning the morals of the population."[38]

Busby's concerns were shared by many contemporary leaders in settler society. Daniel Wheeler, an English Protestant missionary who made extensive voyages around the South Pacific in the 1830s (meeting with Busby in the New Zealand), wrote extensively about the evils of "ardent spirits" in his published travel diary. His ship stopped in many ports, and he met both European settlers and indigenous people. "It is satisfactory to know, that some of the strangers who have attended our [religious] meetings on board, have, in more than one instance, remarked, (as if of rare occurrence,) that our sailors look more like healthy, fresh-faced farmers, than men come off a long voyage: the generality of those we see daily, have a thin and worn-down appearance, particularly when they belong to ships that supply them daily with ardent spirits; while our sailors have each a quart of beer per day, of weak quality," he assured his readers.[39] Temperance writers warned that the ways in which people drank wine, and the type of wine they drank, was troubling. Wine itself was not necessarily the problem; cheap wine, and strong wine, was the problem. "To drink wine largely has long been customary and fashionable, and to bring it within the reach of as many as could be, it had to be made as cheap as possible," argued a British temperance activist in 1831, "and when the middling classes entered generally into its use, it had to compete and compare with the spirituous liquors they had been accustomed to."[40] British commentators on colonial Australia and New Zealand shared identical concerns, and official promotion of wine was partly due to the belief that it would tame the population. They were quick to point out that unfortified wine was better than other, higher-alcohol beverages. If you could get rum drinkers to start drinking wine, the logic went, they would behave like wine drinkers. Thus Australian winemakers envisioned that their wine be a civilizing beverage that would have a positive influence on the unruly members of the settler population, who normally craved beer and spirits. Edward Wakefield, in an early history of the British Antipodes, wrote with frustration about New South Wales in the 1830s, that "the great majority of the colonists have yet to learn that the free use of a light unadulterated wine, will not only strengthen their bodies and clear their minds, but weaken or destroy the relish for those stronger stimulants," meaning hard liquor and spirits, "which are now poisoning the morals of the population."[41] This argument was clearly class-based. Wine consumption was less common among working-class people, who made up the bulk of the European population in the young convict colony.

These moral concerns may have propelled the glorification of the wine farmer in the Australian press. Rather than a working-class scourge on Australian society, the wine farmer was a social hero to celebrate. He brought savage land under control and produced. "Every farm-settler is now adding a vineyard to his estate," the Australian colonist Edward Wilson Landor crowed in 1847, that "we almost fear that the colonists are giving too much of their attention to the cultivation of grapes."[42] Landor was writing about Western Australia, and his call for moderation—for diverse agriculture, such that settlers would guarantee themselves the best security—strikes a note of false alarm. He was proud of viticulture as evidence that Western Australia was being transformed, in the eyes of European settlers, from an overwhelming frontier to a place of settled agriculture and industry.

In a short book aimed at encouraging British immigration to South Australia in the 1840s—the new colony, centered around the city of Adelaide—G. B. Wilkinson described an idyllic scene of tired but proud settlers arriving in the South Australian bush, their horses and carts laden with "good seed wheat and potatoes; flower seeds for a garden; vine cuttings and fruit trees to plant." They were optimistic farmers, and they were confident in their civilizing mission: they "speculate that they will astonish the natives with their neat house and superior culture."[43] As with Marsden's claiming of "astonishing" the Maori in New Zealand with his orchard, we have little record of the indigenous response. Thomas Hardy, his company would nonchalantly remark a century later, built part of his South Australian estate on an Aboriginal graveyard,[44] probably belonging to the Kaurna people. If this astonished them, it was because it was an act of desecration.

According to Wilkinson, who observed an agricultural fair in February 1847 in Adelaide, there was "keen competition for the wine prize," although the "samples were rather in bad condition, having been brought from a long distance; some of them, however, give promise of the production of superior wines by the vine growers." The winner, a Mr. Anstey, also won prizes for his orchard fruits, and a close second, Mr. Duffield, won prizes for his vegetables, bacon, and hops.[45] This was almost certainly Walter Duffield, an English-born settler who farmed and later became a politician.[46] He is believed to have been the first to produce wine in South Australia, and, as we have seen, he celebrated his venture in what was the ultimate promotional move in the nineteenth-century British world: he sent a sample of his "Echunga hock" to Queen Victoria. Agricultural fairs were social events in which settler communities took stock of their own progress. Australia's cities also organized learned societies to celebrate and promote agriculture. The Floral and Horticultural Society was established in Sydney, and its shows attracted "nearly the whole of the respectable persons of Sydney," and the patronage of the colonial governor. At its 1839 show, there were "several samples of colonial wine," the journalist reported with some amusement for these new and unusual products. He (presumably) reported that the "claret and burgundy were tolerable wine, but the sherry—all we have to say is, that if it had not been labelled nobody would have known what it was. There was a bottle labelled champagne, but our reporter laments that it was emptied before he arrived."[47] One wonders whether it was emptied into glasses, or into the potted plants that "tastefully adorned" the hotel ballroom.

Landor also wrote sentimentally about the family aspects of wine production in Western Australia, and how the settler would come to love "the easy, independent life which he was accustomed to lead, when his children used to run about in brown holland, and his wife looked becoming in printed cotton, and thought no beverage so good as the wine which she had assisted to make."[48] Hubert de Castella, a Swiss-born winemaker in Australia, picked up this refrain, writing about winemaking in New South Wales in the 1880s. In echo of tropes of wine's positive role in social engineering, de Castella argues that the cultivation of the grape brings health, peace, and prosperity to the Australian vigneron and his family: "The more sober a man is—and he must have been so, otherwise his vineyard would not have been properly kept and would have borne him no early crop—the more there is joy in the family. For wine is food, and he gives it, diluted with water, to his wife and his young children, for whom the acidulated taste is freshness in the mouth, like chickweed to the birds. This cask of wine lasts him the whole year, and the children grow to like only the fruity liquid which they get at home; they will never care for strong drinks afterwards."[49] Both Landor's and de Castella's rural imaginaries, written nearly forty years apart, celebrate the family as an independent social unit, with a strong patriarch who cares for his wife and children by supplying them with wholesome wine.

An 1870 painting and chromolithograph, from a series published in London called *Ten Australian Views,* also showed this very image of Australian family life (see fig. 2). Two women sit on a blanket in the foreground, sorting deep-purple grapes, calmly looking up as a child teeters toward them, holding a basket full of ripe fruit. In the background a man steers a wheelbarrow full of grapes, another adds grapes to be crushed by a wooden hand press, and another pours grape must into a wooden barrel. The scene is calm and productive; the sun shines down on this happy, intergenerational band of European workers, and most of them wear pristine white garments (including, most improbably, the child). Wine that was made by European settlers was clean and wholesome, this image suggests; we should contrast this with the writings about Cape wine made by native Africans and colored people, which was frequently described as dirty.

It is not certain whether the unknown artist had ever visited Australia or observed winemaking firsthand. But this idealized scene illustrated many ideas that Australian wine lovers were trying to promote in Britain, of a family-friendly and civilized life. Indeed, the Wyndhams, a major Hunter Valley wine producer, advertised their wines in the 1870s as "Good Pure

FIGURE 2. *The Vineyard* (artist unknown). An idyllic (and imagined) scene of an Australian family making wine. From *Ten Australian Views* (London: n.p., 1870). Used with permission from the National Library of Australia, nla.obj-139535117.

Australian Wine," suited for "families."[50] This wholesome image that the industry perpetrated was in keeping with government promotion of wine as a civilized beverage.

Furthermore, the wine itself was extolled by settler-winemakers as a symbol of deep loyalty and imperial pride. Duffield, famed sender of Echunga hock, wrote that his vinous gift to Queen Victoria was "literally first fruits of our vineyards, so loyally rendered as a tribute of respect and gratitude."[51] The image of winemaking as a civilized and wholesome pursuit was not only for colonial self-affirmation, but to promote positive images of the colonies in Britain. Landor's writing, for example, was syndicated in many British newspapers (the *Glasgow Herald* ran an excerpt that emphasized that "it is of so comforting a nature, that the laborers in harvest prefer the home-made colonial wine to any other beverage"). James Fallon, another booster for Australian wine, whom we will meet in the next chapter, had his remarks published in both Australia and in London.[52] Fallon was not alone in writing about Australian wine for a British audience: his better-known, Swiss-born contemporary, Hubert de Castella, penned a book, *John Bull's Vineyard,* dedicated to the Prince of Wales and extolling the virtues of Australian wine. McIntyre argues that this kind of literature is "booster literature," meant to entice new settlers to join the wine industry; the volume of the literature does not *reflect* the existing level of interest in the topic, but aims to *create* interest and, in doing so, to mold the type of colony that its authors desired: prosperous, peaceful and civilized.[53] She sees James Fallon's writing as evident of this "settlerist rhetoric."[54]

How accurate was this romantic portrayal of winemaking? Certainly, families did harvest grapes together, but this was of economic necessity given labor constraints, especially in more remote areas. It was not a reality that underpaid black and colored laborers in nineteenth-century South Africa would have recognized. Racial and ethnic divides between employers and workers were common and were considered by white employers to be grounds for treating their workers without dignity. In addition, one of the more controversial developments in South Africa's postemancipation era was the creation of the "dop" or "tot" system in the Cape. This was a system where wine workers received all or part of their wages in the form of alcohol. The dop system should not be confused with the custom, still common in the twenty-first century, of winemakers celebrating the end of a successful harvest with a boozy party for their field laborers (known as *la Paulée* in Burgundy, for example). Rather, the dop system tied workers to estates, because it limited their cash purchasing power and thus ability to exercise any freedom of movement; indeed, wine farmers argued that they needed the dop system to recruit and retain workers.[55] It also created a crisis of alcoholism within black and colored communities, especially among men. As in New Zealand and Australia, settlers worked to expand the market for alcohol sales among indigenous people, and simultaneously decried the susceptibility of indigenous people to alcohol abuse. The solution, many settlers and colonial governors believed, was to take control over indigenous people's lives, to save or "protect" them from a social problem that settlers themselves had introduced. Alcohol abuse was real, but European social control was real, too.

The curiously named Echunga hock reveals many stories about the early nineteenth-century wine industry. It links the monarch of the world's largest empire, and her German husband, to a small farmer in the budding colony of South Australia, by means of barrels, bottles, carts, and ships. The hopes and dreams of this settler were buoyed by his local newspaper, itself a self-conscious civilizing mechanism of settler society—for what is a modern society without a vibrant press? Indeed, much of what we know about wine in the Cape and Australia in the early nineteenth century comes through newspapers, which both created and reflected the ideals of their communities, and which were entwined in the dense communication webs of the empire. In the spaces and silences of these texts, we can train our eyes to bring the hazy background into focus, and there we can also see the stories of the indigenous workers who slaved over the vineyards, or whose livelihoods were disfigured by the booming settler communities. The "earthiness" of early colonial wine was blended from these many varieties of human experience.

EIGHT

Have You Any Colonial Wine?

AUSTRALIAN PRODUCERS AND BRITISH TARIFFS

THE "PRESENT HIGH DUTY PAID upon foreign and colony wine," a member of Parliament for Yorkshire declared in 1854, was "contrary to the principles of free trade, adverse to the social and moral improvement of the people, and injurious to the [national] revenue."[1] It was, one might even say, un-British. It is worth noting that this statement came from a politician whose constituency had no coast, no ports, and no connection at all to the wine trade.

To a modern reader, customs tariffs may seem an unlikely avenue for moral improvement. But in the 1860s, the British government embraced tariffs for precisely that reason, and these tariffs had a profound impact on colonial producers. Wine tariff debates in the 1820s and 1830s had largely focused on the whether Cape loyalty to the Crown justified a lower rate of tariffs in order to stimulate (or rescue) Cape wineries. The British wine tariff question in the 1860s took the discussion quite a bit further. The legislation that was produced amplifies several surprisingly intertwined topics: the logistics of transporting wine overseas, the styles of wine that were popular in Britain, public health and morality, and food safety and labeling. The public sphere was becoming more complex, just as the balance sheets for British trade were also becoming more detailed and diverse. Some of the discussions of wine in British society (and colonial settler society, too) actually reflect unease about urbanization and poverty. The United Kingdom had experienced a century of unprecedented population growth and had transformed into a country of city dwellers who purchased their staple goods in the market. Legislators and social commentators who wished to improve the fabric of British society honed in on foodstuffs as a tool to shape this growing and unwieldy populace.

The Cape was probably the world's first wine region that was created expressly for an export market. By the late 1850s, there had been forty years of fretting and grumbling about the quality and quantity of wine produced in British South Africa. But in hindsight, this was a first commercial golden period, in which Cape wine had become well established and popular Britain, in spite of the degradations of tariff policy in the 1820s and 1830s. In 1856, nearly half of the wine imported into Britain came from Portugal. But the second-highest place of origin was the Cape. In the 1850s 13 percent of the wine imported into Britain came from the Cape—a fraction higher than the percentage of wine that came from France.[2] Moreover, Cape wine that was imported into Britain tended to remain there for domestic consumption, whereas the finer continental European wines were often reexported as well as consumed domestically.[3] Cape wine, being largely seen as inferior in quality to French wine, was probably purchased for ready consumption, not stockpiled or aged for future profit or pleasure. It is therefore possible that significantly more Cape wine was actually *drunk* in Britain in the mid-nineteenth century than French wine was. In the late 1850s, close observers of the wine trade even expressed concerns about wine prices dropping due to an oversupply of Cape wine in the British market.[4]

This golden age came to an end due to a major change to British tariffs in the 1860s. Tariffs, again, are not simply about prices. They reflect, in this case, deep beliefs about wine's social and civilizing role in both British and colonial societies, and they also offer a glimpse into the emerging field of public health. "Earthy" colonial wines came under scrutiny: though medical professionals and legislators may not have believed that they contained actual dirt, they did increasingly suspect that colonial wines were not entirely clean.

COLONIAL WINE

In the mid-nineteenth century the term *colonial wine* came into general British usage. As we have seen, Cape wines were popular in Britain in the eighteenth and early nineteenth centuries. Gradually, Australian wines started to be exported to Britain, too, especially after 1850. A picture emerges of rather coarse wines, aimed at a middle-class or working-class clientele in the British world, and sold under the names of prominent European styles. There may indeed have been some wonderful Cape and Australian wines making their way into the British market between 1800 and 1860, but overall these two colonies were not marketing their wines based on quality, but on affordability, novelty, and the good effects wine would have on working-class populations.

Even if most exports were not Constantia-quality, Constantia wine continued to appear in well-to-do British homes through the mid-nineteenth century, as a recognizable object of value. In 1850 a domestic servant appeared before the Old Bailey court in London, charged with stealing from her employer this colonial wine, as well as some colonial condiments: "twenty bottles of claret, some bottles of constantia, a sheet, five table-cloths, eighteen tumblers, twenty-four wine glasses, six bottles of chutney, six bottles of cayenne pepper, [and] six bottles of currie powder."[5] The term colonial wine was being used by the 1820s, before Australia was even exporting (and thus, when it referred to the Cape), and it had definitely entered the popular British lexicon by the 1840s. One of the earliest references to wine being exported from Australia appears in the shipping news column of a London newspaper in 1827, noting the departure of "the ship Marquis of Huntley . . . from New South Wales . . . with a cargo of cedar, blue gum plants, tree-nails, Zealand spars, spokes, oil, wool, salted hides, and three half-pipes of Colonial wine."[6] The term colonial wine was used during the tariff debates of 1831, both in Parliament and in the press.[7] It even appears in criminal records, such as when Mary Ann Bamford used a counterfeit coin in a wholesale wine merchant's shop: "'Bamford called for a pint of whisky,' the defrauded merchant's clerk recounted to the Old Bailey Court. 'I told her she could not have so small a quantity, I was a wholesale dealer—she said, "Oh! and by-the-bye, have you any Colonial wine"—I said, "Yes"—she asked for a bottle; I said it was 2s[hillings]., she tendered me a sovereign.'" A sovereign was a pound coin, the equivalent of 20s., much more than the quoted price. But the sovereign turned out to be counterfeit, and Bamford was sentenced to fifteen months' prison for her trickery.[8] Why the wholesaler was prepared to sell a single bottle of colonial wine is unclear, but colonial wine was evidently a request that a hardened criminal did not expect would raise suspicion in a merchant. It was evidently an inauspicious and common item that was not excessively expensive in London.

The term *Cape wine* was still also in common usage in the first half of the nineteenth century in Britain, though it was generally used in a pejorative way, such as another court case for fraud in 1843, which referred to "bad Cape, and it has turned sour."[9] One reason why wines turned sour was when they were contaminated with bacteria, and wines that were shipped long distances in semiporous wooden barrels were susceptible to such contamination. Druitt, the medical doctor whose 1865 book assessed the health and propriety of wine, conceded that Cape port was probably fine to drink, and an acceptable substitute for real (Portuguese) port, and also that Cape wines might be satisfactory if they were drunk on location at the Cape itself. He bemoaned the fact that they were so often, and often secretly, fortified. He related another anecdote about a friend's visit to the Cape, where said friend, "Tasted wine—light, dry, delicious, pure, and unbrandied. Ordered a cask. Gets it home; finds he has to pay the 2s. 6d. duty, indicating that it has lost its virginity as wine. It is now a hot, strong, heady South African, which ought to do long penance in wood and bottle before it is used."[10] This wine was not simply too young to drink, it was morally dubious and salacious, the product of a sultry climate.

Druitt's comment, though steeped in the moralism of temperance campaigning, highlights a practical and methodological issue in assessing the quality of colonial wines in this period. Making wine in South Africa and then exporting it to Britain was really quite difficult. Even the best nineteenth-century producers and merchants could not offer consistent quality and supply. Like all agricultural products, grapes were susceptible to inclement weather, pests, and disease. Shipping exposed wine to further vulnerabilities, especially before the advent of climate-controlled ships' holds. The further the distance, then the longer the time spent in ship, then the greater risk to the wine. In fairness to the Victorian winemakers in the British colonial world, the wine *might* have been just fine when it left the vineyard. It was the importation process, the interference of heat, bacteria, and perhaps importers, that might have spoiled it.

The Australian press itself made great fun of the poor quality of the industry's early efforts. The *Melbourne Punch* solicited reader responses to the question, "Will the Coming Man Drink Wine?" and the responses included, "I offer colonial wine. I am doomed to my fate."[11] Nineteenth-century British wine-writer Thomas Shaw would have agreed. He was unconvinced by any of the good news coming out of Australia: "Notwithstanding the attempt to make it appear that the growth is increasing, and that wine-making may become a profitable investment, the facts do not appear to justify the hope," he argued in 1863, and that those praising the growth of the Australian industry did not know what they were writing about.[12] Dr. Thudichum, a wine-writer whom we will meet again later, did not mince words in reviewing Australian wines in 1873. Pity J. G. Francis, a winemaker in Victoria, whose

1869 vintage Thudichum describes as "thick and undrinkable." He continues mercilessly: "Dirty brownish red colour, fluorescent at margin; very unfavourable aspect; stinks; no Burgundy character; thin to taste; very astringent and bitter. Very bad wine; equal to wine sold at Lisbon at £4 per pipe."[13] Dirty, earthy wine: colonial wine certainly had its detractors. On the other hand, there were major public health debates in Victorian Britain about two related issues in colonial wine production: adulteration and fortification. Fortified wines—those wines that are strengthened by adding hard alcohol for taste, preservation, and style—had long been popular in Britain. The most popular were port and sherry, products of Portugal and Spain, respectively. The fortifying alcohol was often brandy, which is itself made from wine, so distillation was a popular and inexpensive way to deal with an oversupply of table wine in a given year. In turn, using brandy to fortify table wine could be a way to salvage mediocre-quality wine, which was often the result of grapes not ripening sufficiently, since, if grapes do not ripen enough, they will not have enough sugar to convert to alcohol, resulting in a low-alcohol product. That addition of brandy would give body and brawn to insipid wines. Sometimes enough brandy was added to raise the overall alcohol content a few degrees in order to create a sherry or port-style wine, and sometimes just enough brandy was added to boost the wine, while keeping it in the alcohol range of table wines. (This alcohol range was the basis for customs tariffs in the U.K and many other countries: fortified wines were usually taxed at a higher rate.)

The main reason fortification became popular in the British New World was because the higher alcohol content of fortified wines acted as a preservative. Wines that were higher in alcohol were considered more resilient during long ocean journeys, less prone to spoilage and souring. At the cheaper end of the wine market, too, alcoholic content was valued: even if the wine did not taste incredible, it could still be effective for the consumer seeking a relatively refined route to inebriation. The other reason that distillation became popular in the British New World was a means to improve the trials and efforts of new winemakers. We have seen that brandy was distilled in the Cape beginning in the seventeenth century, in an attempt to rescue low-quality wine being produced and to produce something that was marketable. Adding that distilled spirit back into weak wine could be a strategy to avoid losing a vintage and the winemaker's annual income.

Fortification became controversial in nineteenth-century Britain because there was little legal basis for food labeling. That meant that unscrupulous vendors could adulterate food, drink, and medications with other ingredients, defrauding the consumer or even putting health in danger. They could also make claims to the health benefits of their products without providing any kind of scientific process or verifiable proof. When it came to wine, consumers had little way of knowing whether wines had been fortified, and if so with what. Fortifying wine with brandy may have been deceptive, but it was probably not harmful. Fortifying wine with something else could indeed be dangerous. A colonial wine that was relatively high in alcohol was therefore viewed with suspicion; colonial producers clearly had an incentive to add extra alcohol to their wines, in order to strengthen their wines for the long journey; what else might they have added to the mix, and how could they be trusted or even confronted at such distance?

It is difficult to say how widespread fortification was in the wines that Australia and the Cape exported to Britain in the nineteenth century. Most of the sources that discuss fortification are hyperbolic in tone, and there were no comprehensive controls at each stage of the winemaking process. In an extensive British government report on the colonial wine industry written in the 1930s, the author reflected back that the decline of South African wines after the 1830s "was to no little degree due to the fact that the trade had been built up on price rather than quality. Much of the Cape wine had, in fact, been used for blending with British made wines and sold as cheap port and sherry."[14] We do not know on what sources this report based itself, but this was an accusation that the chancellor of the exchequer had used in the 1830s to defend a rise in tariffs (essentially, that Cape wine was party to fraud). Warnings were also issued by some members of the British medical establishment about the risks of adulterated Cape wine, particularly when used for medicinal purposes.[15] In Australia, the colony of Victoria created a special license category in 1868 for "stills for the manufacture of spirits, for the purpose of fortifying colonial wine."[16]

Overall the "authenticity" of wines was not paramount in the nineteenth century, as wine merchants frequently blended and tinkered with wines to improve their taste, and the bulk wine trade made it difficult to verify the precise composition of a wine. However, there were widespread concerns among Britain's chattering classes about *what* wine merchants were using to improve their wine purchases, and whether or not these additives were safe. Adulteration became a much-discussed public health concern in Victorian Britain, one that was directly tied to Britain's growing urbanization: the less people produced their own food, the more they entrusted merchants to provide accurate and healthy products.

Allegations of fraud were common against colonial wines in nineteenth-century Britain, and some of them were probably well-founded. That did not necessarily keep those wines from becoming well known and popular among a segment of the population: a middling sort of consumer, who aspired to drink wine but did not have a large budget. Of course, colonial winemakers had limited control over the state of their wine once it was sold overseas. Wine merchants and off-licenses blended, doctored, and "improved" the wines they received: cue many late-Victorian quips about "chemists who are also wine-merchants (the trades too often are identical)."[17] John Davies' guide to cellaring wine, published in England in 1805, explained that French claret had to be kept in a temperate cellar, and one must "feed it once every two or three weeks with a pint or two of the best French brandy," seasoning to taste, so that the wine does not become fiery, but rather "a little at a time incorporates with the wine, and feeds and mellows it."[18] The same guide advised adding cochineal or sloes to red wines and ports to boost their color, honey to sherry to restore sweetness, and milk to improve lackluster white wine. Davies also gives instructions for how to "fine" wines. Fining is a process to remove harshness from wine; it usually involves adding a substance to the wine which can physically bind with excessive proteins or tannins, and then be filtered out. Davies recommends eggs, milk, and sand in various degrees; of the three, eggs and milk proteins are still commonly used today. He also recommends filtering wine through cloth in order to remove unpleasant sediment. Some of Davies' methods are entirely sound and legitimate, whereas others are clearly designed to deceive the consumer. The most generous interpretation would be that he helped innkeepers and butlers to avoid tragic wastage of spoiled wine. His book went into seventeen editions over the nineteenth century, so no matter how pure his readers' intentions were, his advice was known widely.

LIGHT WINES

Concerns about health, morality, and public finance converged in 1860, a year which was a turning point in wine history. In 1860 Britain entered a new treaty with France and Chancellor William Gladstone subsequently created a new national budget that lowered and made uniform tariffs on wine, to the delight of French producers. The Victorian age's most domineering prime minister, Gladstone was a political force for over fifty years. He led the

Liberal Party's transformation into an ideologically distinct, modern political machine through four successful elections over the second half of the nineteenth century. His reputation was formed in part through his powerful oratory, and also through his meticulous and ambitious budgets, which he presented as chancellor of the exchequer (the second-most important position in British government, and the chief financial role, which he occupied twice, and once while simultaneously serving as prime minister). Gladstone's chief commitments were to retrenchment, the cutting back of excessive spending, and reform, and to molding and improving British society through legislation. Wine had a special role in this mission. As James Simpson has shown, Gladstone's legislation to cut wine duties and create off-licences in the early 1860s was designed to create a "wine revolution," to introduce safe, unadulterated wine to a broader range of consumers, to de-luxurize it and promote it as an act of social engineering.[19]

The tariff changes bring to the surface the moral and civilization arguments around wine consumption in the British world, as well as the costs and class dimensions of the wine trade in Britain itself. These new tariffs, which have been described as an "adventurous and imaginative scheme to open up the wine trade,"[20] differentiated between still table (or "light") wines and stronger spirit-fortified ones. Under the new system, higher-alcohol wines would be taxed at a higher rate than lower-alcohol wines. Until February 1860, there had been two categories for wine tariffs: wine made in "British Possessions" was taxed at 2s. 10d. per gallon, and wine from all other places was taxed at 5s. 9d. per gallon. In 1861, the new regime became based on alcoholic strength instead of country of origin. Still wines up to an alcoholic strength of twenty-six degrees (about 14.8 percent ABV) were taxed at 1s. 9d. per gallon. Wines over twenty-six degrees were presumed to be fortified and were taxed at a higher rate of 2s. 5d. Imperial preference—meaning lower tariffs for British colonies—was thus scrapped.[21]

To put these prices in context, Robert Druitt writes in 1865 that an approximately 750ml bottle of French wine retailed for around 2s. a bottle. The difference between the high and low tariff rate for this amount of wine would only be around 1.5d., or about 6 percent of the retail price. If this cost were passed on to the consumer, 6 percent might seem an insignificant cost difference to the consumer debating between purchasing two bottles. The bigger problem, which the Cape producers had complained about thirty years earlier, was that European wines were now so much cheaper than they had been: Druitt writes that in 1865, "qualities being equal, common Bordeaux may be got at 3/5 the price of 1851."[22] The real problem for colonial producers lay in the fact that their wines couldn't compete with Bordeaux wines, even "common" Bordeaux, in terms of quality or production costs. They needed their wines to be significantly cheaper than French wines to have a real market advantage, and at this point they were not. When added to the relatively high shipping costs (compared to those of nearby European producers), and the uphill battle of reversing consumer perceptions of the poor quality of colonial wines, some merchants saw their businesses completely change. The Gilbeys, British wine merchants who were early importers of Cape wines, "at first could discern nothing but ruin in the destruction of the trade on which their business had been almost exclusively built up."[23] They had been preparing to send a staff member to the Cape to deal with their growing volume of business, and now they found themselves scrambling to sell French wines instead. The result was "a death blow to the popularity of Cape wines, for it opened British markets to the light wines of Bordeaux," which were now competitively priced.[24] This is the context to importers' entreaties to their Australian suppliers to be very careful about the alcoholic strength of their shipments.

Burgoyne never suggests that his suppliers were fortifying their wine, but adulteration continued to be a topic of vigorous debate in Britain. A series of acts were passed to crack down on adulteration of foods and drink, including wine, in 1860 and 1872, with government inspectors and hefty fines imposed on fraudsters. The *British Medical Journal* reported on the terms of this 1872 Adulteration of Food and Drugs Act, and its reporting just happened to appear on the same page as a tragic case of an infant who died after a fatal dose of adulterated cough medicine.[25] There is little evidence that this government crackdown had much impact on wine adulteration; or at least, there is little evidence that the suspicion of wine adulteration retreated very far away from the public consciousness. The topic of additives and alcohol content became a frustrating issue for Australian producers, because they believed that it stemmed from European ignorance about climate and horticulture. Australian wines, then and now, can generally become more alcoholic than continental European wines because hotter climates producer riper, more sugary grapes. Wines of northern France might typically be 12 or 12½ percent alcohol by volume (ABV); Australian reds can easily be 14 percent. A popular Victorian assumption was that strong Australian wines must have been adulterated or fortified to reach such levels. This would be compounded by consumer presumptions that Australian wines were of poorer quality to begin with, and may have been fortified to improve their quality or mask defects, or to guard against spoilage during the long ocean voyage. The reputed "strength" of colonial wines—which referred to their taste as well as to their alcoholic content—may have been a factor in their favor, when it came to building a middle-class market. But it also put them on the radar of temperance activists and other social commentators, who singled them out as problematic wines for their strength and relative cheapness.

In theory, legislation that promoted wine drinking should have been a welcome boon to colonial winemakers. The problem was that Gladstone's legislation promoted light (lower-alcohol) wines, and many colonial wines were too strong, either due to nature or fortification. But the concern of temperance activists in both Britain and British colonies also suggests, again, what we saw in the tariff debates of the early nineteenth century: that colonial wines were creating a middle- and working-class market for wines. If it had not been for the expansion of wine's consumer base, and its early reaches into the middle and working classes, then the temperance movement would have saved its ire for beer and spirits.

It is worth differentiating between temperance movements, which permitted small amounts of alcohol consumption in certain circumstances, and teetotal or abstinence movements, which decried all alcohol as immoral. For the most part, temperance logic prevailed in governance circles in the nineteenth-century Britain and in British colonies. Alcohol was a strong part of British culture, as well as the economy, and total abstinence seemed undesirable and impractical to most legislators. Abstinence culture was probably strongest in New Zealand (which was, probably not coincidentally, the last of the colonies here to really expand its wine industry). New Zealand was particularly earnest in regulating alcohol sales, and working-class people emerge in the records of enforcement. In 1847, for example, a Wellington laborer was convicted of selling wine without a license to a woman, and was sentenced to a £50 fine and four months in prison.[26] Much later in South Africa, in the early twentieth century, wine-farmers tried to use temperance logic to combat the strength of the abstinence movement by trying to relax licensing requirements for sales of "light wines," which they presented as a socially responsible alternative to hard liquor.[27] A writer in an Australian newspaper in the 1870s was at pains to portray how a wine bar in Melbourne was frequented "principally by artisans and labouring men," sometimes accompanied by their wives, and there was "no drunkenness, no bad language, no quarreling." This was thanks to the wine, which was "mild . . . pure and unadulterated."[28]

In considering how wine could have been considered a tool for social improvement, it is also important to bear in mind that alcohol had a long-standing medicinal use, and that using wine as medicine fell within the bounds of what many temperance reformers saw as legitimate usage. News media in the British world was full of heated debated about the health merits of alcohol. Mainstream medical practice in the second half of the nineteenth century viewed alcohol as a tool in the physician's arsenal for treating illness and disease.[29] Alcohol was not viewed as a depressant, as it became known a century later, but as a stimulant that could fortify the constitution. If illness weakened the body, then alcohol, used in moderation and under a doctor's supervision, could strengthen it.

An English country physician, C. R. Bree, writing to the *Times* in 1872, protested teetotal statements signed by his medical colleagues. "I could fill a page of your journal with cases showing the inestimable value of alcohol in the treatment of diseases," he wrote. He went on to pathologize the total-abstinence movement: "The present crusade against alcohol in disease is got up and supported by the same weak-minded people who pretend to argue against the Contagious Diseases Acts and denounce the blessings of vaccination. It is a phase in the morbid sensationalism which will mark the history of the 19th century."[30] For this Dr. Bree, the teetotal movement exercised a kind of dark influence, lobbying doctors to sign on to its principles, without any regard for medical fact or experience.

Morbid sensationalism, perhaps, but these debates also reflect the development of a British state that took some interest in, and responsibility for, public health. In addition, when we include Dr. Bree's invocation of nineteenth-century antivaxxers, we note a corresponding public suspicion about the motivations behind scientific expertise. We have seen how wine, especially "light" wine, was touted as a civilizing beverage in British colonies. The same was true in Victorian Britain. Public drunkenness was a widely debated public health issue in nineteenth-century Britain., particularly its prevalence among working-class residents of Britain's growing industrial cities. According to Seebohm Rowntree's pioneering sociological studies of life in the city of York at the turn of the twentieth century, it was not unusual to see children as young as five purchasing alcohol, even in a "respectable working-class district."[31] When working-class families slipped into poverty,[32] Rowntree found that alcohol was a usually a major factor. Rowntree's data-collection methods were new, but his conclusion that strong drink wreaked havoc on poor communities had been long accepted anecdotally. At the same time, alcohol use was also widely recognized and accepted as a long-standing aspect of British life for all social classes. Temperance reformers like John Dunlap blamed deeply ingrained British traditions of drinking "healths," or toasts, in celebrating both professional and family occasions.[33] Other temperance reformers bemoaned the ubiquitous role of public houses, or pubs, in British community life. Although nineteenth-century pubs usually were not welcoming to women and children, they served multiple roles for men as meeting spaces, restaurants, travelers' lodgings, and places to exchange news and gossip.

There is no reason to believe that drunkenness (or alcoholism) was any more prevalent among the working classes than any other. Rather, it was simply was more disruptive and noticeable than, say, aristocratic men's drunkenness in private members' clubs, since working-class drunkenness was more likely to be carried out in a public space and to have devastating effects on those in financially precarious positions. In addition, the percentage of British society that was working class was much higher than that which was of the middle or professional classes, perhaps 60 or 70 percent of all British people.

What people drank was as class-dependent as where and how they drank (and what social commentators felt empowered to write about it). Whereas wine dominated the drinking habits of the British well-to-do, beer and spirits were cheaper and more widely consumed among the poor and the working classes. Some contemporary critics assumed that consumers were aspirational and emulative in their habits: Dunlap urged his wealthy readers to stop serving wine to their middle-class guests, even as a special treat, for he believed these guests would want to imitate their social superiors, and might acquire bad habits in doing so. But then Dunlap was arguing for total abolition of alcohol in Britain, For many other British thinkers, the logic was a bit different: perhaps wine was a cause, and not just a symbol, of social ease and gentility. If you could get beer drinkers to start drinking wine, the logic went, they would behave like wine drinkers. The antisocial behavior and persistent poverty of Britain's poor cities could perhaps be improved upon, if only ordinary people would give up their light rum for light wine. "As an agency in the cause of temperance the viticultural industry operates powerfully," an Australian viticulturalist claimed, arguing that there was little drunkenness in wine-producing countries.[34]

Were Gladstone's reforms a success in getting British drinkers to switch to "light wines"? For sure, we do not detect any decline in poverty or urban violence as a direct result. The tariffs were modestly effective at raising wine consumption in Britain. At its peak in the 1870s, British wine consumption was about three bottles per person, per year. For comparison, beer peaks at 33.2 imperial gallons, or 265.6 imperial pints, per capita, in the 1870s. This would suggest, for example, that many adult men were drinking several pints a day. Wine consumption rose, but it did not replace beer overnight. Why was wine consumption so low? According to *Ridley's,* a periodical of the wine and spirits trade, it could only be because "three-quarters of the population have never had an opportunity of tasting the sublime liquor."[35]

MYSTIFYING THE PUBLIC

Where Gladstone's reforms were not a success in the short term, was in colonial wine imports into Britain. In terms of the trade, South African wine imports into Britain plummeted, from 788,000 gallons in 1857 to 127,000 gallons in 1861. South African winemakers wrote a petition directly to Queen Victoria, asking for a direct stimulus to save them from the "ruinous effects which the commercial treaty with France must cause to petitioners and the wine trade."[36] In the opposite direction, French wine imports rose from 797,000 gallons in 1857 to 2,187,000 in 1861. It is easy to assume that France had always had a natural advantage over the Cape and that its wines would have long been more popular, but the situation looked completely different to a wine importer in 1861. Rather, surprisingly, France's success in the 1860s was directly at the expense of the Cape. South African wines were more popular in Britain, and for much longer, than they have been given credit for. This is an example of how wine historians should be wary of "whiggish histories" which narrate perpetual progress. Gladstone himself led the political party of progress, but his reforms were felt as a slap in the face by colonial winemakers.

Australian wine was imported into Britain in much smaller quantities but had been on an upward trend through the late 1850s. It, too, saw its imports halved from 1860 into 1861.[37] But the number of Australian producers was growing, and gradually production and exports grew, too. By the 1890s Australia was producing about six million imperial gallons of wine a year, and exporting about seven hundred thousand of them. This was a small amount compared to that of a European producer, but it undoubtedly shows a growing industry.[38] It also exported to New Zealand, which had its own tariff scheme, although in 1878 it lowered its tariffs to give preferential rates to Australian wine.[39]

The debates about tariffs, imperial pride, and adulteration continued for over twenty years. The Australians took a particularly robust opposition to them. Dr. Johann L. W. Thudichum, a pioneering biochemist with a sideline in wine-writing, had concluded in 1872 that "there is a tendency on the part of Australian producers to mystify the public regarding the strength of their wines," which was effectively an accusation that Australian wines were high in alcohol because they were secretly fortified.[40] Thudichum's pronouncement infuriated Australian winemakers. It also led to a public spat with James Fallon, an Irish-born Australian winemaker, who came to Britain to defend Australian wines against such accusations.

Fallon was an unlikely hero of colonial wine, in the sense that he was born in Ireland and emigrated to Australia in 1841, at the age of eighteen, as part of a subsidized immigration scheme to bring labor to Australia. Most of these "bounty immigrants" were of modest backgrounds, and given that Fallon had been born in Athlone, central Ireland, he surely had no previous viticultural experience.[41] He was successful in his new land. He farmed, ran a general store, and even became mayor of the new town of Albury, which is in western New South Wales, close to the border with Victoria. He also purchased a vineyard called the Murray Valley Vineyard, and set about energetically improving his wines and increasing production.[42] He almost certainly was directly involved in the different stages of production. By the early 1870s, Fallon was producing two hundred thousand gallons of wine of ten different varieties: some sold under the name of the grape (riesling, shiraz), and some by style (Burgundy). He sold his wines both bottled and in casks, and was reported to have 150,000 gallons of his wine cellared in the early 1870s, at a time when the annual production of all Australian colonies was around 2 million gallons, and that of New South Wales was around 400,000 gallons.[43] He described himself as "the largest holder of first-class Australian Wines in the world," and claimed that his wines "are superior in soundness and purity to any imported Wines."[44]

Fallon opposed Gladstone's tariffs on several levels: he insisted that his wines were naturally strong and not adulterated or augmented; he argued that the twenty-six-degree cutoff was arbitrary and did not take into account the Australian climate; and he implored British consumers to support their empire by drinking colonial wine. Fallon traveled to London in 1873 to tackle these issues through an extended, widely reported lecture to the Royal Society for Arts. For contemporary wine-writer Charles Tovey the lecture was a watershed moment in Australian wine development.[45] Fallon introduced himself as one not "induced by any selfish motive," but hoped "to benefit the vignerons of Australia; and by so doing, bring under the notice of the mother country the importance of this growing colonial industry," "and, in a humble manner, state the qualifications of Australian wines in England, where their merits and qualities are so little known and recognised."[46] In fact, he said that the initial reason for his visit to London was not to lobby on behalf of the industry—or rather "to make representations," in the parlance of the day—but to conduct his own grand tour of European vineyards as his more privileged colleagues had done before him. Whether this was true or not, that he simply happened to be in Europe when an opportunity arose to defend Australian wine, is impossible to say, but he presented his arguments with gusto and spoke as a self-appointed industry representative. Thudichum, whose comments had perhaps directly inspired the talk, came to respond. In the heated debate following Fallon's speech, Thudichum pulled no punches: he was insistent that Fallon's defense of high alcohol content defied the very laws of nature. He exclaimed that "if in Australia there were grapes which, by a natural course of fermentation, produced the wine with 29 per cent. [*sic*] of proof spirit that ought to be established by a scientific commissioner and thoroughly authenticated, because it would simply upset the whole scientific facts hitherto established throughout the world."[47] Others jumped to Fallon's defense. Mr. David Randall, introducing himself as a winemaker with knowledge of Australia, explained that "the sun was often so hot that the fruit got scorched and dried up." He was also in favor of adjusting the tariffs, for "it seemed rather hard that because nature had done more for Australia than for Europe she should be placed at a disadvantage by fiscal regulations."[48]

It was rather hard, Fallon believed, when considering what Australia had done for Britain. He argued that the growth of Australian viticulture was an economic and social fact to be celebrated. Fallon was not simply defending the natural, unfortified strength of Australian wines. He was also arguing that Australian wines were socially good and that British people had a moral imperative to buy colonial wine, given the phenomenal contribution that the Australian colonies made to the British Empire, and particularly to the British exchequer. After British India, Australia was the prime economic contributor to the Empire, and had far greater trade volume with the mother country than all the North American dependencies together, in spite of having a much smaller population.[49] He argued, then, that supporting the Australian wine industry was a responsibility, as well as an act of patriotic duty. His conclusion, wordy but powerful, was that:

The people of the Australian colonies are either originally inhabitants of this country or their descendants, with purely British feelings. Large sums are expended annually by the several Australian colonies for the introduction of the surplus labor of her Majesty's subjects.... We are as entirely British subjects as the residents of the counties of Middlesex, Surrey or Kent.... These matters should be taken into consideration, and every encouragement afforded to the extension of the growth of this new and important industry. If this were acceded to, it would only be reciprocating the feeling and desire of the colonists generally towards the mother country ... in return [for which Australian has] taken in payment goods manufactured in England, thereby supporting and encouraging the working manufactures of this country.[50]

Nearly a century after the first wine grapes were grown in Australia, Fallon is celebrating imperial economic thought that saw Australia as the agricultural provider and market for British manufactured goods. This moral force argument does not appear to have swayed large numbers of British consumers. But in the meantime, the growth of winemaking encouraged and supported many domestic Australian manufactures, too, and allowed for the diversification of the Australian economy.

NINE

Planting and Pruning

WORKING THE COLONIAL VINEYARD

SOUTH AUSTRALIA GETS HOT. In the Barossa Valley, approximately fifty kilometers inland from the coast, summer temperatures can linger in the nineties Fahrenheit (thirties Celsius). Drought looms. Wineries and cellars are built of stone from local quarries, their cool walls repelling the heat. From atop one of the region's low rolling hills, late-summer fields are a patchwork of golds and greens: sunburned grass, verdant vine leaves. In spite of the dry heat, "irrigation to the vine has only been undertaken in the most tentative way in South Australia," George Sutherland wrote in 1892.[1] Irrigation was expensive, and it was associated with lower-quality grape production. Most vines were allowed to grow dry, in what would become Australia's largest wine region.

The second half of the nineteenth century was a major period of growth for Australian wine. While Cape grape cultivation remained largely clustered in the region surrounding Cape Town, Australian viticulture spread well beyond New South Wales in the mid-nineteenth century: to Victoria, to South Australia, and then later to Tasmania and Western Australia. A British Parliamentary report from 1871 noted that despite some vine plantings, "the time has not yet arrived when Queensland wine is deemed to be a staple production."[2] (We are still waiting; there is very little viticulture in Queensland, a state with a mostly subtropical climate).[3] Until Australia became a single federation in 1901, these were separate colonies, and they spanned nearly a thousand miles from east to west. They were not a free-trade zone, either, but even imposed tariffs on each other's wine. Victoria in the 1880s had "nearly half" of its trade with Britain; another third was with neighboring colonies, principally New South Wales.[4]

In New South Wales, the starter home of Australian wine, the amount of acreage devoted to vines increased steadily in the 1860s. It rose from 1,130 acres in 1862, to 4,152 a decade later, and crept up to 6,745 by 1888. Production of wine rose, too, from 85,000 gallons in 1862 to 667,000 in 1888. In modern terms, these numbers are small. For comparison, New South Wales had 20,000 acres of oats and 177,000 acres of maize (corn) under cultivation in 1888.[5] The population of New South Wales was approaching 700,000 people in 1888, and two-thirds of that population was considered rural, much of it working in agriculture.[6] In annual reports presented to the British Parliament on colonial production, wine ceases to be listed as one of the major products of New South Wales, not because there was so little wine produced, but because the economy had become so diversified, and wine was not one of the colony's principal exports.

Indeed, in the last few decades of the nineteenth century, wine production in Victoria and South Australia surged, far outstripping that of New South Wales (or the Cape, for that matter). In 1885 South Australia exported just 78,000 imperial gallons of wine, but by 1898 it was exporting more than 500,000 gallons per year, most of it bound for the U.K.[7] South Australia had become Australia's premier wine region, in terms of production quantity.

Although the value and amount of wine produced in Australia was much smaller than the amount of wool or wheat, two major agricultural exports, that small number obscures the number of people involved in its production. In Victoria in 1883, the government statistician counted just under three thousand "manufactories": business sites where goods were processed or created. Of these, there were 462 wine presses—by far, the single most common type of manufactory. For comparison, there were 81 breweries, 14 distilleries, and 144 flour mills.[8] What this demonstrates is that there were a lot of small winemakers: far more people worked in mills than in wineries. It also shows that not all who grew wine grapes made their own wine, because there were at least two thousand grape growers active in Victoria in the same period.[9]

Wine industries matured in tandem with colonial economies as a whole, for winemakers needed a whole host of materials and supplies to grow their operations. Even the isolated vineyard on the Australian or South African settler frontier was linked to distant markets. Winemakers benefited from innovations in transport and communications, which helped them move goods faster and build customers.

Indeed, this explains part of the lag in wine growing in New Zealand. As Australian viticulture grew and expanded, New Zealanders followed with interest. In the 1890s the number of people employed in wineries (not vineyards) in New Zealand more than doubled—but only from twenty-four to fifty-nine.[10] Wine production was in the tens of thousands of gallons, not the millions of gallons Australia was making. The New Zealand industry was thus really still in its infancy when the government took an interest in the industry and its commercial prospects, and hired Romeo Bragato, the government viticulturalist of Victoria, as a consultant. He toured New Zealand in 1895 and the government published his report, along with detailed growing instructions, a year later, in order to encourage farmers to expand their knowledge and their vine plantings.

Bragato was impressed by New Zealand's potential for vine growing. He was also startled to find some farmers growing wine grapes in greenhouses ("under glass") to protect them from the elements. New Zealand was not too cold for vines, he explained: it was simply a matter of choosing the correct vines for the climate and pruning them correctly to maximize sun exposure (what would now be referred to as canopy management). He recommended shiraz, cabernet sauvignon, cabernet franc, dolcetto, pinot noir, and Mueller Burgundy for red wines, and riesling, pinot blanc, tokay, and white hermitage for whites.[11] "Mueller Burgundy" probably refers to pinot meunier, one of the three grapes used in Champagne. "White hermitage" could refer to roussanne or marsanne, both used in the Rhône, or perhaps even viognier, which happened to be native to Bragato's birthplace, Croatia. Many of these grapes were evidently selected because they can flourish in cooler climates. "At present," though, Bragato advised, "the demand in Europe is for red wine, therefore it would prove advantageous to plant the larger areas with red varieties." Bragato was an oenologist,[12] not an importer, but it was clear that his brief was to steer the New Zealand wine industry toward export and profits. He was confident that a local market would follow suit. Domestic demand would not be a problem, and nor would climate or lack of interest among farmers be a barrier to growing the industry. Rather, he saw that the biggest disadvantage to winemakers was the lack of railways from rural areas to cities. In order to move produce to market and attract settlers, "railway communication is absolutely necessary," he argued, otherwise prime vine-growing land languished "in little better than its native condition."[13] Good land was cultivated land.

Whereas we lack comprehensive records for eighteenth- and early nineteenth-century plantings in the Cape and Australia, mid-nineteenth-century Australian vineyard records are much more revealing. They show that in Australia, nineteenth-century winemakers were quite promiscuous and adventurous in their plantings. This reflected both the experimental mood that Busby had exemplified, and also the fact that precision was not necessary in a wine that would often be blended by multiple intermediaries. In 1862, Walter Duffield in South Australia was reported as planting six different grape varieties across just five acres of land: "Two acres of vines were planted last year on the east end of the flat, the varieties selected being Black Portugal, Mataro, Shiraz, and Verdeilho. Next year about three acres more will be planted with Black Portugal, Shiraz, and Mataro, for red wine, and Verdeilho and Madeira for white. The whole of the vines already arrived at maturity are staked."[14] James King, in New South Wales, wrote to the Royal Society of Arts in London in 1855 that "I am still experimenting," but was currently growing "Gonais, Verdeilha, and Shepherd's grapes [sic], most extensively, for the growth of white wine; and Black Pineau, Grey Pineau, and Lambrusquat, for that of red wine."[15] Shepherd's grapes was a type of riesling,[16] and "Gonais" was probably a poor transcription of "Gouais," a white varietal that is today extremely rare. Lambrusco, or lambrusca, is a family of grapes that produce both sweet and dry reds in northern Italy. King was not the only one growing these grapes. The 1869 cellar records for Dalwood Vineyard in New South Wales lists casks of verdot, shiraz, malbec, "Pineau" and "Lambruscat." These are all major, recognizable grape varieties, and the record suggests that these were aging as single varietals in their casks. In addition, the cellar held "Burgundy," "Hermitage," "Madeira," "Sherry," "Australian Red," and "Light Red."[17] Given that, for example, shiraz is the predominant grape in the wine of Hermitage, in the French Rhône region, it is not clear how the shiraz casks were different from the Hermitage casks, and so on. Alexander Kelly, who wrote a guide to growing wine in Australia in 1861, listed thirty-six grape varieties that were successfully being grown in Australia at the time.[18] Perhaps surprisingly, these do not include chardonnay, semillon, or sauvignon blanc, three of the major grapes of twenty-first century Australia.[19] Thomas Hardy (no relation to the famous writer) was growing sauvignon blanc near Adelaide in the 1880s, but only producing eight hundred gallons a year of a (sweet) sauternes-style wine (comparatively, he produced ten thousand gallons a year of red "Claret" and fifteen thousand a year of red "Burgundy").[20] Most of Hardy's vines were matara (mourvèdre), carbinet (cabernet sauvignon), doradillo, and shiraz varieties.

The sheer diversity of the wine that was being produced in Australia at this time is striking. There was no single style that was most prominent in the second half of the nineteenth century. There were sweet and dry wines; wines styled after claret, hermitage, and hock; sherry and port-style wines; and all sorts of blends of grapes, including blends of red and white grapes, and many grapes that are now rare. Often the same grapes varieties were used to produce different styles of wine, on the same estates. Consider this entry into the 1886 Colonial and Exhibition in London, proudly displayed in the South Australia section: "Penfold and Co., Magill, near Adelaide. . . . Five cases Frontignac wine; name of vineyard, The Grange; . . . color, red; character, full-bodied, sweet; vintages, 1876, 1881, and 1882; name of grapes from which wine is made, Frontignac, Madeira, and Grenache; . . . age of vines, twenty-five years; . . . of Constantia type."[21] A dry red wine made primarily from shiraz grapes, Penfold's Grange is now probably Australia's most iconic wine. It was a mid-twentieth-century invention, though; in the late nineteenth century, Penfold's was taking its inspiration not just from the Rhône, but also from the Cape. "Constantia type," in this instance, refers to a wine that is sweet but unfortified. Penfold's also made dry red wines, and grew shiraz grapes, which it blended liberally with carbinet or frontignac to make a "Burgundy type" (presumably a medium-bodied red wine; it is not clear what kind of frontignac was planted, whether it was the common white variety, and thus used to mellow and lighten the intensity of shiraz grapes, or a less common red variety). Penfold's also grew riesling, pedro ximenes, tokay, and "Temprano" (probably tempranillo blanco) grapes. Although these grapes are most associated with sweet wines, Penfold's used them to produce three different styles of white wine: "Chablis type" (dry), "Hock type" (sweet), and "Sherry type" (dry).[22]

Thudichum warned Australian winemakers against "losing themselves in excessive variations" at the expense of quality.[23] We can assume that they produced particular wines because they believed these were marketable. Although some individuals had become wealthy in Australia and could sink vast resources into their operations, most wine farmers were looking to make a profit. Making many varieties of wine was possibly a way to hedge one's bets on consumer demand, but it also required more space and more equipment to ferment and age all the different wines. Behind these viticultural experiments were labor, investment, and expertise.

WORKERS

"South Australia could almost supply the world with wine," Mr. E. W. Hawker, a South Australian politician, explained to an English audience at the Royal Colonial Institute in 1889, but "until labour becomes cheaper we shall never be able to make these industries a success."[24] Three decades earlier, Kelly had also bemoaned the lack of labor in some areas, which he complained led some wine farmers to abandon their fields, even as the wine industry was taking off.[25] In early twentieth-century New Zealand, Hawkes Bay winemakers complained to their government that the low tariffs on South African wines were unfair and should be raised to protect domestic viticulture. New Zealand winemakers could not compete because of "the fact that South African wines [were] (the product of cheap coloured labour)."[26] The workers of the world were certainly not united.

In nineteenth-century Australia and New Zealand, where it was often difficult for employers to recruit workers, conditions for wine workers may have been more congenial than they were at the Cape. Cape wine farmers had confronted labor shortages in the seventeenth and eighteenth centuries by importing human beings from across the Indian Ocean to be enslaved. Slavery ended in the nineteenth century, but a general labor shortage persisted across Cape industries and occupations. Colonial administrators frequently drew on examples of what had supposedly worked in other colonies, and Sir James Stirling, a colonial administrator in the mid-nineteenth century, mused that Australian plantation agriculture could be sustained "by means of free labour to be procured from Hindostan, or the neighbouring islands of the Malay archipelago."[27] Although in theory these laborers would be free, they would undoubtedly be paid less than white Europeans.

A government inquiry into labor conditions in the 1890s found that unskilled workers in Britain could earn around 20 s. (£1) a day, but in the Cape (white) workers could expect around 65 s. a day; however, the cost of rental housing was also three times as much at the Cape. Many employers and administrators hoped to attract more settlers from Britain, but given the distance and the cost of living at the Cape, some worried that the Cape "would not get the village laborer [to immigrate] but rather that class which people are only too glad to get rid of."[28] This likely referred to the impoverished, urban working classes, particularly those in Britain's industrial cities. Furthermore, the lure of new opportunities in the Cape (and beyond, into the Transvaal), such as gold mining and working on railroads, made it more difficult for winemakers to recruit and retain white laborers in the second half of the nineteenth century.[29] Most laborers in the Cape wine farms were of the "coloured" population, the specific term used in South Africa for people of mixed racial descent. Some were former slaves from the East Indies or other African regions, some were Khoikhoi people who had been incorporated into this population. None of them were getting rich. It was only through creating a cycle of poverty, combined with restrictive master and servant laws, that landowners were able to force laborers to remain. The tot or dop system of giving alcohol in lieu of wages was instrumental, and was used in Cape agriculture by the mid-eighteenth century, and not only on wine farms.[30]

Records of vineyards suggest that most Australian vineyards in the nineteenth century relied on white, European laborers, though. These workers were often members of the same families, both men and women and probably older children. For example, records from the Ben Ean Winery in New South Wales in July 1903 show several men of the same family doing piecework viticulture: George Bridge worked three days drawing stakes, one day planting and two and a half days bedding [planting] cuttings; Victor Bridge did three days laying stakes, two days cutting cuttings, five days planting and two and three-quarter days ploughing; Joe Bridge worked five days, task unspecified; Ted Bridge did eight and a half days planting; and N. Bridge did nine days of planting. This was possible in part because of the seasonality of winemaking. There is work to be done in vineyards and wineries all year round—blending in the autumn, pruning in the winter, planting in the spring, and so on—but the most labor-intensive period is in late summer or early autumn, when the grapes are harvested and crushed. Winemaking can therefore be a form of complementary agriculture, meaning that vineyard owners often grew other plants and raised pasture animals for market, and vineyard laborers could work in other occupations outside of the few weeks of annual harvest. In the case of the Bridge family, they may have been farmers themselves who picked up vineyard work in the winter, when their own land needed little attention. Indeed, the fact that vine growers could put their own family members to work was what made wine so profitable, George Sutherland argued: "unutilised labour is, by means of vine culture, being put into a sort of savings bank," giving a healthy return on investment in land and vines.[31] What Sutherland is advocating is similar to what Jan de Vries referred to as an "industrious revolution" in eighteenth-century England, when agricultural families took on additional paid work during their downtime, allowing them to become consumers in the growing economy.[32]

The total income for the Bridge family was £7 19 s. 18 p., for a total of 41.75 days of work. These rates of pay, averaging around 3 s. a day, are slightly less than what contemporary British laborers were earning. They were not all paid the same rate—George was paid more than Ted for planting—suggesting that some of these Bridges were children or teenagers, and perhaps George was the patriarch.[33] In the nineteenth-century Anglo world, it was common for workers to be paid based on their social status, rather than for the work completed: adult men, presumed to be family breadwinners, were paid more than women and children, even for the same work. The government statistician for the colony of Victoria noted that average farm laborer rates of pay in the early 1880s were around 20 s. a week for men, but only 10.5 for women.[34]

The lack of rural labor, as well as low levels of expertise, lent support for a liberal immigration policy for wine workers. We saw this in Australia back in the early decades of winemaking, when French and German vine dressers were allowed to migrate. In the 1840s, another wave of German migration began, to South Australia. In the second half of the nineteenth century, 46 of the 225 grape growers in the Adelaide Hills region were German,[35] and deeper inland in the Barossa Valley there was a significant German settlement, most famously through the Seppelt family's Seppeltsfield Winery in Tanunda.

It may seem ironic, even contradictory, that some of the agents of the British viticultural civilizing mission were not British. Indeed, the biggest boosters of Australian wine's civilizing role in this period were of Irish and Swiss-French extraction—Fallon and de Castella. Foreign birth did not mean disloyalty; rather, non-British settlers could also be very appreciative of the British state. Many of the German settlers in Australia migrated due to religious persecution and found freedom to practice their Lutheran faith, and tend their vines, in South Australia. Escaping from the yoke of Prussian imperialism, they were happy to trade for British imperialism,[36] which was relatively permissive toward their community.

Fallon's position as an Irishman is also complicated. Ireland was a part of the United Kingdom at the time, although its Catholic residents were deeply critical of this political union, and Fallon was most likely a Catholic. However, research has shown that many Irish politicians who railed against "imperial" rule in Ireland had no difficulty accepting or even promoting it in other parts of the world.[37] Australian wine was conceived and built as a global and imperial industry, and Irish people were no less a part of these networks and markets as a result of their Irishness. Nor did Fallon appear to try to trade on his Irishness, relying on Irish trust or kin networks; in fact his lobbying appealed to ideas of imperial glory and recognized the centrality of both the British capital and the British consumer market within the imperial system. That said, Fallon was probably the most prominent Irish-born wine producer in the Antipodes in this period. Looking at wine-related trademark applications in Australia in the late nineteenth century, the Irish names that appear as applicants generally tend to be for the production and sale of Catholic communion wine.[38] There were many Scottish people active in Australian wine in this period, though, including Alexander Kelly (born in Leith), Patrick Auld (born in Wigtownshire), and James Johnston (born in West Lothian).

The Anglo system was not without its ethnic hierarchies. In New Zealand, where wine and Catholicism had been intertwined through the Marists, the Catholic magazine the *New Zealand Tablet* fumed that there was not more effort to welcome wine experts. It blamed anti-Catholic bias: "People from wine and olive-growing countries of Europe would be not only desirable but invaluable in many part of the North Island; and yet because such countries are for the most part peopled by Catholics, they are neglected, ignored, whilst immigrants have been eagerly sought in the Protestant countries of the north of Europe."[39] However, in the racial pecking order in the British world, "white" Europeans enjoyed vast social advantages over native Aboriginal and Maori peoples.

Toward the end of the nineteenth century a new immigrant population began arriving in New Zealand, and it would both face the Anglo xenophobia and have a significant impact on twentieth-century wine production. These were immigrants from Dalmatia, a coastal region of modern Croatia, then part of the Austro-Hungarian Empire. Scholarship on Dalmatian emigration notes how the Croatian population chafed against the autocratic Austro-Hungarian rule and sought greater freedoms, and they particularly resented the "Wine Clause" of 1891, which hurt Dalmatian wine production.[40] They were attracted to the comparatively liberal democracy offered in British New Zealand. Many Dalmatians began mining kauri gum—

a fossilized resin that came into high demand for its uses in paints and linoleum—and gradually began acquiring land and planting vineyards. In keeping with Dalmatian custom, small vineyards were planted around farmhouses as part of mixed agriculture, for personal use and for sale of wine;[41] there was not the same commercial plantation mentality that had motivated some British settlers to plant vineyards. But Dalmatian assimilation into New Zealand life was not easy, particularly when the First World War broke out, and they were believed to be Austrian—loyal to the very regime that they had fled.[42]

SCARIFIED BY HORSES

In the nineteenth century, the harvest was done by hand. Near the beginning of this book I described workers enjoying a brief break in an Australian vineyard in the 1880s. They were picking grapes, which were loaded into a cart which was drawn by a horse. Some of the world's oldest surviving, grape-bearing vines are located in Australia's Hunter Valley, and visitors today might notice that the rows of vines are spaced wider apart than is traditional in, say, long-established French vineyards. They were not spaced this way to allow machine harvesters to pass between the rows, but to allow laborers to drive horse-drawn ploughs and carts through. Penfold's specified that its wine made at the Grange vineyard, on the outskirts of Adelaide, was cultivated "by plough and hand," and R. D. Ross's vineyard ten miles away was "ploughed and scarified by horses." (In this context, scarification refers to the earth being scraped and hoed, not the vines).[43] Further inland, in South Australia's Barossa Valley, William Jacob's vine's were "ploughed and trellised," whereas Seppeltsfield's vines were "short pruned, and grown as bushes ten feet each way."[44] Not only was there diversity in what wine-farmers grew, there was evidently diversity in how their vineyards looked.

Cartiers and wheelmakers were important partners to the wine industry. A hardware seller in Cape Town's city center, a mile inland from the quais, took out large advertisements in Cape Town newspapers, "To Grain and Wine Farmers," advertising sales of scythes, sickles, sulphur, double-furrow ploughs, and fumigating bellows.[45] Horses and oxen pulled carts, but all of this work required human labor, too. Henry Davidson Bell's painting from the 1830s, "Stellenbosch Wine Waggon [sic]—Table Mountain in the Background," shows pairs of oxen being driven across a dusty plain, with an open, ox-pulled cart bringing up the rear.[46] Two Black workers drive the cart, which carries just two large barrels of wine. Although the sixteen oxen are much more prominent (and possibly valuable) than the wine, the artist's title draws attention to the cart's cargo, imbuing it with an importance beyond its size or market value.

Oxen and carts were important investments, but there were many other costs and considerations in setting up a winemaking business. Records from Dalwood Vineyard in New South Wales gives insight into the range of supplies and tasks involved. In the 1870s Dalwood incurred expenses for its manager, F. Wilkinson, part of whose job was to visit nearby cities to bring samples to potential clients. In a four-month period in 1870 and 1871 he submitted expenses for postage stamps, accommodation, repairs to an axle when his buggy broke down, and new shoes for the horses who pulled him on his journeys.[47] Trainlines would only be built into the Hunter Valley in the 1870s, and the first record of Dalwood using trains is in 1875, when it began sending cases of wine from the Branxton station to the port city of Newcastle, and receiving supplies in return.[48] For 1891, Dalwood spent about £1,500 on wages, and sold nearly £5,000 worth of wine. But it also spent money on "general expenses," fire insurance, interest (presumably on a loan, not specified), new casks, transportation, and now agents' commissions. The agents were generally based in the port city of Newcastle, where they could arrange shipments directly with ships' captains. Nearby Ben Ean Vineyard also recorded purchases of sulphuric acid, sulphur bellows, caustic acid (probably for disinfecting), fencing materials, plough parts, pruning sheers, engine oil and naphtha (a thinner), and, apparently for the construction of a new cellar, bricks, paint, plaster, Mudgee stone, materials for a retaining wall, and timber.[49] In 1902 Ben Ean built a windmill (£26, plus freight and labor), bought a wine press (£45), and fixed a pump (around £2).

In addition to the tools necessary for growing grapes in the vineyard, there were many more supplies needed for making and cellaring wine. In his 1810 guide to cellaring, John Davies describes at least sixty tools that the cellarmaster needs available for tasting, fining, filtering, portioning, and storing wine.[50] Casks, too, were major investments for both vineyards and those involved in storing, shipping, and selling wine. In 1891, Dalwood Vineyards wrote off £231 worth of "bad casks," presumably full; this was about 15 percent of their annual expenditure on wages, and more than their annual household expenses.[51]

All these businesses were intertwined in a secondhand market, too. Dalwood Vineyards sold casks, presumably used, to Ben Ean in 1900;[52] the following year it had also hoped to sell used casks to a wholesale wine merchant in Sydney, who inquired "if the casks are in perfect condition inside and outside . . . if they have the proper man hole [i.e., cover] . . . if the casks are made of Beech or Cedar [which] are as good as those made of Oak."[53] The type of wood used in wine barrels was a heated topic of debate in colonial Australia. Modern wooden wine barrels are normally made of oak, and most nineteenth-century barrels were, too; Cyrus Redding did note that "in some parts of the Continent [of Europe] beech is employed, because there is an opinion that beech-wood imparts an agreeable flavour to the wine, and brings it earlier to perfection."[54] I have not found documentation of wide use of cedar in nineteenth-century wine casks, although it is used in cellaring Japanese sake (though there is no particular reason to believe Australian winemakers were inspired by Japanese technique).[55] In modern winemaking, winemakers use oak barrels strategically to shape the taste of their wine. New oak barrels can impart a strong spicy or vanilla taste to both red and white wines; older (used) oak barrels are more mellow and impart less flavor.

For colonial Australian winemakers, importing oak barrels from Europe was an expensive prospect, and many began experimenting with native woods that they had locally available. They reported the results of their experiments to scientific societies in the colonies and back in Britain, where there was official curiosity about the sylvanian potential of the Antipodes. Alward Wyndham, a descendant of George, defended his use of beech in a letter to the *Sydney Mail* in 1901. "To import European is to expend three times the cost for a less suitable wood," he argued, and it was unsuitable precisely because it imparted a taste to the wine: "European oak discolours badly, and gives a stronger taste, necessitating at least as much trouble to get rid of it."[56] This will seem deeply ironic to modern wine drinkers, to whom Australia (and the "New World" in general) is sometimes reputed for overuse of oak, particularly in less expensive wines. In addition to beech and cedar, there were also documented attempts to use blackbutt, rosewood, cudgerie, and silky oak (not a true oak) for winemaking and cellaring.[57] And Ben Ean Winery in New South Wales ordered *cement* casks and vats (two specific and separate orders) in 1899, and the casks only cost 12 s. each.[58] Agricultural journals had also documented winemakers' earlier experiments with Portland cement, which had not always been successful (as it "gradually disintegrated by the sugar contained in sweet wines," one farmer despaired).[59]

Colonial winemakers did not take these supplies for granted. In a continental European context, these startup tools would be easily procured, but in a colonial context many would have to be imported, for the demand and the manufacturing capabilities of the colony were not yet established to make these tools readily available in shops. By cataloging these business needs, we do not just see the needs of an individual wine business: we see the complex web of individuals, professions, and international trading networks that supported the burgeoning wine industries. These included construction workers, insurance companies, railway engineers, chemical producers, governments, hotels, the postal service, and many types of manufacturers.

In reports to the Calcutta International Exhibition of 1883, many New South Wales winemakers gave figures for the cost of producing their wine, and averages for the Hunter Valley were between £6 and £8 per acre, with the region around Albury being slightly cheaper, around £4 to £5. Some of these winemakers were small, having fewer than eight acres devoted to vines, and held just a few thousand gallons of their wine in cellar; a few, like Wyndham, Fallon, Lindeman, James Kelman, and the Bouffier brothers, had large estates and tens of thousands of gallons in cellar, although their cultivation costs were similar. The notable exception was James Fallon, who estimated it cost £10 to £12 per acre to cultivate his estate. South Australia only submitted thirteen winemakers, though it included now well-known names like Thomas Hardy and Seppelt, but with no details about growing costs; Victoria submitted dozens of winemakers, but again did not provide financial estimates. George Sutherland's guide to South Australian wine production estimated that even poor land could produce two tons of grapes per acre, and that a ton of grapes could sell for £6 to £8, almost twice as much as the yield for wheat.[60]

According to various official reports, an acre of land in Australia usually produced between 150 and 200 imperial gallons of wine,[61] though some wine-writers praised vineyards that could produce as much as 400 gallons per acre.[62] Official reporters generally believed that higher agricultural yields were simply better, and they offered comparative tables to show where Australians ranked in various yields per acre, boasting where Australian was more productive per acre than other countries. While this may be neutral for grains, it goes against modern wisdom when it comes to wine quality, with lower yields today being seen as a sign of better grapes and, thus, better wine. This was not a logic that nineteenth-century Australians seemed to embrace. High yields meant fertility, prosperity, and success—or so they believed.

Pride permeates the writing about wine in late-Victorian Australia. The Australian man who embarked on vine growing, Sutherland gushed, is "providing for his children or those dependent on him," turning underutilized land to profit and setting idle hands to work. "Vine culture helps bring people together," he concluded, "so that they are enabled to secure for themselves and their children the same advantages which a city offers, but without the great disadvantages that are often associated with city life."[63] This imagined world of Australian viticulture, as pastoral idyll insulated from, even repelling, the vices of the modern world, was shared by many wine-writers, civil servants, and vignerons. Although the Australian and Cape industries fared very differently in this era, a close look at each one shows how they were intertwined in the same webs of imperial and local commerce. The rural idyll imagined by Australian writers like Hubert de Castella might suggest that wine farmers were self-sufficient, but actually they relied on many other tradespeople for supplies. It was a mirage: Australian wine grew because it was connected to the modern world, through networks of people, goods, and services.

TEN

Sulphur! Sulphur!! Sulphur!!!

PHYLLOXERA AND OTHER PESTS

"IT IS SAD TO HEAR that the vine disease is spreading fast," a South African newspaper reported in 1861, "and that there will not be anything like a tithe of last year's crop."[1] This was one of several outbreaks of oidium, a fungal infection of vines leaves capable of destroying the plant. As Cape wine farmers scrambled to treat their vines, they were also faced with the knowledge that demand was shrinking in their British export market.

British import tariffs had created a demand crisis for Cape winemakers in the 1860s, but nature also introduced supply crises, in the form of several diseases and droughts. As a result, the second half of the nineteenth century was a turbulent one for the established wine industry in the Cape. But the situation was very different in Australia, which saw a period of major growth for the wine industry. Although Australia was also afflicted by disease and tariffs, this did not stop the rapid expansion of vineyards throughout the continent. However, the global exchanges in vine growing were also the seeds of the wine industry's greatest crisis, phylloxera.

PHYLLOXERA

Vines in Geelong, in the Australian colony of Victoria, began "presenting a sickly appearance" in 1875. "The leaves afterwards became yellow round the edges, the plants sickened still further, and after a few years died completely," Victoria's secretary for agriculture explained.[2] The cause was phylloxera: a small aphid that feeds on the roots of grape vines. Technically a vine pest, though frequently referred to as a disease, phylloxera is one of the most dreaded afflictions of grape vines, because it is initially invisible and can destroy entire vineyards. It also spreads easily, often imperceptibly, on vine cuttings.

The phylloxera crisis was a product of that imperial-botanical nexus in which winemakers like Busby had participated. Live plants were traded internationally in large volumes in the nineteenth century, purchased by experimental scientists and ambitious farmers, and carried in ships from continent to continent. Phylloxera originated in North America, where many of the native grape varieties are naturally resistant, and was carried to Europe, where the *vitus vinifera* varieties were not. It is not clear if the infected vine imports into Australia came directly from North America or via Europe (and alas, it is too late to attempt contact tracing on nineteenth-century vines). But they certainly came through the same economic and interpersonal systems that fostered trade and exchange.

France was the first country affected by phylloxera. It initially appeared in the Rhône region of France in the early 1860s and then spread throughout the country and beyond its borders. The impact on France was devastating: hundreds of thousands of acres of vines were destroyed, and over the course of fifty years the amount of vineyard acreage decreased by nearly half.[3] Many vignerons and rural workers lost their livelihoods (although it was a boon to the wine industry in French Algeria, which would become one of the world's top wine producers in the twentieth century). There were two problems in halting the spread. The first was the difficulty in identifying the culprit and finding a suitable remedy. Vine growers and scientists tried various methods, including flooding fields, spraying with sulphur, copper, or lime, and burning vines. These methods worried both producers, that the taste of the wine would be altered, and consumers, who were sometimes concerned about the health impact of the chemical treatments.[4] But ultimately, they were ineffective against the nefarious aphid.

The most reliable solution ended up being root grafts: the root of a North American, phylloxera-resistant vine was attached to a cutting of a nonresistant vine, and the two plants encouraged to grow together. The second problem, then, was the patrimonial implications of the solution. A French national commission to study the phylloxera crisis was reluctant to recommend grafting, because it was not "traditional,"[5] and could harm the reputation of French wines. After all, how could a French wine, at its roots, be American? It was a vulgar thought.

Australian responses to phylloxera were relatively swift and decisive. Conscious of being a young country, still learning and growing in the wine

industry, Australians had none of the ancestral baggage of their French coun-
terparts. They also had the advantage of ten years of watching the French
respond (or not) to the crisis. In fact, Victoria's Department of Agriculture
had anticipated a crisis, and published a pamphlet in 1873 to inform vine
growers about the disease. The pamphlet shows the British diplomatic
machine in action: when phylloxera broke out in France and Portugal, the
British ambassadors quickly alerted the foreign secretary and his deputy,
Lord Granville and Viscount Enfield, and who ensured that information was
passed on to other wine-producing lands in the British realm. The resulting
1873 pamphlet, published in Melbourne, contained scientific reports both in
translation and in the original French.[6]

Australia was not caught off guard, then. In response to phylloxera in
Geelong, the legislative assembly of Victoria quickly passed a law, in 1877,
authorizing inspectors to have vines pulled and destroyed. In 1880, a *cordon
sanitaire* was instituted around the infected vineyards, vine importations
were banned, and a commission was formed to coordinate the response with
neighboring colonies New South Wales and South Australia. A compensation program was set up for those vineyards affected, and by mid-1883
Victoria had disbursed £34,000 to two thousand vine owners.[7] For comparison, the total value of the wine exported from Victoria in 1883 was £44,000.

In the Cape, government officials and vine growers watched and waited
nervously. In 1881 there was an international conference on phylloxera held
in Bordeaux, and as a precaution the Cape government sent the director of
the South Africa Museum, Roland Trimen, who was an entomologist as well
as a bureaucrat. Trimen returned with clear recommendations: ban all vine
imports, and ban all other plant imports from countries that had phylloxera,
too. Unfortunately, either because the ban was flouted or because the pest
had already surreptitiously entered the colony, phylloxera was identified at
the Cape in early 1886. It had likely been there for some years previously.

Again, the Cape responded quickly, and brought in a French consultant,
M. P. Mouillefert, who was a professor of viticulture. His recommendations
were extreme: "hand-to-hand contest with the enemy," meaning, destroy all
of the affected vineyards, an estimated ten thousand hectares, producing
more than five million gallons of wine. He argued that simply grafting vines
would not be sufficient, because the pests could still travel to infect other
vineyards. Moreover, it required "a staff of experts for the operation of grafting, the most careful attention and considerable outlay," which he diplomatically suggested would be "out of the reach of the Cape Viticulturalist."[8] The

Cape had actually prepared for this, by buying reserves of vine stock, and it did proceed to set up stations and provide training for farmers in grafting. But Mouillefert was correct: gradually grafting and replanting was not enough to eradicate the pest and stop its spread. This is in fact what happened, and by 1893 nearly 9,000,000 vines had been destroyed, but only 66,300 American vines grafted. Commissioners were appointed to inspect vineyards and enforce bans on vine imports, and were sometimes beside themselves with growers' denial of the extent of the problem. "More astonishing than the comparative slow progress in the cultivation of American vines is the fact, that some farmers in the infected areas still insist in planting Colonial vines, just as if there were no sufficient proof of the phylloxera destroying such vines," an inspector despaired.[9]

In New Zealand, phylloxera made its first appearance in the late 1880s. By this point the disease was widespread in Europe. New Zealand's representative in London, Sir F. D. Bell, was tasked with gathering information to develop an eradication policy. He despaired that "the mass of reports and schemes for dealing with that disease in European countries is so enormous that no one except the most skilled experts could say what would be likely to be useful to New Zealand vine-growers."[10] But Bell had the benefit of those skilled experts, and in his diplomatic role was able to solicit reports on what had been successful in the Cape of Good Hope, Germany, Bulgaria, and Spain. He also corresponded directly with C. V. Riley, the state entomologist of Missouri, United States, who was the acknowledged world expert. Riley recommended killing infected vines with bisulphide injections, and replanting with American root-grafts.[11]

Visiting New Zealand in 1895, Romeo Bragato inspected a vineyard that was said to have phylloxera, and found it was actually free from disease. "I regard it as a criminal act for people, who are not possessed of the necessary knowledge to enable them to judge, to assert that a vineyard is phylloxera affected," he fumed, as rumors of phylloxera could create widespread panic and speculation.[12] At the other extreme, there was also resistance and doubt from farmers about what they perceived as governmental overreach in strict bans, quarantines, and mandatory destruction of vineyards. One disgruntled civil servant in Victoria, François de Castella (son of Hubert), protested loudly that the government was encouraging eradication over grafting. To some historians he was an unsung hero who eventually got his way, but the wider context is that in every wine-producing country, there were vigorous debates about how, when, and on how broad a scale the community should react to phylloxera, and indeed what the role of government was in such an agricultural catastrophe.

There is no doubt that the phylloxera crisis (and the wine industries themselves) was taken seriously both by colonial governments and by the Foreign and Colonial Office in London. British scientists, who had in fact noticed the phylloxera aphid at their botanical gardens in Kew in the 1860s, also followed with interest. The disease was of entomological and botanical interest, and in the case of South Africa, wine was "so important a cultural industry in one of our principal colonies."[13] Indeed, Kew's bulletin bemoaned that the "Cape Colony is the only important British possession which does not possess a fully equipped Botanical Institution," which trammeled its capacity to respond to botanical crises.

There are signs, though, that there were more people who did know what they were doing. Phylloxera energized the scientific community and the evolving world of wine experts. These experts were multiplying. Governments were getting more serious about measuring, testing, and analyzing economic and agricultural output, and there was a growing need for individuals who had the skills to do so. Departments of Agriculture were created in colonies, and the records they produced are fertile sources for wine history. Farmers demanded better experts: in the Cape, wine farmers were complaining in 1880 that a government commission to investigate vine disease was incompetent, because it was composed of a chemist, a farmer, and a military man, but "as in the vast majority of cases the animal assailants are insects, the entomologist should in the first place be associated with the botanist."[14]

Not all agreed. Dr. Thudichum, Fallon's nemesis, had been been deeply critical of the wines coming from Australia in the early 1870s. "The Australian colonists must ascertain the most suitable varieties of wines for their several localities suitable to its culture," he argued to the Royal Society of Arts. "For this purpose they should establish agricultural experimental stations, supported and controlled by the State, to which scientific men, particularly chemists, should be attached."[15] Conveniently, Thudichum was, in fact, a chemist! Thudichum appears to have tried for a second career as an international wine expert, and in fact was offering himself as a wine consultant to the Cape in 1898. Thudichum wrote directly to Lord Alfred Milner, the governor of the Cape Colony, to offer his services in preventing bacterial contamination in Cape wines. Milner's secretary replied, politely declining to employ Thudichum, because the minister of agriculture had already "engaged the services of a gentleman of scientific attainments" to aid in this "subject of great public importance."[16]

Colonial governments did take the next step that Thudichum (and others) had suggested, which was to create experimental stations, which were government-funded laboratories or model farms where scientists could run experiments and provide advice to farmers. (They are similar in principle to the agricultural extension offices established in the United States.) In Australia, oenology had been taught back in the days of Busby, but the premier nineteenth-century institution became Roseworthy Agricultural College, which was established in 1883 in the Barossa region outside of Adelaide, South Australia. The college awarded degrees in oenology, and thus trained a generation of wine experts in the knowledge of that age. In the Cape, Groot Constantia itself was purchased by the government in 1885, and became a state-run experimental station. In New Zealand, a similar venture was undertaken at Te Kauwhata, established in 1886 to study a range of agricultural issues, including wine.

Phylloxera was a unique and comprehensive crisis for the wine industry in Europe and many European colonies. It was not, however, the only environmental stumbling block that settler-vignerons faced. Colonizers often regarded the lands they requisitioned as bizarre, hostile, somehow unnatural. Earlier I warned that we should not consider Australian or South African wines to be an inevitable by-product of an ideal climate. Nineteenth-century observers certainly did not; many were actually skeptical about the prospects of wine-growing in the colonies. "The climate of Australia can hardly be said to be in all respects suited to the successful production of wine," an English writer named C. E. Hawker wrote in 1907, after more than a century of Australian wine production. "Droughts are frequent, as are also heavy rains ... [and] great heat at the time of the vintage" all posed great challenges for the vigneron.[17] Birds also destroyed crops. In South Australia, H. E. Laffer, a lecturer in viticulture, dipped some decoy grapes in strychnine in the hopes of poisoning them. This led to "great numbers of dead starlings lying about," he wrote proudly,[18] like a remorseless villain in a murder mystery.

In South Africa, water and irrigation were often fraught issues. John Crombie Brown, the former Cape government botanist and a much-lauded professor of botany, wrote that the area of Wynberg, which included Constantia, had little difficulty: "in the immediate vicinity of Table Mountain there is a copious supply of water, and no lack of facilities afforded by the ground for storing this and applying it to agricultural purposes." But beyond Wynberg, there were problems. In Stellenbosch, "a rich wine district," in the 1860s, vineyards were accused of drawing water off the top of streams and depriving other residents, who were "thus provoked frequently to take the law into their own hands."[19] In Malmesbury, north of Cape Town, there was severe drought in 1865, which meant the vineyards "suffered" and farmers had no income to pay their laborers.[20] The wine trade was "depressed" by these droughts and conflicts in the 1860s and 1870s, and also fought off several appearances of oidium (a fungal infection to vine leaves that is treated with sulphur). The wine industry's loss was some merchants' gain. "Sulphur! Sulphur!! Sulphur!!!" screamed a Cape Town newspaper advertisement, from merchants who "have just landed a few Casks of Genuine Sublimed Sulphur, as used in Vineyards against the Vine Disease, which they offer to Farmers at low rates."[21]

These news reports certainly understate the problem, in terms of how workers experienced them. Cape vineyard owners were white, and of both Anglo and Afrikaner identities, and workers were poor, of Afrikaner, colored (in the South African sense, meaning of mixed and/or Asian descent), or native identity. There were class and color divides. With discoveries of diamonds in eastern South Africa toward the end of the nineteenth century, white laborers who could afford to do so often moved to try to their luck. But when there were no wages, or when workers were exploited through the dop system, there was little mobility, and in an agricultural depression that meant real human suffering. Hermann Giliomee has explained that diamond wealth encouraged the planting of more vines in the Cape, and that the collapse of wine prices left the Cape extremely vulnerable, as one-third of Cape workers were dependent on viticulture.[22]

We can contrast this reality with the trope of the self-made, bootstrapping farmer, which is common in settler colonial societies. Doubtless, those who established wine farms worked long hours with their hands, and had the satisfaction of building a business from the land over time. In that sense, they showed independence, initiative, and a commitment to hard physical labor. This should not be confused with an embrace of free-market economics. The State, as Thudichum would capitalize it, was involved from the very beginning in colonial viticulture, and as we have seen repeatedly, winemakers sought and expected a degree of governmental support for their work, whether it be in the form of attractive trade arrangements or more direct subsidies. They were self-consciously building the colonial economy, even advancing colonial society, and they expected recognition and support for their endeavors. The State often complied. In 1905 the Cape government commissioned a study of the wine industry. This involved interviewing many involved in wine, and the interviewer asked some of them a leading question: "Would you approve of a scheme whereby a certain number of young Afrikanders [sic] could be sent to Europe in order to gain a practical knowledge of wine-making, after which they would return to this Colony, and by personal assistance and practical demonstration, give the farmers the benefit of the experience and knowledge they had gained; all this to be done with Government aid?" Naturally, the answer was usually affirmative.[23] Which young South African wine maker would not want a free trip to Europe and subsidized education?

In the Cape and Australia, viticulture was state-sponsored at its inception, and time and time against we see that vine growers had expectations of government cooperation and support. Karen Brown has shown how Cape viticulturalists joined with fruit growers to successfully lobby for the appointment of a government entomologist in the 1890s.[24] There were other ways in which Australian governments supported and encouraged the industry: by offering annual prizes for domestic wines, by selling government-owned lands at incentive prices for wine growing, by subventioning some guides for winemakers that were, in themselves, also marketing tools,[25] and by hiring wine experts to the Board of Agriculture to advise growers. The Victoria Water Supply Board sponsored a competition for the best irrigated vineyard (first prize, £50).[26] Indirectly, and in a more reactive way, government aided growers by creating legislation to combat legal uncertainties,[27] and also by licensing and recognizing companies and winemakers.

New Zealand, as we have seen, hired Romeo Bragato, Victoria's state viticulturalist, to advise on expanding the wine industry. Bragato urged New Zealand to implement incentive schemes where "capitalists could be induced to invest some of their money, encouraged and assisted in their enterprise by the Government," to create vineyards.[28] New Zealand hired a vine and wine instructor to work in the Department of Agriculture (and it advertised the job in Australian newspapers).[29] It would also open its own viticultural station in 1893, Te Kauwhata in Waikato, with a vineyard through which it could monitor grape production and advise farmers.[30]

This brings us back to the conditions that created the phylloxera crisis: global trade in plants, people, and ideas. Once wine industries were established, they did not become insulated and aloof, even if their exports remained small. The various wine-producing colonies of the British Empire surveilled and consulted each other; they were warned of the advance of phylloxera in Europe by the Colonial Office, and they sought further international advice. Even in New Zealand, which had the most economically insignificant wine industry, the government looked across the seas for inspiration and assistance. As we will see next, the empire provided other markets, too.

ELEVEN

Served Chilled

BRITISH CONSUMERS IN THE VICTORIAN ERA

IT WAS SLOW AND FRUSTRATING SOMETIMES, to be a British importer of colonial wine in the nineteenth century. In 1884 the London importer Peter Burgoyne wrote to one of his Australian suppliers, Thomas Hardy. Polite but vexed, he complained again that the wine he had received was not appropriate for the British market. "The wine was very dark in color, quite pink. It is very necessary that the *white* wines sent us should be *very pale* in color," he wrote, and he was not convinced by Hardy's rejoinder that the wooden casks were somehow at fault.[1] Purchasing wine directly from individual producers rather than through middlemen or cooperatives gave Burgoyne better traceability in knowing the precise origin of his wine. This was not important because consumers demanded to know the precise terroir of their wine—quite the opposite—but because it created accountability with the producer, allowing Burgoyne to communicate his preferences and adjust his orders as necessary.

Burgoyne's letter demonstrates the delicate task of communicating standards of taste between colonial producers and metropolitan sellers. The British market did not quickly warm to colonial wines. One of the critiques that emerged of colonial wines in the second half of the nineteenth century was not that they were universally bad, but that they were not suited to the British market and its particular tastes. The English wine-writer Thomas Shaw wrote in 1863 that he could "remember well, when I was a boy, hearing the words 'Cape wine' often mentioned," but that many efforts to make "Cape wine agreeable to British tastes" had failed. "For my own part, I have never yet met with anyone courageous enough to place a bottle on his table," he sniffed contemptuously.[2]

Burgoyne was one of London's two main importers of Australian wine. The other, his rival, was W. W. Pownall. Burgoyne's eponymous company represented a number of Australian wineries, including Patrick Auld, Thomas Hardy, and Penfolds. Pownall traded as the Australian Wine Company, developed the Auldana and Emu brands, and bought wine from Benno Seppelt of Seppeltsfield and the Prentice winery at Rutherglen. (The two companies eventually merged in the 1950s.)

The Burgoyne-Hardy correspondence also reveals many of the frustrations of the long-distance wine trade in the nineteenth century. Burgoyne's letter was sent on November 7, 1884, in response to a letter Hardy had written on September 2, which was in turn a response to an earlier letter from Burgoyne, probably on receipt of the wine. The pink wine in question, which may indeed have oxidized and deepened in color during its two-month ocean journey in wooden casks, was probably shipped from Australia in April or May 1884. Hardy probably did not receive Burgoyne's letter until early December. The spring grape harvest in the Southern Hemisphere takes place in March or April, and colonial winemakers were usually anxious to ship their wines as soon as possible, in order to recoup costs as quickly as they could. Importers, in turn, were usually frustrated by haste, and repeatedly insisted that wines should only be shipped after they had been aged for at least several months. But they had to take the winemaker's word that this was the case, and when it took eight or nine months to communicate and discuss the problem with a shipment, it was usually too late to correct the problem. This communication lag would be partly resolved with the extension of telegraph services in the 1890s, but telegrams were expensive and really only suitable for communicating very brief messages.

Ultimately, the twelve thousand mile exchange of colonial wine was built on personal trust, on networks of individuals who relied on each other to deliver the goods promised and to conduct themselves truthfully and in good faith. In many cases, the individuals at either end of these exchanges never met in person, but built their relationships through slow postal correspondence and years of successful transactions. Burgoyne's extended correspondence with Hardy shows that they had, indeed, formed an important business relationship over a number of years, and Burgoyne was willing to forgive occasional lapses in quality. He was generous, for example, when Thomas Hardy had to temporarily leave his son in charge of operations and the subsequent shipment was poor, writing diplomatically, "I am inclined to think that your son in his anxiety to keep us well supplied has drawn from some immature stock."

This left them both in an awkward position, Burgoyne continued: "Altho [sic] I throw the responsibility of these wretchedly bad wines on you, I do not forget what is due between man and man and therefore I shall do my best to get rid of them by degrees so that you may not lose through the carelessness at home in your absence."[3] While Burgoyne sometimes advanced partial payment before or on receipt of wine, the final, pre-agreed price for the wine was dependent on Burgoyne finding a buyer for it. The importer's task of dealing with poor-quality wine had both a technical and business dimension. Burgoyne despaired to Hardy, "The wine is simply unsalable [sic]. I have taken the means you I think suggested of adding charcoal in the hope of removing the most objectionable flavor [sic], but it still comes through everything—the color of the wine too is such that had I not your positive assurances of its being composed of '79, 80 + 81 I should have thought a later vintage had been added."[4] On other occasions Burgoyne attempted to revive tainted wines by blending red and white wines together, fining wine with milk and eggs, and straining it to remove sediment.[5]

This exchange between Hardy and Burgoyne reveals the complexity and precarity of the colonial wine trade. Both the winemaker and the importer carried risk in this transaction. Hardy's wines could spoil on the long voyage, they could be lost at sea, or they could simply fail to please because he had miscalculated what his English client was seeking. Burgoyne had a range of techniques to doctor and market colonial wine, but these were time-consuming and not always successful, and in the meantime he had costs associated with storing the wine and paying customs duties.

The length of the sea voyage had, in fact, improved in the second half of the nineteenth century with the expansion of steam technology. In the 1880s, the journey from London to Sydney could be done in as little as fifty days, down from eighty or ninety days three decades earlier.[6] But it remained dangerous and uncomfortable for passengers, who often shared space with cargo. And a fifty days' journey was still a long one for a hogshead of unstable wine. Burgoyne frequently racked the casks of wine he received. Racking means siphoning the wine from one container to another, in order to remove any sediment that may have formed. This could be expected during a long journey, but it had another purpose: to try and reduce the alcoholic strength of the wine. "The last ten hogsheads of Tintara have been returned as over 26 [degree sign] and must pay I fear the 2/5 duty," Burgoyne complained, but added that "we shall have it racked bright and retested, with the hope that in the operation it will lose some of its strength."[7] Tintara was Hardy's signature wine, and the name of his vineyard, and it needed to be marketable. "Do please be careful on your side to keep the strength down," Burgoyne implored

Hardy, "for it causes so much bother here."[8] That "bother" was due to customs duties, but also due to taste.

Tastes do appear to have been changing, too. One Australian winemaker complained in 1861 that "the wines they produce are too light, and lack the generous property of wine suited to the English taste and the London market."[9] A wine merchant in Bathurst, inland New South Wales, to John Wyndham in 1877 also expressed this frustration: "I am sorry to say that I have not been able to dispose of as much of the Dalwood wines as I would have wished, but the market here has been overstocked with large consignments of Albury wines which from their greater strength have been preferred to yours."[10] (Albury is in eastern Victoria, near the now-famous wine area of Rutherglen.) But by the 1880s Burgoyne was urging his producers to make lighter wines, and not only because of tariffs. Burgoyne explained, "N[ew] S[outh] Wales wines being light or average wines sell most freely. . . . The lighter and more elegant they are the better they are suited for this market."[11] Moreover, Burgoyne was echoing Fallon's call for pride in a colonial product, and for celebrating rather than obscuring the Australian origins of wine. For the British market, branding should emphasize that which was "essentially native" in the wine, he believed, instructing a potential new client to reconsider his wine's name: "Pearl of Australia is fairly good as a brand, but is hackneyed. Some good euphonious native name would be better say 'Hunter River.'"[12] (Burgoyne's frame of reference for "native" refers to a name given by settlers of the British Isles, not by Aboriginal inhabitants). François de Castella also urged vinegrowers in Victoria to coordinate their plantings so that they could establish Australian regions on a named basis. "Everyone admits that the London market is the one upon which we chiefly rely," he wrote in 1891, and "names derived from the sort of grape really mean nothing." To better appeal to that market, "instead of having in each district a host of different names, such as Hermitage, Shiraz, Carbinet . . . we should have, for example, Rutherglen, Great Western, Bendigo."[13] His entreaties were mostly ignored.

One reason winemakers and importers were paying more attention to the naming of their wines was due to international exhibitions, which were gaining in popularity. These were effectively large trade fairs, hosted by a city in a cavernous (and sometimes purpose-built) space. Countries or regions would be invited to set up sections, where their wares would be decoratively and proudly arranged, and where visitors would be able to learn about the goods' production. The fairs in the second half of the nineteenth century, up to the start of the First World War, have become famous both for cultural production (the American St. Louis World's Fair, in 1904, led to the popularization of the hotdog), and equally for racist mockery (such as the importation of Filipinos to live in a "human zoo" at the same fair, and be gawked at by American tourists as they ate actual dogs).[14]

Fairs usually charged daily admission and some attracted hundreds of thousands of visitors. This is why cities were often keen to host fairs, for the influx of visitors and their cash, and the international reputation and media coverage that would be gained. The international exhibition became something of a rite of passage for cities, to demonstrate their competency and arrival on the international stage.

Colonial winemakers were keen to exhibit because it would give them an opportunity to reach new potential customers, and to educate the public about their civic role in building the economy. In the last few decades of the nineteenth century British consumption stood at just over two bottles of wine per capita per annum, compared to beer at an average of 135 liters, or just over 235 imperial pints.[15] Of that wine, over 85 percent came from three European countries: France, Portugal, and Spain. Burgoyne participated in London's International Health Exhibit, which opened in the spring of 1884. This made sense when one remembers that wine was still touted as a health supplement: Burgoyne described his Australian wines "Grown on Ferruginous soil, are recommended for Nutritive, Strengthening and Invigorating Properties."[16] Burgoyne was pleased with this experience, because the passing trade led to many new orders. Business continued through the summer and Burgoyne could reassure his Sydney negociants that the exhibition "continues a great success. The daily attendance averages 20,000 paying persons and we are doing a splendid business."[17] In addition to face-to-face contact with visitors, they benefited from press coverage of the wider event that they otherwise would never have received. Prizes were another important feature, as not only was there often a cash prize, but there was the potential boost to sales from the recognition. Dalwood Vineyards won several prizes at the Centennial International Exhibition in Melbourne in 1888, and would include this in its advertising.

The 1878 Paris Universal Exhibition featured, among its vast displays, some South African wines, and noted in its program that the colony had produced "reputable wines for decades, the most famous of which is

Constantia."[18] This description might well have been lifted directly from the Cape delegation's application to the exhibition, and may not indicate French familiarity with the wine, but it shows the persistence of the Constantia myth.[19]

The most important fair of this era was the massive 1886 Indian and Colonial Exhibition and Australian winemakers jockeyed for space. Burgoyne had clear ideas, based on his experience at the Health Exhibit, of how they should conduct themselves and their trade. He specified all this to an organizer of the exhibition, partly to demonstrate his expertise in an unsuccessful attempt to get himself nominated for the organizational committee: "Casks should if possible be of Colonial manufacture, for these in themselves might be made an effective exhibit. . . . Small boxes of soil will be of interest. . . . Also a map of the Colony showing the wine districts and Vineyards in colours according to soil. Branches of different varieties of grapes in wax of a size natural to the Colony, and models of any article specially Colonial used in the Vineyards will be matters of interest."[20]

An example of such a display was the colony of Victoria's submission to the Calcutta Exhibition of 1883, which made wine the centerpiece of its stand. Visitors were welcomed by "a full size marble statue of Hebe, supported on either side by gilded hogsheads and groups of ferns," and then, arranged in a double-archway, two thousand bottles of Victorian wine with identical blue and gold labels.[21] Hebe was a Grecian goddess of youth, famed for feeding ambrosia to the gods—a reference that the Victorian commission thought needed no explanation. Victorian wines won eleven first-place medals at the exhibition, as did the "Victorian Champagne Company" of Melbourne, which earned gold medals for its "Crème de Bouzy [and] Perle d'Australie, from Victorian grapes."[22] Crème de Bouzy is an actual French champagne, as Bouzy is a premier cru village on the Montagne de Reims in the Champagne region. But in this case, we are dealing with an authentically Australian imitation.

It has been noted that Australian wines won some international competitions in the late nineteenth century, and suggested that these events were a turning point in Australian wine history. They undoubtedly gave a boost to Australia's wine reputation, but they did not attract the level of contemporary attention of, for comparison, the so-called 1976 "Judgement of Paris" on California wines. Colonial wines' reputations would be slower and harder to change. What would be more important to growing Britain's import market was an eventual change to the tariff levels.

In 1879 a Parliamentary Select Committee investigated complaints about the twenty-six degree cut-off and concluded that while the existing tariff levels had been set in order to provide safe wine and good revenue for Britain, it had been "a misleading definition, due solely to the limited practical knowledge as to the nature and character of wine which prevailed in this country at the time."[23] Australian wines were discussed in the five hundred pages of evidence presented by the committee, but the ultimate report of the committee was primarily concerned with French, Spanish, and Portuguese wines, and raised very few questions about the impact upon colonial wines. At the end of a substantial interview with Alfred Baker, a British customs inspector, committee member Jacob Bright did enquire whether "a lighter duty for wines over 26° would produce a large trade in Colonial wines?" to which Mr. Baker replied, "I believe that it would encourage very much the importation of Australian wine. I think it is just the difference between 26 and 28, which affects the question." Evidently satisfied, Bright continued onto another line of questioning.[24] While the committee recommended exactly what Fallon had been advocating, its report does not show the work of Fallon's lobbying. The committee defensively denied "the wish to give preferential advantage to the wine products of any particular country," but rather it anticipated that the suspected beneficiaries would be European: "It is sufficient, in refutation of such a supposition, to point to the fact that the same scale of duties applies to our own colonies."[25] By now Fallon's arguments, that high alcohol was a product of nature and not adulteration, were gaining traction. The *Westminster Review,* a progressive London-based periodical, mused that changing the tariff structure would be good for colonial trade. "It is well known that the bounty of Nature in these fertile Colonies is liberal to the degree of yielding few wines of less strength than the old 26° standard: and as this is a purely natural strength the wholesomeness of these full-bodied wines is assured," it wrote in its quarterly report on British colonies, repeating the lusty language of fecundity we have come to associate with antipodean colonization. Naturally, then, "under the new scale a large and increasing trade in them will probably arise."[26]

When the tariff was ultimately amended in 1886, to broaden the still wine category to incorporate wines up to thirty degrees (about 17 percent ABV), it was after "protracted negotiations with the Spanish government."[27] There is no justification in the official record based on the imperial trade in wine or the welfare of colonial wine producers. Nor was this the final time that colonial wine tariffs would be on the chopping block: again, in 1899, there was fierce uproar from colonial wine producers at the suggestion that wine tariffs would go up. It was the high commissioner of Canada who spoke on behalf of the wine-producing colonies in opposing this proposal. Acknowledging that Canada seemed an unlikely advocate, he argued that increased imperial trade was something all should support, and anyway that Canada had a stake in this fight. Canada "manufactures annually a large quantity of wine, which is consumed locally at present; but the development of the export business is looked upon, however, as one of the probabilities of the near future." And yet colonial wines faced many more challenges than European producers, the commissioner wrote: "They are much farther away from the British markets; freights are three times higher; oak staves have to be imported from England, increasing the cost of casks; large stocks have to be maintained owing to the distance from the sources of supply; and the wine, after the voyage, has to be stored for a longer time before use [to allow it to settle]."[28] In hindsight, Canada's intervention on behalf of other colonial producers is a harbinger of the economic and political cooperation that would arise among British dominions in the 1920s. Canada had become an independent dominion in 1867—self-governing, but still associated with the British Empire—and was assuming a new leadership role as such.

TWELVE

From Melbourne to Madras

WINE IN INDIA, CYPRUS, MALTA, AND CANADA

MOST OF THE VITICULTURAL ACTIVITY in the British world took place in colonies of white settlement, where viticulture was established immediately and deliberately with capitalistic and civilizing zeal. This is how wine's New World was created through settler colonialism. The Cape and Australia were the two largest and most successful of these endeavors, followed by New Zealand, but they were not the only ones. Canada also had a small wine industry, and, perhaps most surprisingly, so did India. But Britain's vast orbit also included several Mediterranean producers that were undeniably "Old World," having produced wine for both local consumption and trade for millennia. This included two Mediterranean islands and wine producers, Cyprus and Malta. In 1860 Cyrus Redding could write of the "the lusciousness of Cyprus," producing wines of which "in England, little is known";[1] this would change after Cyprus became British territory in 1878. The "acquisition" of Cyprus is emblematic of a period of time, from the 1860s up until the start of the First World War, that historians see as something of a peak in British imperialism, both in the rapid accumulation of new lands and in terms of British public enthusiasm for the empire. (The British Empire would technically be larger in the 1920s, in terms of land mass and population, but by that point several of the major colonies had morphed into semi-independent dominions. The mood would change, too.) Settler winemakers, as we have seen, bought into this view of a supportive United Kingdom blessing their efforts, and they fed back images and ideas of their contribution to the imperial bounty.

Winemakers also experienced and viewed the empire as a complex lattice of relationships: theirs was not just a monogamous love for the Mother Country. Good, ideas, capital, and power did not just flow between Britain and individual colonies; it followed among colonies, too. In the case of wine, some of this was just the logistics of travel: ships bound for the Antipodes went through the Cape, or stopped in other colonies in the Indian Ocean, or (after 1869) went through the Suez Canal. But intercolonial trade was also based on a sense of shared kinship and interest.

"In Australia, the settler is not an exile, but a man of energy and resources," the *Times of India* opined in 1879, in an article entitled "An Anglo-Indian in Australia," and "the Australian wine trade is one that should be most profitably increased with India."[2] Just as colonial wine producers were proud to sell their wine in Britain, they viewed white settlements in other British colonies as a natural market for wine. The most obvious of these was India. We have seen how the East India Company began carrying Cape wine to South Asia in the seventeenth century. British rule began to creep into modern-day India in the eighteenth century—from the port cities of Calcutta and Mumbai into the interior—and in 1857, these areas went from being under the control of the British East India Company, to becoming a unified crown colony known as the Indian Raj. Trade and prestige drove these incursions, and small communities of British people followed: traders, merchants, missionaries, civil servants, engineers, and their families.

The flag followed trade, it is sometimes said about British imperialism, and wine followed trade, too. In spite of now being producer countries, New Zealand, Australia, and South Africa all continued to import wine in the second half of the nineteenth century. In 1856, New Zealand made about £7,000 in customs revenue from wine: far less than it made on spirits, but more than it made on beer, tea, or coffee.[3] Rising customs revenue was, the finance minister argued, a proxy for the overall growing prosperity of the colony: "the settler who was contented with his beer, now affords himself the luxury of wine."[4] Not enough, perhaps: the low levels of wine consumption in Australia, one irked English imperialist remarked, revealed "some want of local patriotism."[5]

Build it, trade it, tax it: British civilization and capitalism marched hand in hand. For the colonial wine industry, the next project was India.

CASHMERE RESEMBLES MADEIRA

Unlike in Australia, wine was not introduced into the Indian subcontinent by early modern Europeans. The Mughal Empire, which had roots in Central

Asia and Persia, spread into and ruled much of India over the sixteenth through eighteenth centuries. Mughal culture was highly sophisticated and known for its monumental architecture and decorative arts. Although the Mughals were Muslim, wine consumption was common among elites. There was a tradition of wine poetry, and wine and wine cups appeared frequently in Mughal iconography.[6] The wine that Mughals consumed in northern Indian cities like Delhi and Agra was generally "Shiraz" imported from modern-day Iran; after Dutch traders' expansion into the Indian Ocean, wine from the Canary Islands also entered the market.[7]

Cyrus Redding claimed in the 1830s that wine was being produced in India. Redding's work is probably the best-known wine-writing of nineteenth-century Britain, but his popularity does not give any indication of his credentials or research process. Still, his confident description, rooted in orientalist fascination with ancient Indian religion and scholarship, is intriguing: "Suradévi is the Hindoo [sic] goddess of wine. India at present [1834] produces little or no wine, except in the northern parts between the Sutledge and the Indus, bordering upon the former river; indeed to the southward the climate is hot and the soil too rich for vine culture. . . . At Lahore, beyond the Sutledge, wine is made of good quality, and all the way from thence to Condahar [sic], and northward to and in Cashmere [sic], vines are planted and wine is manufactured. That of Cashmere resembles Madeira."[8] How did Redding know this? Was it true? There are reports from a British visitor to Kashmir in the 1830s that refer to locals' memory of a recent, extensive wine-making tradition, since abandoned.[9] But Kashmir was not under British occupation in the 1830s, and its traditional wine making had little impact on the consumption patterns of British settlers in India, who seem to have obtained their wine through import.

On the whole, poverty, religious prohibitions, and lack of a major domestic supply meant that most Indians did not ordinarily consume wine. Therefore, wine consumption among white settlers in Asian and African colonies could serve an important social and cultural role in how they saw themselves. By consuming wine, a "civilized" beverage, Anglo people could reinforce their social distance from the native peoples over whom they purported to rule, and with whom they had to negotiate on a daily basis. Their wine imports were a symbol of their success and of their civilized lifestyle in the face of what they believed to be a bewildering and foreign culture. The French explorer Dumont D'Urville noted that in his travels through the Himalayas in the 1830s, "all the luxuries of a sumptuous life" were available to the English inhabitants of Calcutta who summered in Simla, and that these luxuries were "port, sherry, Bordeaux [wine], Champagne, Rhine wine, and Cape wine."[10]

In 1832 the British Parliament made an enquiry into the affairs of the East India Company, the state-backed private corporation that enjoyed monopoly trading rights in British India. The enquiry was very interested in the subject of wine importation into India, and its potential for expansion. The company's imports into India for the period 1814–20 were described as mainly being metals, cloth, and "such articles as blankets, woollen nightcaps, Madeira, claret, port, Cape wine and brandy."[11] (The woollen nightcaps were probably clothing, not a comforting bedtime cocktail.) A company official précised, in his evidence, that "the exportation of wine to India, which commenced in 1808, arose in consequence of complaint, that good wine could not be procured at reasonable prices."[12] There was also testimony that in the early 1830s, wine was one of the principle commodities transported on Indian rivers, from Calcutta to cities in Uttar Pradesh, Farrukhabad on the Ganges and Agra on the Jumna.[13] This wine came both from East India imports, and from imports by French vessels. An official argued that the wine trade was ripe for expansion, in part because there was demand among Indians themselves, particularly in Calcutta where the natives "being so much more with Europeans, are divested in a much greater degree of their prejudices and habits than others," and were willing to consume wine even though it was not customary.[14] For this official, openness to wine consumption was a civilizational continuum, with "European" and "native" at opposing extremes.

Most intriguingly, the parliamentary enquiry reveals that an Italian named Giuseppe Mutti was granted land around 1829 by British officials in Mumbai in order to experiment in producing silk, "Mocha coffee," and wine. He describes his "plantation" as being called Kathoor Bagh, which a later author identifies as being near Pune,[15] so within trading distance of Mumbai. He had some success with silk, due to his long previous experience in the silk trade in Italy; of course, India had been home to a thriving silk industry for a millennia. His experiments with wine were, as of 1830, inconclusive, because grapes "are a species of plant which require some time before you can form an opinion." But he claimed to tend a "large plantation" of grape vines on a daily basis.[16]

This single piece of evidence is too isolated to speak of a British wine-making tradition in India, although it does repeat patterns we have seen elsewhere: allow a skilled foreigner to experiment in producing goods that are luxurious and profitable for export, and simultaneously culturally essential for civilized living by settler-colonizers. But in terms of official support for wine growing, I have not unearthed evidence that British officials were proactively promoting the planting of vines in India. The reason for this may have been that India was not a British colony of white settlement. There were indeed thousands of Europeans who lived in India under British rule, but they remained a microscopic minority in the vast country. Unlike in Australia or New Zealand, there was no concept in the British official mind of India as an underpopulated state, ripe for civilizing settlement, and thus no vision of a viticultural future. Nor were most British residents in India necessarily planning to stay: they were "merely birds of passage," to quote the Lady Hariot Dufferin, an industrious vicereine of India who was born in Northern Ireland.[17] Unlike settlers in the Antipodes and the Cape, Europeans in India usually intended to carry out service or make a fortune, and then return home.

The degree to which colonies were categorized in the British official mind became more starkly apparent in the late nineteenth and early twentieth centuries, when the colonies of white settlement began demanding representative government (for people of European descent) and transforming into independent dominions in the empire. Canada came first when it confederated in 1867, followed by the Australian federation of 1901, New Zealand in 1907, and the Union of South Africa in 1910. Indian demands for representative government had been politely pitched by groups like the Indian National Congress since the 1880s, but were rebuffed and ridiculed by many British officials. A highly organized anticolonial movement gained momentum in the twentieth century and India became an independent state in 1947. The rate of progress toward self-governance underlines the distinct differences in the way the United Kingdom regarded its colonies based on whether or not they were heavily settled by white people. This was equally reflected in the levels of investment and interest in viticulture.

Still, Australian appeals to the Indian wine market were pitched as a reminder of transimperial white solidarity, reassuring settlers of their role in the empire and the economy. Many newspaper articles on the Australian wine trade in Indian Anglo newspapers in the late nineteenth and early twentieth centuries—editorials masquerading as news articles—encouraged its expansion. The *Indian Daily News* noted Australian settlers' enterprising efforts to sell to India, and that they were "bent on popularising the

Australian wines, which are now very generally drunk throughout the colonies, and which quite recently received very big commendation at the Bordeaux Exhibition."[18] The underlying message is not just that the British in India should buy Australian wine, but that they should do so because Australian settlers embodied what is good about colonial settlement.

Household management guides and cookbooks for Anglo women in India demonstrate that wine was considered a household staple, a basic provision, both for social consumption and for medicinal use. The Calcutta artist Muhammad Amir created a series of watercolors of household servants in the 1840s, including a man whose job was to serve wine. The servant is pictured wearing a long white apron and holding a bottle and tumbler.[19] Flora Steel and Grace Gardiner's classic *Indian Housekeeper and Cook,* first published in 1888, lists both "wine" and "spirits of wine" in its "Hindostani" glossary of essential words ("the more common articles of general consumption"),[20] and recommends that hostesses serve claret and hock punches to refresh their guests. But I have not found instances of such guides specifying which kinds of wine, or arguing that they must be European in origin. There was a degree of snobbery about colonial wines which may indeed reflect poor quality. One Australian journalist worried in 1846, still early days in Australian wine production, that "it is a well ascertained fact that really good wine is the product of old vineyards only," and flattered his readers that Australian wine was young, and probably "too simple a concoction to suit the palates of your curry-loving Anglo-Indian."[21] But mixing wines into punches was an excellent way to stretch wine and use cheaper wines—thus colonial wines were well suited to what were, apparently, popular drinks in colonial India. Another London journalist wrote in 1849 that while "hitherto our experience of colonial wine has not been very cheering," the wine was improving, and newer Rhenish-like wines produced in Australia had a "general character . . . well-adapted to the East Indies."[22] Some journalists claimed that the cheapest, poorest quality Australian wines were sent to India, rather than to Britain, and that as a result Australians had earned themselves a poor reputation, and squandered a potentially good market.[23] This was anecdotal, but it may reflect a view that there was less competition in the Indian market, and that consumers there would have to take what they could get.

In theory, too, it would be a great deal easier for the Cape and the Antipodean colonies to export their wine to India than to Britain. There would be less competition from European wines and potentially lower shipping costs. The Cape would be able to take advantage of ships already en route to India—as it had done since the 1660s—and Australia was a great deal closer to India than it was to Britain. James Busby had propounded this very theory as early as 1825, when he wrote of the potential to ship Australian wines to India: "ships which go out [from Britain to Australia] with convicts and emigrants would obtain a freight home; or, instead of going in ballast to seek a return cargo in India, might carry thither a cargo of wines."[24] Redding, in the 1860 edition of his book, was also feeling more positive, and reported that "Australian wines, it is gratifying to learn, have been made so successfully as to sell in the market at Calcutta for thirty-two shillings per dozen."[25] When James Fallon wished to demonstrate in the 1870s that his wines were high quality enough to withstand ocean journeys, he solicited written testimonies and certificates from a variety of wine experts in the specific markets that he wished to enter, which he then published in a collection entitled *Australian Vines and Wines.* This included a certificate of quality from "Messrs John Davies and Co., the eminent wine tasters of Calcutta," who testified that they had tasted a variety of his wines and that they were "pure and of good quality, and will stand fair comparison with those of European manufacture."[26]

Once the Australian wine industry had expanded appreciably in the 1860s and 1870s, Australian wine agents were therefore on the lookout for such opportunities. The Wyndham family, which owned Dalwood Vineyards in Australia's Hunter Valley, used an agent in the nearby port city of Newcastle to arrange the shipping and sale of their wine overseas. The agent wrote to Wyndham in 1872 with excitement about an order from British Ceylon (modern-day Sri Lanka): "I have a commission from some friends of mine in Ceylon to take up for them a selection of wines for them to taste, and I should be glad if you will let me know what sorts you think would be best. My two friends want 8 dozen between them and leave all about details to me, except they would prefer a larger quantity of the *white* than of the *red* wines."[27] However, he was often stymied by shipping logistics. John Wyndham's shipping agent had found him a number of clients in Madras, Bombay, and Calcutta, and tried to send frequent small shipments. Nonetheless, he frequently had difficulty in filling these Indian orders: "This week *no vessels* for any port but California, vessels are detained in Port for want of freight, . . . there have been no ships for India for the last five weeks, and only two for China ... there are *eighteen* vessels now engaged for *California* all *American,* so I shall not be sorry when we have some more English ships in port bound for any other place but *California.*"[28] On a different occasion he bemoaned, "There is no vessel bound for Madras at present and it is hard to say when a charter will be effected for that place—The 'Rialto' starts from *Melbourne* for Madras on the 14th of September ... — otherwise you can ship from here to *Ceylon* and thence re ship [*sic*] at that place by one of the steamers trading between Ceylon and Madras; a ship proceeds to Ceylon next week from here, but it is the most expensive way, I certainly would advise the direct shipment from Melbourne."[29] Shipping from Melbourne was harder than it sounds, for Victoria and New South Wales were different colonies, and the trip between Sydney and Melbourne was over six hundred nautical miles.

Still, Australian winemakers persisted in trying to crack the Indian market. Four Australian colonies—Victoria, New South Wales, South Australia, and Tasmania—exhibited at the 1883 Calcutta Exhibition, and dozens of winemakers submitted their products for display and competition. The participants considered such an exhibition to be a serious business that could bring substantial trade and respect to Australia, and the colonies established official committees and committed funds to create dramatic stands.

The Victorian commission's findings reflected on the potential and the challenges of building Australian wine imports to India. On the whole it argued that a "lucrative business" could be established, but that it required two things. First, an Australian deputation would have to establish its own wine depot in India, to ensure that Australian wines were handled with care and then properly marketed and sold; simply selling them to long-established wine merchants would not do, because these merchants had little incentive to build the Australian trade, and the wines would languish. A second recommendation by the commission gives great insight into the naming practices of Australian wines. The wines sent to the exhibition were named after the dominant grape varieties: "comprising for the uninitiated such bewildering names as Dolcette [*sic*], Malbec, Mataro, Pedro Ximenes, Gouais, Muscat of Alexandria, Shiraz, Verdheilho, Aucarot, Carbinet [*sic*], Grenache, Roussillon, and Sauvignon. Not one in twenty of the ordinary wine consumers in India would select any of the foregoing wines from the labels alone, simply because they would be ignorant of the description of wine indicated."[30]

Many contemporary wine lovers will also be mystified by some of these names, and it is striking how many different kinds of grapes were then being grown in Australia. Gouais is now truly obscure,[31] as is aucarot; mataro is now better known as monastrell or mourvèdre, and in Australia is commonly a silent partner in a blend with shiraz. No one proposed, in 1884, that Australian producers should label their wines as more well-known varietals, though. The trick for exporters, the commission argued, was to stick to "say, half-a-dozen well-known kinds—such, for instance, as claret and hock, tokay and madeira, port and sherry."[32] This was proposed as a marketing strategy, and not as a directive to growers: presumably, the prize-winning "Sauvignon, 1879, red, resembling chauteau lafitte [sic]," exhibited by de Castella and Rowan,[33] would simply be relabeled as claret. Styles were easily recognized; most grapes were not.

The Calcutta International Exhibition was also the next time that Indian wine gained international attention. The Maharajah Ranbir Singh of Jammu and Kashmir, a noted British ally, is credited with importing French vines to Kashmir, only to have them later succumb to phylloxera and need to be replaced with American root stock. At the exhibition, he presented red and white wines, and won a medal for the white. There were no further details as to the grapes, quantities, or style of the wines he exhibited. An 1898 tourist guide to Kashmir noted that wine was made in Gopkar from grapes grown "near Chishma Shahi," and could be purchased at the following prices: "Claret Rs [rupees] 14 per dozen bottles; White Wine Rs. 12 per dozen. Cognac Rs. 3 per bottle, and Brandy No. 1 Rs. 2, and No. 2 Rs. 1."[34] Marion Doughty, an Englishwoman who visited Kashmir in 1900, wrote that its vineyards produced "large quantities of Barsac and Medoc" under the direction of an Italian winemaker, and "though the flavour is still a little rough, they are good strengthening wines, and at the rate of about one rupee for a bottle will create a large demand."[35] This is a familiar refrain we have heard in infant wine industries, extolling the strength and cheapness of colonial wine, and promising future growth. Transport, though, was a problem, given the relative isolation of Kashmir from major markets.

"The idea of India coming into the market as a wine-producing country seemed to amuse most persons," the Calcutta official report noted, "and was even viewed with considerable suspicion by some of the colonial exhibitors."[36] The Australians, the principal wine producers present at the exhibition, knew how truly difficult it was to make wine, and may have been skeptical about Indian capabilities and climate. But they also may have had their eye on the Indian market and did not welcome potential competition.

How successful was the wine trade between Australia and India? This is a methodological issue, in part. Imperial and colonial history has refocused its attention on connections between and among colonies, but nineteenth-century sources still reflect a core-periphery official imagination: for example, the most widely available statistics for colonial production and trade tend to be those commissioned by Parliament in London, and they record each colony individually, or in terms of how much each colony traded with Britain, I have not yet been able to find precise data on the amount of Australian wine imported into India in the nineteenth century. This in itself shows us that it was a near-negligible amount, and given the challenges in nineteenth-century shipping, it is not hard to see why. Why did colonial winemakers persevere, in spite of the persistent rejection of their products? A lot of writing about imperial commodities naturally emphasizes plenty: of voracious British appetites for colonial goods, of vast markets, of wealth and mobility. In practice, the Australians identified a clear market for their wine in India, but appeared stymied in their attempts to conquer it. This recalls the argument made by historians Andrew Thompson and Gary Magee, that colonial markets could be very difficult to penetrate, and that we should not assume that trade was always smooth or automatic across the world of white settlement.

That said, there were clear webs of international exchange in the colonial world that entirely bypassed the Britain itself. According to a nineteenth-century French geographer, the French colony of New Caledonia could not produce wine for its consumption, and was "obliged to purchase a prodigious quantity of wine overseas, in Australia and New Zealand,"[37] to the tune of 1,600,000 French francs in 1883, which was more than the total sum the colony imported of grain, fruits and vegetables, sugar, and animals. Unlike for British settlers, wine was a staple good for French settlers. Australian wine was also significantly cheaper in most New Zealand wine markets than European wines were; in Wellington, European wine was twice the price of Australian wine,[38] and this gave Australian wines an advantage and an easy market. Dalwood's records show that sales were being made overseas: in one week, shipments of wine were sent to Hong Kong, Mauritius, Bombay, Batavia, Singapore, London, and New Zealand.[39] Dalwood was a larger vineyard, but it still carried out many small, local sales; with the help of a well-networked agent, it was also able to sell throughout the British Empire.

In 1844 the famed English poet Elizabeth Barrett Browning wrote an enthusiastic (and perhaps slightly tipsy) poem entitled "Cyprus Wine," in which
drinking the wine is analogous to imbibing rich Greek classical poetry.[40]
"Sooth, the drinking should be ampler," she writes in the second stanza,
"when the drink is so divine."[41] Henry George Keene, an East India Company
minor bureaucrat turned writer, published a volume called *Poems Written in
India,* in which he also extolled the virtues of Cypriot wine. He, too, appealed
to Hebe, that ancient goddess who had looked over Australian wines at the
Calcutta Exhibition, to "fill a cup for me, with smiling face, / For all the gods
were born of Cyprus wine."[42]

Cyprus is a Mediterranean island with both Greek and Turkish-speaking
populations. It was under Ottoman rule until 1878, when a backdoor deal
between Britain and the Ottoman Empire led to it becoming a British protectorate (still technically Ottoman territory, it was governed by the British
as a strategy to prevent Russian encroachment). If Australians and South
Africans could sell their wine in India, surely Mediterranean islands should
be able to shift their wine to Britain? Colonial administrators in the late
1870s agreed: the drinking should be ampler, in the sense that Cyprus and
Malta should be encouraged to make, sell, and pay taxes on more wine.
Cyprus was much larger than Malta and, of the two, its wines had more
prominence in the British market.

Just as the Cape had Constantia, Cyprus had a reputed and mythical wine
called Commandaria, a sweet dessert wine. The wine shared a name with the
land where it was grown, which claimed medieval crusading knights in its
heritage. Commandaria appears in eighteenth- and nineteenth-century
British popular culture, similarly to Constantia but with less frequency. It
was considered a "ladies' wine,"[43] and according to Dr. Druitt could be prescribed "for nursing mothers, children recovering from illness, etc."[44] In the
1870s an Irish journalist even described a white wine made from Frontignac
and Muscat in Gawler, South Australia, as "a sweet white wine closely resembling Cyprus in bouquet and flavour."[45] Commandaria was, a London newspaper declared in 1824, the "choicest sweet wine," and Cyprus was a place of
great viticultural potential, according to one journalist: "Candia [Crete] and
Cyprus alone, if properly cultivated, would be capable of supplying us with
every variety of wine."[46] Could natives ever be trusted to cultivate properly,
without British supervision?

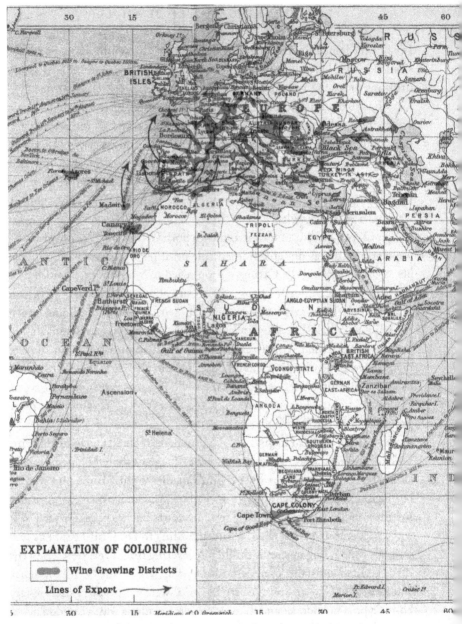

FIGURE 3. Map of wine-producing countries, with major trade routes. Note that New Zealand's vineyards have not been marked on the map. J. G. Bartholomew, "Wine-Producing Countries," *Atlas of the World's Commerce, A New Series of Maps with Descriptive Text and Diagrams* . . . (London: George Newnes, 1907). Courtesy of the David Rumsey Map Center, Stanford Libraries.

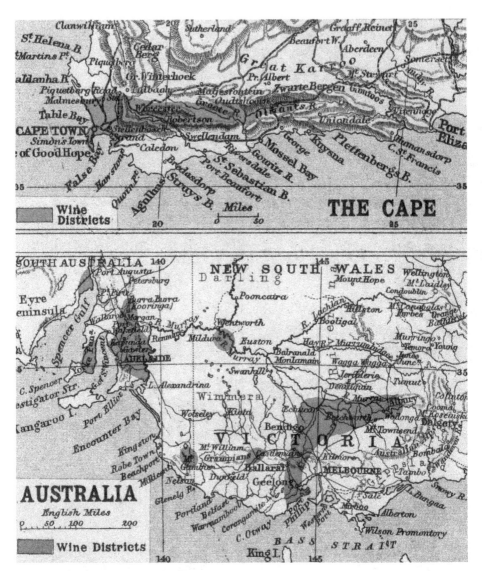

FIGURE 4. Detail, Australia and the Cape, from the map in figure 3. South Australia and Victoria are now of much greater commercial importance for wine producing than New South Wales, and wine in South Africa has spread far beyond Constantia.

Proper cultivation was also somewhat lacking in nearby Malta: perhaps the Maltese had been making wine for several thousand years, but they weren't making money—which was the sign, to a British bureaucrat, of underperformance. The Mediterranean island chain had been producing wine for millennia, from indigenous grape varieties like gellewza and ghirgentina. Malta had become a British possession in 1800 and it exported very small amounts of wine to Britain. In the nineteenth century the British provincial newspaper subscriber could read occasional reports of ships bringing wine from Malta into southern ports like Falmouth and Plymouth.[47] This wine was not necessarily Maltese in origin, but may have been reimports of wines from other Mediterranean islands, like Sicily. Indeed, by the end of the nineteenth century, wine was actually one of the main imports *into* Malta: £138,000 sterling worth of it in 1896, for example, mostly from Italy, Greece, and Turkey. For an archipelago with a population of around 160,000 people, mostly poor, this was a large sum, and was not necessarily all consumed by locals: Malta had a modest tourist industry already, and it also could reexport goods to other destinations.[48] In the same year, Malta exported just £2,000 sterling worth of wine.[49] Wages for dock workers in the wine trade had been dropping over several decades, and were among the lowest in Malta's port.[50]

The Maltese wine industry was hardly a commercial success, but there is no evidence that the British administrative mind had plans to make it profitable. This is curious, but it may have to do with the demographics and geography. Unlike in the Cape and Antipodes, where colonizers believed that there were vast amounts of land theirs for the taking, Malta was not terra nullius, even to the most ambitious official imagination. The small archipelago was already densely settled and had little room for agricultural expansion. Nor was there much question of removing existing farmers from their land, as there was no frontier or outback to which they could be removed or banished; besides, they were European, with institutions that British officials recognized and begrudgingly respected, like the Catholic Church. The plantation-exportation mentality that the British exercised in other colonies was not extended to Maltese viticulture.

To the extent that Maltese wine enters the British legislative record, it is in discussions about a fair rate of duty and the charge for licenses to sell alcohol. On the one hand, it was recognized that Malta was poor and could not realistically produce much income; on the other hand, it was a British colony and would be expected to contribute its fair share to public coffers. Enquiries were made in the 1870s and the evidence presented to Parliament.

Wine, it noted, was consumed regularly; a spokesperson for the Catholic Church spoke in opposition to any increases to wine duties, "because wine is nearly as necessary as bread" for Maltese workers.[51] A local professional also gave Parliamentary evidence in opposition to wine duties, arguing that while for the English, "wine is a luxury, but in Malta it is a necessity," and a vital source of calories for working people.[52] Indeed, a further report argued, the imperial state should ease up the license fees on small grocery shops that sold wines to ordinary Maltese peasants, and instead crack down on "grog shops," run by "applicants of bad character who are known to sell adulterated and unwholesome liquors."[53] The Victorian obsession with adulteration, and the differentiation between "wholesome" wines and "unwholesome" strong alcohol, extended to tiny Malta, too.

Cyprus, being a larger island, was viewed with more industry potential, and even of desperate need. "The agricultural prosperity of Cyprus is a matter of the gravest interest to the Government, for on that prosperity the revenue entirely depends," the former high commissioner explained to the Royal Geographical Society. Wine grapes were one of the principal agricultural products, and 80 percent of the island's wine was exported (largely to Egypt and Turkey), but he viewed the industry as unsustainable. This was partly because of the custom of partible inheritance, in which lands were subdivided equally among children, with some of the resulting plots becoming impracticably small. Moreover, the vine-growing was "most primitive," and "the wine is manufactured in the rudest way," he wrote with disgust.[54]

As with Malta, much of the discussion of Cypriot wine in British official sources boils down to the correct methods and levels of taxation. Ottoman rulers had extracted a tithe on grape-growers, but British tax collectors found this very labor-intensive and easily cheated, and transitioned to imposing excise taxes on alcohol instead. There was a lack of investment, the Royal Colonial Institute discussed, which stymied trade; some argued that Cyprus already received sufficient government subsidy, and others countered that it required stimulus in the form of government grants, in order to upgrade the harbor facilities and attract investors.[55] (In the late 1870s group of "English gentlemen" had placed advertisements in English newspapers seeking investors for a wine export business from Cyprus, which in itself suggests traditional sources of capital investment were nonplussed by the island's prospects.)[56] Underlying both sides was a regret and frustration that Cyprus was not more "developed," more prosperous, after nearly twenty years of British custodianship. There was also a distinct lack of kinship with the native population, referred to as "peasants," in British official sources, and that seemed to underlie discussions of investment and funding. Australian and Cape producers stressed their loyalty, their Britishness, in appealing for assistance, and that type of discussion just did not take place in the official sphere when it came to Cypriot wine.

Gods were not born of this wine. It was a disappointment for eager bureaucrats, and some of it was even toxic. A small scandal erupted in the early years of British rule when a consignment of Cypriot wine exported to France was found to be adulterated with aniline dye, presumably to enhance the color.[57] (France, deep in the phylloxera crisis, was desperate for cheap wine, though not desperate enough to drink this: it was dumped in the Marseille harbor.) Adulteration, that scourge of the Victorian consumer, had struck again.

There are occasional mentions of Cyprus wine in the late nineteenth-century press, but usually they are advertisements for estate sales and auctions, not for wine merchants' direct sales. One exception are a handful of British newspaper advertisements for a Cyprus red wine, sold under the name of Chateau Pera, a "special value" in the 1890s.[58] James Denman, a wine merchant who also specialized in South African wines, sometimes advertised a range of Greek wines, "which are absolutely Pure, and not strengthened by the addition of Spirit," and this range included a Cyprus wine.[59] But on the whole, Cyprus exported only miniscule amounts of wine to Britain in the last few decades of the nineteenth century, not even enough for Cyprus to be itemized in parliamentary accounts.[60]

CANADA

Canada's nineteenth-century wine industry was based in lower Ontario, near the cities of Hamilton and St. Catharine's, a region that curves west and south of Toronto and hugs the shore of Lake Ontario. This was a region that primarily produced grain and had a complementary milling industry. The wine industry was not significant enough to be included in the description of St. Catharine's in an 1873 gazetteer.[61] There was, however, a Hamilton-based "Canada Vine Growers' Association," which was not actually a cooperative or lobbying group, but a private company. It was legally incorporated, the parliamentary edict citing the general wish for "the encouragement of the cultivation of vines and the manufacture of wine in the Dominion [of Canada]."[62] It applied for space at the Paris Exhibition of 1878 to exhibit its wines, although it did not appear in the final program,[63] and it also followed precedent in seeking medical opinion on the excellence of its wines. In a fluff piece published in the *Canadian Journal of Medical Science,* it found two university professors prepared to state that its wine were "perfectly pure" and even "equal to many of the best wines of France."[64] They were therefore suitable for medical treatment. The Vine Growers' Association swept up the prizes for "commercial wines" at the Ontario agricultural exhibition in 1883. The categories were dry wine, sweet wine, sparkling wine, and "Canada claret." There was a separate prize category for amateur winemakers using "hardy" grapes (native *vitis labrusca* grapes, like Concord). The combined professional and amateur categories had just thirty-three entrants.[65]

There was some official curiosity about the prospects for an Ontario wine industry, with an official report proclaiming that the wine industry in the early 1880s was "growing steadily" and would soon be of "considerable importance".[66] The Canadian Commissioner of Agriculture procured wines (and cereals) from the Melbourne International Exhibition of 1881,[67] suggesting that it was interested in knowing more about Australian efforts in these domains.[68] And the Ontario Legislature gathered information on a variety of agricultural products, to inform itself of the market potential. Grapes were one such product: growers were brought forward to the Fruit-Growers' Association of Ontario in 1883, to give testimony on the best grapes to grow for market. The growers were not very cooperative: few had kept precise records of yields, many complained of pests like thrips that snacked on vine leaves, and several expressed astonishment that official bodies would be interested in their amateur exploits. Most professed to growing Concord, Isabella, and Delaware table grapes, and not European wine grapes ("The farmer wants a pure native. . . . Foreign blood is not for him").[69] The few who engaged in winemaking described adding sugar and water to their grape must. One winemaker boasted that an English visitor who had lived in Oporto had tasted his Canadian port and declared it excellent. Others compared their techniques for retrofitting household equipment for the operation:

> Mr Haskins: Might it not be better to press [the grapes] through a very coarse sieve than through a sausage machine?
> Mr Switzer: That might be done, perhaps, but we put the machine over the tub, and grind them through it.[70]

There was, indeed, a nineteenth-century British product known as "meat wine", in which meat extract was added to wine to give it additional nutritional value (supposedly),[71] but it did not involve a sausage machine. "If you let it go four or five years," Switzer continued, "you will have a wine that you will be surprised at."[72] This was doubtlessly true.

The language of wine making in other settler-colonial contexts is familiar here: the promises of a bright future, the bold claims that the wine was as wholesome and as good as anything European, the official curiosity as to the profitability of the entire scheme. One winemaker who gave official testimony even proposed that his wine would contribute toward temperance; he did not elaborate, but this was probably in steering people away from spirits, which were very popular in Canada. Despite these identical tropes, the Ontario version of this viticultural project was much smaller, and much more amateur, than the contemporary projects in Australia, the Cape, or even New Zealand. It was certainly not ready for export. And there was no urgency: since Canada had already established itself as one of the major grain suppliers of the empire, it did not need to be looking to export wine. Each dominion and colony would do its part for the whole. That would become clear as the empire found itself in a global war.

PART THREE

Market

C. 1910–1950

THIRTEEN

Plonk!

COLONIAL WINE AND THE FIRST WORLD WAR

IN THE SUMMER OF 1914, the carefully cultivated European alliance system flopped like a house of cards, and the United Kingdom was at war with Germany.

Major Gerald Achilles Burgoyne was the second son of the wine importer Peter Bond Burgoyne. Gerald, born in 1874, was a young child while his father was building his colonial wine business in the 1880s, and even accompanied him on a wine-buying trip to Australia. Gerald did not enter the family business but became a career soldier who commanded a Royal Irish Regiment and was sent to the Western Front in 1914, near the southern Franco-Belgian border. He kept a careful diary of the first year and a half of the war that frankly documented the harsh experience of soldiering.[1]

The picture Burgoyne created of the war was bleak: death, disease, boredom, little communication, no hot water, tasteless rations that went wasted, stumbling over severed limbs in muddy fields. Anxiety and desperation were common, with one of Burgoyne's soldiers attempting suicide before their ship had even left British waters for France. Burgoyne believed that strict discipline was essential to prevent a descent into total chaos, but he had some sympathy for his troops who panicked in the desperate circumstances.

His experiences at the Front, which he chronicled for his family back in Britain, are a far cry from his father's world of wine warehouses and tastings, of international shipments and lobbying for better tariff rates. Gerald's high-ranking position in the army though, and his portraits by the famed photographer Bassano hanging in the National Portrait Gallery, show how his family had risen to social prominence by the success of his father John's colonial wine importation business. The wine business was not particularly high status. It did not require formal qualifications or degrees, it involved a great deal of manual labor, and it had a certain seedy association with drunkenness and adulteration. Burgoyne, however, was commercially successful, and his wealth gave him a respectability and status which he passed on to his sons. Peter Burgoyne had four sons and four daughters. Three of his sons served during the First World War, at the rank of either major or lieutenant, as did all four of his sons-in-law. The anomaly was his son Cuthbert Burgoyne, who resided in England and had taken over the family wine business. Cuthbert was excused from military service on the recommendation of Andrew Fisher, Australia's first Labour prime minister and its wartime high commissioner to Britain, because "his work was of much importance to the Australian wine industry."[2] This was an exceptional exemption, the Australian press noted with pride. Britain had mandatory conscription, and it was not typical for business owners to be exempted from military service. This was surely a sign of how important colonial wine was, the loyal press wanted to believe, even during a war.

The First World War was a war of imperialism and colonialism. In the first instance, it was a war that broke out among European imperial powers, and which concerned the fate of their colonies. The immediate catalyst for the war was the assassination of the Archduke Franz Ferdinand, the heir to the land-based Austro-Hungarian Empire, by an anticolonial nationalist in subject Serbia. When other European powers mobilized in response to this incident, they were not simply honoring a diplomatic balance-of-power agreement in Europe, but were mindful of the power vacuums and imperial opportunities created when one empire lost control of their colonies and subordinate states: Russia was eyeing Austro-Hungarian territories in the Balkans, and France and Britain had clashed with German ambitions in Morocco a few years earlier. This is ultimately what happened: several empires collapsed in the war and the victorious empires scooped up their captured colonies. The First World War had dramatic political and demographic effects on the European victors France and the United Kingdom, and this included their seizure of former German and Ottoman territories. The result was that the British Empire was at its largest ever in terms of territory and population in the 1920s, with the addition of new territories like Mesopotamia and Palestine.

The war was also a colonial war in the sense that when imperial powers went to war, their colonies and territories were mobilized as well, whether they wished to be or not. Even though the white dominions now had control over most of their domestic affairs, their subordinate status meant that

Britain retained command over foreign policy. Britain thus mobilized troops from colonies across the globe: about 6 million people from Britain (slightly over 10 percent of the total population) served alongside 2.5 million troops from across the empire. White dominions Canada, Australia, New Zealand, and South Africa contributed around 1 million troops—a significant number given the size of their populations of around 14 million.[3] For the Antipodes in particular, the ANZAC troops, as they were known, were a source of national pride, and became renowned in myth for their fighting at battles in Gallipoli. But India, with a total population larger than Britain's, also contributed 1.5 million troops. In some ways, the South Asians' sacrifice was the least lauded and recognized. During the war the white dominions were privy to and part of decision making in the British Cabinet. After the war several dominions were awarded former German colonies to manage, like little imperial apprentices who were given more responsibilities in recognition of their grown-up behavior. German South West Africa, for example, became a South African territory and remained one until the 1960s. India, instead, expected to be recognized with significant progress toward democratic participation and self-government, and was sorely disappointed.

Colonial regions were also affected by the war by dint of being deeply enmeshed in webs of imperial trade and transport, and this is one way in which the wine industry was directly crippled by the war—although not immediately or uniformly. The temporary closure and then devastation of many European vineyards during the First World War actually gave a short-term comparative boost to colonial wines. The battlegrounds of the Western Front were close to the vineyards of Champagne, and international newspapers described troops marching through vineyards and laborers picking ripe grapes under the sound of shelling.[4] Many agricultural laborers left their posts to serve in the military, and this deprived vineyards of their workers—this was true of Australia as much as France, although Australian vineyards were spared actual fighting. German wines, which had been popular in Britain before the war, became somewhat taboo.

THEIR LOSS, OUR GAIN

In the decade before the First World War, only about 8 percent of wine imports into Britain came from the empire. These were predominantly from Australia, with a much smaller fraction from the Cape, Malta, and Cyprus.

The rest came from European producers, dominated by France, Germany, Spain, and Portugal. This, as we have seen, was a significant shift from the mid-nineteenth century, when half of the wine in Britain came from Portugal, Cape wine was more popular than French, and Australia had not yet entered the market.

By 1915, overall wine imports into Britain had fallen about 20 percent, from every country, but the percentage of wine from the empire had actually risen to over 10 percent of imports. This was a small rise, and the overall volume was not larger than it had been, but it meant that colonial producers (principally Australian) held their own, and even enjoyed a relative market boost, due to the war's impact on the competition.

Imports continued to drop throughout the war, partly due to production and trade conditions, but also because of British restrictions on alcohol purchases. When the war ended in late 1918, and European vineyards began producing again and also exporting wine from prewar and wartime vintages, British wine imports skyrocketed. Overall imports of colonial wine climbed, too, but their brief wartime advantage was lost. It would not be until a decade later that colonial wines would reclaim their market share, as we will see in the next few chapters.

There were deep fears in Britain that alcohol consumption would weaken the war effort, distracting workers or making them less efficient. Joseph Yeomans has described how "drinking was the object of borderline hysteria during the First World War,"[5] and how national politicians, army generals, and Christian prelates joined with temperance societies, and issuing dire warnings that alcohol use could cost Britain the war. Alcohol consumption was presented as wasteful and immoral, as taking resources directly from the war effort, whether they be individuals' pocket money, or crops that went into domestic beer production that could have been used for food. During the war the government both set price controls and rationed foodstuffs, yet the cost of living still went up, even as many families learn to live with less income.

With nearly five million young men enlisted in the military (over the course of the war, out of a total British population of forty-four million), agriculture and industrial work were both increasingly entrusted to women. Working-class women had always done paid work (and most British women were working class), but there were specific wartime schemes to recruit women into new roles. The Women's Land Army recruited young women from cities and towns to work on understaffed farms, and there were munitions factories staffed entirely by young women. One morale-boosting

government poster trumpeted how "of the 500 different processes in muni-
tion work, upon which women are engaged, two-thirds had never been performed by a woman previously to a year ago."[6] Overall, 1.5 million women
formally entered the workforce, most with no provision for childcare. The
British economy was being held together by a thread; if these women workers
were tempted by drink, would it all fall apart?

Not every British elite was in favor of the abstinence movement. Gerald
Burgoyne wrote that on the Western Front, alcohol was hard to come by, and
he was deeply critical of men in his troops who would hoard new rum deliveries and not share evenly with the entire group. He viewed small amounts of
alcohol as fortifying and comforting in the dark, damp, and dangerous conditions of the Front, where he was burying soldiers on a regular basis. "A drop
of rum in our tea worked wonders," he wrote, and he grumbled that "Sir
Victor Horsley and all the drink cranks can say what they like about the issue
of rum to the troops, and drink generally, but if instead of writing from the
comforts of a nice cosy room, they'd put in a few days in the trenches I am
sure they'd change their mind."[7] Horsley, a pioneering neuroscientist and a
high-profile temperance campaigner, did in fact serve in the First World War,
both in the Western Front and the Middle East, and in spite of being in his
late fifties. He died a field surgeon in Mesopotamia.[8] But this experience did
not, as far as we can tell, temper his temperance.

For the first year of the war, British abstinence from alcohol took on a
patriotic element with a voluntary pledge campaign championed by the
Church of England and temperance groups (in which individuals, many of
them women, would pledge to abstain for the duration of the war).[9] In May
1915, the government took things a step further by creating the Central
Control Board (CCB) through the Defense of the Realm Act. The CCB was
empowered to enact restrictions on alcohol in the name of "national effi-
ciency," and it began by restricting open hours of licensed premises in cities
and regions that were vital to the war effort (mainly ports and the locations
of major munitions factories). This meant that in some cases, pubs could only
sell alcohol during five hours specific hours in a day, down from eighteen
continuous hours before the war. Restrictions on off-license sales followed,
which impacted wine merchants and department store food halls. P. B.
Burgoyne registered his dissent in a London newspaper, and the article was
reprinted in Australian papers. He trotted out the familiar civilizational
argument: that while drunkenness caused by cheap spirits should certainly
be curbed, colonial wines should not have to suffer restrictions because they

were "the pure wines so much recommended and favoured by the late Mr. W. E. Gladstone," the products of an "innocent and valuable" imperial industry.[10] His protests made no headway in Britain, although that might not have been the point, anyway: his intended audience might have been his Australian producers and partners, to galvanize them and maintain their loyalty and business. The business records of wine sellers during the war show correspondence with suppliers who were suspending and amending contracts that they could no longer meet, due to import restrictions.[11]

Although the CCB's strictures seem to have been widely accepted, the CCB was also criticized for disproportionately targeting working-class people: "It is people who do not require to use the public house for refreshment who bring in rules of this kind."[12] This was certainly true. For Britain's wine-drinking elites, well-stocked cellars buffered the impact of the war and made CCB restrictions inconsequential. King's College, a constituent college of the University of Cambridge, maintained large wine cellars for its resident academic fellows and its students. The cellars provided both for official college feasts and events, and for purchase by residents through an internal off-license. King's had the following on hand in 1912: 1,604 bottles of French claret, 1,272 bottles of French champagne, 576 bottles of "Rudesheimer Hock" (German white wine from the northern Rheingau, almost certainly riesling), 846 bottles of sherry, and smaller quantities of whiskey (and whisky) and Madeira. Most reassuringly, there were twelve different types of port, for a total of 7,858 bottles.[13] This was for, at the very most, a few hundred residents. There were no bottles of colonial wine in this wealthy and discerning space.

As an asset, the King's College cellar lost about 10 percent of its total value over the course of the war, and the decline in the number of bottles must have been higher as wartime prices had become inflated. But the damage was minimal and short-lived. By 1920 the wine account had grown, and the College had patriotically purchased even *more* port: 111 dozen bottles of "Victory Port," a 1916 vintage bottled in 1919.[14] The economist and post-war negotiator John Maynard Keynes, who was also a fellow and the bursar at King's, did his part to stimulate European economies by spending £35 on wine in 1920—what kind of wines, we don't know, but he was fond of claret, and in 1920 this could have purchased twenty dozen bottles of claret. Perhaps he was hosting a party.[15]

For ordinary consumers, the beginning of the war even appeared to offer good deals. Whiteley's, a large West London department store that catered to a middle-class clientele, advertised special bargains that it had procured at auction in January 1915. These included: "French clarets from 12s. to 39s. per dozen . . . Swiss and Australian hocks, French white wines and burgundies." Some of these wines and spirits had never been intended for the colonial market, and had been auctioned because they could not be shipped. One bargain was "'Highland Breeze,' a Scotch whisky which was intended for Australia, but was cancelled when war broke out, is being sold at 48s. instead of 60s. per dozen."[16]

Domestic restrictions on alcohol aside, wine was still in circulation in the British world, although the very records that demonstrate the persistence of the wine trade also show how risky it had become. The First World War was fought on several fronts, including in the northern Atlantic, where ships were often diverted or sunk due to naval battles. Insurance records for one British ship downed in the war, for example, showed a payout for £160 in 1916 for the wine that was guzzled by the sea (worth approximately £11,000 in 2018 money).[17]

Any short boost to wine sales in Britain, and indeed most enthusiasm for a war that many had predicted would be over by Christmas of 1914, dwindled in 1915. By the end of 1915 the tone of Whiteley's advertising was shifting from gleeful to almost sober frugality. Advertising French clarets in October 1915, it counseled, "In these days of economy there is no better beverage than this beautiful and wholesome wine."[18]

In Australia, 1915 brought mixed predictions about the wine industry's fate. In addition to the direct effects of the war on trade, sales, and labor, there were environmental problems dogging some winemakers. The 1914–15 vintage in South Australia had been wracked by frost and then drought. The results were deplorable, and wine production would be about a quarter of what it had been a year or two before, an Adelaide newspaper warned. It interviewed an expert, who offered this analysis: "The outlook for supplies of wine for export is certainly gloomy. In one sense, the restriction of trade with the United Kingdom brought about through war, means that for the time being curtailed supplies do not represent such a serious matter to the London merchants. . . . On the other hand, looking ahead, we must anticipate in the United Kingdom a swinging back of the pendulum, and a large increase in trade as soon as the war is over." In a stiff-upper-lip, cheerily patriotic tone, the expert concluded on a high note: "I am entirely optimistic regarding the future of the great wine-producing industry of the Commonwealth [of Australia]. The London merchants are even now straining every nerve to secure that portion of the wine trade of Great Britain which was in the hands of the enemy."[19] This reference to the "enemy" meant German wines, and here the expert believed that South Australia was poised for export greatness, because it produced some white wines that were similar to German whites.[20] Would Echunga Hock finally have its moment of glory?

But the expert summoned by the Adelaide newspaper was, we should not be surprised to learn, a Mr. D'Arbley Burney, the Australian manager of P. B. Burgoyne's wine business. He had, therefore, both an excellent overview of the British import market for Australian wines, as well as a clearly vested interest in promoting it and even exaggerating its potential. But he was not the only one thinking so wishfully. The *Mudgee Guardian* newspaper wrote that Mudgee should increase its viticultural production in 1915, since "With the wine trade of France shattered by the ravages of war . . . there seems to be an unique opportunity of extending a branch of rural production which should be highly profitable." (Robinson and Johnson describe Mudgee as having an long-established wine industry that "dwelt in obscurity" until the 1970s,[21] so this was not to be in the short-term). For the rest of the war, though, Australian wine sellers faced similar problems to those of both France and Britain. Like France, Australia saw thousands of agricultural laborers depart for military service, many never to return. Like Britain, the Australian federation limited the opening hours of licensed premises, and in particular hotel bars. This was also in the name of decreasing drunkenness to support a cohesive war effort, and it drew vigorous criticism from industry groups. A dramatically-titled Citizens' Defense League was formed in Sydney to protest, and it argued that closing hotels early just fueled the black market in illicit booze, exposing street children to poisonous brews and putting the following jobs at risk: "hotel employees, barmen, barmaids and general brewers, carters, coopers, engineers, engine-drivers, firemen, greasers, fitters, architects, bottlers, brick-makers, bricklayers, laborers, plasterers and general builders, glass-blowers, produce merchants, wheelwrights, coachbuilders, blacksmiths, saddle and harness makers, tobacconists, ham and beef, shops, fish and oyster saloons. . . . [And] also affects vineyards, vineyard employees, and the great Australian Industry of wine-making."[22] This awareness of how alcohol production and consumption were knitted deep into many other trades has been stressed in previous chapters. It did not have much success with colonial legislators, though, especially in an era where many countries were restricting alcohol access. Other contemporary prohibitions—some due to the war, some due to the strength of temperance movements and moral panic—took place in Norway, Russia, Canada, Estonia, Sweden, and, in 1919, the United States. These were lauded by temperance activists and deplored by winemakers.[23] It is difficult to put a cash value on the cost of such restrictions, if any, on the colonial wine industries. New Zealand was the worst-off of all the colonial producers, when it came to prohibitionist tendencies. Individual alcohol-licensing districts could ban alcohol licenses, and several wine-producing districts around Auckland did so in the run-up to the First World War, creating a labyrinthine "depot" system whereby many vineyard owners were unable to make and sell their own wine, but could (at much cost and hassle) ship their grapes to wineries in another location.[24] Furthermore, New Zealand came close to enacting prohibition twice, in 1911 and 1919, in national referenda.

Some New Zealand winemakers had an even more immediate problem during the War, though, as Dalmatian immigrants were considered to be "Austrian." While they had, in fact, migrated to New Zealand from the Austro-Hungarian Empire, that was precisely because they were *not* loyal Austrians, and on the declaration of war some had demonstrated in support of Serbia separatism and organized fundraisers for the New Zealand (and thus British) war effort.[25] These New Zealand residents were now considered enemy aliens, though. Not being of British extraction, they were pressed into "national service" in camps instead, and dozens were interned for the "menace" they supposedly posed to Anglo society.[26] Their wine was referred to as "Austrian wine" by New Zealand's wartime prime minister, W. F. Massey, who portrayed it as a dangerous and menacing beverage that, like its creators, threatened the health and stability of New Zealand society.

VIN BLANC

On the whole the First World War was not good for colonial wine industries. However, it has frequently been credited with producing a new word for wine that is still used widely in Britain and the Antipodes today. That term, *plonk,* meaning a cheap or poor-quality wine, appears to be a distinct creation of the war. Many have argued that the word emerged as an anglified version of the French *vin blanc,* meaning white wine. Some attribute this specifically to Australian troops, others to "English" or "British Tommies."[27] The real history is both more varied and more interesting than the myth.

The *Digger Dialects* is a dictionary of wartime slang published by a veteran of the Australian Imperial Force, which fought in several fronts in Europe and the Middle East. This 1919 volume says that white went by *vin blank* and *von blink,* with *von-blinked* an adjective meaning inebriated. (Red wine was *vin roush.*) Plonk, on the other hand, meant "an artillery ammunition column."[28] A 1917 New Zealand source refers to *whizzy plonk* meaning, not champagne, but the sound of artillery shells falling through the sky.[29] In general plonk referred in Australian and New Zealand wartime sources to a sudden, loud sound, especially one caused by explosions or ammunition.[30] It was apparently also used as an expletive, or as a journalistic euphemism for an expletive: "Plonk you!" shouted the drunk before punching his landlady, an Australian court heard in 1925.[31]

None of this suggests, of course, that Anzac soldiers were using these slang terms because they were encountering wine for the first time. Rather, they were attempting to pronounce the French term so that they could order wine in a French establishment while on leave during the war. There is plenty of evidence that ordinary Australians had access to wine at home, and that if Anzac troops had never tasted it before going overseas, it would have been due to lack of interest rather than lack of opportunity. Burgoyne's war diaries recount how he and his troops were billeted in farmhouses of ordinary French and Belgian countrypeople, officers sleeping in the main house and common soldiers barracked in requisitioned barns. They would occasionally be sent to a village to retrieve supplies or messages, and this provided an opportunity to frequent villages shops and cafés, and have a drink if any were available.

If the "plonk" was used by soldiers to mean "wine," it seems to have taken a few years to percolate into general practice. It was definitely in common usage to mean terrible wine in 1937, when it was used by an Australian newspaper to describe the drinks consumed by homeless vagrants: one such "plonk" was a blend of "methylated spirits, ginger beer and boot polish."[32] In 1944, plonk appeared on a satirical menu of the Bread and Cheese Club in Melbourne, in keeping with the rest of the meal, which punned and poked fun at wartime shortages; for instance, "Fish: Soles (apply, with coupons, to Manager, Boot Department."[33] The two references to footwear appear entirely coincidental. In 1936 a New Zealand newspaper reported Australian wine merchants were angered at having their wine described as plonk or "pinkie"[34]—the latter which might be reasonably assumed to emerge from *von blink.* In a sensational 1937 article about the wide availability of cheap "wine" in Sydney—cheap enough that children had purchased a bottle and were "in a stupor"—the journalist noted that "pinkie" referred to cheap claret or port, and "paint" referred to a sticky, syrupy red wine that tasted like lead. Plonk, though, was "the genuined bottled headache, syrupy as paint, with a dynamite aftermath." The term derived from "the distinctive thud made when the steady drinker flops on the floor. Plonk!"[35]

The term seems to have been revived, with these connotations, among troops during the Second World War. An Anzac veteran described finding wine, cigarettes, and tinned food in Tobruk, Libya, after defeating Italian forces in 1941. "We called the Italian wine 'plonk,'" Sapper William Yates explained: "You drank a lot of it, and then—plonk!"[36] This does not refer to the wine being necessarily of poor or indifferent quality, but to the powers of its alcohol. The effect of finding this cache of wine, possibly warmed by the desert climate, on dehydrated, exhausted, and exhilirated troops, was probably a very big plonk indeed.

It is not clear how, and why, this term then entered the civilian British vernacular. The *Oxford English Dictionary* describes it as "an example of a word of Australian derivation adopted in Britain, and elsewhere, with little awareness of its origin," and gives early British uses as being in the 1960s.[37] Actually, there is some awareness of its origin among wine-writers, but it is true that the term evolved and entered the wine lexicon gradually and probably over both world wars, and not just the first. Its prominence in modern British speech may be a testament to the long and enduring links between British and Australian drinking cultures, and to how closely bound Britain, colonies, and dominions were during the First World War, and indeed throughout the twentieth century.

FOURTEEN

Fortification

THE DOMINIONS AND THE INTERWAR PERIOD

THE FIRST WORLD WAR WAS A WATERSHED for the empire in many ways. At least 1.25 million people across the empire died in fighting; more than 2 million were documented as injured.[1] These numbers do not include the millions who were psychologically scarred from the experience and struggled to readjust to everyday life, nor the number who perished from the Spanish flu in 1918. In addition to this human toll, the British Empire shifted its borders once again, as Ottoman and German colonies were redistributed to the European victors. The result was an empire that was physically larger and more populous than it had ever been.

For the wine-producing colonies of white settlement, though, the war came on the heels of other major changes in their status. Canada had become an independent federation in 1867. Australia followed next, fusing into a commonwealth of states in 1901, and New Zealand became self-governing in 1907. These processes were peaceful and democratic, to the extent that only white, male settlers were fully involved in the democratic process. The Cape emerged as part of the much larger Union of South Africa in 1910, a decade after a war Britain had fought to subdue Afrikaner nationalism in the mineral-rich plains of eastern South Africa. This had been an embarrassing pyrrhic victory for Britain—longer and much more costly than the imperial power could have imagined at the start. It was a dead loss for native South Africans, who got nothing out of the new state, and a win for white supremacism in the long term.

With self-governance, these colonies became dominions. Dominion status meant that although they were independent as far as domestic policy was concerned, they still maintained loyalty and deference to Britain. This included aligning foreign policy with that of Britain, and maintaining many of the symbols of Britishness—such as the monarch's profile adorning the currency. These four were generally enthusiastic dominions; the Irish Free State, on the other hand, also became a dominion in 1923, but to the chagrin of its leadership, and following four years of brutal anticolonial warfare. As a result of the creation of all these dominions, we start to see the use of a new term: the British Empire and Commonwealth, used to describe the fact that Britain had both colonies and independent partners, and projecting an image of them all joined together for their collective well-being. In 1931, the Statute of Westminster recognized that the dominions were, in fact, self-governing states.

The dominions began slowly, gingerly testing the boundaries of their new status. Their economies remained strongly intertwined with that of Britain and of each other; in that regard, there was little change. But the dominions were fortifying themselves in several ways. One was in their newfound assertiveness in colonial trade negotiations. The other was in the actual types of wine they were producing. In the 1920s, many colonial producers recommitted themselves to brandy production, both for sale as brandy itself and for fortification of their table wines for sale as "sherry" and "port." This was in response to supply issues, particularly in the case of South Africa, and also to reflect changing tastes in Britain. The dominions remained hungry for the Britain drinks market, and these beverages became more and more popular into the middle decades of the twentieth century.

SOUTH AFRICA

While colonial wines, especially Australian wines, had enjoyed a surge in popularity in the early years of the war, they were momentarily cast aside in the celebrations that followed the Armistice in November 1918. Both French and German wines were fervently restocked by retailers by 1921,[2] once new vintages were available. South Africa, anyway, had been muddling through its own existential and export crisis. In 1905 the Board of Horticulture assembled a committee to investigate and report on the status of the Cape wine industry, which was in "an alarming state of depression."[3] There were several reasons for this, most obviously the cost of responding to phylloxera and a season of overproduction in 1904. The committee, however, was keen to shift responsibility away from the farmers and onto specific policy issues, like the levels of excise taxes.

The Cape wine industry had suffered a triple punch in the late nineteenth and early twentieth centuries: bad weather conditions, pests, and diseases that attacked vines, and less reliable labor due to the expansion of industry and the glittering promise of better jobs in the diamond mines. What to do? Cape winemakers knew they were not alone in their struggles. Paul Nugent explains that at the turn of the twentieth century most wine farmers were "almost parochial,"[4] but "maintained an acquaintance with international events through the Afrikaans press."[5] There was even more: when wine workers in France went on strike, the English language press covered the developments in close detail. Although wine farmers might have been parochial in their personal relationships and travel experience, they were exposed to a lot of information about fluxes in international wine markets.

Cape Town newspapers hungrily slurped up news from France's Champagne region, where the wine industry was also in crisis and where a "war" was raging between wine growers and champagne houses in 1911. Following riots in some villages and the deployment of French troops, the government brokered rules for champagne production based on the precise origin of the grapes, protecting vine growers from being undercut by the importation of cheaper grapes from outside the region.

The Cape did not share Champagne's reputation for quality—indeed, throughout France's phylloxera crisis it had been alleged that poor-quality Cape wines were being fraudulently blended with French wines.[6] The French example, then, offered little hope to the Cape. And despite all of the Cape's problems with pests, mildew, and fungus, the catalyst to the 1905 commission was actually the overproduction of Cape wine, not crop failures.

Overproduction is a counterintuitive but common problem in wine. Knowing that, for example, South Africa was very keen to boost its wine exports, one might imagine that a very large bounty in one year would be a boon for exporters. Rather, overproduction could be devastating for wine producers. As we have seen, many colonial producers took a financial risk in producing wine: vines take three to five years to bear fruit, there is financial outlay in labor, storage, equipment, and so on, and it can take several years for a winemaker to receive payment for a vintage. This is true of wine making anywhere in the world, but for colonial winemakers targeting the British market, the particularly long distances in shipping were extra onerous. Winemakers also expected a certain price for their wine in order to make a profit, and, following basic laws of supply and demand, a sudden glut of wine in the market could drive the price down, meaning that all winemakers received less money for their wine. For those wine-makers already burdened with loans or debt that they expected to recoup once their wine was sold, a massive drop in price could be financially ruinous.

The great advantage of growing vines was a poisoned chalice, the 1905 South African report showed: vines could grow in areas that were unsuitable for agriculture, allowing the farmer to make a profit on poor land. But once there had been investments in machinery and vines, and the bottom fell out of the grape market, the farmer had little hope of converting vineyards into any other kind of profitable agriculture.[7] The farmer was stuck, having invested capital, and losing money.

One obvious solution for a savvy winemaker would be to withhold wine from the market, and cellar it for sales in a future year. There were several reasons this generally did not happen at the Cape. Many winemakers needed to sell their wine and could not wait a year or more to be paid. As they witnessed the herd rushing to offload wine, they followed suit, worried that the prices might get worse, rather than better. The other apparent reason was that most Cape wine was not suitably high quality for cellaring and keeping. All wine changes with age, but most wines do not improve with age. Cape wine producers were worried that if they didn't sell their wine young and fresh, they would be left with vinegar. One response was to shift toward brandy production to help salvage an overproduction of wine. Brandy would keep longer than bad wine, due to its higher alcohol content, and distillation might also hide the faults in the original wine. The Cape had always produced brandy, both on purpose and as a fallback plan for poor wine. However, as we have seen, its export reputation in the nineteenth century was for (supposedly) unfortified table wines.

By 1905, the committee noted, the quality of Cape wine was generally so poor that the committee recommended merchants put their export businesses on pause, and that the government assist in helping winemakers develop the skills to make their wine "more palatable to the European taste."[8] In the meantime, it had an ingenious plan to offload the terrible wine: sell it to the natives. "Permitting the sale of Colonial [sic] wine amongst that class of inhabitants" would assist in the "immediate relief of the wine-farmer."[9] It was quite clear whose livelihood was a priority for the state. The wine farmer, the committee believed, was a major employer and a generous patrician in the moral economy. It praised the vine grower's "superior social status and environment, his educational tastes and in many instances his advanced ideas on all matters connected with agricultural development."[10] This committee worked of and for the growers' interests, and it echoed the foundational arguments that transforming colonized land to vineyards was in the interest of civilizational advancement. There was no consideration for the rights, health, or desires of the native population. The actual recommendation about liquor laws was ultimately not accepted, and Black alcohol purchases remained criminalized.

Another recommendation of the committee that did eventually become a reality was the creation of cooperatives, "as a means of securing a uniform good quality of Cape Wine and Brandy." Across wine regions, it is not unusual for vine growers to sell some or all of their grapes to winemakers; several South Australian winemakers in the nineteenth century noted that they bought in grapes to supplement what they grew themselves. The agricultural cooperative movement had become popular across Europe and the larger British world in the nineteenth century. It had been successful in New Zealand in organizing dairy farmers to export butter, and had attracted many adherents in rural Ireland. The concept of a cooperative, as far as wine was concerned, was that the growers would sell their grapes to the cooperative, in exchange for a fair or set price. This would give the growers some stability and a reasonable expectation of income. In theory, it would lead to better wine, since by horizontally integrating the industry each intermediary could develop expertise in one area. Growers could be growers, and would not have to develop expertise in wine making, too, which the committee recognized was beyond most growers' current skill levels.

The cooperative movement in Europe was loosely associated with socialism,[11] even "crackpot utopianism,"[12] but in the Cape wine industry it was created to entrench the power of an elite and to maintain the racial order. It was created under the leadership of a Cape winemaker named C. W. Kohler, who had emerged as one of the main voices of the Cape wine lobby in the early twentieth century. Kohler advocated a multifaceted strategy to solve what he saw as the ills of the industry and, by extension, Cape society. First, winemakers should form a cooperative, which would ensure they could weather moments of over- and undersupply. Second, the cooperative should set price controls, to ensure that prices would not plummet below cost. And third, the cooperative should aggressively pursue distillation, both to preserve wines through fortification and avoid total loss of a harvest, and also to salvage wines that were probably unsaleable. Distillation yielded lots of Cape brandy, Cape "sherry," and Cape "port." That cooperative, established in 1918,

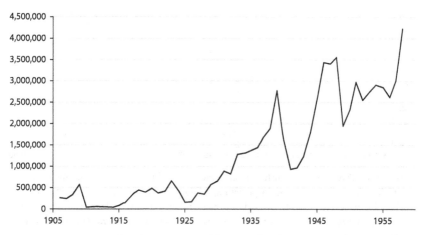

FIGURE 5. Quantity of total wine exported from South Africa, 1906–61. In imperial gallons. Twentieth-century South Africa was actually quite export-oriented, with most of its wine going to Britain and British territories. Source: South African Customs Statistical Bureau, *Annual Statements of Trade and Shipping*, 1906–1961 (Cape Town).

was known as the KWV (the Koöperatieve Wynbouwers Vereniging van Suid-Afrika, or Associated Cooperative of South African Winegrowers). Kohler became its first president.

It is often assumed that for most of the twentieth century, South Africa did not export much wine at all: that its export market had dried up in the late nineteenth century, that both farmers and merchants turned their attention to the South African domestic market, and that from 1918 until the early 1990s, "wine from the Cape . . . . hardly featured on overseas shelves."[13] Many scholars have taken this for granted. Starting with this assumption, they have emphasized the internal dynamics of the KWV. From this viewpoint, the KWV's strong emphasis on distillation appears to be a knee-jerk response to oversupply and domestic pressures.

While it is true that the KWV wanted to grow the domestic market, and that it did increasingly produce brandy and fortified wines, looking closely at the export data shows a very different story. Although the Cape did indeed go through some rough years in the early twentieth century, it recovered, and the volume of wine exported in the 1920s and 1930s rose steadily. Exports fluctuated between two hundred thousand and five hundred thousand imperial gallons between 1900 and 1922, before steadily beginning to climb, reach three and half million gallons in 1938 (see the charts in figs. 5 and 6). Increasingly, this wine was fortified.

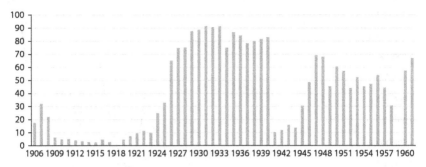

FIGURE 6. Percentage of South African wine exported to the U.K., 1906–61. Following tariff changes in the late 1920s, the percentage of South African wine bound for Britain sky-rocketed. The Second World War had a dramatic impact on this trade relationship. Source: *Reports of the Imperial Economic Committee, Twenty-third Report: Wine* (London: HMSO, 1932), appendix 4, table A.

Before the First World War nearly half of South African exports were unfortified—also referred to as "light" wines, or described as "claret" in the official documents.[14] Wines classified as "heavy," over "20 percent," "sherry" or "port," are counted as fortified. But that also meant that half of South African wines were *not* fortified. In the 1920s, the proportion of light wine plummeted, and by the early 1930s only about 15 percent of South African wine exports were light, making the remaining 85 percent fortified. South Africa thus became overwhelmingly associated with fortified wines, but not until the late 1920s.

This coincides with another important trend, which is the main destinations for South African wine exports. From 1906 to 1926, the single largest destination for South African wine was Mauritius. Mauritius, like the Cape itself, had been a Dutch colony, then a French one, and then became a British one officially in 1814. The hundreds of thousands of gallons of wine that were shipped to Mauritius were probably not for local consumption; rather, this large island in the Indian Ocean was an important shipping point, and wine was sent from Mauritius to other points east. (This is a problem with most export data: it tells us where wine was going when it left South Africa, and not where it eventually ended up.) Mauritius was followed by New Zealand, Britain, and several African territories: Belgian Congo, South West Africa (German and then British), and British East Africa. Cape wine was primarily sent to British colonies, followed by other European settlements in Africa. It was a colonial product for a colonial world.

A tricky question is what proportion of South Africa's wine was exported. Taking official customs export data, and comparing this to some recently published production data, shows that while less than a quarter of South Africa's wine was exported in 1918, it steadily climbed to 50 percent in the 1930s.[15] This flies in the face of the traditional view of South African wine exports, although there are gaps in data and sources that leave some uncertainty.[16] It makes sense, though, and South African wine continued to have a small but distinct cultural significance in Britain in the early 1920s. By 1920, the *Financial Times* reported its pleasure that after lean years, the wine industry in South Africa was "flourishing."[17] Kohler himself was quite savvy about international markets. In 1921 he made a visit to Britain, in coordination with the Union of South Africa Trade Commission, and, in his words, "laid the foundation for considerable expansion of trade in Cape wines and spirits."[18] His efforts were given a major boost by a new era of British tariffs, known as "imperial preference."

The question of customs tariffs on colonial goods had been simmering for some time. Tariffs continued to be an issue that resonated with ordinary voters in Britain, because people understood that tariffs were directly related to the price that they paid for food. The 1906 British general election was a shocking victory for the Liberal Party, in part because it campaigned on a free trade platform, promising a "big loaf" of bread over a Conservative-protectionist "little loaf." However, a small number of items had always been treated separately when it came to import duties, and that included alcohol. Even though Britain was largely dedicated to "free trade" between the end of the Corn Laws and the 1920s, wine had always been subject to duty. For wine producers, Britain had never been a truly free-trade economy, and for colonial wine producers, the lobbyable issue had long been why they were not consistently charged lower ("preferential") tariffs than countries like France or Spain.

One effect of the war, though, was that it accustomed people to a greater degree of government oversight of the economy. There were rationing and alcohol restrictions during the war, and the British public was generally compliant. After the war, the state accepted a higher level of responsibility for social services—including, for example, pensions for soldiers and their families—and that needed to be paid for through tax revenue. Ultimately, too, there seems to have been an increased awareness on the part of British people of the role that colonies had played in the war effort. Combined with some existential threats to the empire—the independence of Ireland, formerly an integral part of the United Kingdom, and increasing calls for self-rule in Asian and African colonies—the urgency of protecting the empire and the imperial economy seems to have converted much of the populace toward more economic intervention. On top of that, there was a global recession. In the 1920s, there had been an initial economic boom after the war, but by 1925 trouble was brewing. First, there was a general strike of British industries, which lasted well into 1926 and cramped the economy. Britain had pegged its currency to gold during the war, but it became clear after the war's end that the pound was overvalued, and it went off the gold standard in 1925. Then, in 1929, there was the infamous stock market collapse in the United States, which sent economic shockwaves throughout the world. Britain was on better economic foundations than some countries, but British people certainly felt the economic distress in the 1920s and 1930s.

Colonial trade became more difficult as a result of the worldwide recession, and this was frustrating and embarrassing to the empire. It was a time "when Great Britain is facing active competition of all kinds," a trade advisory committee warned in 1929, on the subject of British colonies and dominions exhibiting in a major trade fair in Antwerp: "the exhibition presents an opportunity of maintaining our national prestige which it would be unwise to neglect."[19] Furthermore, as the British secretary for colonies wrote in 1934, international trade deals were becoming more complex, and "for some time past it has been becoming increasingly difficult for the Colonial producer to sell his goods in certain foreign markets." This was a matter of interest to the United Kingdom itself, he argued to his colleagues in the Government, in large part because the colonies were critical buyers of British goods. If colonies sold fewer goods, colonial subjects would have less income. Any reduction in colonial purchasing power would both lessen the demand for British goods, and create resentment about preferential treatment for British goods.[20] The "bargaining position of the Colonial Empire is . . . a weak one," whereas "the bargaining position of the United Kingdom vis-à-vis the great majority of foreign countries is exceptionally strong."[21] If dominions and colonies could not help themselves, then Britain would have to help them directly.

However, the dominions did not watch these events unfold, but played an active role in asserting their own needs. At an Imperial Economic Conference in 1923 they lobbied for some reduction in tariffs on foodstuffs. This was granted but implemented in an unusual form, not as a direct cut, but through the creation of a promotional body, the Empire Marketing Board (EMB). Established in 1926, the EMB had a block grant to promote imperial goods in Britain and to sponsor research and development. This creative compromise was because the Conservative government did not have the parliamentary strength to implement the reductions, but still wished to address what its leader, Stanley Baldwin, called the urgent problem "of maintaining the moral and political unity of so widely scattered and diverse a commonwealth of nations."[22]

There was also a readjustment to wine tariffs in 1927, to the satisfaction of colonial producers. There was still a scheme to incentivize the production and consumption of lower-alcohol wines, but recognizing that "Empire wines naturally develop a higher alcoholic strength," the bar was set higher for them.[23] Foreign wines paid a 3s. duty per gallon up to twenty-five degrees (14.3 percent ABV), and then paid 8s. a gallon. For empire wines, the higher rate did not kick in until they reached twenty-seven degrees (15.43 percent ABV), and they only paid 2s. on wine up to twenty-seven degrees. For Empire wines between twenty-seven and forty-two degrees, the rate was 4s. a gallon. This was thus a doubly preferential duty, allowing higher alcoholic strength and also charging less duty on wines of equal strength.

The adjustment was what winemakers like Fallon had been pleading for fifty years earlier: the recognition that their wines could be naturally strong, and should not be considered to have been fortified when they were simply the product of a hot sun and ripe fruit. However, the real advantage with this new tariff scheme was for wines that *were* fortified. This was bad news for Portugal and Spain: colonial "port" and "sherry" would pay half as much duty as the original, genuine article.

No wonder, then, that Australia and South Africa began producing and exporting more fortified wines. As we have seen, most colonial wines in the nineteenth century were not styled as fortified wines, but as still table wines. The shift is evident in South African exports, the transition to fortified wines and to British markets intensifying after 1927. Whereas up until 1926 South African wine was dispersed to many destinations, though principally Mauritius, after 1927 it became overwhelmingly a U.K. trade. In 1925 only about one-third of South African wine went to Britain; by 1932, over 90 percent of it was U.K.-bound (see fig. 7). In other words: the new British tariffs fundamentally changed the type, volume, and destination of South African wine exports, toward large quantities of fortified wine going directly to Britain. (Most of this wine, incidentally, was bulk wine, not wine shipped in bottles.) Looking closely at this data, we can clearly see how South Africa became associated in Britain with fortified wines, particularly "port" and "sherry" styles. Sociologist Joachim Ewert concludes that it was the KWV's

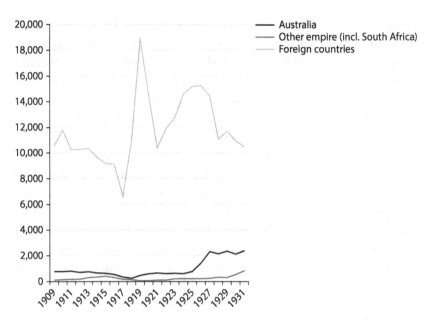

FIGURE 7. Australian, other empire, and foreign (European) wine imports to the U.K., 1909–31. In thousands of gallons. The impact of the First World War on European wine supply, and the decreases in tariffs on colonial wines in the 1920s, meant that colonial wine rose to one-quarter of British imports by 1931. Source: *Reports of the Imperial Economic Committee. Twenty-third Report: Wine* (London: HMSO, 1932), appendix 4, table A, *United Kingdom: Wine Entered for Home Consumption.*

price-fixing, rigid production quotas, and "quasi-export monopoly" that created South Africa's twentieth-century reputation for low-quality fortified wine and brandy. As a result, he concludes, with few exceptions, "wine from the Cape passed as a characterless product and hardly featured on overseas shelves." This is not wrong, but it was the British market that made this strategy appealing. In fact, looking at the trends in South African wine exports, it is clear that the South African wine industry was acutely impacted by international events in general. Exports dropped dramatically during both the First and Second World Wars. They rose sharply in the late 1920s with the creation of the new British preferential tariff. There are two dips in 1948 and around 1960, possibly when the declaration of apartheid and then the Sharpesville massacre made British consumers momentarily hesitate on whether it was ethical to buy South African wine. [24]

The 1927 tariffs were intended to encourage empire trade in an era of instability and uncertainty. As far as colonial wine was concerned, they were a resounding success. In the late 1920s the proportion of British wine imports that came from colonies and dominions rose to over 20 percent, the largest it had ever been. The EMB boasted in an internal report that imports of colonial wine into Britain had risen 94 percent between 1924 and 1931.[25] The EMB noted this with particular satisfaction that it was fulfilling its mission, because wine is one of the products "of which, broadly speaking, the country of origin can be ascertained by a customer in the retail shop."[26] People knew that they were buying empire with their colonial wine.

By 1931 23 percent of the wine entering Britain for domestic consumption was from the empire, with the largest single supplier being Australia (17 percent). This means, too, that the South African trade was very asymmetric, as it had been in the nineteenth century: South African wine was not very important to the British market, but the British wine market was critically important to South African wine. The tariffs allowed importers of colonial wine to express optimism in the face of general economic challenges. After all, as with the First World War, colonial wine also stood to gain from disruptions to European wine producers. In 1936 the chairman of the Victoria Wine Company, one of the largest wine and spirit merchants in Britain, noted that, "The unsettled nature of world politics has caused us a certain amount of anxiety with regard in particular to the buying of our bulk wines from Continental countries," whereas, "I am pleased to report that Empire products are in increasing demand and our agency arrangements with leading Australian shippers enable us to offer extremely good value in these wines."[27]

When a major Imperial Economic Conference was convened in Ottawa in 1932 to negotiate imperial trade deals, the dominions were ready, and they won long-term concessions for imperial preference. In preparation for the conference, an Imperial Economic Committee had prepared a series of lengthy research reports on different empire goods. The twenty-third report was on wine and was an extensive ninety-two pages long. Wine, as a commodity of the empire, was taken seriously and decisions about its trade trajectory would increasingly be data-based, not anecdotal or sentimental.

The Ottawa trade deals marked, for historian Frank Trentmann, the ultimate "decline of Free Trade as a secular religion" among the British public.[28] Tariffs and trade were a very divisive issue in British party politics in the 1920s and early 1930s, but were less and less exciting to British consumers. They were greatly exciting to colonial wine producers and their advocates and, as we shall see, brought new tastes to a new type of British consumer.

FIFTEEN

Crude Potions

THE BRITISH MARKET FOR EMPIRE WINES

"CYPRUS WINES WERE JUSTLY FAMOUS for ten centuries up to the Middle Ages," a columnist for the *Financial Times* wrote in 1928, "Then the Turks took the island and destroyed the industry." For shame! Thank goodness for British initiative: "Fifty years ago it was revived, but it is only within the last five years that attempts have been made to recover the overseas popularity which it once enjoyed."[1] The journalist recounted how Imperial Preference had whetted the appetites of both Cypriot exporters and London importers, and that the search was on to find a port-style wine "to suit the British palate."[2]

Whose palate was that, and what did it want? This question has absorbed both interwar wine merchants and modern historians. Of course, taste is reflexive: just as retailers try to sell wines that consumers want, consumers learn what they want through advertising, trying new things, and social influence. The expansion of public transportation and the press created numerous opportunities for retailers to promote their wines to the British public, and to convince them that wine should be part of their lives.

In the interwar period, it was an increasingly middle-class palate, and, as we have seen, it was increasingly for the fortified colonial wines. Echoing much older advice about the social benefits of good wine, a 1922 British wine guide wrote approvingly about South African wines: "not precisely wine for connoisseurs, they are sound and wholesome beverages for citizens of modest means."[3] On the other hand, a feature in the London *Times* in 1922 on South African wines concluded, somewhat snobbishly, that the young country had great potential for excellent wine production, but that currently it was a "'canteen' trade," and producers would have to increase quality if they hoped to sell to an English market.[4] It is clear that these two different writers are

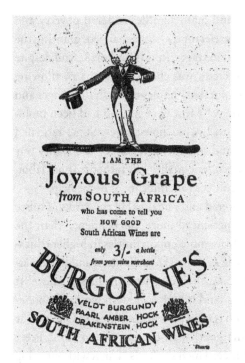

I AM THE

Joyous Grape

from SOUTH AFRICA

who has come to tell you
HOW GOOD
South African Wines are

only 3/- *a bottle*
from your wine merchant

BURGOYNE'S

VELDT BURGUNDY
PAARL AMBER HOCK
DRAKENSTEIN HOCK
SOUTH AFRICAN WINES

FIGURE 8. "The Joyous Grape"; an advertisement for Burgoyne's wines, emphasizing European wine styles, conviviality, and affordability. "Burgoyne's South African Wines," *Sunday Times,* April 10, 1927.

assessing South African wine for different audiences. For ordinary British people who needed a "wholesome" wine, who would benefit socially from a wine that transmitted respectability and thrift, then colonial wine was absolutely appropriate. But those with refined palates would turn up their noses at this same beverage. In fact, the *Times,* a newspaper quite confident in its own superior taste, had a habit of jeering at colonial wines. Reviewing an art exhibition in 1928, its culture journalist remarked that moving from beautiful paintings to some weaker ones, was "like drinking Empire Wine after Tokay."[5] Both Australian and South African wines were still referred to in the British press as "colonial wines" up until the Second World War. Importers and advertisers preferred the more imposing term "imperial wine," perhaps feeling that "colonial" was pejorative, and official government documents often wrote "Empire wines" to stress solidarity and to chime with "Buy Empire" sentiments.

It is really not surprising that the market for colonial wines in Britain changed during the interwar years, because British society had been profoundly jolted by the First World War. Many young people were killed or permanently disabled by the war, and many families suffered poverty and deprivation. On the positive side, the electoral system changed, granting the vote to all men in 1918 and to women in stages, in 1918 and 1928. And despite the global economic constrictions, credit was cheap in the 1920s, allowing more middle-class British people to purchase homes through mortgages and to indulge in a new era of domesticity.[6] Most women who had been mobilized into wartime work returned to lives as housewives. Some returned home with regret and frustration, and some with relief, for the reality was that most paid work did not offer gender equality but rather manual labor, no chance of promotion, and no resources for childcare or home help.

Some young women, though, entered and remained in the ranks of office work and the professions. They experienced more independence than the previous generation and benefited from more opportunities in higher education. This meant, too, that they made decisions as consumers, and wine marketing start to shift to take into account their interests. The mystery novelist Dorothy Sayers's character Ann Dorland is such a modern woman, a bohemian Londoner who works and who is used to drinking "horrid Chianti" at parties. When she dines with the gentleman-detective hero Lord Peter Wimsey, he offers her Romani-Contée, which she finds "harsh without being thin."[7] She does not have an educated palate, but she is a woman out in the world who is unafraid to try new things.

Lord Peter graciously demurs at this sacrilegious condemnation of one of Burgundy's great wines. Other men of his social class were vexed and befuddled. W. K. Haselden, a cartoonist for the very popular middle-class tabloid the *Daily Mirror*, gently satirized the changing social milieu with a cartoon entitled "Are the Good Club Days Ended?" His cartoon showed a gentleman seated for lunch expressing shock at this "new day," where a waitress casually handed him a bottle wine, instead of a butler formally presenting it.[8] *Punch* poked fun at "A speaker at a Wine Luncheon [who] suggested that it would greatly help if wives were to be given wine money, as well as a dress-allowance, in order that they might be able to soothe their husbands with vintages." *Punch* found the idea absurd. Writers who felt threatened by demographic and social changes in the interwar period had a tendency to romanticize and overstate the "good club days." What could be more ridiculous, these two journalists are asking, than leaving something as important as wine selection to women? The *Punch* snippet is a reminder not only that wine expertise was associated with men, but also that many upper-middle-class British women lacked financial independence in the interwar era.[9]

However, wine had never been the exclusive preserve of the clubbable, wealthy, white Englishman. It may have been strongly associated with this class of people, and it might have been consumed more frequently by this group than by other social groups, but upper-class Englishmen did not have a monopoly on wine. Port wine was strongly associated with middle-class men in the eighteenth century,[10] women (and children!) drank wine, and we have seen in the nineteenth century how colonial wines were affordable options that appealed specifically to middle-class drinkers. This class profile for colonial wines became all the more apparent in the late 1920s, when colonial wine became a much more significant proportion of British wine consumption. The interwar period was also a time of widening participation in public drinking: David Gutzke has argued that the "improved pubs" of the interwar period (those that offered seating, carpeting, and a lounge area) were designed to attract more female clientele, and were increasingly frequented by middle-class women and what he calls "respectable working-class ones as well."[11] A growing acceptance of the respectability of drinking would open the door for more domestic consumption, too.

OFF-LICENSES

Indeed, Britain also saw the expansion of "off-licences" that catered to people of ordinary means. These are businesses that have a license to sell alcohol for consumption off of the premises, as distinct from the "on-trade," which refers to restaurants, bars, and hotels that serve alcohol on location.

In the interwar period most foods for home consumption were still purchased through a range of specialized dealers: fruits and vegetables from greengrocers, meat from butchers, wine from off-licences, and so on. If a historian only looked at the records of famous and exclusive wine merchants, they would erroneously conclude that no one was drinking colonial wine in the interwar period. Berry Brothers and Rudd, one of Britain's longest-established wine merchants, had rich cellars of exquisite fine wines, all of them European. Food halls tell a different story. Buying wine in a food hall or a large, national chain of off-licences could offer a more impersonal buying experience than the small wine-merchant. To a consumer who was not very familiar with wine, that could be attractive: there would be less fear of judgment from the sales staff, less embarrassment about prices, and perhaps more ability to browse independently. Department stores were not coy about the prices for their wines. Harrods, not quite as famous in the 1920s as it would be later, was loudly advertising the "Champagne of Australia!" in 1924 (in the *Times*, no less), "a unique opportunity to obtain a fine Empire Wine for Christmas Festivities" at special low prices.[12] The low prices were because Harrods purchased the wine as a job lot after the Wembley Imperial Exhibition; it was probably better for the producer, Romalo, to sell it cheap than to ship it home.

Whiteley's, located in West London in Bayswater, was another large department store with a food hall, and it catered to a diverse clientele in a neighborhood that had de-gentrified over the late Victorian and Edwardian period. Sarah Cheang, an art historian who has studied Whiteley's marketing of furniture and orientalist objects, has shown how the department store catered to a middle- and working-class clientele that wanted a bit of exoticism for their homes, but presented in a safe and nonintimidating way.[13] The same is true of Whiteley's wine advertisements, which were simultaneously enthusiastic, bland, and reassuring. Wine writing in general in the interwar period (and indeed, up through the 1970s) was vague and gave very little description of what the wines actually tasted like. The extent of the vocabulary used to describe wines was usually: fruity, sweet, dry, light, or heavy. Beyond that, consumers are told that wines are flavorful, or beautiful, or of excellent quality; there is no discussion of particular aromas or structures. This suggests the retailer's low expectations of the consumer's wine knowledge and the consumer's desire to be reassured in their choices. One of the most detailed descriptions in a Whiteley's advertisement from this period was for a 1920 Graves Superior, described as "A full round wine which will please the most fastidious."[14] One can easily imagine this description resonating with a nervous wine buyer who was entertaining. This customer does not need to know that the Graves has notes of citrus and balanced acidity; this customer needs to know that the wine will meet the approval of her exacting mother-in-law, who might also be full and round.

In general, wine lists of this era—that is, the flyers with the names and prices of wines offered by a merchant—contained scant description of the wines themselves. They were almost always divided by region, and by the 1920s the empire constituted a single, separate region within most lists. Generally there were the following styles of colonial wines on offer: hock, burgundy, claret, port (red, white, and tawny), and sherry. Although some colonial wines had names—Burgoyne sold a "Kangaroo Burgundy" and "Tintara," for example—wine lists of retailers and merchants tell us little else: not the alcoholic volume, not the vineyard of origin, and certainly not the vintage year. "Australian burgundy" was a common name for a wine, and that was as much as the consumer would learn, along with the price.

European styles remained the benchmark and, frequently, the name of the style, although there were some musings in the industry about breaking out on their own. France was starting to assert its domain over its own place names, although it would be unable to defend this right for several decades.[15] Percy Wilkinson, director of the Commonwealth Laboratory, was worried about the intellectual property dimensions of Australia continuing to use French names, and he also saw this as "a marked obsession for a mistaken ideal".[16] Australian wines had different characteristics from European wines, and their names should reflect this. He suggested instead that Australia copyright its own names that were inspired by European styles but distinctly Australian—distinct in the sense that they would all end in *ia*. Australian Burgundy would become "Burgalia," hock would become "Hokalia," and Hermitage "Hermalia." Curiously, or perhaps for brand consistency, he thought that Shiraz should become "Shiralia"; this is surprising because in this case the word Shiraz is referring to the grape, not the place, and referring to it as Shiraz was distinctly not French.[17] Even more curiously, and perhaps disappointingly, Wilkinson's scheme never caught on.

Another commonality in wine lists is that colonial wines were usually not the cheapest, but the second cheapest wines on the wine lists. For consumers who know nothing about wine and are on a budget, choosing the second cheapest wine often seems like a clever strategy. Perhaps retailers knew this, and priced their colonial wines accordingly, so that buyers would feel reassured rather than cheap. The Army and Navy Stores offered, in the early 1930s, an "Empire Wine" Christmas hamper, significantly cheaper than its standard all-European one.[18] The Army and Navy Stores was located in London's upscale Victoria; open to the public, it had been initially established as a cooperative to provide affordable goods for military families, so it combined respectability with frugality. Whiteley's 1934 Christmas offerings included an own-brand sparkling wine called "Empress of Britain," a white-label muscatel from French grapes (supposedly), advertised right under its empire wines.[19]

Indeed, good value for money was one of the main messages that wine merchants tried to convey about colonial wine in the interwar period. The other message was that choosing colonial wine was vaguely patriotic, which in itself is a message that aims to reassure the buyer in the wisdom of their choice. "You can combine patriotism and economy," a British wine writer trilled in 1924, "And you get the added satisfaction in buying Empire wines in realizing you are keeping the money in the family."[20]

One of the major proponents of this message was Victoria Wine, a large chain of off-licenses, established in the 1860s to provide "rich wine for people who were not (necessarily) rich." Victoria Wine was a pioneer of both new selling techniques (such as free tastings) in its shops, and also an early adopter of Australian wines.[21] Its headquarters were in Whitechapel, East London, and by 1924 it had 104 shops, most in the Greater London area.[22] This made it one of the most significant actors in British wine retailing. One of its main selling points was its keen prices, thanks to its large purchasing power and cash-only sales. Unlike an independent wine merchant who might recommend certain wines based on his or her palate alone, Victoria Wine worked out individual contracts with each supplier that specified how the wines would be marketed. Burgoyne had a premium contract, in that he supplied ten different wines to Victoria Wine, was guaranteed his wines listed at the top of the price list, and would have a "showcard (not less than 12″ × 10″) exhibited in good position in window and shop."[23]

Victoria Wine also sold individual bottles, which assumed that most of its customers did not have cellars and were buying wine to consume soon. This was a different model from a wine merchant who had a more personalized and long-term relationship with a client who purchased wine in cases or casks for cellaring. "Our branches are your wine cellar," was the Victoria Wine Company advertising slogan in 1924, and the chairman of its board of directors congratulated his colleagues that the company "is serving a very real need of present-day life."[24] In 1938, the chairman was explaining the need to purchase more motor vehicles for deliveries: "While in the past our customers bought their requirements by the dozen, today they often require daily deliveries as they have no cellar accommodation for storage."[25]

Daily deliveries mean daily consumption, but selling single bottles also was attractive to customers who could not afford to buy wine by the case. In fact, Victoria Wine offered wines in both bottles and half-bottles, as did Whiteley's, and for its Australian wines it also offered flagons and half-flagons. Bottle sizes were not standardized until the 1870s (and since most wine was sold in bulk, this made little differences to many consumers), when a "wine bottle" was set at one-sixth of an imperial gallon, or 26.67 ounces. This is equivalent to 760ml, which is slightly larger than the now-standard 750ml wine bottle. The flagon was bigger: two imperial pints, or 40 imperial ounces, or a bottle-and-a-half. A half-flagon was therefore one imperial pint, or 20 ounces. Flagons were good value for consumers, the wine costing about 15 to 20 percent less per ounce than for a bottle. Arthur and Co., an independent wine merchant and off-license located on slightly seedy Ladbroke Grove in North Kensington, also sold colonial wines in flagons and in individual bottles.[26]

Burgoyne ran an advertisement in British newspapers in the early 1920s about the flagon bottle, which the firm claimed its venerable founder had created for Australian fine wines. The distinctive bottle design, the advertising copywriters claimed, was based on a bottle found in the archaeological remains of the Great Fire of London. Perhaps because it was grounded (literally) in the bedrock of London, "this particular form of bottle greatly helped to break down the prejudices of a conservative people against new articles," and this was one of the reasons Burgoyne was "the founder of the Empire Wine Industry." Burgoyne's company marketing strategy is transparent and relentless: draw on an emotive and dramatic moment in London history, appeal to empire pride, laud Burgoyne for his industriousness, and associate it with good health. Yes, Burgoyne's flagons were wholesome and civilized: Tintara Burgundy, "grown on ferruginous soil, is the most remarkable natural tonic known—and it is as good as a dinner beverage as a recuperative."[27] Wine does contain small amounts of iron, although the tannins in red wine might prevent its absorption, and anyway it is not clear that iron-rich soil results in iron-richer wine. That did not matter. Nutritional science was in vogue in Britain, with vitamins having been discovered and recently popularized, so while this advertisement continues in a century-old tradition of promoting colonial wines as healthy, the specific appeal to nutrition would have been a modern spin in 1923.[28]

Many British people were not drinking colonial wine for the nutritional benefits. A buyer for Whitbread Brewers, which was a major owner of pubs, wrote in his notes for a South African wine in 1947: "Sweet rather sickly with fiery after taste [sic] and the same S.A. nose. No doubt popular with the lower classes."[29] This was certainly snobbery, but it also reflected how the affordability of colonial wines made them popular for those who sought strong alcohol at a low price. In a 1939 photo essay about Glasgow, the *Picture Post* reported that in Glasgow's working-class pubs and working men's clubs, "'Red Biddy'—methylated spirits and Empire wine—once popular, is now being suppressed."[30] Perhaps Burgoyne's advertisements were aimed at reclaiming respectability for his wines, so that middle-class consumers could purchase it without embarrassment.

In the 1930s the London Tube introduced new trains on its Circle Line, with moquette seats running the length of the carriage. During crowded peak hours, standing passengers would grab handrails that hung from the ceilings and try not to sway into their fellow passengers. They might pass the time by perusing the border of ads above the windows: "Drink and enjoy Lipton's Tea ... Learn to drive at the British School of Motoring ... Fearons. Holborn Viaduct EC1. Wine merchants for 250 years."[31]

Likewise, Burgoyne's advertisements were popping up everywhere in Britain: in newspapers, in trams, at train stations and bus stops.[32] Cities continued to grow and so did public transportation, and with it advertising opportunities. The Empire Marketing Board's "Buy Empire" campaign produced, among other things, a wide range of colorful and iconic posters that plastered public transport in the late 1920s and 1930s. The London Underground subway system, or Tube, invited travelers to visit the empire by Tube, noting the imperial associations of various stops. Its posters showed the names of colonies and dominions decorated with flora and fauna, and South Africa and Australia hang heavy with scrolls of vines and bunches of grapes.[33] The EMB also produced several colorful posters of vineyards and still lifes with wine.

The EMB and associated government agencies dedicated to imperial trade produced a good body of literature, too, that tells us about efforts to promote wine. An extensive government-commissioned report concluded that reductions in colonial wine tariffs had doubled British demand for Australian and South African wines, and that this market share was directly at the expense of European wines.[34] However, the advertising and marketing of colonial wines in the interwar period shows that colonial wines were not being targeted at the traditional wine-drinking elite, but toward people who did not normally drink wine; that if lowering the price of colonial wine boosted sales, it was not from encouraging drinkers of fine French wine to change their preferences, but by introducing new drinkers to colonial wine.

By the mid-1930s the apparent success of colonial wines was causing some alarm, not to the European wine importers, but to domestic brewers of beer. A major brewery chairman raised the alarm in 1936 that low tariffs were harming his trade: "the preferential duty being so light ... taking into account the high percentage of alcohol they contain, [colonial wines] are the cheapest form of alcoholic beverage that is offered to the public at the present time. They are displacing drinks such as beer and cider."[35] Wine was a long way from displacing beer in British alcohol consumption—Britain was still largely a nation of beer drinkers—but wine was becoming popular enough among working- and middle-class consumers that brewers were worried.

Complementing the work of the EMB (though entirely separate from it), in 1929 Australia created an Overseas Wine Marketing Board to focus on selling more wine in the British market. In 1936 its name changed to the Australian Wine Board. The Wine Board established a London office, set agreed minimum prices for two types of wine ("sweet red" and "sweet white"), and paid for newspaper advertising and networking with wine retailers. In 1936, it contributed material for many "Pageants of Empire" in British schools. The board was very satisfied with the state of the British market by the late 1930s: "Consequent on returning prosperity to the country with decreased unemployment resulting in freer spending, the public naturally again began to buy more wine."[36] The Canadian market was much less satisfactory for Australian exports, though, "and it is difficult to determine the reason." If the many complaints made to the Canadian premier by alcohol importers are to be believed, the reason was that Canada put high duties on imported alcohol, and sales tax, too, both of which hurt empire producers.[37]

The EMB's efforts were complemented by agricultural research. The Imperial Institute was chaired by Lieutenant-General Sir William Furse, and he described it as "a clearing house of information regarding the economic utilisation of all manner of raw products—animal, vegetable or mineral." Wine was vegetable. The institute had scientists who could answer enquiries from both growers and government, and laboratories to test samples, and Furse reported that it had received enquiries about wine.[38] Research into fruit production was carried out by scientists at a research institute in East Malling, Kent (a county in the southeast, known as the "garden of England"). Grapes fell under its aegis, although there were no major EMB-funded projects related to wine quality or production, except for a memorandum on Viticultural Research and a longer "Chemistry of Wine Making [sic]: A Report on Oenological Research." On one level this would suggest that wine was relatively marginal in imperial trade, compared to fruit and grain production. But this would be true even in a country with very high wine consumption; modern-day France, one of the world's largest wine producers, still only devotes 3 percent of its agricultural land to vineyards.[39] If anything, U.K.-based research stations were late to the game and possibly superfluous, because by then the dominions had their own stations and viticultural experts.

N.Z. WAERENGA WINES

MANUFACTURED AND BOTTLED BY
THE DEPARTMENT OF AGRICULTURE

Distributed by   TELEPHONE 41-587
JAMES J. JOYCE,
Depot: COLWILL CHAMBERS,
SWANSON ST., AUCKLAND,C.1.
Telegraphic Address, STATWIN, Auckland.

Mr. W. Field,   1st November, 1934.
The Terrace,
WELLINGTON.

Dear Sir:
          Wines produced at the Government Farm, by
the Department of Agriculture, will be forwarded
to your district in December, care of the N. Z.
Express Co., Wellington. Should you desire
to share in the distribution the enclosed requisi-
tion, together with remittance, must be posted
in the Wellington district not later than the 15th
December.

          For your further information the Department
has been producing wine for over thirty years, and
in view of the fact that the Government has now
decided to dispose of the vineyards, the oldest and
best wine produced at the farm will be made available to purchasers under this special Group
Delivery.

          The quality of the above is such, that
during my association with the product, as
distributor, I have never offered such remarkable
value; undoubtedly in the hands of private enterprise, this wine would be double or treble the
price fixed by the Department, and would still be
good buying. A trial will definitely convince
you that New Zealand can produce a quality wine
that compares more than favourably with the
imported article.

Postal Orders should be addressed:— Box 1806, G.P.O., AUCKLAND.

                              Yours faithfully,

                              James J. Joyce
                                   Distributor.

FIGURE 9. Waerenga wines, 1934. "N.Z. Waerenga Wines, manufactured and bottled by the Department of Agriculture. Distributed by James J. Joyce ... Auckland." Circular letter to Mr. W. Field, The Terrace, Wellington, November 1, 1934. Ephemera of quarto sizes relating to alcohol and alcoholic beverages and drink, in New Zealand. Courtesy of the Alexander Turnbull Library, Wellington, New Zealand.

That did not stop an enthusiastic civil servant and chairman of the EMB, Stephen Tallents, from undertaking his own little experiment in 1928. "We made it a rule, whenever we gave an official entertainment in the Board's name, to serve such drinks as light wines of a hock type from Australia or Paarl Amber from South Africa," he explained, but he noticed that many of his colleagues were reluctant to drink these "rather crude Empire potions."[40] A passing conversation with a chemist led Tallents to believe that bottling colonial wine in better-quality glass bottles would improve its maturation and allow it to keep longer. Eager to do his part for the empire, Tallents assembled an eight-man team of chemists and wine experts, including writer André Simon, Francis Berry of Berry Brothers, and Alfred Heath, the wine buyer for the Army and Navy Stores. The experiment was hushed in the officials records, because a board member—"a Scotsman, if I remember rightly," Tallents recalled, "demurred on temperance grounds."[41] He managed to finagle £1,230 of funding, though, which would have bought around twenty-seven hundred bottles of the Army and Navy Stores's finest claret (a 1924 Château Durfort-Vivens, a Margaux).[42]

The experiment involved three types of red wine—a French, an Australian, and a South African—and three different types of bottles, of varying qualities of glass. Each wine was placed in each of the types of bottles, and then laid down in a cellar near Charing Cross station in central London. After six months, the wines were tasted, "solemnly," but none of the experts could detect any difference in the wines. When the EMB was dissolved in 1933 and some of its duties passed on to the Imperial Economic Committee, Tallents hoped that it would take over the grave responsibility of tasting the wine at regular intervals.[43] This was not to be. As late as 1944, when most civil servants were otherwise preoccupied, Tallents had not given up the dream: he was writing to the committee to let them know that the Army and Navy Stores would host a tasting, if necessary.[44]

The EMB chairman's zest for colonial wines is both touching and pathetic. It does not seem to have generated any information or results that had an impact on the colonial wine industries. Like the foundation of these industries themselves, it was a scheme grounded in idealistic imperial principles rather than economic reality. Some people might like empire wines, the English poet W. H. Auden quipped in 1936,[45] in a way that suggested that those people had very dubious taste. Perhaps those people were very keen on the empire.

SIXTEEN

Doodle Bugs Destroyed Our Cellar

WINE IN THE SECOND WORLD WAR

A SOUTH AUSTRALIAN WINEMAKER NAMED HENRY MARTIN made a major visit to England in 1938.[1] He went by ship, leaving Adelaide on April 10 and arriving in Cape Town on May 20. In Cape Town, he disembarked to visit vineyards for a few days. He attended a rugby game, enjoyed taking photographs of the Paarl region until he ran out of film, and visited a viticultural station in Stellenbosch where experiments were being conducted on vine resistance. His impressions of the wines were mixed; some were "too acid," but he enjoyed, in Groot Drakenstein, "two dry whites 1930 [vintage], a light Burgundy and 3 l[ight] Reds."[2] He finally anchored in Southampton, England, on June 16. ("It is indeed a very melancholic fact that in 25 years practically no curtailment of the length of the voyages to and fro has been achieved," Winston Churchill had grumbled in 1926, "and that Australia still remains deeply plunged in the abyss of ocean as at the end of the last century.")[3] Martin was fascinated by what he saw in southern England. There were tidy villages, pretty houses, and manicured parks. One of the highlights of his trip—which edged out any description of the actual work he was doing—was a pageant put on by the Royal Air Force in the Hendon Aerodrome. "One of the most spectacular events was the sky-writing," he marveled, and he sketched out the formation of the planes in his diary.[4]

Just a year later, those airplanes would be mobilized to protect Britain in a second total war, one that was fought in the skies as well as on land and sea. Only twenty-one years after the First World War ended, Britain and all of its colonies and dominions were again at war with Germany. Many of the men and women who would fight in the war were born during or just after the First World War, products of their parents' joyful reunions. Most adults could remember the previous conflict; some remained traumatized by it, and in Britain many civilians felt a desperate aversion against another war.[5] This is why when the British prime minister Neville Chamberlain declared, in 1938, that he had successfully negotiated a compromise with the German chancellor Adolf Hitler, many British people were jubilant. This strategy of partly capitulating with the German leader in order to maintain peace was known as "appeasement." In 1939 it failed, and hopes of avoiding war were sunk as Hitler invaded Poland in September, and war was declared.

Appeasement has been a much-debated strategy. In hindsight, Chamberlain's trust in the German leader seems like an inexcusable blunder. In reality, Chamberlain did not have the benefit of hindsight, and he was leading a British public that had few delusions about the reality of war. Some historians have suggested that appeasement was a means of buying time in order to build up the British military. Colonial wine played a bit part in the buildup. It had become ritual to christen new naval vessels with a bottle of empire wine, which would be ceremoniously smashed on the hull of the ship.[6] When the First Lord of the Admiralty launched a new ship in Plymouth in 1932, an unspecified bottle of colonial wine was handed to his wife to christen the ship. The colonial bottles proved their substance, too: "There was a strong breeze blowing . . . when Lady Eyres-Monsell attempted to break the flower-covered bottle of Colonial [sic] wine. . . . On the third attempt she was successful."[7]

The first nine months of the war were known in Britain as the "Phoney War" or the "Bore War" (a wordplay on the Boer War, forty years earlier): after the tense buildup to the declaration of war, the initial, limited military action was eerily anticlimatic. That changed in the late spring of 1940, when the German army raged across the Netherlands, Belgium, and northern France. Paris fell to the Germans, a collaborationist government was established in France, and resistant "Free French" leaders took refuge in London and in the French territory of Algeria. In the summer of 1940, British and German aircrafts bombed each other's cities, leading to tens of thousands of civilian deaths and massive destruction to homes, businesses, and infrastructure. During the 1940 Battle of Britain, or Blitz, as it became known, civilians across Britain endured six months of aerial bombing, including seventy-six nights of consecutive bombing in London's East End. Tens of thousands of civilians died, and many more lost their homes. One small casualty was the Victoria Wine Company's headquarters and warehouse on Osborn Street, near Aldgate High Street, where a parachute mine and a high explosive bomb both detonated.[8] Victoria Wine, shaken but not deterred, moved its headquarters to North London, promising shareholders that there had been "very little noticeable effect so far as our retail branches are concerned."[9] Parts of Osborn Street remain derelict today.

The Second World War was in some ways very similar to the First World War, and in other ways very different. In terms of similarities, it was equally a war of imperialism and colonialism, the Allied Powers (including Britain) mobilizing to protect their imperial possessions, and the Axis Powers seeking to satisfy their own imperial ambitions. It marshaled millions of British subjects to fight for the Allied cause, and it marshaled their economies, too, as secure supplies for Britain food production took on a patriotic importance. Trade was disrupted and food was rationed.

This time, the fighting was even more geographically distributed, and it took place by land, sea, and air, across Europe, North Africa, South Asia, and in the Atlantic and Pacific Oceans. It lasted longer, too, by two years, commencing in 1939 and concluding, in stages, in mid-1945. Whereas the First World War left many of its participants with a sense of futility and waste—millions had died, but the victors had gained little—the Second World War was more obviously ideological. Now, Allied citizens could buoy themselves in the belief that they were fighting fascism; after the war, the knowledge of German death camps reassured them that they had been waging a noble battle.

Keeping civilian morale up was a concern for British and dominion leaders, especially as the war dragged on with a heavy human toll. Unlike in the First World War, alcohol was not rationed or restricted in Britain, although it did become more expensive and hard to find. Pubs were viewed as community venues that raised spirits, and the government considered an alcoholic beverage to be a well-earned booster to the self-sacrificing British population. (That the British prime minister for most of the war was an alcoholic did not hurt the cause.) Pubs remained open, although they were sometimes short on drinks, glassware, and staff. The pub even served as a sentimental image that linked imperial troops together. In a 1941 cartoon in the *Daily Mail,* an Australian soldier is seen standing on his head in a pub. His English colleague, seated normally, explains to the barmaid that "he likes to be the same way up as the folks down under, when he is dreaming of home."[10]

Some argued that not restricting licensing hours actually encouraged moderation in drink. Quoted in an Australian newspaper, a London publican said, "We are anxious to avoid the sort of thing that happened in the last war. Hotels then often closed for days, and when they re-opened people drank them dry in a half-hour or so."[11] With dark humor, the cartoonist David Low drew a man being thrown up into the air surrounded by flying bottles,[12] joking that pub "closing time is to be observed even during air-raids."

LABOR PROBLEMS

If there was more crush in the pubs, there was less in colonial wineries. The Second World War would have a massive impact on the global wine trade. Some of this impact was felt immediately in the vineyards, as men and women across the British Empire left their jobs among the vines to contribute to the war effort. "Picking presents a labour problem," the New Zealand press noted, as grapes grew heavy but workers were thin on the ground.[13] One New Zealand winemaker in Whangarei, in the Northland region, successfully petitioned to have his sons' military conscription deferred until after the wine harvest.[14] "Pensioner or youth wanted immediately for vineyard work," ran one desperate advertisement in a New Zealand paper in 1942, as military-age men could not be recruited.[15]

International trade was also disrupted, as merchant ships and sailors were redirected toward military duties and some routes became too dangerous for commodity traffic. Vital, incoming agricultural supplies were caught in this clogged shipping web, too. Sugar, which is sometimes used in wine making as a catalyst for fermentation, was rationed and in short supply. But food production also took on a patriotic shine across the empire, as the need to secure food supplies became quickly apparent, and tens of thousands of women were mobilized to work fields and farms. A 1940 British Ministry of Information film, which would have been shown as a trailer in a British cinema, praised the dominion food producers who strove to keep the British "housewife" provided with a variety of foodstuffs.[16] In an era when many young British people went to the cinema at least once a week, these short films reached large audiences. They appear designed to stir up feelings of imperial pride and brotherhood, while also asserting the United Kingdom's central leadership role in the war. Colonies and dominions adapted their food production to supply British needs, and as far as British consumers went, it worked. "And if British civilians were well fed as a result of the policy of importing condensed, high-energy foods," like New Zealand cheese and Canadian bacon, "this was because the country was able to draw on farms in the settler colonies, which extended the nation's agricultural estate over vast tracts of the world's lands," historian Lizzie Collingham writes.[17]

While it was true that the United Kingdom was the command center for government-military decision making, and that civilians living in Britain experienced conflict and bombings in a way that other parts of the empire did not, the narrative of colonies existing only to proudly provide for the British table was imaginary. It was also sometimes resented. An Australian civil servant named J. G. Crawford argued in 1942 that "the disabilities of a cut in local [Australian] civilian consumption . . . must be balanced against the gains to, say, the British civilian population." In other words, the Australian population should not suffer out of proportion to the British population, and Australian needs should not come last. But he argued that it was imperative that Commonwealth countries work together to set realistic targets and strategies for wartime production and trade, to ensure that "production goals and man-power proposals can be subjected to critical and useful discussion before incorporation in the 'national' [i.e., Commonwealth] plan."[18] In closed Cabinet discussions (before Japan entered the war), it was noted that Japan was a large buyer of Australian and South African wool and Indian cotton, and that the impact on these producers would have to be considered in view of Britain's strategic desire to control trade with Japan in order to cut off supplies to Germany and Russia.[19] Dominions counted on trade to keep their economies afloat, and were anxious that their needs not be ignored in Britain's war strategy.

Indeed, South Africa entered the war as an Allied member of the Commonwealth, but its population was deeply splintered over the war. Politics was controlled by the state's white minority, but many of the white Afrikaner population felt hereditary and linguistic affinity with Germany, and Prime Minister Jan Smuts split his own political party by bringing South Africa into the war. For the majority Black population, poor living conditions continued to deteriorate, even as the demands on those in low-skilled manufacturing jobs rose. The South African government undertook extensive propaganda campaigns to encourage support for the war, highlighting South Africa's critical strategic position in sea routes, and likening war volunteers to both Zulu warriors and Afrikaner heroes of the Great Trek.[20]

There were fewer fears about the population of German descent in Second World War Australia than there had been in the previous war. Most of the population was now "mixed thoroughly and happily with the British people," multiple Australian newspapers reported in 1938, trying to quell the fears that German-Australians were being recruited to Nazism.[21] Internment camps were reestablished, though. Some Australians of German and Italian descent were interned, when they were suspected of being "fifth columnists," or clandestine supporters of the Axis who were working to sabotage the Australian cause from within. Australian camps primarily housed prisoners-of-war from Europe. Christine Winter has argued that Australia's participation reinforced its history, "built on Australia's origins as a penal colony, a depository for the British unwanted," while asserting its future, "as an important member and dominion of the empire,"[22] contributing toward the greater war effort.

It is, of course, possible to find a wine angle, even to the internment camps. At camps in Cowra and Leeton, New South Wales, Italian internees tended vineyards and made wine.[23] Conditions for European internees were not terrible, and good behavior and cooperation on their part led the Australian government to stage a gradual release of POWs in order to alleviate the severe labor shortages in agriculture. POWs worked "in vineyards, pineapple and tobacco plantations, and dairy and mixed farms" in Queensland, where the first release of six hundred prisoners netted over a thousand applications from farmers.[24]

A NOBLE HOARD

Britain's market for wine shriveled like so many raisins in the sun, and far more significantly than it had done during the First World War. This was devastating for many colonial wine producers, who had come to depend on the British market. Already in the autumn of 1940, South Australian winemakers were petitioning the Wine Board to consider shuttering its London office and using its resources on advertising wine in other markets.[25]

In 1941, the U.K. Ministry of Food instituted a partial ban on wine imports, and set quotas for the amounts British wine merchants could sell to their customers. This left South Australia with an oversupply of wine. There was a desperate scramble for new markets, because "the home market will not by any means replace the British market which has been lost," the Adelaide *Chronicle* reported.[26] "Canada, the East Indies, Indo China [*sic*], Vietnam, New Caledonia—all of which formerly bought large quantities of wine from France—have turned to Australia as an alternative source of supply." Still, there was excess, and no storage space or labor to deal with it, and the *Chronicle* editorialized that the government should purchase the excess and distill it into alcohol for industrial use, to assist wine farmers and make up for petrol shortages.[27] This was not an entirely original idea: the KWV had produced industrial alcohol in the First World War, so much that it still had some in storage at the start of the Second.[28]

South Africa, too, saw a large drop in export demand for its wine. Its exports had risen steadily in the 1930s, and had been primarily bound for Britain, when they plummeted in 1942. Toward the end of the war, they began to rise again, and by 1946 surpassed their previous high in terms of quantity.[29] South Africa had, effectively, recovered during the interwar period from the crises of the late nineteenth century, but it was still economically vulnerable because of its strong reliance on Britain's market to sell its wine and brandy.

The collapse in the maritime trade in wine during the war did not mean that British people went entirely without. Some resorted to making "English wines," from orchard fruits and foraged berries. As with the First World War, the secret to having real wine was to have a full cellar at the ready. Victoria Wines's chairman reassured his stockholders in 1942 that business was still brisk, because "Our extensive trade in home-produced beers, wines and spirits, together with our stocks on hand, carried us through a difficult year in spite of the prohibition of imports of both foreign and Empire wines."[30]

The wine elite had no problems. The Saintsbury Club was a London-based association of fifty-odd men who worshiped at the memory of George Saintsbury, literary critic, wine connoisseur, and author of *Notes on a Cellar Book*. The club's members included the prolific wine writer André Simon, the Irish barrister and author of the wine book *Stay Me with Flagons,* Maurice Healy, authors Hilaire Beloc and Alec Waugh, cartoonist David Low, and men of the Harvey and Berry wine-retailing families. None of the wines in their cellars were colonial: indeed, they only stocked Bordeaux, Burgundy, Champagne, Moselle "Rhenish" (so French, but German in style), port, and Madeira. Their annual dinners were multicourse affairs with exquisite wines, and the war did not put a damper on festivities. The one amendment to the 1942 dinner was that neither cheese nor cheesecake was available to the bon vivants, given wartime shortages, so "a somewhat dry cake is provided as a kapok bolster to rest the heads of our Port and Madeira" (which were from 1909 and 1848, respectively).[31] Truly, sacrifices were made.

King's College, Cambridge, had weathered the First World War, and its wine cellars were equally well prepared for the Second World War. The records from the 1920s and 1930s show a community with quite expensive, and entirely European, taste in wine. Particularly popular were red wines from Bordeaux and Burgundy, and white wines from Germany and eastern France. In December 1939, its senior wine stock (that which was reserved for academic staff, or fellows) consisted of 3,588 bottles of claret, 600 bottles of Burgundy (mostly red), 1,776 bottles of hock (German white wine), and a smaller quantity of other whites. In addition, it held nearly eight thousand bottles of port, 564 bottles of sherry, and smaller stocks of other fortified wines and spirits (including whisky, Madeira, Marsala, gin, and vermouth).[32] Once again, King's was ready.

The number of residents in the college fluctuated during the war. Both students and younger fellows were called up for military service, so the number of resident students ranged between 100 and 170, and the number of fellows probably in the range of 30 to 50 at a time. King's welcomed scholars from Queen Mary, University of London, who had decided to evacuate from their East End campus. It also billeted members of the Royal Air Force in its now-empty student rooms. Support for these troops was dampened by frequent squabbles, mainly around staff and food shortages.

King's is a useful barometer for changing tastes and drinks availability over time, because the consumption was so frequent and regular. It is also an excellent case study for a wine historian, because it kept detailed records over a long period of time. There was a fixed schedule of dinners that required wine, and daily sales of wine and spirits to both fellows and students (who, at the time, were all men). Through the 1920s and 1930s, the college's stocks were entirely European. Like the Saintsbury Club, the College prioritized the wines of select French regions—Bordeaux, Burgundy, Champagne, and Moselle—and also had German wines. Port, sherry, whiskey, gin, and rum rounded out the selection. King's began the war with 4,200 bottles of French red wine (mostly claret) and 2,028 bottles of white wine (mostly German hock), plus 7,670 bottles of port and an assortment of smaller quantities of other fortified wines and spirits.[33] The main difference with the Saintsbury Club is that while the college did have fine bottles for special occasions, it also had a selection of cheaper wines for everyday drinking and for student consumption. But, like with the Saintsbury Club and upper-crust wine merchants like Berry Brothers, there were no stocks of colonial wine in the interwar period. Colonial wine was clearly the preserve of retailers to the hoi polloi, like Victoria Wine Company and its ilk.

A humorous poem in *Punch* bemoaned the diminishing availability of wine in late 1941:

> When supplies are running short
> Of every kind from pop to port...
> 'Tis well for him whose bins are stored
> With red and white, a noble hoard.[34]

King's had a noble hoard, but not an infinite one. The wine accounts show the fellows slowly dipping into the college stores of Lafite and Pommard, but by December 1943, the war showed no sign of ending and the cellars were emptying out. Over four years, the college had emptied out around half of its cellar, having drunk 3,600 bottles of port, 2,000 bottles of claret, 348 bottles of Champagne, and 1,380 bottles of hock.[35] The German wine had already been purchased and paid for, so apparently there was no harm in drinking it.

Ever connected and clever, the college ordered from ten different suppliers during the war. Despite this resourcefulness, there were still marked shifts in consumption. By 1943 there was a noticeable uptake in the college's purchases of spirits and decline in purchases of wine. Whisky, gin, brandy, vermouth, Pimm's No. 1, and rum were bought by the case, but there was no champagne and no fine French wines. This may have been completely dictated by availability, but spirits also were an economical purchase during tough times, because they could be drunk neat or mixed, kept longer once opened, and offered more alcohol per bottle than wine. The real watershed came in December 1943, with an order from wine merchants Williams, Standring Ltd: ninety-six bottles of whiskey, ninety-six bottles of gin, a few bottles each Pimms, brandy, rum, and vermouth, and 192 bottles of Algerian wine. Algerian was the first non-European wine to pass through the King's cellars, and it was not cheap: 77/6 for twelve bottles, when ten years earlier that amount would have purchased a dozen bottles of very fine French claret at Whiteley's, or two dozen bottles of Australian wine.[36] Algerian wine was colonial wine, just not from a British colony. Algeria had been claimed by the French in 1830 and, during the phylloxera crisis of late nineteenth century, had grown into a major wine-producing area, supplying metropolitan France with its hearty reds. Now, in another crisis, it was supplying the British, too.

The fortress had been breached and the floodgates opened. The college ordered more Algerian wine again in June 1944, September 1944 and in January 1945—small quantities each time, as if just to tide them over, and now at an eye-watering 96 shillings per dozen bottles. In October 1944, the first South African red wine appeared, followed by South African sherry. In January 1945, it splurged on forty-eight bottles of South African red wine (90s.) and thirty-six bottles of South African white wine (96s.).[37] This wine was then sold to fellows and students in the College off-licence, called the buttery. The fellows indulged, a bit: Professor Frank Adcock, an ancient historian and wartime cryptographer, went first, buying a bottle of Algerian red wine in December 1943; others followed, and in 1944 the college off-licence was selling a bottle or two a week. Hock and claret were still available, but they cost about twice as much as a bottle from South Africa.[38]

Most of the colonial wine was purchased by students, not fellows.[39] Anthony Berry, who was a student at neighboring college Trinity Hall in the 1930s, and later of Berry Brothers and Rudd, recalled that his own father kept him "liberally supplied" in sherry and port, "but, except for occasional parties in my rooms, I drank very little red and white wine even though I already knew that I was destined for the wine trade." Students generally preferred beer, he explained, because it was cheap and abundant.[40] Colonial wine was the next best thing, then, and there are no records of students buying noncolonial still wine in the last two years of the war: what they bought was Algerian, South African, or Australian.

Supplies of European wines did not return to normal immediately after the war, which was a continued boon to colonial producers. In 1946 the wine purchasers for Whitbread Brewers, which owned a major chain of pubs across Britain, tasted three Cypriot wines. The sherry and the ruby port were deemed of very poor quality, but the Cyprus white port (-style) was better, and deemed "worth buying as long as the shortage lasts."[41] King's began purchasing its old French favorites as soon as it could, but it also continued to purchase colonial wine. On June 12, 1945, a few days after Britain declared victory in Europe, King's ordered some fabulous French wines (Pichon Longueville and Lafite, both 1934, both from Pauillac). But it also ordered South African sherry.[42] In late 1946, it ordered seventeen dozen bottles of vintage St. Julien claret and four dozen bottles of Burgundy, as well as four dozen bottles of "Stellenbosch W[hite]" and two dozen "Stellenbosch R[ed]."[43]

Students and young fellows continued to buy colonial wine up through the early 1950s. The historian Eric Hobsbawm, then a PhD student, bought two bottles of Algerian red wine in June 1946. The computer scientist, cryptographer, and polymath Alan Turing bought two bottles of "S.A. Stellenbosch" (color unknown) in 1947. E. M. Forster, the novelist and an honorary fellow at King's, purchased fifteen bottles of the same in the summer of 1948, perhaps for entertaining students, since it was recorded in the student wine accounts.[44] The largest purchase of this Stellenbosch wine was, appropriately, for a "Colonial Dinner" in July 1948. This was two months after the National Party had been elected to power in South Africa, promising (and then implementing) a system of racial segregation.

Student accounts also show that port was starting to fall out of favor by the end of the Second World War, although King's shifted a good number of bottles of Australian port. Sherry was on the rise. On June 6, 1946, the second anniversary of the D-Day landings and probably a cause for some celebration, King's students bought fifteen bottles of South Africa sherry, seven bottles of Algerian red wine, two bottles of whisky, three bottles of Australian port, and three bottles of champagne (provenance unknown). By 1950 the students were confirmed sherry drinkers. South African sherry, the cheapest sherry available, became the most popular drink, with the buttery selling fifty-nine bottles to students in November 1947. It was about 20 percent cheaper than the alternative, "Bristol milk sherry." Algerian red wine began to disappear by the end of 1948 in favor of South African wines and "Australian Burgundy."

The interwar period had seen colonial wines gain considerable popularity with middle- and working-class consumers. At an elite college that was living with and through the Second World War, colonial wine had a clear profile: it was a drink of students and young people of more limited means, and it was what more mature wine lovers stooped to consume when they did not have much choice. There was also, increasingly, an association with fortified wines from the dominions and colonies, which had begun in 1927 but was very much cemented during and after the war.

THE FINEST SILICA

Remarkably, in spite of the dramatic disruptions to both daily life and international trade, official discussions about wine continued. In May 1944, as Allied troops organized in southern England for what would be the D-Day landings, Stephen Tallents maintained a lively correspondence about the colonial bottles he had laid down in 1928. Writing to Sir David Chadwick, of the Imperial Economic Committee, he asked that the experiments be resumed, and explained that "Heath would be provisionally willing to make all arrangements for a further tasting of the wine in his own tasting room at the Army and Navy Stores, and Hetherington has ascertained that D.S.I.R. would be willing to make the concurrent chemical laboratory tests."[45] These hopes were dashed, though, a month later, when Heath learned that the cellar holding the bottles had been destroyed.[46] "I must plead the 'doodle bug' for it drove us out of London," he apologized to Tallents for not informing him sooner, sadly explaining that the "bottle test can be carried no further."[47]

For an experiment that probably never met the highest standards of scientific procedure, this was still a pathetic end, as sixteen years of patient waiting had become collateral in a total war. As the young Princess Elizabeth famously remarked following the bombing of her home at Buckingham Palace, Tallents, too, could now look the East End in the eye. Wistfully, hopefully, perhaps even defensively, Tallents noted in a 1946 speech that "If enemy action has spared our vault, there must still lie neglected, somewhere near Charing Cross, some useful unclaimed wines and a valuable stock of flasks of the finest silica."[48] While recent archaeological digs in London have turned up thousands of glass bottles of early-twentieth century picallili and chutney, this author is not aware of Tallents's colonial wine bottles having been unearthed.[49] One waits in hope.

PART FOUR

Conquest

C. 1950–2020

SEVENTEEN

And a Glass of Wine

COLONIAL WINES IN THE POSTWAR SOCIETY

IN 1976 THE *FINANCIAL TIMES* reviewed a new play in London by Jim Rand, entitled *Sherry and Wine*. The plot revolved around a "nice West Indian laborer," his wife, and daughters. The laborer "has done well for himself, he has moved his family from Brixton to a pretty home in Finchley; but he is still happy to sit around in his boiler-suit and Wellingtons, eat peas and rice, drink beer." His wife, on the other hand, "believes that in Rome you do as the Romans do," and that means that when her daughter brings a young man home for dinner, "it has to be a slap-up do with sherry and wine." That, apparently, is what respectable British people did in Finchley, a middle-class neighborhood of greater London. What follows in the play is a "prolonged dispute about this cultural conflict," between white society and Black society, between immigrant parents and first-generation children.[1] And not just immigrant families of the rising middle classes, either: an *Irish Times* columnist recalled a contemporary television advertisement for inexpensive French wine brand Piat d'Or, "where a posh, suspicious father is won over by his daughter's suitor when he turns up for dinner with a bottle of—surprise, surprise—Piat d'Or."[2]

The cultural distance between 1945 and 1976 was substantial. Wine and sherry serve as proxies, or as shorthand, for this thirty-year period of deep social change in the United Kingdom. Demographically, millions of British citizens from colonies and dominions resettled in Britain, just as millions of British-born people tried their prospects in former colonies of white settlement. British consumption patterns changed, with the arrival of supermarket-style shopping and the introduction of more new foods. Conservative commentators bemoaned a "permissive society" emerging, one where personal relationships became less formal.

These were not great years for colonial wines. If winemakers and importers had expected the upward trend of the 1930s and the war years to continue, they were disappointed: colonial wine consumption in Britain stumbled, then fell, after 1945, and it did not pull itself up again until the 1980s. Its association with the war probably did long-term harm to its reputation. Ironically, a foundation for a true appreciation of wines from former colonies was being slowly laid down in the postwar period. This took several forms: the growth in standards of living and consumer purchasing power, the rise in migration throughout the British Commonwealth, and the introduction of many new foods and flavors into British life through "ethnic" restaurants.

Colonial wines ceased, of course, to be actually colonial in this period. The dominions remained members of the Commonwealth (except for South Africa, as we will see in the next chapter), but they had become unmistakably independent, sovereign states. India became independent in 1947, Palestine (as Israel) in 1948, Cyprus in 1960, and Malta in 1964. For simplicity, though, we will continue to refer to them as colonial wines, which by the 1960s was a quaint anachronism.

SIXTY-SEVEN QUARTS

When the war ended a cartoonist predicted a surge of people participating in that great British leisure activity of going to the pub. He depicted a tour bus emptying its passengers into a quiet pub and the passengers demanding, "Sixty-seven quarts, landlord, please!"[3] The wine trade slowly resumed, but government quotas remained on individual wine purchases to ensure enough to go around. As Anthony Berry reminisced many years later, there was "at the end of 1945, a complete 'sellers' market' in the sense that demand was far in excess of supply. A reflection of this was that we published no price list of any kind for no less than ten years from 1940 to 1950."[4] There was too little choice to justify an extensive list, and too many people wanting wine.

Still, while there was a return to consumer spending, Britain did not experience immediate and widespread prosperity, and when it did it was not to the benefit of colonial wines. A vigorous debate ensued in Parliament in 1949 about wine duties, which had skyrocketed during the war. The Labour government was considering reducing them to encourage consumption and to boost tax revenue, which it needed to fund its exciting (and expensive) portfolio of new social programs. As with the tariff discussions in Parliament in the 1880s, most of the discussion was of the responsibilities that Britain had toward European allies like France and Spain, although a few members tried to steer the debate back toward the empire. "I am perfectly certain that very few gatherings in this Palace could have functioned in recent years had it not been for South African sherry," Captain Harry Crookshank, a Conservative MP, admonished his colleagues. His Conservative colleague agreed, and echoed arguments about imperial preference that had been made repeatedly over 140 years: that colonial wines needed preferential tariffs over European countries, not equal ones, if they hoped to compete at all, and that having encouraged wine production, Britain now had a responsibility to empire farmers to look after their imports. The tariff "differential remains the same, but the cost to the consumer is such that, *the taste being what it is,* the Empire wine is prejudiced," argued the Conservative MP for Cheltenham, Arthur Dodds-Parker. He continued, "throughout the war the Empire played the greatest part in producing wines which we in this country consumed, because the Empire was the only place where we could get wines. . . . I cannot see how under the present system there is likely to be any encouragement to the wine-producing industries which have grown up in the Empire and which had considerable encouragement during the last 10 years or so."[5] Although the Conservatives were flying their imperial flag in support of colonial wine producers, they were damning the wine itself with faint praise. Their defense of the producers seemed to owe more to guilt and a sense of patrician responsibility, than to a respect for them as business owners or a real admiration for their wine. "Encouragement" was another war debt to be repaid.

There was also an understanding in official circles that the wine industry was an employer, and that encouraging empire trade had an impact on British jobs (for example, a Conservative MP suggesting that preferential tariffs would "also help to build up the home bottling trade").[6] Much wine was still imported in large containers, wooden barrels, and then bottled in Britain.[7] The South African Wine Farmers' Association, for example, imported South African wines into Britain on Union Castle steamers into Southampton, from which the wines were pumped by hoses into warehouses and bottled.[8] The same organization also had its own warehouse and depot in South London.[9] Each of these employed local people: as dockhands, bottlers, warehousers, drivers, and managers, for instance. Colonial independence did not unravel the economic connections that fed both British and overseas economies.

To later generations, the thirty-year period after the war is frequently seen as a stain on the monumental landscape of British food history. Rationing continued in Britain until 1954, and some of the infamous processed foods of the war lasted much longer. Vegetables, fruits, and meats came in tins (cans), and were accompanied by powdered custard, margarine, and industrial sliced bread. This is not to say that many British people did not eat delicious, high-quality, home-cooked food, but the trend in the postwar period was toward convenience and an increasing reliance on processed food. The "meat and two veg" diet of bland, boiled food gave Britain a global culinary notoriety. Colonial wine became damned by association in this gastronomic purgatory: it had been popular during the war, it was relatively cheap, and it was usually sold as a quasi-generic product of unspecific origin. Australian burgundy had become the Spam of drinks.

Colonial wines slipped so far off the cultural radar in Britain in the postwar period that they lost their history. The popularity of colonial wines steadily declined, so that by the early 1980s Australia and South Africa had less of a market share in Britain than they had had in the 1880s. When, as we shall see, they again became popular in the 1980s, many assumed that they were entirely new products. Their vast popularity before and during the Second World War had been forgotten.

Indeed, colonial wines even became associated in the popular imagination with the unsophisticated. In Barbara Pym's 1950 satirical novel *Some Tame Gazelle*, the hapless spinster Belinda wakes up ill, and wonders whether it might be due to "the half-empty bottle of Empire port that Edith had found in the back of a cupboard or the damp walk home in thin shoes. She was inclined to think it must be the last, for what else could have given her such an unromantic, sniveling cold?"[10] The Australian flagons that must have lubricated many happy gatherings in working-class, interwar U.K., and the bottles of South African port that buoyed student parties in Cambridge, were becoming the domain of maiden aunts and provincial vicars. It was a world that had narrow aspirations and smelled of wet wool.

The Australians were very concerned about this reputation and did endeavor to change it. Citing a drop in sales of two million gallons since 1939, the industry decided to recycle the exhibition model, and opened an "Australian Wine Festival" in 1955. Its target market, for reasons that have not emerged from the archives, was Newport, Wales, a town (now city) just east of the city of Cardiff, on the Severn Estuary. Of all the possible locations in Britain, this may seem an improbable one: why not London, or Birmingham? But Newport, an industrial port that had suffered catastrophic unemployment in the 1930s, was rebounding economically, and its working-class population may have been seen as a market with lots of potential growth. More prosaically, it was across the estuary from Bristol, a which had long been a port for wine imports and was home to some iconic British merchants, like Harvey's and Averys. Nine importers of Australian wine participated, including Burgoyne, Emu, Penfolds, and Seppelt, and the trade press noted that they were satisfied with the good crowds.

A similar event followed in Leicester, a city in England, "in conjunction with the finals of the East Midlands Gas Board area 'Bride of the Year' competition," where fifteen hundred attendees sampled Australian wines.[11] If such an event sounds farcical, it actually suggests a keen eye for new customer bases. After the wartime destruction of so many civilian homes, housing became an intense election issue, and in the 1950s British popular culture reembraced domesticity. British culture encouraged newlyweds to establish their own, independent living situation, and young brides were encouraged to entertain in their homes. Most women married in their early twenties,[12] and retailers seemed to think it a duty to educate these women in the finer arts of house-keeping and hostessing. Wine was a step up from beer or cider, and serving it was a sign of a young person's maturity and assumption of the trappings of adult life. It was in this mood in 1957 that the satirical magazine *Punch* published a humorous "guide to [wine for] those about to graduate from beer."[13]

Whiteley's reflected this demographic in its advertisements, too. A cheerful 1950s era brochure called *Wine Cups and Punches* encouraged the serving of wine-based, chilled drinks for "informal entertaining," because they were "most economical and easily varied to suit individual tastes." The names revealed a strong colonial and "exotic" theme: the Bush Ranger, the Tropical Sparkler, and the Barossa Punch, which served twenty-four:

> 2 bottles burgundy or claret; 1/2 pint lemon juice; 1/2 pint orange juice; 1/2 cup sugar; 4 sliced peaches; 1 sliced orange; about 2 dozen halved strawberries or equal number raspberries; diced pineapple; 3 pints soda water. Method—Mix sugar into wine in mixing bowl, add fruit juices, stir. Pour this over large lumps cracked ice in punch bowl. Add fruits. Just before serving add the soda water. Fix slice of cucumber to rim of glass.[14]

Conveniently, Whiteley's had a range of wine specially selected for these treats, suggesting either a bottle of French burgundy at 7/9, or a flagon of Australian burgundy at 11/6 (which actually was the same unit price). A South African sherry and an Australian tawny dessert wine were available for other recipes, and were presented as cheaper alternatives to European versions.[15]

Colonial wines also fell back on their old advertising strategy, which was to advertise the health benefits of their wines. Burgoyne was advertising its "Harvest Burgundy" as an "aid to digestion" to accompany meals. "Enjoy good health—with me!" the distinctive flagon chirped in one of Burgoyne's many newspaper advertisements.[16] Much wine was still imported in large wooden barrels and then bottled in U.K., allowing Britisher bottlers to blend and style the wines as they wished, and Harvest Burgundy was now a blend of both Australian and South African wines.[17] By promoting its wine as an accompaniment to meals, Burgoyne was also dodging the association with heavy drinking that trailed behind cheap wines.

Journalism and print media also show the rise of wine in British life. Wine advertisements started appearing regularly in the magazine *Punch* in 1969 (there had only been four in the previous century), peaking at 113 in 1987.[18] Burgoyne also branched into new media, advertising on television in 1957.[19] Burgoyne's advertisements were not coy: they actually listed the retail prices of their flagons in their newspaper advertisements, and they are identical to the prices that Whiteley's was advertising for its own Australian burgundy flagons. Low price was its selling point. Likewise, the South African Wine Farmers' Association ran some advertisements in the 1950s and 1960s stressing the high calibre of its sherries ("These South African people keep improving the quality of their wine—especially the sherry. It's a credit to them").[20] But it also, especially in the later 1960s, stressed value and price, with the tagline "South African sherry—the luxury *you* can afford."[21]

The pricing of wine in Britain was in for a major change, though, with the abolition of resale price management in 1964.[22] Resale or retail price maintenance (RPM) is the agreement between producers and retailers that goods will be sold at a particular price—in the case of wine, generally above a particular minimum price floor. The abolition of price floors meant that wine retailers could sell wine below the recommended retail price, and even below cost. Large retailers could afford to sell goods below cost as "loss leaders": low prices on certain goods would entice customers into their stores, but the customers could be counted on to buy other things at retail cost to compensate.

FIGURE 10. Burgoyne's Harvest Burgundy, advertised as an affordable health drink in a distinctive flagon bottle. *Picture Post*, March 24, 1951.

Many small retailers opposed the abolition of RPM, arguing that it favored larger retailers.[23]

Small, independent wine merchants had a reason to be worried, because in the longer term this legal change would be of enormous benefit to a new type of retailer, the supermarket. Large, brightly lit spaces with wide aisles and huge freezers, supermarkets arrived from the United States in the post-war period and gradually came to dominate over the traditional style of retailing food in small shops dedicated to single types of food. The supermarket is often directly credited with rising levels of wine consumption in Britain, but the sources show a more complex trend.[24]

Supermarkets are eligible to apply for off-licences in Britain, so legally they are no different from the food halls that had long sold wine. In the 1960s, two alcohol licensing acts—a first act in 1961 followed by a major consolidation in 1964—liberalized alcohol sales in Britain by extending the hours that off-licenses could sell, up to fifteen hours a day.[25] The previous 1921 licensing act had limited sales to nine hours per day.[26] The 1964 act made alcohol sales more convenient and potentially lucrative for all retailers, including supermarkets. Combined with the abolition of RPM, large retail chains were best positioned to lure in the public with very low promotional prices on wine.

While it is true that by the 1980s, half of the wine sold in Britain was sold in supermarkets, and supermarkets did not immediately dive into wine selling. Marks and Spencer, an iconic British department store chain, had begun selling food by counter service in 1931, moving to self-service in 1950 and becoming a major grocery retailer in the postwar era. It pioneered quality convenience foods, particularly "ready meals" (prepackaged meals that just need reheating). In doing so it both reflected and drove changing tastes in U.K., for example by first offering Indian food in 1974. But Marks and Spencer only began selling wine in 1974, a decade after the changes to licensing laws and RPM. It did so gingerly, starting with just two wines, and gradually adding a few more. Although grocery stores had purchasing power and the ability to shape taste, they also were reluctant to launch a range that would not find a willing public.

Demand for wine was growing, though, without supermarkets' assistance. In 1961 Britain imported about two and a half bottles of wine per capita; these are 750ml bottles, and for the entire population including children, so we would expect average adult consumption to be higher. By 1970, that number had doubled, to about five bottles per capita, and by 1980 it had doubled again, to about ten bottles per year (see fig. 11). As we have seen, colonial wines had over a century and a half of consumption amongst people of ordinary means. Although we lack sources that would allow us to track the precise wine purchases of masses of individuals, the volume of wine alone being sold in Britain shows that it was not the preserve of the elite. The fraction of British society that could be considered wealthy was simply too small to sustain this level of consumption without the declaration of a public health crisis.

Increasingly, though, wine lists demonstrate that rising British wine consumption was in European wines, not in colonial ones. Whereas prewar wine lists generally showed mostly French, some German, and some colonial unfortified wines, in the 1960s France dominated but a much more diverse range of European wines start to appear, too. Augustus Barnett, a London-based chain that billed itself as "Britain's Biggest Selling [sic] Independent Wine and Spirits Retailer," carried almost exclusively French wines in the 1970s. A March 1972 flyer, for example, listed ninety-two still wines, all French except two which were recognizably Italian, two German, one Hungarian, and one Austrian. Of the whites, sweeter Alsatian wines were prominent.[27]

Oddbins, another London-based national off-license chain, had a similar selection. Oddbins initially specialized in "bin ends," limited quantities of wines at discount. Their wine lists from the 1960s and 1970s are almost exclusively French, with the inclusion of a small number of Greek, Turkish, and Moroccan wines. There were no Australian, South African, New Zealand, or Cyprus wines.[28]

In 1974 Marks and Spencer trialed two wines in a select number of shops, before rolling out a full range a few months later. This initially included twelve still table wines, two sparkling wines, three sherries, and two vermouths, plus some beers and hard ciders. The wines were presented thematically rather than regionally. "Party wines" were a "trio of attractive, reliable wines carefully blended to appeal to British palates and bottled in litres for drinking continental style [sic] at informal get-togethers with family and friends." These unknown varietals of imprecise origin were sold by the liter: "Spanish red wine" and French "Vin Supérieur Rouge" and "Vin Supérieur Blanc."[29] For still reds, there were three French and two Italian. Dry whites included Italian soave and French Macon Villages and a Loire. There was a wider range of sweet whites: a French Moselle riesling, a German Liebfraumilch, a "French Sweet White" and, appearing in November 1974, a Yugoslav riesling. The Yugoslavian wine was the cheapest, at 75p for 750ml, and the most expensive still wine was a Chianti Classico at 99p. (In February 1971 Britain finally disbanded its pound-shilling-pence currency in favor of a decimal system.) The only New World wines were three sherries from South Africa.[30]

The emphasis in Marks and Spencer's early wine lists is firmly on the functionality of the wines, echoing the earlier descriptions found in Whiteley's lists. They are described in terms of appropriate food pairings and social events, evoking the mood of the wines rather than referencing particular tastes or aromas. The Spanish red is "a robust sunny wine . . . that will cheerfully hold its own" with a range of dishes, and the Côtes du Rhône "will bring a touch of sun to your entertaining in cold weather."[31] This chimes with Johnson's reminiscences about professional wine writers, that they "used to be alarmingly vague."[32] Marks and Spencer's seems to be targeting nervous consumers ("Do you enjoy wine but find buying it a confusing, hit-or-miss affair?"), who are presumed to be female. They reassure them that "the customer has a double guarantee for her M&S wines," as some of these own-brand wines were also protected appellations,[33] though as their wine grew in popularity and range through the 1980s there were still many bottles of vague origin: liter bottles of "White Table Wine," for example, at only 9 percent ABV and labeled as "[a] light fruity medium sweet wine bottled in W. Germany. Wine from different countries of the European Community."[34]

What is striking in this collection is the range of European countries represented: there were many Yugoslavian, Austrian, Bulgarian, and German wines, as well as French and Spanish.[35] Marks and Spencer even carried a Lebanese wine in 1990.[36] By 1984 the chain carried nearly fifty different wines, and boasted annual wine sales of £35,000,000.[37]

Marks and Spencer's clientele might have warmed to the idea of "dining Continental style" for several reasons. One was a food movement spearheaded by the diplomat-turned-writer Elizabeth David, who reacted against the prevailing taste (or lack thereof) in British foods and championed Mediterranean ingredients, in particular olive oil. Her journalism and books particularly celebrated the cuisine of rural France. Like her American counterpart Julia Child, David had been exposed to new foods and cooking through her wartime experience in the intelligence services, and churned this into books that introduced her homeland to new ways of eating. Unlike Child's effervescent prose, David's journalistic voice was that of a displeased school mistress. Many modern British chefs and cookery writers cite her as a crucial inspiration, and to be sure, her tone would not disturb anyone accustomed to working in a professional kitchen. David liked wine, too, and considered it a normal and regular accompaniment to meals. One of her collections was entitled *An Omelette and a Glass of Wine*, which was her ideal Christmas meal, preferably consumed alone. She also penned magazine columns and short pamphlets about cooking with wine. In one, commissioned by the wine merchants Saccone and Speed, she argued that "Cheap wine is better than no wine at all, at any rate for cooking," but that a simple wine of Burgundy or Beaujolais was much preferable to a "fiery Algerian wine."[38]

Probably more than Elizabeth David, trips to the Continent exposed British people to new types of food and cooking, and certainly gave them access to inexpensive wine in wine-producing countries. If British winters seemed lonely and dreary, the rise of affordable package holidays to continental Europe in the 1960s and 1970s was an antidote.[39] By 1976, over 20 percent of British people went on holiday abroad, and that percentage would double by 1985.[40] Hugh Johnson, the famed wine writer, actually did occasional travel journalism early in his career, recommending German country hotels and good-value ferry crossings to France for English Sunday newspapers.[41]

Another trend that had an impact on British cultural value of wine was the growth of migration. Britain had relatively open borders from the end of the Second World War until the late 1960s, and it encouraged migration from the empire and parts of Europe. The gastronomic impact of this was the marked expansion of Indian and Italian restaurants in British cities and towns. Hugh Johnson, then a twenty-three year-old rising journalist, wrote an article called "What to Drink with Exotic Food," in the summer of 1962. With great enthusiasm for the growing variety of restaurants in Britain, he noted that the "only snag is that our wine-play, so carefully conned from the old soup-fish-meat routine, leading up to port and nuts, is old hat."[42] He recommended mostly French wines, or, for those who enjoyed spicy curries, Guinness, as "the bitter malty bubbles have something like a scouring action, laying bare the tastebuds for the next ecstatic forkful."[43] Guinness: it's good for you! Bubbles were also recommended by contemporary New Zealand wine makers: "said to be good for digestive troubles . . . [sparkling wines] are the only wine to serve with curries, Chinese foods and other well seasoned [sic] dishes."[44]

Culturally, then, new food and wine habits were creeping into British leisure time. Continental Europe itself was edging politically closer, too. In 1952 France, West Germany, Italy, Belgium, the Netherlands, and Luxembourg established a community for the free trade in coal and steel. The states hoped to facilitate their wartime recovery by removing barriers to trading fuel and construction supplies, and ensuring long-term peace through economic cooperation. In 1957, the Treaty of Rome elevated this group into the European Economic Community, with a wider remit for economic policy. An article in the popular London *Picture Post* in 1957 argued in favor of Britain joining a European customs union, opining that such a union would expand Britain's market and lower production costs. Food, drink, and tobacco would be exempt from a Free Trade Area, however, "Therefore Britain and Dominion farmer will continue to be helped: and this country will remain loyal to her old 'Imperial Preferences', whereby, for example, South African and Australian wine, and Rhodesian tobacco, enjoy a Preferential Tariff."[45]

The British desire to have its preferential wine tariff and drink it, too, would be problematic. Britain first applied to join the European Community in 1961, and its application was rejected two years later. The British accused the French leader Charles de Gaulle of vetoing their application because it threatened his own power; de Gaulle countered that the UK's main loyalties were to its colonial empire, and not to its European neighbors. Britain tried again, and in 1973 it acceded to the EEC along with the Republic of Ireland and Denmark (an event which I personally refer to as the "Bacon Accession"). This was, according to one scholar, "a kind of betrayal" for Australia (and other former colonies).[46] One of the major changes in the EEC since 1957 had been the creation of the Common Agricultural Policy, which broadly aimed at ensuring farmers' livelihoods and increasing food availability through subsidy programs. These policies, including those which concerned wine, were and continue to be some of the most controversial, but in the aftermath of the deprivations of the war, it is not difficult to see why they were considered vital by French and German farmers. For former British colonies that were major exporters of agricultural products to Britain, the accession was a major blow to their easy access to the Britain market, and their overall competitiveness in European markets. Frustrated, the Australians looked towards Asia for wider trading relationships, and cofounded the Cairns Group in the 1980s to improve the negotiating power of agricultural exporters.[47]

As far as wine was concerned, the empire's defenders were sounding the alarm about the adoption of the EEC's CET, or Common External Tariff (a tariff on goods coming into the EEC, which would replace Britain's existing tariffs with EEC membership). According to Sir Ronald Russell, a Conservative MP, this "would be disastrous to the wine industry of Cyprus, would drastically affect the whole industry of South Africa, and would be a setback to trade in Australia."[48] This would be largely true in the medium term. But EEC membership contributed to the growing thirst for wine in Britain, and in the longer term colonial wine would reap those benefits. Colonial wine had introduced ordinary British people to wine many decades before, and it would return in popularity to a nation of confirmed wine drinkers in the 1980s.

EIGHTEEN

Good Fighting Wine

COLONIAL WINES BATTLE BACK

AUSTRALIAN WINE WAS AN EASY TARGET for Eric Idle, member of the British comedy troupe Monty Python, in the late 1970s. By this point, its reputation among British drinkers-in-the-know was abysmal. This is how he could invent and satirize a "a prize-winning 'Cuiver Reserve Chateau Bottled Nuit San Wogga Wogga', which has a bouquet like an Aborigine's armpit."[1] Idle may not have known that he was continuing a centuries-old tradition of associating the taste and smell of colonial wine with filth, and of filth with the bodies of indigenous people. For indigenous Australians, this was no joke. From the early twentieth century into the 1970s, a white Australia policy aimed at shaming and eradicating Aboriginal culture had sanctioned the kidnapping of thousands of indigenous children. These "Stolen Generations" were forced to assimilate into white homes and institutions. A flippant, satirical sketch about poor-quality Australian wine is a reminder of how indigenous bodies were denigrated and devalued, with traumatic consequences.[2]

After all, wine appreciation never exists outside of a human context. The people who make wine, and the people who consume wine, help shape its perception as a cultural good. Thus, wine's proximity to undesirable people was something to be overcome and erased. In terms of the British market, there was a more innocuous association that winemakers wished to avoid. A. J. Ludbrook, an Australian wine writer and publicist, wrote to Hugh Johnson in 1972 of the "old time when Australian burgundy [sic] was sold to anaemic old ladies in England at corner stores as a cure for all their troubles." He hoped that these days were over: "I would have thought that although it has always been very difficult to live this down, we had at last reached the stage of living it down, with the quality of wines we can offer today."[3] To be sure, this was a statement about the Australian wine industry's successful efforts to make better-quality wines that would earn the respect of the world's top wine critics. But the dig at "old ladies" writes off the wine's established demographic in Britain as unsophisticated, impressionable, and undesirable.

Even if their exports to Britain were declining between the 1960s and late 1980s, winemakers in Australia, New Zealand, and South Africa were busy. This was a period of expansion and improvement. Colonial wine's triumphant conquest of the British wine market in the late 1980s was not simply due to changes in British consumption; it was also down to a new mindset and major upgrades among wine producers. "Knowing the likelihood of Britain's entry to E.E.C., the Wine Board and exporters had for two years sought new or increased outlets elsewhere," the *Australian Wine, Brewing, and Spirit Review* reported in 1971. "Trade with Canada had increased but most of the wine now exported to Britain would have to be absorbed within the Australian market."[4] This is indeed what happened. Just as Britain was becoming a wine-drinking country in the 1970s and 1980s, consuming more and more European wines, building on a foundation that had been laid by colonial wines, Australia was becoming a wine-drinking country, too. The biggest changes in this time period, though, were in New Zealand, where there was exponential growth in the acreage and the production of wine.

South Africa's path was somewhat different, because of the political path taken by its white minority population. The proud, celebratory spirit of wine bodies stands in contrast to some of the darker social currents in what were now postcolonial societies. The postwar era was marked by long-term growth and prosperity for Britain and the former colonies of white settlement, but this success was not evenly distributed. In fact, the racial hierarchies that had defined European colonialism persisted in new forms. The most obvious and extreme version of this was South Africa.

RACISM AND APARTHEID

South Africa had become a "Union" and a dominion in 1910. The Union stretched from the Cape and its fertile winelands on the western, Atlantic side, across a vast interior plateau, to the coast on the Indian Ocean. It was a large country of geographic and climatic diversity. What tied it together politically was an uneasy accommodation between the two white communities: one of British extraction and loyalty, and the other Afrikaner. Together, these two communities made up around 20 percent of the total population, but they claimed all of the political power. The Union was swift in consolidating white supremacy by passing acts which created reservations for Black Africans, limiting their rights to own land and to live in certain urban areas. This discrimination was a prelude to the official policy of separation, known as apartheid, which took hold with the election of the National Party in 1948. Apartheid mandated racial segregation and sought to repress people of color. The apartheid state was a brutal one that operated through oppression and violence. Some British leaders publicly rebuked the apartheid state—notably Prime Minister Harold Macmillan, whose 1960 "wind of change" speech indicated that he would not support South Africa's policies. When it became apparent that its continued membership of the Commonwealth would not be supported by other members, South Africa withdrew in 1961.

Apartheid is critical to understanding South African wine in the twentieth century, yet it is conspicuously absent from many studies. As far as the Cape winelands were concerned, the native land restrictions did not have much impact: most of the good land was already in the hands of white owners by the 1910s. Hermann Giliomee has shown how wine and wheat farmers in the Western Cape were critical to the development of Afrikaner nationalism, which fueled the white supremacist architecture of apartheid. Agriculturalists remained some of the most fervent supporters of the National Party through the second half of the twentieth century. Apartheid guaranteed them cheap colored laborers whom they could treat with impunity. Historian Bill Nasson found one Stellenbosch wine farm was only paying its workers R4 (rand) per day in the early 1980s.[5]

Apartheid eventually made South Africa into a pariah state on the international stage, and that had some impact upon its wine exports—though not as much as might be expected. The United Nations passed resolutions in favor of sanctions against South Africa, but these were voluntary and had little teeth. In Britain, an anti-apartheid movement formed in the 1950s to encourage boycott of South African goods, including fruit, cigarettes, and wines. Christabel Gurney has noted that in 1959, student groups in Cambridge urged colleges not to stock South African wines in their butteries.[6] Thirty years later, though, the battle was still waging: in the spring of 1989, anti-apartheid protesters gathered outside off-licenses in Bristol, carrying signs that read "Boycott South African Wine."[7]

Now that apartheid has ended and its abusive character is well known, it is logical that scholars would want to know more about the people who had opposed apartheid in Britain. It is not unusual for groups that go against the grain to receive an outsize amount of scholarly attention. It might surprise us, then, that most people in Britain did *not* boycott South African goods for the duration of apartheid (and it is difficult to write about that fact, without seeming to point fingers).

South African wines were not anathema to the British in the 1960s and 1970s; if they were, it was primarily for reasons of taste and quality, not political ethics. Rather, South Africa was still appearing on many lists for major retailers, although by the 1970s it had mostly been relegated to the sherry column, and only small independent merchants stocked its still table wines. Augustus Barnett stocked South African sherry in 1972.[8] Cape Province Wines was another British importer of South African wines, based in Staines, Middlesex. It boasted "one of the largest selections of Cape Wines available in the United Kingdom," and noted that its buyers had personally visited some of the estates. It also carried Australian and New Zealand wines, and offered worldwide delivery. Its selection included an "Oude Libertas Pinotage '77—Soft dry red with a 'nutty' flavour."[9] Jancis Robinson, a London-based wine expert and writer, visited South Africa in 1977, scribbling notes about the different plantings and yields ("Pinotage yield 2x Cab yield"), and that some farmers were expanding their vineyards ("No problem w/ land short-age").[10] Oz Clarke, who wrote a number of popular wine books in Britain in the 1980s, and hosted a television show about wine, waxed lyrical about South Africa in his 1984 *Essential Wine Book*, gushing about the beauty of the landscape and the exciting potential of the wines. He did refer to "torrid sweat-shop conditions," but this was regarding the climate near the Orange River, not the labor environment.[11]

In 1986 the United States and the EEC imposed sanctions on South Africa, in spite of British reluctance. Whether these sanctions actually had an impact on bringing about political change is debatable, but they did seem to have an impact on the consciences of British wine sellers. Berry Brothers and Rudd had stocked South African wine in the early 1970s, but these had silently disappeared from the lists by 1984. There could have been other reasons not to stock South African wine (a decline in quality, for example), but from a range of stockists' lists, it appears that it did not look good to be selling South African wine between 1986 and 1991. Oz Clarke's 1987 *Sainsbury's Book of Wine*, produced for a major grocery chain, included South Africa but demoted it to a short section, tucked discreetly between Morocco and

Mexico.[12] (Jancis Robinson described Sainsbury's approvingly in 1995 as "the UK's favourite wine merchant with an upmarket image, a good range of wines and a mail order business.")[13] As we will see, British wine retailers reembraced South African wine in 1991, as if after a long absence, when it fact it had been a brief intermission.

RAW AND VIGOROUS

Although Australia did not have an apartheid policy with the notoriety of South Africa's, the postwar era is now acknowledged as one of cruel and regrettable policies toward Aboriginal people, including one of separating children from their families in order to assimilate them into Anglo society. This is not tangential to wine production, because the racial attitudes seep deeply into the wine literature, too. In a celebratory centenary volume produced by Thomas Hardy and Sons in 1953, we learn how young Thomas arrived in the "raw, vigourous [sic] young colony" of South Australia, where "half-naked natives clustered round the shops or lounged about the streets with waddies in their hands, filthy and greasy. Hanging to them were packs of hungry, vagrant dogs. At the back of the Botanic Garden, the nursery of South Australia's first vines, was a corroboree ground."[14] The nineteenth-century civilizing trope had thus continued well into the 1950s: Hardy, it is implied, built a wine business where there had been savages, and the vines were a breakwater, with native festivities continuing beyond the pale.

The fact that many Australian wineries began producing official histories and collectors' volumes to mark milestones shows their self-confidence in the mid-twentieth century. It was a confidence in their businesses, their longevity, their futures, and their superiority over native Australians. They were beacons of civilization, driving industry and entrepreneurship. By the 1960s colonial wine industries were proudly promoting the technological sophistication of their operations. They certainly would not beat the French by trying to sell tradition, but they could portray their industry as clean, modern, and sophisticated. Indeed, John Burgoyne felt the need to defend the Australians'' "factory" of wine, noting that eschewing modern wine-making techniques was like expecting to have the wheat in one's bread cut with a scythe.

The theme of energetic technological advance was also present in postwar New Zealand wine discussions. In 1925 a New Zealand poet described, in patriotic terms, the country as a "teeming land of oil and wine."[15] In reality, viticulture was concentrated in just the northern area of country, primarily around Hawke's Bay. This was where both Busby and the Marist fathers had planted grapes, and where vines were concentrated until the 1970s.

As we have seen, New Zealand's wine industry was created by the original British settlers and augmented by small waves of other Europeans—primarily French priests and Dalmatian farmers. In the late nineteenth century, the industry was small but the state was curious and open to ideas about expanding it: bringing in Romeo Bragato as a consultant, keeping a keen eye on the global phylloxera crisis, and establishing a viticultural research unit at Te Kauwhata. The center at Te Kauwhata was recruiting an assistant vine and wine instructor in 1947, noting that "a degree or diploma in Oenology from a recognized college would be an advantage" to candidates.[16] The New Zealand press also reported on the Australian wine industry's successes and struggles, and New Zealanders bought quite a bit of South African wine (close to a hundred thousand gallons in 1947, which was not nothing in a country of around two million people). Where New Zealand's story diverged, or lagged behind, from Australia's was in the growth rate and volume. New Zealand's wine industry remained small and geographically concentrated for over a century.

The main reason that New Zealand did not follow the path of Australia was because of its highly organized temperance movement. This was a movement that was very skilled, not simply at discouraging consumers from buying alcohol to drink, but also in complicating each step of the wine-making process in order to make it difficult for winemakers to operate. As we have seen, licensing prohibitions in the early twentieth century created barriers to wine production and sales. As Paul Christoffel has shown, national prohibition may have narrowly failed in a 1919 referendum, but the temperance movement did not immediately disappear, and some restrictions were not eased until the 1960s.[17] This included the 6pm closing of pubs, which had been introduced in the temperance-inflected First World War, and led to the notorious "six o'clock swill," when punters would drink as much as they could in the last few minutes before the pubs closed. Closing times were not extended until 1967, and then by a national referendum. The *White Ribbon*, the magazine of the Women's Christian Temperance Union of New Zealand, continued publishing into the 1960s.[18]

The New Zealand environment was therefore not fully conducive to the expansion of the wine industry, although the government continued its support for Te Kauwhata and recognized the value that viticulture could potentially provide to the economy. In 1961, New Zealand's total annual wine production was 4,319 metric tonnes, about the equivalent of 5.75 million bottles of wine (750ml). Cyprus was producing about eight times as much (and Australia thirty-five times as much, and South Africa seventy times as much). New Zealand would catch up with Cyprus in the 1970s, but it would not surpass it until 2000.

However, the dedication that New Zealand put into innovation and technology gave it an edge that would lead to its wines receiving critical acclaim and great popularity in Britain and Australia. In 1948 the Wohnsiedler family's Waihirere Wine Company in Gisborne, New Zealand, invited a local journalist to view its own innovation,[19] "an agitator with an eight-inch blade rotated by a quarter horsepower electric-motor," used by the winemaker's son "to eliminate the tedious work of paddling the sugar into the pulp." A quarter-horsepower motor might be used to power a small home power tool, or perhaps a lawnmower; Waihirere was using it to incorporate sugar by hand into an eight-hundred-gallon vat of crushed pinot meunier grapes. This was a winery that was considered innovative, even internationally-minded. It had also recently changed its aging barrels from Canadian redwood to New Zealand totara, a native evergreen tree. The journalist was duly impressed, describing the winery with dynamism and local pride.

In hindsight, this type of operation seems quaintly rustic, and indeed New Zealand's wine technology would change dramatically over the next few decades. The Corban family estate, called Mt. Lebanon, was located in Henderson, near Auckland. It was established in 1902 by Assid Abraham Corban, a Lebanese immigrant who was an experienced winemaker. His son produced a commemorative pamphlet in the 1960s to celebrate his family's successful winemaking tradition, and contrasted the old technology with the new. "In spite of difficulties of all kinds, the estate developed vigorously [sic]," it wrote, with modernized equipment. In the early years, the grape crusher was turned by hand; now, it was automated and could crush thirty tons of grapes per hour. Stainless steel was now used throughout, "in new pumps, pasteurisation equipment and other installations, which include several firsts of their kind in New Zealand. These are the pneumatic Willmes press; pressure fermentation tanks; a sterile room for bottling table wines, and a refrigeration room with stainless steel capacity for 8,000 gallons."[20]

Whereas earlier accounts of wine making in the colonies often emphasized the relationship with the land and the agricultural nature of the operation, Corban's message was about what was happening in the winery, and not so much in the vineyard. Everything, the Corban brand stressed, was modern, clean, efficient, and technologically advanced—and this was a great source of pride. The family's contribution "to the economy of New Zealand is substantial," both directly and through its reliance on other industries, such as those producing "bottles, cases, cartons, printing and fertilizer."[21]

Technological change happened at the individual initiative of some wine-farmers, and also through the encouragement of government-funded research institutes. These institutes conducted research and usually made their own wine in test vineyards; New Zealand's Cooks Te Kauwhata Riesling was awarded top riesling wine by the French magazine Gault-Millau, its embassy proudly proclaimed in 1979.[22] Australia had the Australian Wine Research Institute, an industry-run and -funded body founded in 1955, which published 270 scientific papers between 1955 and 1985, as well as provided advice directly to winemakers. In 1970, for example, it was investigating the chemical nature of the pigments in shiraz, and supplying winemakers with clean yeast strains.[23] Its output included an influential 1976 study that advocated for "Stevlin" closures on table wine—that is, screw-caps in place of natural corks.[24] In addition, Roseworthy College continued awarding degrees in oenology, and merged with the University of Adelaide in 1991.

Jessica Duong's research into New Zealand scientific research has shown that, in the 1980s, it was a hive of activity and the Department of Agriculture was committed to growth and quality in the wine sector. Dr. Richard Smart, an Australian-born oenologist, was appointed New Zealand's government viticultural scientist in 1982. He was a strong proponent of canopy-management technique. This means carefully pruning and shaping the vines in order to manage the amount of sunlight that grapes receive—in the case of New Zealand, where winemakers had worried for a century that their climate was too cool, it was to maximize sun exposure. Smart's arguments challenged the idea that old vines, low-bearing in fruit, were the best route to wine quality, and he evangelized through publications, open days for winemakers, and by hosting international conferences.[25] New Zealand winemakers needed little encouragement: in the early 1970s, the first commercial wineries had begun on the South Island, led by the winery Montana. Science was catching up with individual initiative. Wine production began growing fast, and almost tripled between 1970 and 1980.

In 1981, New Zealand changed its system of measuring alcohol from the degrees system inherited from Britain, to the new international ABV system. This was one of several changes that would make its wines more friendly toward international markets. When Britain joined the EEC, it also adopted began metric measures for most foods and drink (the coveted exception was the pint, which could be used to measure and serve beer). Standardization helped colonial wines to integrate into foreign markets. In 1974 Australia continued its "metrication" program to include wine, and from that point the standard wine bottle would be 750ml (25.36 oz), instead of the slightly larger "Nett. 1 PT. 6 FL. OZS"—or 26 oz—that had previously been written on Australian wine labels.[26] In this sense Australia was far ahead of Britain. Marks and Spencer wine labels adopted metric measures in the 1970s, but they were not standardized. In labels that probably date from the early 1980s, Yugoslav riesling was sold in 69cl (690ml) bottles and French Meursault in 72cl (720ml) bottles. In 1985 the EEC directed that its members must completely harmonize, which meant that wine bottles would be 750ml.[27]

Although it is a running wine joke that upstart New World wines have fake châteaux on their labels, most colonial wines in the 1960s and 1970s had understated, even whimsical labels, often colorful. Rather than chateaux, crests of arms were popular (the "House of Penfold" crest, for example, aimed to give a touch of class to the "Royal Reserve Hock").[28] Stylized bunches of grapes, bold fonts, and simple animal drawings were also popular, such as springboks on South African labels. (The real "critter wines" of Australia would not dominate until the early twenty-first century.)

Distinctive bottle shapes were also phased out in the 1970s. The Burgoyne company had been purchased by Emu Wines in 1956, which in turn was purchased by Thomas Hardy in 1976,[29] and Burgoyne's famous flagon last appears in advertisements in the early 1960s. In New Zealand, Waihirere was using a distinctive bottle for its Moselle wine—a long, tapered bottle with a short neck—in 1968.[30] When wines were being sold in bulk and bottled overseas, it added cost and hassle to have a distinctive bottle for individual wineries.

One of the greatest changes to apply to colonial wines were with the actual names themselves. Over the course of the twentieth century many European countries, led by France, developed protected geographical origin labels for their wines (and for other traditional food products, like cheeses and cured meats). These labels indicated that the wine had been produced in a precise, limited geographic location, usually under certain production constraints. In French wine, for example, an *appelation d'origine contrôlée* (AOC) can regulate the type of grapes used in its the wine, whether irrigation is allowed, how long the wine must be matured, and so on. Each AOC has its own special criteria and the hundreds of AOCs range in prestige, but the overall effect is to impress consumers that the wine is, at a minimum, of good quality. The French system began developing in 1905 and grew rapidly in the 1930s, the Italian system followed suit, and later the European Union developed a broad system of quality controls for all of its members. Today, the European Union considers its geographical origin labels a form of intellectual property, and it defends them as such in international trade negotiations.[31]

The British New World of wine did not universally adopt such a system to protect its own geographical regions. In the mid-twentieth century, such a system would have made little financial sense to wine producers, whose wines were usually exported under the name of their producing country, combined with the name of the European region or style that had inspired the wine style: Australian burgundy, South African sherry, Cyprus port. John Burgoyne zealously defended this practice and scoffed at the "purists" who opposed it. "The average man," he countered, recognizes these terms as "the only ones in the English language that convey a general description of the *sort* of wine he has in mind."[32]

What the British world did have, and did enforce, was copyright. Ironically, it was a number of long-established *British* sherry importers that copyrighted the names of their wines as a form of quality control. These wines were made in Spain, bottled and marketed by British firms, and sold internationally. The financial interest in having exclusive rights to the word "sherry" thus lay not primarily with the producers in Spain, but with the negociants in Britain. John Harvey and Sons successfully defended their copyright on the term "Bristol Cream Sherry" in 1971.[33] Sandeman and Sons also successfully defended the term "sherry" against International Wines of Emu House, London. In this case Sandeman won a verdict that "sherry" could only refer to a wine coming from the Jerez area of Spain, "otherwise than as part of the phrases 'Cyprus Sherry,' 'British Sherry,' 'English Sherry,' 'South African Sherry,' 'Australian Sherry,' or 'Empire Sherry.'"[34]

This was a small victory, and it did not stop the persistence of colonial sherry. The names that colonial winemakers gave to their wines were, in fact, diversifying and changing, but not in a consistent way. In 1970, for example, South Australia was still selling wines with European names or styles (Stonyfell Claret, Penfolds Dalwood Chablis, Lindemans Bin 45 Claret). It was also naming wines with a mix of Oz and Europe (Wynns Coonawarra Hermitage, Orlando Barossa Moselle), as named varietals (Seaview Cabernet Shiraz, Chateau Tahbilk Marsanne), and various combinations of places and grapes (Leo Buring D.W. 65 Spatlese Rhine Riesling, Seppelts Hermitage Cabernet).[35]

Some Australian marketing professionals were trying similar tactics to associate their wines with a distinctive place. One, of the firm Swift and Moore, defended the name Kanga Rouge, which "was specifically chosen to immediately identify the wine as being Australian" when it was sold in export markets in 1978. In Australia, however, it was sold under "the name Menton Rouge [which] will be observed to have distinct French roots, which seems to be one of many prerequisites for selling red wine in Australia."[36] Consumers wanted to purchase a degree of sophistication, especially more prosperous middle-class Australians who were moving on from "introductory wines" in the late 1970s and into the 1980s.[37]

Sophistication was not Australia's overseas marketing strategy. In the interwar period colonial wines had been promoted by places like Whiteley's as approachable, unpretentious wines that were consistent with popular imperialism. In the postwar period, this evolved into the fun-loving, relaxed, and friendly Australian. "Like so many things Australian, these wines have no need of pretension, fancy names and labels," according to the marketing material produced by the Australian Wine Center in London.[38]

But, starting in 1980, the creation of the Australian Wine and Brandy Corporation (AWBC) created a new, clear requirement: wines made in Australia could not be sold under "false description." Primarily, that referred to wine that "includes the name of a country, or any other indication that the wine originated in a particular country, and the wine did not originate in that country." This was the end of Australian Burgundy. The law anticipated and headed off loopholes: it was false to use a foreign place name even if qualified with a word like "type" or "style"—so, no "Australian Chablis-style" wine—and even if the winemaker's address in Australia was clearly stated on the label. The penalty for flouting this law was two years' imprisonment.[39] The AWBC was a legal body with power to regulate and inspect.

Australia was self-regulating for several reasons. One reason was that Australia had trading agreements with the EEC, and its use of European place names would be seen as a violation of European member states' own appellation schemes. (European brands also defended their intellectual property rights: the Marists in New Zealand faced the threat of legal action in 1991. One of their chardonnays was named Chanel, after a revered priest in their community named Pierre Chanel, but the French luxury brand of the same name claimed potential confusion, and the Marists caved.)[40]

The other reason is that the AWBC was tasked with expanding Australian wine production and exports, and raising quality. It hoped to foster these changes with the creation of its own appellation system, called Australian Geographical Indications (GIs). This subdivided large "zones" into states and then regions (and a few subregions). Thus, Southeastern Australia includes New South Wales, which contains the Hunter Valley region. Unlike in French AOCs, these GIs do not specify production requirements (such as the percentage of particular grapes permitted). Still, James Halliday, the Australian wine-writer, has complained that "procedures for registration were and are inevitably tortuous and slow," as well as potentially expensive when the boundaries were contested.[41] This is undoubtedly true, but it also demonstrates to some degree that the system works, in that certain regions are considered sufficiently prestigious to be worth suing for entry.

South Africa created an appellation system in 1973, which also classified wines based on area of grape production. It, too, has a tiered system. Geographical units are divided into regions, then districts, then wards, so for example the Western Cape is home to the Coastal Region, which contain the district of Swartland and, within it, the ward of Malmesbury. In the 1970s and 1980s South Africa also created a color-coded label system for the necks of its bottles to certify the contents for wines that are sold as a particular varietal, vintage, or estate, with a special gold label for wines judged, by expert blind tasting, to be of superior quality. Meanwhile, in the apartheid era the KWV continued to grow, to the extent that it set and fixed prices, collected payments from farmers, and handled the overwhelming majority of the grapes that were produced in South Africa.[42]

This dualism defined a strange era in wine history. While the labor situation in South African wine looked quasi-feudal, and the country was an international pariah for its racist apartheid system, at the top of the South African wine industry there was an organizational professionalism that poised the country for more export success. In 1991, that would become the new reality.

NINETEEN

All Bar One

THE NEW WORLD CONQUERS
THE BRITISH MARKET

The Cape is a natural viticultural paradise. The dawn of a new
golden age of winemaking is now breaking here and one can only
hope that dark political clouds do not spoil the show.[1]

WINDRUSH WINES WINE LIST, *October 1992*

IT IS INDEED AWKWARD when a racist pariah of a regime is overthrown
to global fanfare and wine markets are vulnerably tossed into the mix. In
1990 the political leader Nelson Mandela was released from prison after
twenty-seven years, and in the spring of 1991 the South African government
began dismantling apartheid legislation. By the time this wine list was
printed in 1992, white South Africans had voted in favor of a full democracy.
The formal era of white supremacy was ending in South Africa.

Windrush Wines—apparently named not after the famous ship bringing
Caribbean immigrants to Britain in 1947, but after a Windrush Lake in the
quintessentially English Cotswold region—was a small, boutique wine
importer that emphasized lesser-known wines. Its 1992 list featured wines
from Australia, New Zealand, South Africa, and California, along with
French standards. The South Africa list was comprised of six still table wines
from five estates: two sauvignon blanc, two chardonnay, a cabernet franc, and
a "Rustenberg Red," all from 1989–91 vintages. Ranging from £4.75 to £8.62
a bottle, these were mid-priced wines for Windrush.

The democratization of South Africa was the most dramatic event that
would have an impact on British wine consumption, but it happened to
occur in a moment of phenomenal change for global wine markets. We have
seen several previous periods of momentous growth in colonial wine production and then consumption in Britain: in the 1820s and then the 1850s for
South Africa, and then in the 1920s and 1930s for all imperial producers. The

FIGURE 11. British per capita consumption, 1961–2013. Source: Food and Agriculture Office of the United Nations; U.K. Office of National Statistics.

final moment, and the most significant of all, happened in the late 1980s through the 1990s. The postwar market slump for Australian and South African wines had erased their market share of the 1930s. This reversal meant that by 1987, over 95 percent of British wine imports came from European countries, and half came from France; less than 3 percent came from South Africa and Australia. The situation looks very different a decade later, when Australian wine comprised around 15 percent of British imports; by 2007, more than half of Britain's wine came from the New World as opposed to European countries, with Australia as the largest single New World importer, followed by the United States, Chile, South Africa and New Zealand.[2] The fact that relatively little colonial wine was drunk in Britain in the 1960s and 1970s gives the false impression that Australia, New Zealand, and South Africa were entirely new market entrants in the 1980s and 1990s. We now know better: the 1960s and 1970s were another downturn in the long-established, volatile, and erratic wine trade between Britain and its (former) colonies. These two decades were a short-term break in a long relationship.

The great irony in the story of colonial wine is that despite two centuries of British support for wine industries, often delivered through preferential tariffs, colonial wines did not conquer the British market until the late 1980s. This was after the colonial relationship had ended, after latent imperial preference policies had been superseded by EEC trade agreements, and after fortified wines had gone far out of fashion.

Between 1970 and 1980 the real price of wine in Britain had dropped 20 percent. Wine consumption in Britain had been steadily rising, too. In 1971 per capita consumption of wine was around five bottles per annum, in 1981 it was ten, in 1991 it was fifteen and in 2001 it was just over twenty. By 1991, then, many adults were consuming wine on a regular basis, such as around a few bottles a month. Consumption levels, once established, only dipped around 10 percent during two major recessions in the early 1990s and early 2000s.[3] Consumption peaked in 2008 at around twenty liters (about twenty-seven bottles) (see fig. 11).[4] Just as important, wine was replacing other kinds of alcoholic drinks: it represented just 6 percent of drink consumption in 1976, but it was 15 percent in 1989.[5]

In the early and mid-1980s, almost all of the wine drunk in Britain came from European countries. Marks and Spencer's emphasis on European wines and particularly sweet whites, with France as the reference, is matched by that of other major retailers. Fortified wines had gone out of favor, but sweet white wines had taken their place. "Liebfraumilch Stars!" referring to a sweet German white wine, was the major Christmas bargain in the Oddbins Christmas catalog for 1986. It also promoted its "party quaffers," magnum bottles priced at less than £3 per liter. These were Italian, French, and German wines, many of them sweet. The Co-Op supermarket had a house-brand range of wines that showed the prevalence of sweet German styles. A wine list from the late 1980s was exclusively European wines, with the largest proportion French, followed by German. The most popular wine and the designated party wine was again probably Liebfraumilch, given that it was the only wine that was sold in four different sizes: a standard 750ml bottle plus 1-liter, 1.5-liter, and 3-liter bottles.[6]

The emphasis on good value reveals quite a bit about the changing demographics of wine. The social elite was too small to contain the massive expansion of wine consumption by the 1980s. Does that mean that the wine-drinking middle classes expanded, or that working-class culture changed to embrace wine? Both are probably true to some degree. John Burnett asserts that wine consumption more socially widespread in the 1970s due to the decline of heavy industry, which led to the "embourgeoisement of society"; for him, "the democratization of wine-drinking is a symbol" of more people considering themselves to be middle class.[7] The wine economist Kym Anderson argues that new wine consumers came from a "new upwardly mobile middle class that arose from former Prime Minister Margaret Thatcher's economic reforms."[8] Thatcher did not become prime minister until 1979, too late to fully explain rising wine consumption in the postwar period. Certain class markers shifted as a result of Thatcherite policies, most noticeably homeownership, but there is no consensus as to whether her monetarist polices created a new or larger middle class. Consumer spending did recover from the global crises of the 1970s (which, in U.K., saw a three-day week, strikes, and high inflation and unemployment rates) and the 1980s saw the rise of particular forms of conspicuous consumption and "yuppie" culture, but historians and economists disagree as to whether the crisis years represent the failure of a postwar Keynesian state, or a cyclical recession in which U.K. fared better than many other countries. We should balance these arguments with the perspective offered, in 1985, by historian Asa Briggs. In his history of the Victoria Wine Company, a large and inexpensive British chain of off-licenses, Briggs noted that the company's own "sophisticated" market research showed that 40 percent of its customers in 1981 were drawn from social classes C2, D, and E (which correspond to manual occupations, skilled through unskilled).[9] Whether or not the class structure of U.K. had changed in the postwar period, there is evidence that wine *already* had its own place in working-class culture. That was, of course, thanks to affordable and approachable colonial wines.

British consumers were, indeed, able to drink more wine thanks to the convenience of supermarkets,[10] although supermarkets were initially to the benefit of European producers, not colonial ones. Berry Bros. & Rudd lamented in their autumn 1983 wine list that, "the growth of wine drinking in this country has brought about a tremendous change in the pattern of retail distribution. . . . Much of the business has passed into the hands of what are called 'non specialist' outlets, such as supermarkets." They underlined the "faceless" and thus unintimidating nature of the supermarket experience, regretting that they had acquired "an undeserved reputation in some quarters, especially perhaps among younger people, for being exclusive and unapproachable!"[11] The fact that one of the premier fine wine sellers in Britain was now bemoaning its "exclusive" reputation shows the great transformations in wine marketing and consumption in U.K.'s postwar era.

While the growth of supermarkets did much to make New World wines accessible, British supermarkets were not responsible for a sudden democratization and export growth of New World wines. However, once British supermarkets had thrown themselves wholeheartedly into wine selling, they had enormous purchasing power and could drive hard bargains with suppliers,[12] pushing prices down, and running specials on wines as loss-leaders. At Murray Edwards College in Cambridge, a women's college then known as New Hall, there was an academic fellow who served as Wine Steward. New Hall was not as old or as wealthy as a college like King's, but it did have a wine cellar. Its wine sales were not intended to make a profit for the college, though, as the Wine Steward explained to their accountant: "There is no point in any case in trying to make a large profit, since our Fellows are extremely conservative as regards paying money for wine . . . [and] it would be difficult and time-consuming to under-cut Sainsburys."[13] New Hall's wine accounts include many clippings from Edmund Penning-Roswell's column on supermarket wines in the *Financial Times,* "High Street Wines."

The ordinary public's tastes and opinions lagged a good decade or two behind those of wine experts, though. They had been tasting colonial wines on location, long before the wines would reach British off-licenses, and they were impressed with what they tasted. Hugh Johnson visited around 1970, and was both enthusiastic and prescient. "It may be too soon to say that great wine is made at Coonawarra," he wrote, "but I will stick my neck out and say that it will be."[14] According to Bristol-based wine importer John Avery, "a lot of Australian fortified wines but not many table wines had already come in; we were pioneers but not exclusive pioneers of Australian [unfortified] wines" in the 1960s, though "Nothing much happened with New World wines for at least ten years from when I started, from 1965 to 1975. But I reckon by the end of the 70's wine journalists were beginning to refer to New World wines."[15] It would take another decade for ordinary consumers to change their preferences, but this interest in New World wines from fine wine experts heralded a shift.

A change was coming to British wine consumption, and the pivotal year was 1987. New Hall only had one Australian wine in 1985, and its Wine Steward was Australian.[16] Now, in 1990, Anthony Berry enthused, "almost every civilised country in the world [is] producing wines of better and better quality in sufficient quantities."[17]

CALL THAT A WINE?

The language of civilization had not disappeared. And why not, since it was Australia's big colonial birthday? Australian wines first appeared in Marks and Spencer in 1987 as a limited collection to celebrate the bicentennial of European colonization. A promotional flyer introduced customers to Australia, the "Lucky Country," whose wines were "full of fruit and openness."[18] The tone generally preached to the nervous neophyte: Australian dry white was described vaguely but enthusiastically as "the ideal aperitif wine, or excellent accompaniment to most foods." However, more precise descriptors were starting to appear for a more knowledgable audience, with red wines described as tannic or "peppery."[19] A full range of New World wines debuted in 1991. Trumpeting a "Brave New World of Grape Expectations," Marks and Spencer introduced wines from South Africa, Chile, Australia, and California. These were described as targeting "an increasingly adventurous consumer" and those who "demand high quality and value."[20]

This "adventurous" language reflected the way that Australian culture, in general, was perceived in Britain. The Jacob's Creek advertisements of the era, shown in cinemas, depicted a laid-back, handsome bush-ranger-cum-winemaker, lounging against a fence in a slouch hat, inviting viewers in to his outdoorsy lifestyle. New Zealand wines were pitched in similarly enthusiastic terms. "New Zealand is ready and waiting for you! Are you ready for New Zealand?" shouted a promotional flyer from 1993,[21] like the announcer warming up a crowd at an international rugby match. Although New Zealand's wine industry was founded through the same ideals, principles, and even individuals of Australia's, it had never exported any quantity of wine to Britain. This would change in the 1990s.

Australian culture made particular inroads with British youth in the 1980s and 1990s. In 1975, Australia and Britain introduced a reciprocal working-holiday scheme, which allowed young people to undertake a year or more of work and travel.[22] Hundreds of thousands of young people have taken advantage of this program; in Australia, working holidaymakers have become vital for agriculture, as the rural population has declined over the past forty years.[23] The scheme has built an impression in Britain of Australia and Australians as fun, youthful, and adventurous.

Complementing that scheme, two Australian soap operas, *Neighbours* and *Home and Away*, began broadcasting on British television in 1986 and 1988, respectively. They aired late in the afternoon and were popular with older children and teenagers. *Neighbours* became one of the most-watched programs on British television in the late 1980s and early 1990s, in part because of two of its break-out stars, Kylie Minogue and Jason Donovan. These two moved to London and became some of the most popular and recognizable pop stars in Britain in the late 1980s and early 1990s, with seven number-one hit songs between 1988 and 1991. But even those who were not particularly young or interested in dancing to "The Locomotion" were probably touched by the Australian entertainment invasion. On Christmas Day in 1989, nearly 40 percent of Britain population retired to their couches for a postprandial broadcast of the Australian film *Crocodile Dundee*.[24]

Many of them were probably drinking an Australian wine with their film. Oddbins began featuring Australian wines in 1986 and quickly made them a focus of their list; over the next decade space given to Eastern European wines waned and sweet white wines went out of style. The "seemingly endless parcels of fabulous Australian that have been appearing for the past five years ... [are] the best value-for-money on the High Street," Oddbins crowed in 1991.[25] Their selection led wine journalist Tim Atkins to affirm that Oddbins had a "brilliant list ... the most cosmopolitan range of wines on the market."[26] This improvement in quality went in tandem with cultural and political changes. According to Oddbins in 1992, "A mere seven or eight years ago, however, to serve an Australian or Chilean wine would have condemned the host to social purdah; the Australian wine industry had for so many years satisfied the Great British public's baser tastes and Chile had sunk into its congenital political miasma and was a lost cause."[27]

"Within a relatively short period of time Australian wines have been firm favourites with Britain wine consumers," a 1990 Augustus Barnett wine list explained, and "fortunately the prices of Australian wines have now generally settled down enabling regular consumption at reasonable prices."[28] Still, Eastern European wines—Bulgarian, Hungarian, and Greek –featured prominently, in greater numbers than the New World wines starting to appear. A few South African wines were available in 1989 and 1990 but at the bottom of the list, without descriptions, as if not to draw attention to them.

The reintroduction of South African wines alongside the deterioration and then collapse of the apartheid state was approached cautiously by some retailers. Berry Bros. & Rudd carried three South African ports in its extensive, French-dominated list from the 1960s up until 1981. In October 1982 it dropped two of those South African wines, and by June 1983 the South African offerings had disappeared and its very first Australian wine was featured. It slowly expanded this selection, and in October 1991 it reintroduced South African wine with the following editorial: "Returning to South African wine after a period of enforced absence has been a thought-provoking experience. South African wines were, after all, once ahead of California and

Australia in terms of reputation. . . . We found, nevertheless, when tasting the wines that we had to be rather more selective in our selection than might have been expected. The three wines with which we are reintroducing South Africa to our list are however superb examples of quality wine-making."[29]

This statement makes an oblique reference to South Africa's discriminatory apartheid system, which was abolished in 1991. Wines sold in 1991 had, of course, been produced under the apartheid system, since wines require some age before shipment and sale. The main point here, however, is that by the early 1990s Australian and South African wines became respectable and appeared on wine lists, and not just those of supermarkets and affordable chains, but also those of retailers specializing in fine and exclusive wines. This was a real first, because while Australian and South African wines had risen and fallen, repeatedly, in the consumption of middle-class British people for a century and a half, they had never received the critical respect of U.K.'s fine wine merchants (with the exception of Constantia in the nineteenth century).

Conclusion

IN 2015, TO MUCH FANFARE in the British press, a company named Gibraltar Wine Vaults announced that it was converting Gibraltar's underground tunnels into wine storage.[1] Gibraltar is a tiny, rocky island that squats in the narrow straits between the Iberian Peninsula and North Africa, where the Mediterranean meets the Atlantic. It has no agriculture, and certainly no vineyards. Gibraltar became a British territory in 1713. It was a vital naval base for the U.K.'s Mediterranean maneuvers—especially, after 1869, for access to the Suez Canal, and onward to the Indian Ocean—and was attacked and besieged dozens of times over the centuries. In the early months of the Second World War the British government authorized an expansion of the island's network of underground tunnels, for safety and storage in the event of an attack. The "Rock" has just twelve kilometers of coastline but fifty-five kilometers of underground tunnels. Because of Gibraltar's relaxed tax regime, wine that is imported into the island can be held in bond at relatively low rates. This allows connoisseurs to store their wine cheaply.

There is no more apt metaphor for the changes that have taken place in the British world of wine over the past two centuries. What was once a military lynchpin facilitating Britain's colonial expansion is now a tax haven for fine wines. The empire is (mostly) gone; the Mediterranean is a holiday destination for British people, not a sea to be crossed and conquered in the pursuit of global power. Free trade stopped being a rallying cry for most British people in the 1920s, but it persists in some of the fragments and remnants of the empire.

This book has rewritten what we think we know about the New World of wine, by demonstrating the long history of wine making in European colonies, and the equally long-standing, if volatile, trade relationships between colonies and the United Kingdom. Wine, for settler colonists in British overseas possessions, was a means of controlling and subduing what they experienced as a strange and exotic land, of making its topography conform to a civilized European model. It was also often a means of controlling and subduing native peoples, by removing their means of independent production, extracting their labor, and creating unhealthy patterns of consumption.

I have taken a broad interpretation of the term "civilizing mission." When historians look at the motivations of those involved in imperial projects, they tend to categorize them as either motivated by profit or by the will to civilize. What wine demonstrates is that these two were never far apart: capitalism was endemic to British imperialism, and the commercial success of wine was viewed as proof of its civilizing success. This was a foundational ethos that existed up through the mid-twentieth century; during and after British decolonization, this civilizing mission was, I have argued, projected back onto Britain, as Britain's new wine-drinking population clutched at excolonial wines as accessible markers of sophistication.

By the mid-1990s, New Hall in Cambridge was serving a sparkling Jacob's Creek pinot noir–chardonnay blend at all of its champagne-worthy events.[2] Winemakers in Australia, New Zealand, and South Africa had plenty to celebrate, too. The dramatic growth in sales meant a growth in revenue as well. Wine making became profitable, and winemakers became more powerful, for the revenue they have created as well as the role their wineries play in countries that make a lot of money from tourism. The face of wine making had changed, from a small, rustic winery of only fifty years earlier, to a bright, modern, stainless-steel operation.

South Africa, Australia, and New Zealand, which have been the main case studies in this book, still grapple with the impact of settler colonialism. In South Africa, stark racial divides and inequality have existed since winemakers began importing people to be enslaved on their vineyards in the seventeenth century. One of the ways in which the modern state of South Africa is trying to reverse several centuries of inequality is through Black Economic Empowerment schemes, which promote the employment of Black people in underrepresented industries, including wine. Land reform is an important political issue, too. The Solms-Delta Vineyard near Franschhoek, which actually has a free museum dedicated to the history of slavery, would seem like a model of a vineyard confronting its past, but it has come under fire in the South African press for allegedly reneging on its promise to make farmworkers co-owners of the land.[3] In Australia, meanwhile, water rights have become a fraught issue. Irrigating vines takes a lot of water, and diverting wine towards commercial vineyards can deprive Aboriginal communities of water access.[4]

These struggles are some of the long legacies of colonialism in the global wine industry. If critics blame external forces for encouraging this activism, that should serve as no surprise: from their inception, wine industries in the New World were woven into global networks of communication and exchange. Australia is often said to have been "born modern." That modernity was colonial in nature, so it is unsurprising that the colonial past still torments modern Australian society.

Some wine lovers might protest that colonialism is a distant historical footnote to the history of wine, and that dredging up colonial history is a buzzkill, a weary intrusion on our enjoyment of wine. Can't we just enjoy a glass of wine without someone introducing controversy? Is colonial history designed to make wine lovers feel guilty? Modern life is fraught and tiring: for once, can we leave politics aside and just drink wine? I hope what this book has demonstrated is that wine has never been apolitical, and that the colonial context in which wine was first created has inflected its production and consumption into the twenty-first century. In Britain, as we have seen, the racial idioms and discussion of "civilized" countries continued to appear in wine literature through the entire twentieth century.

Some of what we have learned about the New World may guide us as modern consumers. More and more consumers in wealthy countries want to know about the ethics of food production: where our consumables come from, how they are produced, and how it is transported. This ethical anxiety partly reflects urbanization, and the fact that many modern consumers feel far removed from food production, just as British consumers did in the 1860s or 1870s, when there were fears about wine adulteration. It is also a status marker. In a world of near-infinite choice, making ethical consumer choices allows us to define ourselves as ethical people. Cynicism should not discourage us, though. It is a good thing to seek out ethically produced and sustainable wine: wine that has been produced by workers paid at fair wages, where both chemicals and natural resources have been used responsibly. In this regard, we are wise to acquaint ourselves with the history of wine, to understand and be alert to the regrettable actions of the past. We might also reconsider some trinkets from the history of colonial wine for our modern needs. Perhaps "bulk wine" need not be a term of derision, if we consider the environmental cost of shipping heavy, cumbersome glass bottles. In light of the climate devastation in modern Australia, people of European extraction might also view with new respect how Aboriginal nations lived harmoniously in an arid land.

Another reason to appreciate the colonial history of the New World is that potted versions of history are still used to sell wine. Now, many Australian wineries offer "cellar door" visits to tourists. Often, tourists can view original nineteenth-century buildings as part of a guided visit that continues to modern vats and a sleek tasting room. At Tyrell Vineyards in Australia's Hunter Valley, which claims some of the world's oldest continuously-producing grape vines from the 1870s, a small cabin in roughhewn wood is presented as the original home of founder Edward Tyrell.[5] The tour continues to the modern vats, and ends in a tasting. It is now a convention for colonial wineries to emphasize their date of founding on their websites and even their wine labels. They know that modern consumers will not associate their wines with the "empire sherry" of the 1950s, but will see that far-off founding date as a mark of quality and character, a selling point for the wine.

This plays well to export markets, too. "In Northern Ireland, some of the best selling wines are McGuigan's. We love them," according to Myra Greer, the then wine columnist of the *Belfast Telegraph*. In 2002, she wrote, the local importer, Gallery Wines, imported almost 1.5 million bottles of McGuigan's, or roughly a bottle per person in the province. McGuigan's "delivers exactly what people want in a red wine and is pitched at exactly the price we want to pay," which was £4.99 a bottle for "an eager to please wine—soft, flavoursome, easy drinking, with no harsh tannins and a nice bit of residual sugar."[6] Fifteen years later, McGuigan's launched one of its new wine ranges in Northern Ireland, in deference to its big market. The press, and McGuigan's, spun this as an enduring historical legacy of Irish emigration: "The chief winemaker of one of Australia's best-known vineyards has said Northern Ireland is the firm's biggest market. Neil McGuigan of McGuigan Wines—whose family originally come from Co Monaghan—said: 'I think people see it as a local boy gone overseas, done good and sent wine back.'"[7] The McGuigans had emigrated to Australia in the 1840s.

British culture and society have been shaped by the experience of colonizing others, whether British people are conscious of it or not. Britain transformed into a country of wine drinkers over the nineteenth and twentieth centuries, and particularly after 1970, and this change in social habits is largely thanks to colonial wines. Colonialism feels so far away and innocuous to some British commentators, that it is a source of lighthearted foodie humor. "They thrashed us at rugby. They thrashed us at cricket. And now they're thrashing us at cooking," Matthew Fort wrote in *The Guardian*, about the rise of Australian restaurateurs in London in the early 2000s: "It seems that they are the latest culinary imperialists ready to colonise their former colonisers."[8] Yet colonialism is a force that continues to shape what it means to be British today—or indeed, what it means to Australian, Kiwi, or South African, or even what it means to drink wine.

Appendix

BOTTLE SIZES

Volume measures have changed repeatedly over time in the U.K. The dominant system until the late twentieth century was the imperial system, which used inches, miles, ounces, and pounds. American readers should note that imperial measures are not identical to American measures, although they use the same names: an imperial pint is 20 fluid ounces, an American one is 16; an Imperial gallon is 160 fluid ounces, and an American one is 128. These imperial measures were standardized in 1824.[1] The Weights and Measures Act 1985 established that an imperial gallon is 4.54609 cubic decimetres; there are 4 quarts in a gallon, 8 pints in a gallon.

For much of the time period covered in this book, in Britain a bottle of wine was one-sixth of an imperial gallon; in the second half of the twentieth century, the 750ml bottle became common and then standard. In 1994 there was a transition to metric units in Britain, although exception was made for the measure of "pint", used in a pub.[2]

ALCOHOL CONTENT

Today alcoholic content is commonly expressed in "alcohol by volume," or ABV. This is expressed as a percentage, and for still table wine the typical range is 11–15 percent. The "degree" system formerly used in the U.K. was based on pure alcohol being 175 degrees.[3] Wine that was 30 degrees contained 30 of proof spirit, and this is equivalent to 17.14 percent ABV. Twenty-six degrees was thus 14.86 percent ABV.

A NOTE ABOUT BRITISH CURRENCY

Until 1971, British currency used the "pound-shilling-pence" system, with 12 pence in a shilling and 20 shillings, or 240 pence, in a pound. This could be expressed a 1.1.1 (one pound, one shilling, one pence), or 1/- (one shilling, zero pence). In 1971 this system was replaced with a decimal system of a hundred pence in a pound.

NOTES

INTRODUCTION

1. Photographs of the Dalwood Vineyards, near Branxton, New South Wales, Australia, 1886. Royal Commonwealth Society Library, Cambridge University Library, RCS/Y3086B.

2. Profit and loss sheet for 1891. Dalwood Vineyard Papers, State Library of New South Wales (hereafter SLNSW), MLMSS 8051, Box 4, Folder 7.

3. Author's photograph, 2017. Costa Coffee, Stansted Arrivals Hall, Stansted Mountfichet, Kent.

4. "John Cunningham reports on the vintage Australian plonk that became U.K.'s wine of the 90s." John Cunningham, "First of the Summer Wine," *The Guardian*, May 13, 1999.

5. Kym Anderson and Nanda R. Aryal, *Growth and Cycles in the Australian Wine Industry: A Statistical Compendium, 1843 to 2013* (Adelaide: University of Adelaide Press, 2015), 12, table 22; National shares of world wine import volume and value, 2007–9 (%); Wine Institute's Per Capita Data, www.wineinstitute.org /files/2010_Per_Capita_Wine_Consumption_by_Country.pdf (accessed June 1, 2018; no longer available). Similar statistics exist via the Organization for Economic Co-operation and Development, https://stats.oecd.org. I then adjusted consumption for adult population (approx. 82 percent) based on Office for National Statistics, table 1: Age distribution of the U.K. population, 1976 to 2046 (projected).

6. With respect, honor, and acknowledgment of Country, Aboriginal readers are advised that this book contains the names of deceased persons, as well as discussion of mistreatment and trauma.

7. Hubert de Castella, *John Bull's Vineyard: Australian Sketches* (Melbourne: Sands and McDougall, 1886), 249–50.

8. Monty Python, "Australian Table Wines," *The Monty Python Instant Record Collection* (London: Charisma, 1977), available at www.youtube.com/watch?v= Cozwo88w44Q (accessed September 2, 2021).

9. *Galium odoratum,* a hardy herbaceous plant common in northern Europe, with sweet-scented white flowers.

10. "May Drink," *Spons' Household Manual: a Treasury of Domestic Receipts and Guide for Home Management* (London and New York: C. and F.N. Spon, 1887), p. 200. See also the "Barossa Punch," in *Recipes Presented By Whiteley's: Wine Punches and Cups* (Whiteley's, n.d. [c. 1950]), Whiteley's Papers, Westminster City Archives, 726/146; and *Entertaining with Wines of the Cape: Choosing, Cellaring, Serving, Cooking, Recipes* (Die Ko-operatiewe Wijnbouwers Vereniging van Zuid-Afrika Beperkt, Paarl, Cape, Republic of South Africa, first published 1959, 4th ed. 1971), Andre Simon Collection, London Guildhall Library (LGL).

CHAPTER 1. WRITING ABOUT WINE

1. Hugh Johnson told me that he was the first person to use the term to write about wine, in the 1960s; this seems probable but I have not found that particular instance in print. Author's conversation with Hugh Johnson, October 2012.

2. FAOStat.org.

3. For example, see the film *Mondovino,* dir. Jonathan Nossiter (New York: Velocity/THINKFilm, 2004).

4. British Broadcasting Corporation, featuring Oz Clarke and Jilly Goolding. *Food and Drink*, broadcast on BBC, April 5, 1994.

5. Hazel Murphy, 2003–4 interview. *In Vino Veritas: Extracts from an Oral History of the U.K. Wine Trade* (London: British Library National Life Story Collection, 2005), audio CD, disc 2, track 19. Indeed, there is evidence of responsiveness in Old World producers: see José Miguel Martínez-Carrión and Francisco Medina-Albaladejo, "Change and Development in the Spanish Wine Sector," *Journal of Wine Research* 21, no. 1 (March 2010): 77–95.

6. Glenn Banks and John Overton, "Old World, New World, Third World? Reconceptualizing the Worlds of Wine," *Journal of Wine Research* 21, no. 1 (March 2010): 60.

7. Ibid., 59.

8. As in the seventeen bans on Chilean vine-planting instituted by Spanish Phillip III, and the tariffs levied on Algerian producers after the end of the French phylloxera crisis. See Kolleen M. Cross, "The Evolution of Colonial Agriculture: The Creation of the Algerian 'Vignoble,' 1870–1892," *Proceedings of the Meeting of the French Colonial Historical Society* 16 (1992): 57–72.

9. See, for more detail, Charles Ludington, *The Politics of Wine in Britain: A New Cultural History* (Basingstoke: Palgrave, 2013); Louis M. Cullen, *The Irish Brandy Houses of Eighteenth-Century France* (Dublin: Lilliput, 2000).

10. Jennifer Regan-Lefebvre, "John Bull's Other Vineyard: Selling Australian Wine in Nineteenth-Century Britain," *Journal of Imperial and Commonwealth History* 45, no. 2 (April 2017): 259–83.

11. Wine Australia, *Directions to 2025: An Industry Strategy for Sustainable Success* (Adelaide: Wine Australia, 2007), 10, 12.

12. James Belich, *Replenishing the Earth: The Settler Revolution and the Rise of the Anglo-World, 1783–1939* (Oxford: Oxford University Press, 2009), 3.

13. James Belich, "Response: A Cultural History of Economics?" *Victorian Studies* 53, no. 1 (Autumn 2010): 119.

14. Whereas the other four maintained very close with and subordinate to U.K. after independence, the new United States severed such ties. Belich argues that the United States' development can be understood in terms of an "Anglo-World"; I put this argument to the side because in terms of wine markets, there appears to have been scant trade among the United States, U.K., and British colonies in the nineteenth and most of the twentieth centuries. On the history of American wine see in particular Thomas Pinney, *A History of Wine in America*, vols. 1 and 2 (Berkeley: University of California Press, 2005); or Erica Hannickel, *Empire of Vines: Wine Culture in America* (Philadelphia: University of Pennsylvania Press, 2013).

15. Two examples from the vast genre include Mark Prendergast, *Uncommon Grounds: The History of Coffee and How It Transformed Our World* (New York: Basic Books, 2010), and Laura C. Martin, *Tea: The Drink that Changed the World* (Rutland, VT: Tuttle, 2007).

16. Sidney Mintz, *Sweetness and Power: The Place of Sugar in Modern History*, 2nd ed. (New York: Penguin, 1986).

17. There is a delightful range of detailed recipes in John Davies, *The Innkeeper's and Butler's Guide; or, A Directory for Making and Managing British Wines: With Directions for the Managing, Colouring and Flavouring of Foreign Wines and Spirits, and, for Making British Compounds, Peppermint, Aniseed, Shrub, &c. . . . 13th ed.*, rev. and corrected (Leeds: Davies, 1810).

18. Examples include Julie McIntyre, "Camden to London and Paris: The Role of the Macarthur Family in the Early New South Wales Wine Industry," *History Compass* 5, no. 2 (2007): 427–38; Vincent Geraci, "Fermenting a Twenty-First Century California Wine Industry," *Agricultural History* 78, no. 4 (Autumn 2004): 438–65; Julius Jacobs, "California's Pioneer Wine Families," *California Historical Quarterly* 54, no. 2 (Summer 1975): 139–74; Erica Hannickel, "A Fortune in Fruit: Nicholas Longworth and Grape Speculation in Antebellum Ohio," *American Studies* 51, nos. 1–2 (Spring–Summer 2010): 89–108.

19. Julie Holbrook Tolley, "The History of Women in the South Australian Wine Industry, 1836–2003," 119–38, and Gwyn Campbell, "South Africa: Wine, Black Labour and Black Empowerment," 221–40, both in Campbell and Nathalie Guibert, eds., *Wine, Society and Globalisation: Multidisciplinary Perspectives on the Wine Industry* (Basingstoke: Palgrave, 2007).

20. Hugh Johnson, *Vintage: The Story of Wine* (London: Mitchell Beardsley, 1989); Paul Lukacs, *Inventing Wine: A New History of One of the World's Most Ancient Pleasures* (New York: Norton, 2012); John Varriano, *Wine: A Cultural History* (London: Reaktion, 2011); Marc Millon, *Wine: A Global History* (London: Reaktion, 2013).

21. Bruce Robbins, "Commodity Histories," *PMLA* 120, no. 2 (March 2005): 456.

22. A few examples: William Gervase Clarence-Smith, *Cocoa and Chocolate, 1765–1914* (New York: Routledge, 2000); Ericka Rappaport, *A Thirst for Empire: How Tea Shaped the Modern World* (Princeton, NJ: Princeton University Press, 2017); Rachel Laudan, *Cuisine and Empire: Cooking in World History* (Berkeley: University of California Press, 2013).

23. Jenny Diski, "Flowery, Rustic, Tippy, Smokey," review of *Green Gold: The Empire of Tea,* by Alan Macfarlane and Iris Macfarlane, *London Review of Books* 25, no. 12, June 19, 2003, 11–12.

24. Lukacs, *Inventing Wine,* 128.

CHAPTER 2. WHY BRITAIN?

1. Two classic and powerful expressions are Edward Said, *Culture and Imperialism* (New York: Vintage, 1994), and Partha Chatterjee, *Nationalist Thought and the Colonial World* (London: United Nations University, 1986).

2. A. Gordon Bagnall, *An Account of Their History, Their Production and Their Nature, Illustrated with Wood-Engravings by Roman Waher* (Paarl: KWV, 1961).

3. Oddbins Christmas Catalogue, 1999, p. 23. Guildhall Wine Lists, COL/LIB/PB29/72, LGL.

4. Charles Ludington, *The Politics of Wine in Britain: A New Cultural History* (Basingstoke: Palgrave, 2013).

5. Kolleen M. Guy, *When Champagne Became French: Wine and the Making of a National Identity* (Baltimore: Johns Hopkins University Press, 2003).

6. For a good overview of the literature, see Joanna de Groot, "Metropolitan Desires and Colonial Connections: Reflections on Consumption and Empire," in *At Home with the Empire: Metropolitan Culture and the Imperial World,* ed. Catherine Hall and Sonya Rose (Cambridge: Cambridge University Press, 2007), 166–90. A recent intervention in imperial commodity history is John M. Talbot, "On the Abandonment of Coffee Plantations in Jamaica after Emancipation," *Journal of Imperial and Commonwealth History* 43, no. 1 (2015): 33–57.

7. Maxine Berg. "From Imitation to Invention: Creating Commodities in Eighteenth-Century U.K.," *Economic History Review,* n.s., 55, no. 1 (February 1, 2002): 1–30.

8. For a particularly potent representation of this image, see Ministry of Information short film, *Food from the Empire* (1940), on www.colonialfilm.org.uk.

9. A debate that crystalized around Bernard Porter, *The Absentminded Imperialists* (Oxford: Oxford University Press, 2004).

10. This should not be misconstrued to mean that the rest of U.K. was a backwater—far from it. But the capital city is a powerful magnet.

11. Explored in meticulous detail in John Nye, *War, Wine, and Taxes: The Political Economy of Anglo-French Trade, 1689–1900* (Princeton, NJ: Princeton University Press, 2007).

12. Motoko Hori, "The Price and Quality of Wine and Conspicuous Consumption in England, 1646–1759," *English Historical Review* 123, no. 505 (December 2008): 1468.

13. John Burnett, *Liquid Pleasures: A Social History of Drinks in Modern U.K.* (London: Routledge, 1999), 153.

14. Charles Ludington, *Politics of Wine in Britain: A New Cultural History* (Basingstoke: Palgrave Macmillan, 2013).

15. See David Gutzke, *Women Drinking Out in U.K. since the Early Twentieth Century* (Manchester: Manchester University Press, 2013).

CHAPTER 3. DUTCH COURAGE

1. Charles Davidson Bell, *Jan van Riebeeck Arrives in Table Bay in April 1652* (n.d. [c. 1840–80]), https://commons.wikimedia.org/wiki/File:Charles_Bell_-_Jan_van_Riebeeck_se_aankoms_aan_die_Kaap.jpg (accessed September 1, 2021).

2. Giulio Osso, "Rare portrait of Simon Van Der Stel highlight of the National Antiques Faire" (n.d. [2012]), Wine.co.za, https://services.wine.co.za/pdf-view.aspx?PDFID=2505 (accessed September 1, 2021).

3. Rod Phillips, *French Wine: A History* (Berkeley: University of California Press, 2016), 69–71.

4. André Jullien, *Topographie de tous les vignobles connus* (Paris: Madame Huzard and L. Colas, 1816), 428.

5. Roger Beck, *The History of South Africa* (Westport, CT: Greenwood Press, 2000), 28

6. André L. Simon, ed. *South Africa,* "Wines of the World" Pocket Library (London: Wine and Food Society, 1950), 7.

7. A Gordon Bagnall, *Wines of South Africa: An Account of Their History, Their Production and Their Nature, Illustrated with Wood-Engravings by Roman Waher* (Paarl: KWV, 1961), 10.

8. Ibid., 10.

9. George McCall Theal, *Chronicles of Cape Commanders; or, An Abstract of Original Manuscripts in the Archives of the Cape Colony.* (Cape Town: W. A. Richards, Government Printers, 1882), 89–90.

10. Ibid., 87.

11. Ibid., 296.

12. Ibid., 62. A stiver is a coin of small value.

13. Ibid., 180.

14. Johan Fourie and Dieter von Fintel, "Settler Skills and Colonial Development: The Huguenot Wine-Makers in Eighteenth-Century Dutch South Africa," *Economic History Review* 67, no. 4 (November 2014): 932–63.

15. Theal, *Chronicles of Cape Commanders,* 275.

16. Richard Hemming, "Planting Density" in "Wine By the Numbers, Part One," 15 September 15, 2016, at the Jancis Robinson website, www.jancisrobinson .com/articles/wine-by-numbers-part-one?layout=pdf (accessed July 23, 2021).

17. Phillips, *French Wine*, 79.

18. For example, as in the seventeenth-century Languedoc-Roussillon. Ibid., 80.

19. "Our History," Groot Constantia, www.grootconstantia.co.za/our-history (accessed July 23, 2021).

20. Theal, *Chronicles of Cape Commanders*, 268.

21. Beck, *History of South Africa*, 33.

22. Gerald Groenewald, "An Early Modern Entrepreneur: Hendrik Oostwald Eksteen and the Creation of Wealth in Dutch Colonial Cape Town, 1702–1741," *Kronos* 35 (November 2009): 6–31.

23. Nigel Worden, "Strangers Ashore: Sailor Identity and Social Conflict in Mid-18th Century Cape Town," *Kronos* 33 (November 2007): 72–83.

24. John Ovendish, *A Voyage to Suratt, in the Year, 1689: Giving a Large Account of that City and its Inhabitants, and the English Factory There* (London: Jacob Tonson, 1696), 503.

25. D. Fenning and J. Collyer, *A New System of Geography; or, A General Description of the World* (London: S. Crowder et al., 1766), 357.

26. Sylvanus Urbanus, *The Gentleman's Magazine and Historical Chronicle,* vol. 8 (London: Edw. Cave, July 1738), 371.

27. Mary Barber, *Poems on several occasions* (London: C. Rivington, 1734), 170.

28. For good discussions of wine as medicine, see David Hancock, *Oceans of Wine: Madeira and the Emergence of American Trade and Taste* (New Haven, CT: Yale University Press, 2009), 318–32.

29. William Chaigneau, *The History of Jack Connor,* 2 vols. (London: William Johnston, 1753), 2: 10.

30. Jane Austen, *Sense and Sensibility* (London: Thomas Egerton, 1811), vol. 2, chap. 8.

31. Also known as Belvedere raisins, from western Greece. "Belvedere," entry in John Walker, *The Universal Gazeteer* (London: Ogilvy and Son et al., 1798).

32. Hannah Glasse, *The compleat confectioner: or, the whole art of confectionary made plain and easy. Shewing, The various Methods of preserving and candying, both* ... (London: Printed and sold at Mrs. Ashburner's China Shop, 1760), 197.

33. Jancis Robinson, Julia Harding, and José Vouillamoz, *Wine Grapes* (London: Allen Lane, 2012). Entries for muscat de frontignan, p. 683, and muscat of Alexandria, p. 689.

34. Simon, *South Africa,* 11.

35. Jancis Robinson, *The Oxford Companion to Wine,* 2nd ed. (Oxford: Oxford University Press, 2006), entry on "Sémillon," 626.

36. Classified ads, *Daily Advertiser* (London), Saturday, June 11, 1743.

37. "The Stock of Wines of Mr. Jos. Thorpe," *Daily Advertiser* (London), September 14, 1743.

38. Thomas Salmon, *Modern history; or, the present state of all nations. Describing their respective situations, persons, habits, Buildings, Manners, Laws and Customs* (London: Thomas Wotton, 1735), 128.

39. Johan Fourie, "The Remarkable Wealth of the Dutch Cape Colony: Measurements from Eighteenth-Century Probate Inventories," *Economic History Review* 66, no. 2 (May 2013): 419–48. On wine, see p. 429.

40. Fourie actually writes that slaves are "a proxy for total wealth." Ibid., 431–32.

41. Salmon, *Modern history*, 128.

42. Mary Rayner, "Wine and Slaves: The Failure of an Export Economy and the Ending of Slavery in the Cape Colony, South Africa, 1806–1834," PhD diss., Duke University, 1986, 4.

43. Lady Anne Barnard, cited in Bagnall, *Wines of South Africa*, 18. Barnard was well aware of the movement to abolish slavery at home in U.K., and her diaries reference William Wilberforce, one of its leaders. Margaret Lenta, "Degrees of Freedom: Lady Anne Barnard's Cape Diaries," *English in Africa* 19, no. 2 (October 1992): 65.

44. Beck, *History of South Africa*, 42.

CHAPTER 4. FIRST FLEET, FIRST FLIGHT

1. David Collins, *An Account of the English Colony in New South Wales, from Its First Settlement in January 1788, to August 1801: With Remarks on the Dispositions, Customs, Manners, &C., of the Native Inhabitants of That Country*, 2nd ed. (London: T. Cadell and W. Davies, 1804).

2. Charles Tuckwell, "Combatting Australia's founding myth: the motives behind the British Settlement of Australia," Senior thesis, Trinity College, Hartford, CT, 2018.

3. Maggie Brady, *First Taste: How Indigenous Australians Learned about Grog*, 6 vols. (Deakin, Australia: Alcohol Education & Rehabilitation Foundation, 2008), 1: 6

4. Arthur Philip and John Stockdale, eds., *The voyage of Governor Phillip to Botany Bay; with an account of the establishment of the colonies of Port Jackson & Norfolk Island; compiled from authentic papers, which have been obtained from the several Departments. To which are added, the journals of Lieuts. Shortland, Watts, Ball, & Capt. Marshall, with an account of their new discoveries* (London: John Stockdale, 1789).

5. George Barrington, *A voyage to New South Wales; with a description of the country; the manners, customs, religion, &c. of the natives, in the vicinity of Botany Bay* (Philadelphia: Thomas Dobson, 1796), 77.

6. Philip and Stockdale, *The voyage of Governor Phillip*, 21–22.

7. See, for example, "Wine glass stem from the Zeewijk wreck site, before 1727," Australian National Maritime Museum, object no. 00016341.

8. Julie McIntyre argues this, too, and I agree, *First Vintage: Wine in Colonial New South Wales* (Sydney: University of New South Wales Press, 2012), 36.

9. Killian Quigley, "Indolence and Illness: Scurvy, the Irish, and Early Australia," *Eighteenth-Century Life* 41, no. 2 (2017): 139–53.

10. Phillip and Stockdale, *Voyage of Captain Phillip,* 281, 330. Spruce-beer was a lightly fermented beverage made from the needles of evergreen trees.

11. Based on Basic Report 14096, Alcoholic beverage, wine, table, red. National Nutrient Database, April 2018, U.S. Department of Agriculture, Agricultural Research Service, https://ndb.nal.usda.gov (accessed September 2, 2021).

12. *Report from the Select Committee on Transportation,* Parliament, House of Commons, London): Ordered by the House of Commons to be printed, 1812. Digitized on Trove.

13. Collins, *Account of the English Colony in New South Wales,* 153–54.

14. "Method of Preparing a Piece of Land, for the Purpose of Preparing a Vineyard," *Sydney Gazette and New South Wales Advertiser,* March 5, 1803, https://trove.nla.gov.au/newspaper/page/5656 (accessed September 2, 2021).

15. The French source is not attributed and is unknown, but it *could* be a sloppy paraphrase of parts of Jean-Antoine Chaptal, *Traité théorique et pratique sur la culture de la vigne* (Paris: Delalain, 1801).

16. "Cultivation of the Vine," *Sydney Gazette and New South Wales Advertiser,* March 12, 1803, https://trove.nla.gov.au/newspaper/page/5660 (accessed September 2, 2021).

17. McIntyre, "Resisting Ages-Old Fixity as a Factor in Wine Quality: Colonial Wine Tours and Australia's Early Wine Industry," *Locale* 1 (2011): 43.

18. Drawn from McIntyre, *First Vintage,* passim and pp. 73–75.

19. Ibid., 75.

20. Jessica Moody, "Liverpool's Local Tints: Drowning Memory and 'Maritimising' Slavery in a Seaport City," in *Britain's History and Memory of Transatlantic Slavery: Local Nuances of a "National Sin,"* ed. Katie Donington, Ryan Hanley, and Jessica Moody (Liverpool: Liverpool University Press, 2016), 161.

21. McIntyre, *First Vintage,* 43–53.

22. Ibid., 50.

CHAPTER 5. ASTONISHED BY THE FRUIT

1. UCL Legacies of Slavery-ownership Database, www.ucl.ac.uk/lbs.

2. Eric Ramsden, *James Busby: The Prophet of Australian Viticulture* (Sydney: Ramsden, 1940).

3. James Busby, *A Treatise on the Culture of the Vine and the Art of Making Wine* ([Sydney?]: R. Howe, Government Printer, 1825), ix.

4. Ibid., xxviii.

5. James Busby, *A Journal of a Tour through Some of the Vineyards of Spain and France* (Sydney: Stephens and Stokes, 1833), appendix, p. 117.

6. Ibid., 72.

7. Ibid., 107.

8. James Busby, *Report on the Vines, Introduced into the Colony of New South Wales, in the Year 1832: With a Catalogue of the Several Varieties Growing in the Botanical Garden, in Sydney* (Sydney: William Jones, 1834).

9. No title, *Hobart Town Gazette and Southern Reporter,* June 29, 1816, 2, https://trove.nla.gov.au/newspaper/page/40422 (accessed September 2, 2021).

10. Also discussed in Julie McIntyre and John Germov, *Hunter Wine: A History* (Sydney: NewSouth, 2018), 3–4.

11. Kristen Maynard, Sarah Wright, and Shirleyanne Brown, "Ruru Parirao: Mäori and Alcohol; The Importance of Destabilising Negative Stereotypes and the Implications for Policy and Practice," *MAI Journal* 2, no. 2 (2012): 79.

12. Marsden quoted in John Buxton Marsden, *Memoirs of the Life And Labors of the Rev. Samuel Marsden: Of Paramatta, Senior Chaplain of New South Wales; and of His Early Connection with the Missions to New Zealand and Tahiti* (London: Religious Tract Society, 1838), 33.

13. John Rawson Elder, ed., *The Letters and Journals of Samuel Marsden, 1765–1838* (Auckland: Coulls, Somerville Wilkie, 1932), 180, 181.

14. Ibid., 181.

15. Dumont D'Urville, cited in Keith Stewart, *Chancers and Visionaries: A History of Wine in New Zealand* (Auckland: Godwit, 2010), 33.

16. Ibid., 48.

17. Committee on New Zealand, *Report,* May 23, 1844, HC 556 1844, Q87–88, p. 6.

18. William Williams, D.C.L., Archdeacon of Waiapu, *A Dictionary of the New Zealand Language, and a Concise Grammar, to which is added a Selection of Colloquial Sentences,* 2nd ed. (London: Williams and Norgate, 1852), 310.

19. Ibid., 318–19.

20. James Belich, *Making Peoples: A History of the New Zealanders from Polynesian Settlement to the End of the Nineteenth Century* (Honolulu: University of Hawai'i Press, 1996), 197–200.

21. Raewyn Dalziel, "Southern Islands: New Zealand and Polynesia," in *The Oxford History of the British Empire,* vol. 3, *The Nineteenth Century,* ed. Andrew Porter (Oxford: Oxford University Press, 1999), 581–82.

22. W. Jackson Hooker, "The Late Mr Cunningham," *Companion to the Botanical Magazine: Being a Journal, Containing Such Interesting Botanical Information As Does Not Come Within the Prescribed Limits of the Magazine; with Occasional Figures* (London: Printed by E. Conchman ... for the proprietor, S. Curtis, 1835–36), 215.

23. My translation. "Que pensez-vous que j'aie fait du premier raisin qui ait muri à Tonga? que je l'ai donné? conservé? Non rien de tout cela: je l'ai cueilli religieusement, je l'ai pressé dans un linge très-propre, puis après en avoir clarifié le jus, je m'en suis servi pour dire la messe, le premier janvier 1844." Révérend Père Grande, Missionary of the Society of Mary, to a fellow priest, Tonga, March 1844. Reprinted in

Annales de l'Association de la propagation de la foi (Lyons: M.P. Rusand) 18 (1846): 37.

24. Mgr. Douarre, New Caledonia, to the Members of the Central Committees [of the Catholic Church] in Lyon and Paris, January 1, 1844. Reprinted in *Annales de l'Association* 17 (1845): 50.

25. M. Thiersé to his mother, Perth, February 8, 1846. Reprinted in *Annales de l'Association* 18 (1846): 542.

26. Address of Fr. Yardin, Hawkes Bay Philosophical Institute, *Hawke's Bay Herald,* August 1890.

27. James Busby, *The Rebellions of the Maories Traced to Their True Origin: In Two Letters to the Right Honourable Edward Cardwell . . .* (London: Strangeways & Walden, 1865).

CHAPTER 6. CHEAP AND WHOLESOME

1. Ebenezer Elliott, *Corn Law Rhymes* (Sheffield, Yorkshire: Mechanics' Anti-Bread-Tax Society, 1831), 10.

2. Thomas Perronet, *A Catechism on the Corn Laws, with a List of Fallacies and the Answers,* 18th ed. (London: Westminster Review, 1834).

3. Editorial, "Glasgow and Edinburgh Anti-Corn Law Demonstrations," *Liverpool Mercury,* January 20, 1843.

4. Timothy Keegan, *South Africa and the Origins of the Racial Order* (Cape Town: David Philip, 1996), 52; United Kingdom, House of Commons, *Account of Value of Imports from Cape of Good Hope, 1812–16,* 1817, 225, 14: 149.

5. Mary Rayner, "Wine and Slaves: The Failure of an Export Economy and the Ending of Slavery in the Cape Colony, South Africa, 1806–1834" (PhD diss., Duke University, 1986), 8–9.

6. *Account of Value of Imports from Cape of Good Hope, 1812–16,* 1817, 225, 14: 149.

7. "Proclamation by His Excellency, the Rt. Hon. General Lord Charles Henry Somerset," *Cape Town Gazette and African Advertiser,* April 26, 1823.

8. "Proclamation by His Excellency, the Rt. Hon. General Lord Charles Henry Somerset," *Cape Town Gazette and African Advertiser,* November 15, 1823.

9. Keegan, *Origins of the Racial Order,* 58; on previous office of wine taster, see George McCall Theal, ed., *Records of the Cape Colony from May 1801 to February 1803, Copied for the Cape Government, from the Manuscript Documents in the Public Record Office, London,* vol. 4 (London: Printed for the Government of the Cape Colony, 1899 [University of Michigan Digitization], 226–27.

10. Keegan, *Origins of the Racial Order,* 52.

11. Grant, Peter Warden, *Considerations on the State of the Colonial Currency and Foreign Exchanges at the Cape of Good Hope: Comprehending Also Some Statements Relative to the Population, Agriculture, Commerce, and Statistics of the Colony* (Cape Town: W. Bridekirk, Jr., 1825), 108.

12. "Wanted for the island of St Helena," *Cape Town Gazette and African Advertiser,* December 30, 1815.

13. Charles Ludington, *The Politics of Wine in Britain: A New Cultural History* (Basingstoke: Palgrave, 2013), table A.1, pp. 264–65.

14. This is not to suggest that European countries were dominated by large protocorporations. Rather, even when they were dominated by small family-run vineyards and wineries, wine was generally not exported under those wineries' names, and they had longer-established systems for getting that wine to market. One excellent case study is Thomas Brennan's *Burgundy to Champagne: The Wine Trade in Early Modern France* (Baltimore: Johns Hopkins, 1997).

15. "Cape Town," *Cape Town Gazette and African Advertiser,* October 25, 1823.

16. Helpfully summarized in Ludington, *Politics of Wine,* 264–65.

17. Despatch from the Governor of the Cape of Good Hope to the Right Hon. Lord Viscount Goderisch, April 2, 1831. *Representations from Cape of Good Hope to H.M. Government respecting Duties on Cape Wine,* HC 1831, 103, 17: 485.

18. Memorial and Petition of the undersigned Wine Growers, Wine Merchants, and other Inhabitants of the Cape of Good Hope. Ibid., 103.

19. HC Deb, September 7, 1831, 6: 1216–40.

20. Memorial and Petition of the undersigned Wine Growers ..., *Representations from Cape of Good Hope to H.M. Government respecting Duties on Cape Wine,* HC 1831, 103.

21. Mr Keith Douglas MP, "Wine Duties," HC Deb, September 7, 1831, 6: 1216–40.

22. Calculated 1s. 6d. in 1820 to £102.1 using the simple purchasing power calculator. "Purchasing Power of British Pounds from 1270 to Present," MeasuringWorth, 2021, on MeasuringWorth.com, www.measuringworth.com/ppoweruk.

23. My emphasis. Sir J. Stanley, HC Deb, September 7, 1831, 4: c1008–76.

24. Cyrus Redding, *History and Description of Modern Wines,* 2nd ed. (London: G. Bell, 1836), 290.

25. C. I. Latrobe, *Journal of a Visit to South Africa, in 1815, and 1816: With Some Account of the Missionary Settlements of the United Brethren, Near the Cape of Good Hope* (Cape of Good Hope: L. B. Seeley, and R. Ackermann, 1818), 331. Christian Latrobe (or La Trobe) was the father of Charles Latrobe, the future lieutenant-governor of Victoria, Australia.

26. John Campbell, *Travels in South Africa: Undertaken at the Request of the Missionary Society* (London: Black and Parry, 1815), 85.

CHAPTER 7. ECHUNGA HOCK

1. "South Australian Wine," *South Australian,* March 4, 1845.

2. John Campbell, *Travels in South Africa: Undertaken at the Request of the Missionary Society* (London: Black and Parry, 1815), 85–86.

3. C. I. LaTrobe, *Journal of a Visit to South Africa, in 1815, and 1816: With Some Account of the Missionary Settlements of the United Brethren, Near the Cape of Good Hope* (Cape of Good Hope: L. B. Seeley, and R. Ackermann, 1818), 331.

4. W. H. Roberts, *The British Wine-Maker and Domestic Brewer; a Complete Practical and Easy Treatise on the Art of Making and Managing Every Description of British Wines*... 5th ed. (Edinburgh: A. & C. Black; London: Whittaker, 3rd ed., rev., 1836; and 5th ed., rev., 1849). Note that this Constantia recipe was not featured in the 3rd edition of 1836, and was invented in the intervening years.

5. Menu, "The Fourteenth Meeting of the Saintsbury Club," April 27, 1938, London. Francis Meynell Papers, MS Add.9813/F7/1, Cambridge University Library.

6. Fay Banks, *Wine Drinking in Oxford, 1640–1850: A Story Revealed by Tavern, Inn, College and Other Bottles; with a Catalogue of Bottles and Seals from the Collection in the Ashmolean Museum.* British Archaelogical Reports (BAR) British Series 257 (Oxford: Archaeopress, 1997), 1.

7. James L. Denman, "Wine Merchant," *Sunday Times* (London), May 20, 1860.

8. Troy Bickham, "Eating the Empire: Intersections of Food, Cookery, and Imperialism in Eighteenth-Century Britain," *Past and Present* 198, no. 1 (February 2008): 74.

9. A few examples: Flyers for sale of rum and wines, 1821 and 1823, Matthew Clark and Sons Papers, MS 38347, London Metropolitan Archives; Advertisements, *Liverpool Mercury*, Friday, April 11, 1817.

10. Campbell, *Travels in South Africa,* 221. Nowadays known as Genadendal, it is about eighty miles east of Cape Town and outside recognized wine areas.

11. Sir Henry Trueman Wood, "The Royal Society of the Arts. IV—The Society and the Colonies (1754–1847)." *Journal of the Royal Society of Arts* 59, no. 3071 (September 29, 1911): 1043. This refers to wines of the Canary Islands, which were usually "Malmsey" or Malvasia-grape-based, yielding a sweet wine similar to Madeira.

12. "Australasia," *Times* (London), May 5, 1823, 3.

13. *Sydney Gazette and New South Wales Advertiser,* February 26, 1824.

14. Committees of Inquiry on Administration of Government and Finances at Cape of Good Hope, *Documents Referred to in the Reports of the Commissioners,* HC 1826–27, 406, 21: 287.

15. United Kingdom, House of Commons, testimony of Rev. Mr. H. P. Hallbeck, Gnadenthal, May 12, 1825. *Papers relative to Aboriginal Inhabitants of Cape of Good Hope. Part I. Hottentots and Bosjesmen; Caffres; Griquas. HC* 1835, 50, 39: 301. The closest modern wine regions to Genandandel are Franschoek, about fifty miles to the west, and the newer Cape South Coast area, which starts about twenty miles southwest. Regions based on Hugh Johnson and Jancis Robinson, *The World Atlas of Wine,* 7th ed. (London: Mitchell Beazley, 2013), 371–72.

16. Advertisement, E. K. Green's Bottle Store, *Cape Town Mercantile Advertiser,* May 10, 1858.

17. "Wines! Wines! Wines!" *Cape Town Mercantile Advertiser,* September 21, 1861.

18. *Zuid-Afrikaan Vereenigd Met ons Land* (Cape Town), July 20, 1865, 4; *Cape Town Mercantile Advertiser* (Cape Town), September 4, 1861, 1.

19. "Groendruif stokken," advertisements, *Zuid-Afrikaan Vereenigd Met ons Land* (Cape Town), August 27, 1846.

20. Advertisements, *Zuid-Afrikaan Vereenigd Met ons Land* (Cape Town), October 3, 1850.

21. Advertisements, *Cape Times,* December 15, 1881.

22. "Muscat of Alexandria," Jancis Robinson, Julia Harding, and José Vouillamoz, *Wine Grapes* (London: Allen Lane, 2012), 689–90.

23. Thanks to Joanne Gibson, DipWSET, for suggesting the "klipp" and "steen" connection.

24. Cyrus Redding, *History and Description of Modern Wines.* 2nd ed. (London: G. Bell, 1836), 291.

25. Robert Druitt, *Report on the Cheap Wines from France, Italy, Austria, Greece, and Hungary; Their Quality, Wholesomeness, and Price, and their Use in Diet and Medicine. With Short Notes of a Lecture to Ladies on Wine, and Remarks on Acidity.* (London: Henry Renshaw, 1865), 91.

26. *Cape Town Gazette and African Advertiser,* December 28, 1822.

27. "To Be Sold by Public Sale," *Cape Town Gazette,* September 13, 1800.

28. Italics in original. *Cape Town Gazette and African Advertiser,* October 10, 1828.

29. Romita Ray, "Ornamental Exotica: Transplanting the Aesthetics of Tea Consumption and the Birth of a British Exotic," in *The Botany of Empire in the Long Eighteenth Century,* ed. Yota Batsaki, Sarah Burke Cahalan, and Anatole Tchikine (Washington, DC: Dumbarton Oaks Research Library and Collection, 2016), 259.

30. "Sir Charles Bunbury," *The Spectator,* January 12, 1907, 21.

31. Charles J. F. Bunbury, *Journal of a Residence at the Cape of Good Hope, with Excursions into the Interior, and Notes on the Natural History, and the Native Tribes* (London: John Murray, 1848), 3.

32. Ibid., 5.

33. Alfred W. Cole, *The Cape and the Kafirs; or, Notes on Five Years' Residence in South Africa* (London: R. Bentley, 1852), 391.

34. Ibid., 392.

35. Joanna de Groot, "Metropolitan Desires and Colonial Connections," in *At Home with the Empire: Metropolitan Culture and the Imperial World,* ed. Catherine Hall and Sonya Rose (Cambridge: Cambridge University Press, 2007), 166–90.

36. James Busby, "Letter on the Emigration of Mechanics and Laborers to New South Wales, to the Rt. Hon. R. William Horton, MP," in his *Authentic Information Relative to New South Wales and New Zealand* (London: Joseph Cross, 1832), 10.

37. Ibid., 10.

38. Ibid.

39. Editor unknown, *Extracts from the Letters and Journal of Daniel Wheeler, while engaged in a religious visit to the inhabitants of some of the islands of the Pacific Ocean, Van Dieman's Land, New South Wales, and New Zealand, accompanied by his son, Charles Wheeler* (Philadelphia: Joseph Rakestraw, 1840), 49.

40. John Dunlop, *On the Wine System of Great Britain* (Greenock, Scotland: R. B. Lusk, 1831), 6.

41. Edward Jerningham Wakefield and John Ward, *The British Colonization of New Zealand: Being an Account of the Principles, Objects, And Plans of the New Zealand Association, Together With Particulars Concerning the Position, Extent, Soil And Climate, Natural Productions, And Native Inhabitants of New Zealand* (London: John W. Parker, 1837), 396.

42. "Western Australia," an excerpt from E. W. Landor's book *The Bushman. Glasgow Herald* (Scotland), November 29, 1847.

43. George Blakiston Wilkinson, *South Australia: Its Advantages and Its Resources* (London: J. Murray, 1848), 121.

44. *The Hardy Tradition: Tracing the Growth and Development of a Great Winemaking [sic] Family through Its First Hundred Years* (Adelaide: Thomas Hardy & Sons Limited, 1953), 7.

45. Wilkinson, *South Australia,* 90.

46. Molly Huxley, "Duffield, Walter (1816–1882)," *Australian Dictionary of Biography,* National Centre of Biography, Australian National University, http://adb.anu.edu.au/biography/duffield-walter-3449/text5239, published first in hardcopy 1972 (accessed June 13, 2019).

47. "Australia," *Morning Chronicle* (London), July 15, 1839.

48. Edward Wilson Landor, *The Bushman: Life in a New Country.* First published 1847, London: Richard Bentley; Gutenberg online edition, December 2004. Quote from chapter 10 (no ebook pagination).

49. Hubert de Castella, *John Bull's Vineyard: Australian Sketches* (Melbourne: Sands and McDougall, 1886), 70.

50. Flyer for Dalwood Vineyards, c. 1870, SLNSW MLMSS 8915, Folder 1, Item 2.

51. "South Australian Wine," *South Australian,* March 4, 1845.

52. "Western Australia," *Glasgow Herald* (Glasgow, Scotland), Monday, November 29, 1847; Issue 4678. J. T. Fallon, *The "Murray Valley Vineyard," Albury, New South Wales, and "Australian Vines and Wines"* (Melbourne: n.p., 1874).

53. McIntyre, *First Vintage,* 95–100.

54. Ibid., 103.

55. See, for example, Paul Nugent, "The Temperance Movement and Wine Farmers at the Cape: Collective Action, Racial Discourse and Legislative Reform, c. 1890–1965," *Journal of African History* 52, no. 3 (January 1, 2011): 341–63; Pamela Scully, *Liberating the Family? Gender and British Slave Emancipation in the Rural Western Cape, South Africa, 1823–1853* (Cape Town: David Philip, 1997).

CHAPTER 8. HAVE YOU ANY COLONIAL WINE?

1. "The Wine Duties Reduction," *Morning Post* (London), August 5, 1854. The MP was Benjamin Oliviera of Pontefract.

2. *Spirits and Wine: Returns of the Quantities of British Spirits Used for Home Consumption in the United Kingdom.* HC 1862, 168.

3. *Account of the Quantity of Foreign Wine Imported, Exported, and Retained for Home Consumption.* HC 1851, 427.

4. "Cape Wines and Their Effects on the Wine Trade," *Morning Chronicle* (London), January 13, 1858; "Prince Alfred at the Cape of Good Hope," *Morning Post* (London), August 26, 1860.

5. Trial of Thomas Savage, Elizabeth Savage, November 1850 (t18501125–104), Old Bailey, London. Old Bailey Proceedings, www.oldbaileyonline.org.

6. *The Standard* (London), June 25, 1827. Three half-pipes are roughly 715 liters, or around 950 modern 750ml bottles.

7. *The Standard* (London), July 12, 1831.

8. Trial of Mary Ann Bamford (34), Jane White (220, May 1860), (t18600507–414), Old Bailey Proceedings.

9. Trial of George Tenant, April 1843, (t18430403–1203), Old Bailey Proceedings.

10. Robert Druitt, *Report on the Cheap Wines from France, Italy, Austria, Greece, and Hungary; Their Quality, Wholesomeness, and Price, and Their Use in Diet and Medicine: With Short Notes of a Lecture to Ladies on Wine, and Remarks on Acidity* (London: Henry Renshaw, 1865), 14.

11. "Will the Coming Man Drink Wine? Corks," *Melbourne Punch*, January 14, 1869, 11.

12. Thomas George Shaw, *Wine, the Vine, and the Cellar* (London: Longman, Green, Longman, Roberts & Green, 1863), 343.

13. Thudichum, "Report on Wines," *Royal Society* (1873), 928.

14. *Reports of the Imperial Economic Committee, Twenty-third Report: Wine.* (London: HMSO 1932), 43.

15. On medicinal use, see "Weekly Chronicle of Sales, Commerce etc," *The Morning Chronicle* (London), September 28, 1827; response of Mr Hunt, "if given to sick persons, would only make them worse," HC Deb, September 7, 1831, 6: c1216–40.

16. Distillation Act 25 Vic., No. 147. *Victoria Government Gazette,* November 27, 1868, 2256.

17. [Henry Silver], "Wine and Electricity," *Punch,* January 29, 1870, 35.

18. John Davies, *The Innkeeper's and Butler's Guide; or, A Directory for Making and Managing British Wines: With Directions for the Managing, Colouring and Flavouring of Foreign Wines and Spirits, and, for Making British Compounds, Peppermint, Aniseed, Shrub, &c.* . . . 13th ed., rev. and corrected (Leeds: Davies, 1810), 63.

19. Revolution on p. 101 of James Simpson, *Creating Wine: The Emergence of a World Industry, 1840–1914* (Princeton, NJ: Princeton University Press, 2011); Gladstone on luxury, p. 86. "Social engineering" is my term.

20. Brian Howard Harrison, *Drink and the Victorians: The Temperance Question in England, 1815–1872,* 2nd ed. (Keele, Staffordshire: Keele University Press, 1994), 228–30.

21. *Returns of the Quantities of British Spirits Used for Home Consumption,* 168.

22. Druitt, *Report on Cheap Wines,* 59.

23. Herbert Maxwell, *Half-a-century of Successful Trade: Being a Sketch of the Rise And Development of the Business of W & A Gilbey, 1857–1907* (London: W & A Gilbey, 1907), 14.

24. Ibid., 13.

25. "Child Killed by Cough-Medicine" and "The Adulteration Of Food," *British Medical Journal* 1, no. 640 (April 5, 1873): 380–81.

26. "Police Office," *New Zealand Spectator and Cook's Strait Guardian,* March 20, 1847.

27. Paul Nugent, "The Temperance Movement and Wine Farmers at the Cape: Collective Action, Racial Discourse, and Legislative Reform, c. 1890–1965," *Journal of African History* 52, no. 3 (January 1, 2011): 347–49.

28. "A Colonial Wine Shop," *Wagga Wagga Advertiser and Riverine Reporter,* NSW, July 22, 1871.

29. A few examples: "Alcoholic Drinks," *Times* (London), August 14, 1884, 12; "Alcohol in Health and Disease: A Lecture," *Times,* January 1, 1881, 6; Alfred Carpenter et al., "Drinking and Drunkenness," *Times,* September 18, 1891, 5.

30. C. R. Bree, "Who Shall Decide When Doctors Disagree?" *Times* (London), January 10, 1872, 6.

31. B. Seebohm Rowntree, *Poverty: A Study of Town Life* (London: Macmillan, 1908), 332.

32. Ibid., 142.

33. John Dunlop, *The Philosophy of Artificial and Compulsory Drinking Usage in Great Britain and Ireland* (London: Holston and Stoneman, 1839).

34. Romeo Bragato, *Report On the Prospects of Viticulture In New Zealand: Together with Instructions for Planting and Pruning* (Wellington: S. Costall, Government Printer, 1895), 12.

35. "Cape Wines and Their Effects on the Wine Trade," [From *Ridley's*], *Morning Chronicle,* January 13, 1858.

36. "Prince Alfred at the Cape of Good Hope," *Morning Post* (London), August 26, 1860.

37. *Returns of the Quantities of British Spirits Used for Home Consumption,* 1862, 168.

38. Board of Trade, *Production and Consumption of Alcoholic Beverages (Wine, Beer and Spirits) in the British Colonies (Australasia, Canada, and the Cape),* 1900, Cd 72, p. 15.

39. "Exportation to New Zealand of Australian Wine," *Victoria Government Gazette,* January 3 1879, 56.

40. Cited in George Bell, "The South Australian Wine Industry, 1858–1876." *Journal of Wine Research* 4, no. 3 (September 1993): 148; J. T. Fallon, "Australian Vines and Wines," *Journal of the Society of Arts* 22, no. 1098 (December 1873): 47.

41. On assisted emigration schemes see John McDonald and Eric Richards, "The Great Emigration of 1841: Recruitment for New South Wales in British Emi-

gration Fields," *Population Studies* 51, no. 3 (1997): 337–55; Robin Haines, "Indigent Misfits or Shrewd Operators? Government-Assisted Emigrants from the United Kingdom to Australia, 1831–1860," *Population Studies* 48, no. 2 (1994): 223–47.

42. W. P. Driscoll, "Fallon, James Thomas (1823–1886)," *Australian Dictionary of Biography*, National Centre of Biography, Australian National University, https://adb.anu.edu.au/biography/fallon-james-thomas-3496/text5365, published first in hardcopy 1972 (accessed September 3, 2021).

43. J. T. Fallon, *The "Murray Valley Vineyard," Albury, New South Wales, and "Australian Vines and Wines"* (Melbourne: n.p., 1874), 7, 20, 33–34.

44. Ibid., 1.

45. Tovey, *Wine and Wine Countries,* 49.

46. Fallon, "Australian Vines and Wines," 21, 22.

47. Thudichum cited in ibid., 48.

48. Ibid., 49.

49. Ibid., 34.

50. Ibid., 35.

CHAPTER 9. PLANTING AND PRUNING

1. George Sutherland, *The South Australian Vinegrower's Manual: A Practical Guide to the Art of Viticulture in South Australia; Prepared under Instructions from the Government of South Australia, and with the Co-operation of Practical Vinegrowers of the Province* (Adelaide: C. Bristow, Government Printer, 1892), 108.

2. *Reports to Secretary of State on Past and Present State of H.M. Colonial Possessions, 1869 (Part II. N. American Colonies; African Settlements and St. Helena; Australia and New Zealand; Mediterranean Possessions; Heligoland and Falkland Islands).* 1871, 415, 67: 101.

3. Queensland wine is produced at cooler high altitudes in the South Burnett and Granite Belt geographic indications. Hugh Johnson and Jancis Robinson, *The World Atlas of Wine,* 7th ed. (London: Mitchell Beazley, 2013), 334.

4. Henry Heylyn Hayter, "Facts and Figures," in James Thomson, *Illustrated Handbook of Victoria, Australia* (Melbourne: J. Ferres, Government Printer, 1886), 26.

5. New South Wales Bureau of Statistics and Economics, *Official Year Book of New South Wales* (Sydney: W. A. Gullick, 1887), 239, 237.

6. Ibid., chart: "Estimated Population of the Colony," 321.

7. *Statistical abstract for the several colonial and other possessions of the United Kingdom in each year from 1885 to 1899.* 1900 Cd 307.

8. Victoria Bureau of Statistics, *Victorian Year-Book* (Melbourne: Government Printer, 1883, 1888, 1889), 11 (1883–84): 453–57.

9. This was the number compensated for phylloxera in 1883. Ibid., 433–35.

10. *Statistical Report on the Population of the Dominion of New Zealand for the Year 1907* (Wellington: John Mackay, Government Printer, 1908), 2: 502.

11. Romeo Bragato, *Report On the Prospects of Viticulture In New Zealand: Together with Instructions for Planting and Pruning* (Wellington: S. Costall, Government Printer, 1895), 13.

12. Ibid.

13. Ibid., 5.

14. "Mr Walter Duffield's Vineyard, near Gawler Town, etc," *South Australian Advertiser* (Adelaide), March 26, 1862.

15. Probably a poor transcription of "Gouais." James King, "On the Growth of Wine in New South Wales," December 14, 1855, reprinted in *Journal of the Society of Arts* 4, no. 189 (July 4, 1856): 576.

16. A. C. Kelly, *The Vine in Australia* (Sydney: Sands and Kelly, 1861), 179.

17. Inventory of Wine at Bukkulla, 1869, Dalwood Mss, SLNSW, MLMSS 8051 Box 1, Folder 2.

18. Kelly, *Vine in Australia*.

19. Kelly does include "Aucarot", or Auxerrois, which Robinson et al. note can be confused with Chardonnay. Kelly also lists grapes I have been unable to identify, such as "Miller's Burgundy," which is probably pinot meunier. Jancis Robinson, Julia Harding, and José Vouillamoz, *Wine Grapes* (London: Allen Lane, 2012), "Auxerrois."

20. *Official Catalogue of Exhibits in South Australian Court, Colonial and Indian Exhibition* (Adelaide: Government Printer, 1886), 36–37.

21. Ibid., 38.

22. Ibid., 38–40.

23. J. L. W. Thudichum, "Report on Wines from the Colony of Victoria, Australia," *Journal of Society of Arts* 21, no. 1094 (November 7, 1873): 929.

24. "Australasian Public Finance," Fifth Ordinary General Meeting, Tuesday, March 29, 1889, 261. *Proceedings of the Royal Colonial Institute*, vol. 20, 1888–89.

25. Kelly, *Vine in Australia*, 6–7.

26. Editorial in *The Farmer*, New Zealand, 1911, cited in Dick Scott, *Winemakers of New Zealand* (Auckland: Southern Cross Books, 1964), 63.

27. Stirling quoted in Angela Woolacott, "A Radical's Career: Responsible Government, Settler Colonialism and Indigenous Dispossession," *Journal of Colonialism and Colonial History* 16, no. 2 (Summer) 2015: [n.p., online only].

28. Testimony of Mr C. B. Elliott, 3 March 1893, *Minutes of evidence and minutes of proceedings, . . . v.1.* (Cape Town: W. A. Richards, 1893–1894), 162.

29. John Crombie Brown, *Water Supply of South Africa and Facilities for the Storage of It* (Edinburgh: Oliver and Boyd, 1877), 236

30. Russel Viljoen, "Aboriginal Khoikhoi Servants and Their Masters in Colonial Swellendam, South Africa, 1745–1795," *Agricultural History* 75, no. 1 (2001): 45.

31. Sutherland, *South Australian*, 13.

32. Jan De Vries, "The Industrial Revolution and the Industrious Revolution," *Journal of Economic History* 54, no. 2 (1994): 249–70.

33. Cash Book, MacDonald Family Papers, Capricornia CQ University Collection, Digitized, MS A2/2–17/4, http://libguides.library.cqu.edu.au/macdonaldfamily (accessed September 2, 2021).

34. *Victorian Year-Book* (1883–84), II: 440.

35. Geoffrey C. Bishop, "The First Fine Drop: Grape-Growing and Wine-Making in the Adelaide Hills, 1839–1937," *Australian Garden History* 13, no. 5 (2002): 4–6.

36. Gordon Young, "Early German Settlements in South Australia," *Australian Journal of Historical Archaeology* 3 (1985): 43–55.

37. Jennifer Regan-Lefebvre, ed., *For the Liberty of Ireland at Home and Abroad: The Autobiography of J. F. X. O'Brien,* Classics in Irish History Series (Dublin: University College Dublin Press, 2010); [as Jennifer M. Regan], "'We could be of service to other suffering people': Representations of India in the Irish Nationalist Press, 1857–1887," *Victorian Periodicals Review* 41, no. 1 (Spring 2008): 61–77.

38. Applications for Trade Marks, digitized, National Archives of Australia.

39. "Financial Statement," *New Zealand Tablet,* August 16, 1873.

40. Ljubomir Antić, "The Press as a Secondary Source for Research on Emigration from Dalmatia up to the First World War," *SEER: Journal for Labour and Social Affairs in Eastern Europe* 4, no. 4 (2002): 25–35.

41. Martin J. Jones, "Dalmatian Settlement and Identity in New Zealand: The Devcich Farm, Kauaeranga Valley, near Thames," *Australasian Historical Archaeology* 30 (2012): 24–33.

42. Carl Walrond, "Dalmatians," *Te Ara: The Encyclopedia of New Zealand,* Auckland, New Zealand: Minister for Culture and Heritage, https://teara.govt.nz; Jason Mabbett, "The Dalmatian Influence on the New Zealand Wine Industry," *Journal of Wine Research* 9, no. 1 (April 1998): 15–25..

43. See Sutherland, *South Australian.*

44. *Official Catalogue of Exhibits in South Australian Court,* 38–41.

45. R. M. Ross and Co., advertisement, *Cape Times,* December 2, 1892.

46. Charles Davidson Bell, "Stellenbosch Wine Waggon [*sic*]—Table Mountain in the Background,"1830s, watercolor, University of Cape Town Libraries, BC686: John and Charles Bell Heritage Trust Collection, https://digitalcollections.lib.uct. ac.za/collection/islandora-26368 (accessed September 2, 2021).

47. F. Wilkinson's Traveling Expenses, Dalwood Vineyard Records, SLNSW MLMSS 8051 Box 1, Folder 2.

48. Great Northern Railway bill for merchandise carriage, April 1875, Dalwood Mss, SLNSW MLMSS 8051 Box 4, Folder 7.

49. Cashbook, 1899–1904. MacDonald Family Papers, Capricornia CQ University Collection, Digitized, MS A2/2–17/4.

50. John Davies, *The Innkeeper's and Butler's Guide; or, A Directory for Making and Managing British Wines: With Directions for the Managing, Colouring and Flavouring of Foreign Wines and Spirits, and, for Making British Compounds, Peppermint, Aniseed, Shrub, &c. . . .* 13th ed., rev. and corrected (Leeds: Davies, 1810), 182–91.

51. Profit and Loss a/c for January 1 to December 31 1891. Dalwood Mss, SLNSW, MLMSS 8051, Box 4, Folder 7.

52. Entry for January 1900. Cashbook, 1899–1904. MacDonald Family Papers, Capricornia CQ University Collection, Digitized, MS A2/2–17/4.

53. The Busby Wine Cellar, wholesale wine merchants, to the manager of Dalwood Vineyards, September 23, 1901. Dalwood Mss, SLNSW, MLMSS 8051, Box 5, Folder 3.

54. Cyrus Redding, *History and Description of Modern Wines*, 1833 edition, p. 32.

55. I would love to be proven wrong on this point.

56. Alward Wyndham, "Australian Woods for Wine Casks: to the Editor of the *Sydney Mail*," reprinted in the *Queensland Agricultural Journal* (January 1, 1900): 38–39.

57. Identified in Latin as Blackbutt (*Eucalpytus pilularis*), Cudgerie (*Flindersia australis*), Silky Oak (*Grevillea robusta*), and White Beech (*Grivillea leichhardtii*). See the *Queensland Agricultural Journal* (January 1, 1900): 38–39. European oak used in modern winemaking is *Quercus petraea* or *Quercus robur*, and the American oak is *Quercus alba*. Silky oak is a tree that resembles oak but is of a different genus; it is also known as Australian silvery oak.

58. Entry for December 1899. Cashbook, 1899–1904. MacDonald Family Papers, Capricornia CQ University Collection, Digitized, MS A2/2–17/4.

59. "Wine Tanks," *Illustrated Sydney News and New South Wales Agriculturalist and Grazier*, March 19, 1873.

60. Sutherland, *South Australian*, 13.

61. *Official Year Book of New South Wales*, 256. This includes acreage for vines that were not exclusively for wine, but may also have contained table grapes.

62. Modern oenology estimates that a ton of grape yields 120 to 180 American gallons, or 100 to 150 imperial gallons. Chris Gerling, "Conversion Factors: From Vineyard to Bottle," *Cornell Viticulture and Enology Newsletter* 8 (December 2011): n.p.

63. Sutherland, *South Australian*, 13–14.

CHAPTER 10. SULPHUR! SULPHUR!! SULPHUR!!!

1. "Cape and Frontier News," *Natal Witness*, February 1, 1861.

2. Note that this is two years earlier than normally dated in secondary sources. Victoria Bureau of Statistics, *Victorian Year-Book* (Melbourne: Government Printer, 1883, 1888, 1889), 11 (1883–84): 434.

3. Rod Phillips, *French Wine: A History* (Berkeley: University of California Press, 2016), 162.

4. Augustine Henry, "Vine Cultivation in the Gironde," *Bulletin of Miscellaneous Information (Royal Botanic Gardens, Kew)*, 33 (1889): 227–30.

5. Phillips, *French Wine*, 163.

6. *Papers Respecting the Phylloxera Vastatrix or New Vine Scourge / Published by the Department of Agriculture for the Information of the Public Generally* (Melbourne: John Ferres, Government Printer, 1873).

7. *Victorian Year-Book* 11 (1883–84): 433–35.

8. "Phylloxera in South Africa," *Bulletin of Miscellaneous Information* (Royal Botanic Gardens, Kew), no. 33 (1889): 230–35.

9. "Phylloxera and American Vines," *Argus Annual and South African Gazeteer* (Cape Town: Argus Printing and Publishing, 1895), 298.

10. New Zealand Department of Agriculture, *Phylloxera and Other Diseases of the Grape-Vine: Correspondence and Extracts Reprinted for Public Information* (Wellington: G. Didsbury, Government Printer, 1891), 2.

11. Ibid., 5.

12. Romeo Bragato, *Report on the Prospects of Viticulture In New Zealand: Together with Instructions for Planting and Pruning* (Wellington: S. Costall, Government Printer, 1895), 7.

13. "Phylloxera in South Africa," *Bulletin*, 231.

14. "Notes by the Editor," *Natal Witness,* February 26, 1880.

15. J. L. W. Thudichum, "Report on Wines from the Colony of Victoria, Australia," *Journal of the Royal Society of Arts* 23 (November 7, 1873): 929.

16. [Illegible], letter to J. L. W. Thudichum, February 28, 1898, Thudichum Papers, National Library of Medicine, Bethesda, MD, MSC 122.

17. C. E. Hawker, *Chats about Wine* (London: Daly, 1907), 128.

18. H. E. Laffer, "Report of the Lecturer on Viticulture and Fruit Culture, Etc.," *South Australia: Report of the Department of Agriculture for the Year Ended June 30th, 1911* (Adelaide: R. E. E. Rogers, Government Printer, 1911), 16.

19. John Crombie Brown, *Water Supply of South Africa and Facilities for the Storage of It* (Edinburgh: Oliver and Boyd, 1877), 235.

20. Ibid., 243–45.

21. Advertisement for Wm. Kuhr and Co., *Cape Town Mercantile Advertiser,* August 27, 1862.

22. Hermann Giliomee, "Western Cape Farmers and the Beginnings of Afrikaner Nationalism, 1870–1915," *Journal of Southern African Studies* 14, no. 1 (1987): 38–63.

23. Cape of Good Hope, Department of Prime Minister, *Report of Committee Nominated by the Western Province Board of Horticulture to Inquire into the Wine and Brandy Industry of the Cape Colony, 1905* (Cape Town: Government Printers, 1905. Reprinted Delhi: Facsimile Publisher, 2019), 14.

24. Karen Brown, "Political Entomology: The Insectile Challenge to Agricultural Development in the Cape Colony, 1895–1910," *Journal of Southern African Studies* 29, no. 2 (June 2003): 529–49.

25. François de Castella, *Handbook on Viticulture for Victoria* (Melbourne: Government Printer, 1891).

26. *Victoria Government Gazette* 118 (November 8, 1888): 3804.

27. George Bell, "The South Australian Wine Industry, 1858–1876," *Journal of Wine Research* 4, no. 3 (September 1993): 147–64.

28. Bragato, *Report on the Prospects of Viticulture,* 6.

29. Advertisements, *Daily Telegraph* (Sydney), January 1, 1915.

30. Waihirere District Council, "Te Kauwhata & District," *Built Heritage Assessment Historic Overview,* November 2017, https://wdcsitefinity.blob.core

.windows.net/sitefinity-storage/docs/default-source/your-council/plans-policies-and-bylaws/plans/district-plan-review/section-32-reports/historic-heritage/appendix-10-4---s32-historic-overview-of-waikato-district.pdf?sfvrsn=e22480c9_2 (accessed September 1, 2021), 81.

CHAPTER 11. SERVED CHILLED

1. P. B. Burgoyne to Thomas Hardy, November 7, 1884, Burgoyne Mss LMA CLC/B/227-143.

2. Thomas George Shaw, *Wine, the Vine, and the Cellar* (London: Longman, Green, Longman, Roberts, & Green, 1863), 337.

3. P. B. Burgoyne to Thomas Hardy, February 22, [1884?], Burgoyne Mss, LMA, CLC/B/227-143.

4. Ibid.

5. For example, P. B. Burgoyne to Thomas Hardy, March 21, [1884?], Burgoyne Mss, LMA, CLC/B/227-143.

6. "A Comparison of Vessels and Journey Times to Australia between 1788 and 1900," Australian National Maritime Museum, www.sea.museum/collections /library/research-guides/passenger-ships-to-australia (accessed September 2, 2021).

7. Burgoyne to T. Hardy, September 11, 1885, P. B Burgoyne Letter Book, Burgoyne Mss, LMA, CLC/B/227-143.

8. Ibid.

9. Cited in George Bell, "The South Australian Wine Industry, 1858-1876," *Journal of Wine Research* 4, no. 3 (September 1993): 155.

10. Letter from James Fitzpatrick, Bathurst, January 10, 1877, to John Wyndham. Dalwood Mss SLNSW MLMSS 8051, Box 1, Folder 1.

11. Burgoyne to Sir Thomas Elder, Adelaide, n.d. [March 1884], Burgoyne Mss, LMA, CLC/B/227-143.

12. Burgoyne to Mr E. Adcock, Esq. Managing Director, Victorian Champagne Co., n.d. [August 1884], Burgoyne Mss, LMA, CLC/B/227-143.

13. François de Castella, *Handbook on Viticulture for Victoria* (Melbourne: Government Printer, 1891), xiii-xiv.

14. See Nancy J. Parezo and Don D. Fowler, *Anthropology Goes to the Fair: The 1904 Louisiana Purchase Exposition* (Lincoln: University of Nebraska Press, 2007).

15. I have used Pinilla's figures for 1886-1905. Table C.1. Evolution of Alcoholic Beverage Consumption, 1886-1929. Vicente Pinilla, "Wine Historical Statistics: A Quantitative Approach to its Consumption, Production and Trade, 1840-1938," *American Association of Wine Economists Working Paper* 167 (August 2014) .

16. *The Standard* (London), October 21, 1889, 8.

17. Burgoyne to Peate and Harcourt, Sydney, August 11, 1884, Burgoyne Mss, LMA, CLC/B/227-143.

18. "Venaient ensuite des échantillons de vins du Cap, vins renommés depuis des siècles et dont le plus fameux est celui de Constance." My translation. Jules Brun-

faut, ed., *L'Exposition Universelle de 1878 illustrée*, vols. 173–74, Paris: n.p., December 1878, 937.

19. Memo about Canada Wine Growers Association application, July 1877. Agriculture Department Correspondence for 1881, Archives Canada, RG17 Document number 20115. And the exhibition appears to have been selective: the Canada Wine Growers Association applied for space, but never appeared in the program.

20. Burgoyne to Sir A. Blythe K.C.M.G., Executive Commissioner for S. Australia, July 1885, Burgoyne Mss, LMA, CLC/B/227-143.

21. *Calcutta International Exhibition, 1883–84: Report of the Royal Commission for Victoria, at the Calcutta International Exhibition, 1883–84* (Melbourne: John Ferres, Government Printer, 1884).

22. Ibid., 36.

23. Select Committee on Wine Duties, *Supplementary appendix to the report from the Select Committee on Wine Duties*, 1879, HC 1878–79, 278, 14: iii.

24. Ibid.

25. Ibid.

26. "India and Our Colonial Empire," *Westminster Review* 113–14 (July 1880): 95.

27. *Customs Tariffs of the United Kingdom from 1800 to 1897: With Some Notes upon the History of the More Important Branches of Receipt from the Year 1660* (London: Printed for Her Majesty's Stationery Office by Darling & Son, 1897), 144.

28. The High Commissioner for Canada and the Agents-General for the Australasian Colonies, the Cape of Good Hope, and Natal, to Colonial Office, April 26, 1899, *Correspondence Respecting the Increase in the Wine Duties*, May 1899, C 9322, 6.

CHAPTER 12. FROM MELBOURNE TO MADRAS

1. Cyrus Redding, *History and Description of Modern Wines*, 3rd ed. (London: Henry G. Bohn, 1860), 26.

2. "An Anglo-Indian in Australia," *The Times of India*, August 18, 1879.

3. "Finance. Customs Revenue, General Revenue," *Votes and Proceedings of the New Zealand House of Representatives*, January 1, 1856, Papers Past, https://paperspast.natlib.govt.nz/parliamentary/VP1856-I.2.1.47 (accessed July 25, 2021).

4. Financial Statement by the Hon. the Colonial Treasurer, *Appendix to the Journals of the House of Representatives*, New Zealand, January 1, 1865, 11b no. 1A. https://paperspast.natlib.govt.nz/parliamentary/AJHR1865-I.2.1.3.2 (accessed September 2, 2021).

5. G. Collins Levey, in "Wine-Growing in British Colonies," Eighth Ordinary General Meeting, Royal Colonial Institute, June 12, 1888, *Proceedings of the Royal Colonial Institute* (London) 19 (1887–88): 322.

6. For example, gold coin depicting Jahangir with wine cup, Mughal Empire, ca. 1611 A.D., University of Washington Libraries, Special Collections, C. Krishna Gairola Indian and Asian Art and Architecture Slides, PH Coll 744, https://

digitalcollections.lib.washington.edu/digital/collection/ic/id/7395 (accessed September 2, 2021).

7. Divya Narayanan, "Cultures of Food and Gastronomy in Mughal and Post-Mughal India" (PhD diss., University of Heidelberg, January 2015). See particularly chap. 5 and pp. 187–89. In this instance I believe "Shiraz" refers to geographical origin in a region, not necessarily the shiraz grape variety.

8. Redding, *History and Description*, 2nd ed., 283.

9. Godfrey Thomas Vigne, *Travels in Kashmir, Ladak, Iskardo, the Countries Adjoining the Mountain-Course of the Indus, and the Himalaya, north of the Panjab with Map* (1842), quoted in Vinayak Razdan, "Wine of Kashmir," www.searchkashmir .org, blog post October 24, 2010 (accessed October 12, 2019).

10. My translation. Jean-Baptiste-Benoît Eyriès and Alfred Jacobs, *Histoire générale des voyages: Publié sous la direction du contre-amiral Dumont D'Urville,* vol. 4, *Voyage en Asie et en Afrique* (Paris: Furne, 1859), 198.

11. Select Committee on the Affairs of the East India Company, *Report from the Select Committee on the Affairs of the East India Company; with Minutes of Evidence in Six Parts, and an Appendix and Index to Each,* HC 1831–32, 734, Finance, 2: 80, q882.

12. Testimony of William Simons, *Report from the Select Committee on the Affairs of the East India Company,* HC 1831–32, 734, Finance, 2: 80, q882.

13. Testimony of T. L. Peacock, *Report from the Select Committee on the Affairs of the East India Company,* HC 1831–32, 734, Finance, 2: 130, q1627.

14. Testimony of Thomas Bracken, *Report from the Select Committee on the Affairs of the East India Company,* HC 1831–32, 734, Finance, 2: 160, q1933–38.

15. "Kathoor Bagh" may translate as "austere garden"; fortunately Mutti claimed his language skills were limited. On Mutti at Pune, see George Watt, *The Commercial Products of India: Being an Abridgement of "The Dictionary of the Economic Products of India"* (London: J. Murray, 1908), 1016.

16. Letter from Guiseppe Mutti, Bombay, December 2, 1830, *Report from the Select Committee on the Affairs of the East India Company,* HC 1831–32, 734, vol. 3, Revenue, Appendix no. 137.

17. Daniel Sanjiv Roberts, "'Merely Birds of Passage': Lady Hariot Dufferin's Travel Writings and Medical Work in India, 1884–1888," *Women's History Review* 15, no. 3 (2006): 443–57.

18. *Indian Daily News,* August 6, reprinted in "The Calcutta Exhibition," *The Times of India,* August 9, 1883.

19. Muhammad Amir, Shaikh, of Karraya, *Wine and Water-Cooler Holding a Tumbler and Bottle,* c. 1846, painting, British Library Digitized Manuscripts Add Or 176.

20. Grace Gardiner and F. A. Steel, *The Complete Indian Housekeeper and Cook: Giving the Duties of Mistress and Servants, the General Management of the House and Practical Recipes for Cooking in All Its Branches,* 3rd ed. (Edinburgh: Edinburgh Press, 1893), 18.

21. "New South Wales: Our Own Correspondent," *Bombay Times and Journal of Commerce,* September 9, 1846.

22. "Australian Native Wine," *Morning Chronicle* (London), December 8, 1849.

23. For example, "Australian Wine," *Dublin University Magazine* 87 (1876): 237–40.

24. James Busby, *A Treatise on the Culture of the Vine and the Art of Making Wine* ([Sydney?]: R. Howe, Government Printer, 1825), xxix.

25. Redding, *History and Description*, 1860 ed., 310.

26. Certificate reprinted in J. T. Fallon, *The "Murray Valley Vineyard," Albury, New South Wales, and "Australian Vines and Wines"* (Melbourne: n.p., 1874), 16.

27. Letter from George C. [Burne?], Campbell Lodge, Potts' Point, to [John?] Wyndham, April 11, 1872. Dalwood Mss, SLNSW, MLMSS 8051, Box 1, Folder 1.

28. Letter from E. H. Simmons, shipping agent in Newcastle, to John Wyndham, Mar 31, 1894. Dalwood Mss, SLNSW, MLMSS 8051, Box 1, Folder 3.

29. E. H. Simmons to John Wyndham, August 26, 1874. Dalwood Mss, SLNSW, MLMSS 8051, Box 1, Folder 3.

30. *Calcutta International Exhibition, 1883–84: Report of the Royal Commission for Victoria, at the Calcutta International Exhibition, 1883–84* (Melbourne: John Ferres, Government Printer, 1884), 14.

31. Although Gouais is now recognized genetically as the "mother" of Chardonnay. See "Gouais Blanc," in Jancis Robinson, *The Oxford Companion to Wine*, 2nd ed. (Oxford: Oxford University Press, 2006), 319.

32. *Calcutta International Exhibition . . . Victoria,* 14.

33. *Official Report of the Calcutta International Exhibition, 1883–1884*, vol. 1, (Calcutta: Bengal Secretariat Press, 1885), 182–83.

34. John Collett, *A Guide for Visitors to Kashmir: Enl., Rev. and Corr. Up to Date by A. Mitra; with a Route Map of Kashmir* (Calcutta: W. Newman, 1898), 77.

35. Marion Doughty, *Afoot through the Kashmir valley* (1901), quoted in Vinayak Razdan, "Wine of Kashmir," www.searchkashmir.org, blog post October 24, 2010 (accessed October 12, 2019).

36. *Official Report of the Calcutta International Exhibition,* 313.

37. "La Nouvelle-Calédonie ne produit pas pour suffire à sa consommation. Elle est obligée d'acheter à l'étranger, en Australie, en Nouvelle-Zélande, une quantité prodigieuse de vin." My translation. *Revue de géographie* (Paris, 1888): 107.

38. "Average prices of produce, live-stock, provisions, etc., in each provincial district of New Zealand during the year 1891," E. J. von Dadelszen, ed., *The New Zealand Official Handbook, 1892* (Wellington: Registrar General, 1892). Unpaginated, digital copy at https://www3.stats.govt.nz/historic_publications/1892-official-handbook/1892-official-handbook.html (accessed September 2, 2021).

39. "Private Memorandum: Sales effected this present week to date," n.d. [c. 1880–1900], Dalwood Mss, SLNSW, MLMSS 8051, Box 4, Folder 7.

40. Marjorie Stone, "Lyric Tipplers: Elizabeth Barrett Browning's 'Wine of Cyprus,' Emily Dickinson's 'I Taste a Liquor,' and the Transatlantic Anacreontic Tradition," *Victorian Poetry* 54, no. 2 (Summer 2016): 123–54.

41. Elizabeth Barrett Browning, "Asia Minor: Cyprus, the Island Wine of Cyprus" (1844), available on www.bartleby.com/270/11/135.html (accessed July 25, 2021).

42. H. G. Keene, "A Poet's View of Cyprus," in *Peepful Leaves: Poems Written in India* (London: W. H. Allen, 1879).

43. "Cyprian Dreams" (poem), *Pall Mall Gazette* (London, July 19, 1878).

44. Robert Druitt, *Report on the Cheap Wines from France, Italy, Austria, Greece, and Hungary; Their Quality, Wholesomeness, and Price, and Their Use in Diet and Medicine: With Short Notes of a Lecture to Ladies on Wine, and Remarks on Acidity* (London: Henry Renshaw, 1865), 86.

45. "Australian Wine." *Dublin University Magazine* 87 (1876): 237.

46. "Greek Wines," *Morning Post* (London), September 9, 1824.

47. For example, "Ship News," *Morning Post* (London), January 6, 1815; "Shipping Intelligence," *Royal Cornwall Gazette* (Truro, England), July 14, 1821.

48. On population, "Malta," *Hampshire/Portsmouth Telegraph,* January 22, 1887.

49. United Kingdom, House of Commons, *Malta: Annual Report for 1896,* C 8279–20, 59: 18–19; *Malta: Annual Report for 1895,* C 172.

50. United Kingdom, House of Commons, "Return Showing the Daily Earnings of Laborers in Malta Harbour between 1837 and 1877," *Malta: Correspondence Respecting the Taxation and Expenditure of Malta,* 1878, C 2032, 55: 377, appendix G.

51. United Kingdom, House of Commons, "Memorandum of Interview with the Vicar-General and the Bishop's Assessor, at Valetta," *Malta: Correspondence Respecting the Taxation and Expenditure of Malta,* 1878, C 2032, vol. 55, appendix U.

52. Letter from C. B. Eynaud, Esq, *Malta: Correspondence Respecting the Taxation and Expenditure of Malta,* 1878, C 2032, vol. 55, appendix R.

53. United Kingdom, House of Commons, *Report on the Civil Establishments of Malta,* 1880, C 2684, 49: 24.

54. Robert Biddulph, "Cyprus," *Proceedings of the Royal Geographic Society* (December 1889): 10.

55. Charles Christian. *Cyprus and Its Possibilities* (London: Royal Colonial Institute, 1897).

56. Multiple classified ads, *Morning Post* (London), July 27, 1878.

57. United Kingdom, House of Commons, Sr R. Biddulph to the Earl of Kimberley, November 30, 1882, *Papers Relating to the Administration and Finances of Cyprus,* 1883, C 3661, 46: 106.

58. "Xmas Hampers," *Financial Times,* December 16, 1898.

59. For example, ad for James Denman, "Greek Wines," *Preston Chronicle,* July 1, 1865.

60. United Kingdom, House of Commons, *Trade and Navigation. For the Month Ended 31st January 1890,* 1890, C 14-I-XI.

61. "St Catharine's," P. A. Crosby, ed., *Lovell's Gazeteer of British North America* (Montreal: John Lovell, 1873).

62. "An Act Respecting the Canada Vine Growers' Association, May 22, 1868," *Statutes of Canada,* 1868, Part Second (Ottawa: Malcolm Cameron, 1868).

63. Jules Brunfaut, ed., *L'Exposition Universelle de 1878 illustrée,* vols. 173–74 (Paris: n.p., December 1878).

64. "Canada Vine Growers' Association," *Canadian Journal of Medical Science* (October 1878): 348.

65. Department of Industries (Ontario, Canada), "First Official Report to the Commissioner of Agriculture," *Sessional Papers of the Legislature of Ontario,* no. 3, A, 1883, 137.

66. Ibid., 23.

67. Ibid., 21.

68. R. W. Cameron, Commissioner for Canada, Archives Canada, to the Secretary of the Department of Agriculture, Ottawa, April 19, 1881. Archives Canada, Department of Agriculture Correspondence, RG17, 1881.

69. Appendix to Report of the Commissioner of Agriculture and Arts, Appendix C: Annual Report of the Fruit-Growers' Association of Ontario, 1882, *Sessional Papers of the Legislature of Ontario,* no. 3, C,1883, 23.

70. Ibid., 21.

71. "The Composition Of Some Proprietary Dietetic Preparations. I," *British Medical Journal* 1, no. 2517 (1909): 795–97.

72. Appendix to Report of the Commissioner of Agriculture and Arts, 21.

CHAPTER 13. PLONK! COLONIAL WINE

1. Gerald Achilles Burgoyne, *The Burgoyne Diaries* (London: Thomas Harmsworth, 1985).

2. "Vinegrowing Items," *Rutherglen Sun and Chiltern Valley Advertiser* (Victoria), February 1, 1918, 3.

3. Population estimates: "Canada's Contribution," Canadian War Museum, www.warmuseum.ca/firstworldwar/history/going-to-war/canada-enters-the-war/canada-at-war; A. J. Christopher, "The Union of South Africa Censuses, 1911–1960: An Incomplete Record," *Historia* 56, no. 2 (2011): 1–18.

4. Associate Press article, "Near Relatives Fight Each Other in Europe . . . Vintage of 1914 Is under the Press While the Cannon Boom toward the North," *Lexington Herald* (Lexington, KY), no. 362, December 28, 1914, 6.

5. Henry Yeomans, *Alcohol and Moral Regulation: Public Attitudes, Spirited Measures, and Victorian Hangovers* (Bristol: Bristol University Press, 2014), 15.

6. Detail from poster celebrating U.K.'s war mobilization, c. 1916. First World War posters collection, Watkinson Library, Trinity College, Hartford.

7. Burgoyne, *Burgoyne Diaries,* 131.

8. Arthur MacNalty, "Sir Victor Horsley: His Life and Work," *British Medical Journal* 5024, no. 1 (April 20, 1957): 910–16.

9. See Yeomans, *Alcohol and Moral Regulation,* chap. 3, 97–128.

10. P. B. Burgoyne letter, published as "War and Wine," *The Register* (Adelaide), June 24, 1915, 6.

11. For example, Brown, Gore and Co. writing to the Victoria Wine Company, suspending its contract to supply gin, March 25, 1916, Victoria Wine Company papers, LMA/4434/V/01/038.

12. Trade representative quoted in *The Scotsman,* August 16, 1915, cited in Robert Duncan, *Pubs and Patriots: The Drink Crisis in Britain during World War One* (Liverpool: Liverpool University Press, 2013).

13. Final Summary of Wine Account for the year ended December 13, 1912, Wine Supply Stock List—Senior Account, King's College, KCAR/5/6/11/4.

14. Ibid. It was either not very good, or was being aged for a special occasion, since most of it was still in stock in 1932.

15. Ibid., KCAR/5/6/11/2.

16. "Whiteley's Great Sale," clipping from *The Star,* January 11, 1915, Whiteley's Mss, Westminster City Archives, Acc 726/118.

17. Chantala, 1916. Board of Trade and successors: War Risks Insurance Records, National Archives U.K., T 365/2/144. Consulted online. Price determined using www.measuringworth.com, using the consumer price index. *SS Chantala* was sunk in the Mediterranean, off the Algerian coast, in April 1916. www.uboats.net.

18. "Whiteley's Important Sale . . .," clipping from *Evening Standard,* October 30, 1915, Whiteley's Mss, WC, Acc 726/118.

19. "The Man on the Land," *Adelaide Register,* January 16, 1915, 13.

20. Ibid.

21. "New South Wales," in Hugh Johnson and Jancis Robinson, *The World Atlas of Wine,* 7th ed. (London: Mitchell Beazley, 2013), 354.

22. "For Late Closing: Advocates Give Reasons," *The Sun* (Sydney), April 6, 1916, 3. For a similar statement of outrage against wartime restrictions, see "Wine Industry: State Encouragement Wanted; Australia Could Supply Empire," *Evening News* (Sydney), March 15, 1917.

23. Ernest H. Cherrington, "World-Wide Progress toward Prohibition Legislation," *Annals of the American Academy of Political and Social Science* 109 (1923): 208–24.

24. Dick Scott, *Winemakers of New Zealand* (Auckland: Southern Cross Books, 1964), 62–64.

25. Judith Bassett, "Colonial Justice: the Treatment of Dalmatians in New Zealand During the First World War," *New Zealand Journal of History* 33, no. 2 (1999): 157.

26. Ibid.

27. Jancis Robinson, *The Oxford Companion to Wine,* 2nd ed. (Oxford: Oxford University Press, 2006); Julian Walker, "Slang Terms at the Front," BL.uk, January 29, 2014, www.bl.uk/world-war-one/articles/slang-terms-at-the-front (accessed September 1, 2021). "English Tommies," in Paul Lukacs, *Inventing Wine: A New History of One of the World's Most Ancient Pleasures* (New York: Norton, 2012), 191; "British Tommies" in Iain Gately, *Drink: A Cultural History of Alcohol* (New York: Gotham, 2008), 361.

28. W. H. Downing, *Digger Dialects: A Collection of Slang Phrases Used by the Australian Soldiers on Active Service* (Melbourne and Sydney: Lothian, 1919). Digitized by the State Library of Victoria.

29. "Whizzy Plonk," *Auckland Star,* May 12, 1917.

30. "Behind the Lines," *Poverty Bay Herald,* October 19, 1916.

31. "Criminal Sessions: Alleged Assault," *The Register* (Adelaide), October 2, 1925, 14.

32. "Plonk," *Grenfell Record and Lachlan District Advertiser,* April 22, 1937, 1.

33. Bread and Cheese Club (Melbourne), "Bread and Cheese Club Dinner, 9th December 1944," Monash Collections Online, http://repository.monash.edu/items /show/33552 (accessed September 2, 2021).

34. "Wine Trade," *Bay of Plenty Times,* August 12, 1937.

35. "Bottled Headaches," *Evening Star* (Dunedin), August 28, 1937.

36. "They Called It 'Plonk,'" *Gisborne Herald,* July 31, 1941.

37. "Australian English in the Twentieth Century," OED blog post, posted August 2012: https://public.oed.com/blog/australian-english-in-the-twentieth-century (accessed July 24, 2021). See also the OED entry for "plonk."

CHAPTER 14. FORTIFICATION

1. Nadège Mougel, "World War I Casualties," Centre européen Robert Schuman, 2011.

2. *Whiteley's Great Spring Sale* flyer, n.d. [1920–21], Whiteley's Mss, WCA, MS 726/118; John Turner, "State Purchase of the Liquor Trade in the First World War," *Historical Journal* 23, no. 3 (September 1980): 589–615.

3. Cape of Good Hope, Department of Prime Minister, *Report of Committee Nominated by the Western Province Board of Horticulture to Inquire into the Wine and Brandy Industry of the Cape Colony, 1905* (Cape Town: Government Printers, 1905; repr., Delhi: Facsimile Publisher, 2019), 1.

4. Paul Nugent, "The Temperance Movement and Wine Farmers at the Cape: Collective Action, Racial Discourse, and Legislative Reform, c. 1890–1965," *Journal of African History* 52, no. 3 (January 1, 2011): 344.

5. Ibid., 345 n. 20.

6. Cape of Good Hope, *Report of Committee,* 2.

7. Ibid.

8. Ibid., 7. This refers to Europeans in Europe, not in South Africa.

9. Ibid., 10–11.

10. Ibid., 2.

11. For a nuanced discussion of the term in a British context, see Peter Gurney, "The Middle-Class Embrace: Language, Representation, and the Contest over Co-operative Forms in U.K., c. 1860–1914." *Victorian Studies* 37, no. 2 (1994): 253–86.

12. James J. Kennelly, "The 'Dawn of the Practical': Horace Plunkett and the Cooperative Movement," *New Hibernia Review / Iris Éireannach Nua* 12, no. 1 (2008): 73.

13. Joachim Ewert, "A Force for Good? Markets, Cellars and Labour in the South African Wine Industry after Apartheid," *Review of African Political Economy* 39, no. 132 (June 1, 2012): 225.

14. *Union of South Africa Annual Statements of Trade and Shipping.* I have included sparkling wines in the unfortified calculations.

15. Export data is from the *Annual Statements of Trade and Shipping.* The production data is from Vink et al., "South Africa," in *Wine Globalization: A New Comparative History,* ed. Kym Anderson and Vicente Pinilla (Adelaide: University of Adelaide Press, 2018), 384–409.

16. When I presented these findings at a conference for wine economists, the editors and contributors of the production data (ibid.) told me flat out that I must have made calculation errors, because *everyone knew* that South Africa was not a significant wine exporter in this period. One economist who had worked on the production data asked me to make a public statement disavowing my results. That production data employed two common economic techniques: first, extrapolation—where you "fill in" missing years of data in a series—and second, data smoothing—where you remove abnormal "noise" from the data to better see a trend. Data smoothing is common in agricultural economics where you have small seasonal fluctuations. The problem I saw with their application of these techniques is that they had interpolated all the data from 1935 to 1948. Those are significant years in imperial and South African trade history: taking in global depression, the Second World War, and the establishment of the apartheid regime. Lacking data for these years, the production data was not reliable. Furthermore, the only sources given for the Vink et al.'s South African data is "Blue Books," which is not sufficiently precise: this refers to government publications, but there are many different types of publications that contain data.

17. "African Banking Corporation," *Financial Times,* January 16, 1920.

18. Kohler paraphrased in "Expansion of Trade in England," *Mafeking Mail and Protectorate Guardian,* November 4, 1921.

19. Advisory Committee to the Department of Overseas Trade (Development and Intelligence), "Maritime and Colonial Exhibition in Antwerp, 1930: Lack of Participation by Dominions and Colonies," Board of Trade and Foreign Office, BT 90/25/10, National Archives, Kew.

20. Philip Cunliffe-Lister, Secretary of State for the Colonies, "The Foreign Trade of the Colonial Empire." Memorandum to the Cabinet, September 19, 1934, 2. National Archives, Kew, CAB 24/250/37.

21. Ibid., 3.

22. "Mr Baldwin's Original Statement to the House of Commons about the Origin of the Empire Marking Fund [*sic*]." Three-page typescript, extract from Hansard: December 17, 1924, Cols 1064/1068, University of London Senate House Library, London, Senate House Tallents Papers ICS79/1/2.

23. *Reports of the Imperial Economic Committee, Twenty-third Report: Wine.* London, HMSO (1932), 23.

24. Export data from *Union of South Africa Annual Statements of Trade and Shipping.* Cape Town, Government Printer, annual 1906–61, missing 1959.

25. "Confidential. The Empire Marketing Board. Part I: General," appendix 5, Leo Amery Papers, Churchill College Archive, CHURCHILL/AMEL1/5/13.

26. Ibid.

27. Report of the Proceedings at the Twelfth Ordinary General Meeting of the Members ..., May 8, 1936, Shareholders Minute Book, Victoria Wine Mss, LMA/4434/V/01/022.

28. Frank Trentmann, *Free Trade Nation* (Oxford: Oxford University Press, 2009), 333.

CHAPTER 15. CRUDE POTIONS

1. Owen Tweedy, "Commercial Development of Cyprus," *Financial Times,* March 23, 1928.

2. Ibid.

3. W.J. Todd, *A Handbook of Wine: How to Buy, Serve, Store, and Drink It* (London: Jonathan Cape, 1922), 68.

4. "South African Wines: A Critical Survey; Growing for Quantity (from a Correspondent)," *The Times* (London), May 24, 1922.

5. "Miss Marian Clarke," *The Times* (London), June 21, 1928, 12. Tokaji is a very well-regarded sweet wine from Hungary.

6. See Peter Gurney, *The Making of Consumer Culture in Modern U.K.* (London: Bloomsbury, 2017), especially chapter 7.

7. Dorothy Sayers, *The Unpleasantness at the Bellona Club* (London: Ernest Benn,1928), chap. 21, "Lord Peter Calls a Bluff," n.p., Kindle ed.

8. William Haselden, "Are the Good Club Days Ended?" *Daily Mirror,* November 24, 1920.

9. "Woman and Wine," *Punch,* October 18, 1933, 431.

10. Charles Ludington, *The Politics of Wine in Britain: A New Cultural History* (Basingstoke: Palgrave, 2013).

11. David Gutzke, *Women Drinking Out in Britain since the Early Twentieth Century* (Manchester: Manchester University Press, 2013), 31.

12. Harrods advertisement, *The Times* (London), November 18, 1924.

13. Sarah Cheang, "Selling China: Class, Gender and Orientalism at the Department Store," *Journal of Design History* 20, no. 1 (Spring 2007): 1–16.

14. Whiteley's Great Spring Sale flyer, n.d. [1920–21], Whiteley's Mss, WCA, MS 726/118.

15. See Wilkinson discussed in Stephen Stern, "A History of Australia's Wine Geographical Indication Legislation," in *Research Handbook on Intellectual Property*

and Geographical Indications, ed. Dev Gangjee (Cheltenham, Gloucestershire: Edward Elgar, 2016), 245–91.

16. W. Percy Wilkinson, "The Nomenclature of Australian Wines," in *Harper's Manual* (London: Harper, 1920), 10.

17. W. Percy Wilkinson, *The Nomenclature of Australian Wines: In Relation to Historical Commercial Usage of European Wine Names, International Conventions for the Protection of Industrial Property, and Recent European Commercial Treaties* (Melbourne: Thomas Urquhart, 1919).

18. Army and Navy Stores Christmas Wine List, 1934, 21. Wine Lists, LGL, COL/LIB/PB28/1.

19. Whiteley's Christmas Wine List 1934, Whiteley's Mss, WCA, MS 726/123.

20. Diner-Out (pseud. of Alfred Edye Manning Foster), *Through the Wine List* (London: Bles, 1924), 65–66.

21. Asa Briggs, *Wine for Sale: Victoria Wine and the Liquor Trade, 1860–1984* (Chicago: University of Chicago Press, 1985), quote 54; 83.

22. Newsclipping, Shareholders Minute Book, 1924, Victoria Wine Mss, LMA/4434/V/01/022.

23. Burgoyne contract terms, c. 1907, Victoria Wine Contract Book, Victoria Wine Mss, LMA/4434/V/01/038.

24. Sir Charles Cottier quoted in "Victoria Wine: Company's High Reputation: Gratifying Progress," press clipping, no name, May 29, 1924, Victoria Wine Co. Shareholders Minute Book, Victoria Wine Mss, LMA/4434/V/01/022.

25. Report of the Proceedings at the Fourteenth Ordinary General Meeting of the Members . . ., May 5, 1938. Victoria Wine Co. Shareholders Minute Book, Victoria Wine Mss, LMA/4434/V/01/022.

26. Arthur and Co. Wine List, early 1920s. Wine Lists, LGL, COL/LIB/PB28/1.

27. Burgoyne's advertisement, *Times* (London), May 25, 1923.

28. On the growth of nutrition science, see Elizabeth Neswald, David F. Smith, and Ulrike Thoms, eds., *Setting Nutritional Standards: Theory, Policies, Practices* (Woodbridge, Suffolk: Boydell & Brewer, 2017).

29. Tasting Book, Whitbread and Company Papers, London Metropolitan Archives, LMA 4453/K/08/001.

30. Andrew Lothian, "Glasgow," *Picture Post* (London), April 1, 1939, 43.

31. Topical Press, "Interior of Metropolitan 1913/1921-Electric Stock Car, after Refurbishment for Use on Circle Line," August 15, 1934, London Transport Museum, digital collection, 1998/46235, www.ltmuseum.co.uk/collections/collections-online/photographs/item/1998-46235 (accessed September 2, 2021).

32. Unknown, photograph, *Platform View at Hammersmith Station, with a Number of Passengers Waiting for a Train, 1913,* London Transport Museum, digital collection, 1998/74131, www.ltmuseum.co.uk/collections/collections-online/photographs/item/1998-74131 (accessed September 2, 2021); Southern Railway, b/w print, *Interior of Waterloo and City Railway Motor Car (Possibly No. 15),* January 1940–March 1940, London Transport Museum, digital collection, 1998/88431,

www.ltmuseum.co.uk/collections/collections-online/photographs/item/1998
-88431 (acccessed September 2, 2021).

33. Ernest Michael Dinkel, *Visit the Empire,* poster, 1933. London Transport
Museum, www.ltmuseum.co.uk/collections/collections-online/posters/item/1983-
4-3552 (accessed September 2, 2021).

34. "Clearly the decrease in consumption of all kinds of wine has been born
entirely by foreign [i.e., not empire] wines." *Reports of the Imperial Economic Committee, Twenty-third Report: Wine.* London, HMSO (1932), 20.

35. "Colonial Wine Imports: Brewery Chairman's Statement," *The Times* (London), November 21, 1936, 18.

36. *Annual Report of the Australian Wine Board, Year . . . : Together with Statement . . . Regarding the Operation of the Wine Overseas Marketing Act* (Canberra:
Government Printer, 1936–37), no. 21, 7.

37. For example, "Prime Minister's Office Canada. Subject Sales Tax on Wine,"
Bennett Papers, Archives Canada, M-1426/469601.

38. "Raw Products," *Financial Times,* April 24, 1929.

39. "La Viticulture," Minister of Agriculture and Food [Ministère de
l'Agriculture et de l'Alimentation], France, 2018 infographic, https://infographies
.agriculture.gouv.fr/image/175576923037 (accessed May 2019).

40. Stephen Tallents, draft essay, marked December 1936 [1946], Tallents Papers,
University of London Senate House Library, ICS79/38/1 Empire Wines.

41. Ibid.

42. Whiteley's Christmas Wine List 1934, Whiteley's Mss, WCA, MS 726/123,

43. "Empire Wines," typescript, April 1944, Tallents Papers, ICS79/38/9.

44. Letter from Stephen Tallents to Sir David Chadwick (Imperial Economic
Committee), May 8, 1944, Tallents Papers, ICS79/38/11.

45. W. H. Auden, "Letter to Lord Byron" (1936), second stanza.

CHAPTER 16. DOODLE BUGS DESTROYED OUR CELLAR

1. Martin was the owner of Stonyfell Winery in Langhorne.

2. R. H. M. Martin, diary of a trip to England [1938?], Martin Papers, State
Library of South Australia, BRG 309/1/2, 57.

3. C.P. 115 (26) Cabinet, Empire Marketing Grant, Memorandum by the Chan-
cellor of the Exchequer, March 17, 1926, [Marked Secret. Stamped "TO BE KEPT
UNDER LOCK AND KEY"], Tallents Papers, University of London Senate House
Library, ICS79/1/13.

4. Martin, diary of a trip to England.

5. An excellent study is Richard Overy, *The Morbid Age: U.K. between the Wars*
(London: Allen Lane, 2009).

6. "Launch of the Orion: New Cruiser Named by Lady Eyres-Monsell," *The
Times* (London), Friday, November 25, 1932, 16. "Our Correspondent: 'On This Day:

October 31, 1947; Appeal for Spirit of Unity—U.K.'s New Battle.'" *The Times* (London), October 31, 2002, 41.

7. "Launch of the Orion. New Cruiser Named by Lady Eyres-Monsell," *The Times* (London), Friday, November 25, 1932, 16.

8. See the Bombsight Project's website, Mapping the WW2 Bomb Census, bombsight.org.

9. Chairman's remarks, *Minutes of the Seventeenth Ordinary Annual General Meeting of Shareholders of the Victoria Wine Company Limited*, August 7, 1941, Shareholders Minute Book, Victoria Wine Mss, LMA/4434/V/01/022.

10. [Ronald Niebour], "He Likes to Be the Same Way Up As the Folks Down Under, When He Is Dreaming of Home," *Daily Mail*, May 12, 1941, British Cartoon Archive, NEB 0030, University of Kent, cartoons.ac.uk.

11. "The London 'Pub' Is Not What It Used to Be," *Western Star and Roma Advertiser* (Toowoomba, Queensland), January 30, 1942, 7.

12. David Low, "Low's Topical Budget," *Evening Standard*, October 14, 1939, British Cartoon Archive, LSE0823.

13. "The Grape Crop," *Evening Post* (Wellington), February 18, 1943.

14. "Manpower Cmte: Deals with Whangarei Appeals," *Northern Advocate* (Northland, New Zealand), December 13, 1940.

15. Advertisements, *New Zealand Herald*, February 7, 1942.

16. Ministry of Information, U.K., *Food from the Empire*, 1940, short film, available on Colonial Film website, www.colonialfilm.org.uk (accessed July 21, 2021).

17. Lizzie Collingham, *The Hungry Empire: How Britain's Quest for Food Shaped the Modern World* (London: The Bodley Head, 2017), 255.

18. J. G. Crawford, "Some Aspects of the Food Front," *Australian Quarterly* 14, no. 3 (September 1942): 18–32; 24.

19. War Cabinet Conclusions, March 14, 1940, National Archives, Kew, CAB 65/6/13.

20. Suryakanthie Chetty, "Imagining National Unity: South African Propaganda Efforts during the Second World War," *Kronos*, no. 38 (November 2012): 106–30.

21. "THE GERMAN 'VOLK': NAZIS ABROAD; Solidarity Sought," *Sydney Morning Herald*, February 16, 1938.

22. Christine Winter, "Removing Danger: The Making of 'Dangerous Internees' in Australia," in *Home Fronts: U.K. and the Empire at War, 1939–45*, ed. Mark J. Crowley and Sandra Trudgen Dawson (Woodbridge, Suffolk: Boydell & Brewer, 2017).

23. Geoffrey McInnes, "Italian Prisoners-of-War from No. 15 Prisoner-of-War Camp [Leeton] Working in the Camp Vineyard among Vines Bearing White Muscatel Grapes," February 1944, Australian War Memorial Photograph Collection, www.awm.gov.au/collection/C282426 (accessed September 2, 2021).

24. "Heavy Demand for P.O.W. Labour," *Townsville Daily Bulletin* (Queensland), June 14, 1944, 1.

25. "Problems of Wine Industry Discussed," *Australian Brewing and Wine Journal*, November 20, 1940, clipping in Lloyd Williams Evans Papers, State Library of South Australia, PRG 1453/56.

26. "Wine Industry Problems," *Chronicle* (Adelaide), June 19, 1941.

27. Ibid.

28. Graham Knox, *Estate Wines of South Africa,* 2nd ed. (Cape Town and Johannesburg: David Phillip, 1982), 16.

29. *Union of South Africa Annual Statements of Trade and Shipping* (Cape Town: Government Printer, annual 1906–61).

30. Chairman's Statement to AGM, Victoria Wine Company [n.d., sent ahead of meeting of June 4, 1942], Victoria Wine Shareholders' Minute Book, Victoria Wine Mss, LMA/4434/V/01/022.

31. Menu, "The Nineteenth Meeting of the Saintsbury Club," January 2, 1942, London, Francis Meynell Papers, Cambridge University Library, Meynell MS Add.9813/F7/12. Kapok is a cottonlike fiber from a tropical tree.

32. "Senior Wine Stock, December 15th, 1939," Senior Acct., King's College Archives, Cambridge, 5/6/11/4.

33. Entry for December 15, 1939. Senior Acct., King's College Archives, 5/6/11/4.

34. Dum-Dum, "Wine," *Punch,* December 17, 1941, 532.

35. Entry for December 10, 1943, Senior Acct., King's College Archives, 5/6/11/4.

36. Entry for December 6, 1943, Senior Acct., King's College Archives, 5/6/11/2; Whiteley's Autumn Sale, 1934, Whiteley's Mss, Westminster City Archives, MS 726/121.

37. Senior Acct., King's College Archives, 5/6/11/2.

38. Senior Wine Day Book, King's College Archives, 5/6/11/1.

39. Junior Wine Account Books, vols. 1 and 2, King's College Archives, 5/6/11/3; Senior Acct., King's College Archives, 5/6/11/4.

40. Anthony Berry, "Wine at the Universities," "Number Three Saint James's Street" (Autumn 1989), no. 71. Published by Berry Bros & Rudd Ltd., London. Anthony Berry Papers, Trinity Hall, Cambridge, THHR/1/2/BER.

41. Tasting notes, September 24, 1946. Whitbread & Co. Ltd. Brewers Tasting Book, 1946–48, Whitbread Mss, LMA/4453/K/08/001.

42. Entry for Williams, Standring, June 12, 1945, Senior Acct., King's College Archives, 5/6/11/2.

43. Entry for Findlater M. Todd and Co., December 3, 1946, Senior Acct., King's College Archives, 5/6/11/2.

44. Junior Wine Account Books, vol. 2, King's College Archives, 5/6/11/3.

45. Letter from Stephen Tallents to Sir David Chadwick, May 8, 1944, Tallents Papers, ICS79/38/11.

46. Letter from A.M.P. Hodsoll to Alfred Heath, 28 June 1944, Tallents Papers, ICS79/38/17.

47. Alfred Heath to Tallents, July 30, 1944, Tallents Papers, ICS79/38/15.

48. Draft typescript, "Empire Wine," December 1946, Tallents Papers, ICS79/38/1.

49. "Preserved in Time: 13,000 Crosse & Blackwell .Containers Discovered at Crossrail Site," January 9, 2017, Museum of London Archaeology, mola.org.uk.

CHAPTER 17. AND A GLASS OF WINE

1. "Sherry and Wine," *Financial Times,* February 19, 1976, 3.

2. John Cunningham, "Right Up Our Creek," *Irish Times,* May 29, 1999.

3. Joseph Lee, "London Laughs: Charabancs Return," *Evening News,* July 10, 1945, British Cartoon Archive, JL3091, cartoons.ac.uk (accessed September 2, 2021).

4. Anthony Berry, "Thespian Royalty and Rationing: The Wine Trade in 1945," *Number Three* (Autumn 1990), reprinted on the Berry Brothers and Rudd blog. http://bbrblog.com/2016/03/02/wine-trade-in-1945 (accessed September 2, 2021).

5. My emphasis. HC Deb, June 1949, 244–45.

6. Lieutenant-Commander Braithwaite, HC Deb, June 22, 1949, vol. 466, 247.

7. Photograph, "Handling Hogsheads of Sherry, at the Crescent Bonded Wine Vaults at London Docks, in Preparation for Transportation to Shops and Warehouses," *Financial Times,* November 21, 1963, 2.

8. Photograph, "South African Wine Farmers' Association Depot: West Bay Road, Southampton, 1965," Southampton City Council Libraries digital collection, no. 5191, southampton.spydus.co.uk/cgi-bin/spydus.exe/ENQ/WPAC/BIBENQ? SETLVL=&BRN=1302557 (accessed September 2, 2021).

9. Photograph, "Entrance to the Former Bonded Warehouse of the South African Wine Farmers Association at Nine Elms Goods Yard off Wandsworth Road, Vauxhall," March 31, 1966, Borough of Lambeth, Ref. 13959, https://boroughphotos .org/lambeth/south-arfican-wine-growers-bonded-warehouse-nine-elms (accessed September 2, 2021).

10. Barbara Pym, *Some Tame Gazelle,* chapter 17. Google Books e-version, n.p., in *The Barbara Pym Collection,* vol. 1, *A Glass of Blessings, Some Tame Gazelle, and Jane and Prudence* (New York: Open Road Media, 2018).

11. "Australian Wine Festival," clipping from *Harper's,* November 1955, Jack Kilgour Papers, State Library of South Australia, PRG 1279/5.

12. A. Barrington and J. Stone, *Cohabitation Trends and Patterns in the U.K* (Southampton: ESRC Centre for Population Change, 2015).

13. B. A. Young, "Working Up to Wine," *Punch,* October 9, 1957, 416.

14. *Wine Cups and Punches,* n.d. [1950s], Whiteley's Department Store Papers, Westminster City Archives, London, 726/146.

15. Ibid.

16. "Burgoyne's Harvest," *Picture Post* (London), April 21, 1951.

17. "Handling Hogsheads of Sherry . . . ," *Financial Times,* November 21, 1963, 2.

18. Term frequency for "wine" in publication section "advertising," *Punch Historical Archive, 1841–1992,* Gale Cengage Group (accessed May 28, 2019).

19. "Campaigns in Brief," *Financial Times,* December 5, 1957.

20. SAWFA advertisement, *The Economist,* December 19, 1953.

21. South African sherry ad, SAWFA, *The Blue: The Journal of the Royal Horse Guards*, no. 6 (1969): 2.

22. Confirmed and amended in 1976. Resale Prices Act 1976. Full text on www.legislation.gov.uk.

23. Helen Mercer, "Retailer-Supplier Relationships before and after the Resale Prices Act, 1964: A Turning Point in British Economic History?" *Enterprise and Society* 15, no. 1 (March 2014): 132–65.

24. I unpack this argument in more detail in Jennifer Regan-Lefebvre, "From Colonial Wine to New World: British Wine Drinking, c. 1900–1990," *Global Food History* 5, nos. 1–2 (2019): 67–83.

25. Licensing Act of 1964. Full text on www.legislation.gov.uk. For a review of licensing laws see Roy Light and Susan Heenan, "Controlling Supply: The Concept of 'Need' in Liquor Licensing," *Final Report for Alcohol Research Development Grant*, Bristol, 1999, available on www.researchgate.net/publication/265990013_Controlling_Supply_The_Concept_of_'Need'_in_Liquor_Licensing (accessed September 2, 2021).

26. John Burnett, *Liquid Pleasures: A Social History of Drinks in Modern Britain* (London: Routledge, 1999), 124; "Licensing Act, 1921," in Army and Navy Stores, Christmas Wine List, 1934, Wine Lists, LGL, COL/LIB/PB28/1.

27. Augustus Barnett Wine Sale Bulletin, March 1972, Wine Lists, LGL, COL/LIB/PB29/9.

28. Oddbins lists, 1960s–70s, Wine Lists, LGL, COL/LIB/PB29/72.

29. Marks and Spencer Wines, Sherries and Beers Price List, October 1974, Marks and Spencer Company Archives (MSCA), HO/11/1/2/70.

30. Marks and Spencer Wines, Sherries and Beers Price List, November 1974, MSCA, HO/11/1/2/1.

31. Marks and Spencer Wines, Sherries and Beers Price List, October 1974.

32. Hugh Johnson, *Wine: A Life Uncorked*, 2nd ed. (London: Phoenix, 2006), 44.

33. My emphasis. Lin Randall, "Through the Grapevine," *St Michael News*, October 1974, 8; MSCA.

34. 'White Table Wine' etiquette, n.d. [pre-1989], MCSA T500/473.

35. Various wine etiquettes. MCSA T500/428–550.

36. "Hochar Père et Fils" etiquette, n.d. [c. 1990]. MCSA T500/535.

37. Asa Briggs, *Marks and Spencer, 1884–1984: A Centenary History* (London: Octopus Books, 1984), 61.

38. Proofs of Elizabeth David, *The Use of Wine in Fine Cooking* (London: Saccone and Speed, c.1950), 4, in Elizabeth David Papers, Schlesinger Library, Radcliffe Institute, Harvard University, MC 689, Box 48 Folder 12.

39. John K. Walton, "Another Face of 'Mass Tourism': San Sebastián and Spanish Beach Resorts under Franco, 1936–1975," *Urban History* 40, no. 3 (2013): 483–506.

40. Data on holidays from Chris Ryan, "Trends Past and Present in the Package Holiday Industry," *Service Industries Journal* 9, no. 1 (1989): 61–78; 67, table 2. Population data ONS.

41. Hugh Johnson Papers, University of California Davis Special Collections (hereafter Johnson Mss, UCD), D-599, Box 1, Folder 6.

42. Hugh Johnson, "What to Drink with Exotic Food," clipping from *About Town*, marked June 1962, Johnson Mss, UCD, D-599, Box 1, Folder 1.

43. Ibid.

44. *Father to Son Tradition in Wine Making*, A.A. Corban & Sons, "Mt. Lebanon" Vineyards, Henderson, New Zealand. n.d. [early 1960s]. Author's own copy, 14.

45. Edward Hulton, "Is Economic Union Possible?" *Picture Post* (London), January 14, 1957, 18–19.

46. Gonzalo Villalta Puig, "Australia and the European Union: A Brief Commercial History," in *Potential Benefits of an Australia-EU Free Trade Agreement: Key Issues and Options,* ed. Jane Drake-Brockman and Patrick Messerlin (Adelaide: University of Adelaide Press, 2018), 4.

47. See also Alan Swinbank and Carsten Daugbjerg, "The Changed Architecture of the EU's Agricultural Policy over Four Decades: Trade Policy Implications for Australia," in *Australia, the European Union and the New Trade Agenda,* ed. Elijah Annmarie et al., 77–96 (Canberra: Australian National University Press, 2017).

48. Ronald Russell, "The Commonwealth and the Common Market," *Journal of the Royal Society of Arts* 119, no. 5177 (1971): 312–18; 314.

CHAPTER 18. GOOD FIGHTING WINE

1. Monty Python, "Australian Table Wines," in *The Monty Python Instant Record Collection* (London: Charisma, 1977), available at www.youtube.com /watch?v=Cozwo88w44Q (accessed September 2, 2021).

2. For an introduction to the Stolen Generations, it is worth reading the testimony in Australian Human Rights Commission, *Bringing Them Home: Report of the National Inquiry into the Separation of Aboriginal and Torres Strait Islander Children from Their Families* (Sydney, April 1997).

3. A.J. Ludbrook to Hugh Johnson, April 12, 1972, Hugh Johnson Papers, University of California Davis Special Collections, D-599, Box 5, Folder 9.

4. "U.K. Entry to E.E.C.—Effect on Australian Wine Trade," *Australian Wine, Brewing and Spirit Review,* November 26, 1971, in Johnson Mss, UCD, D-599, Box 5, Folder 9.

5. Bill Nasson, "Bitter Harvest: Farm Schooling for Black South Africans," Carnegie Conference Paper no. 97, *Second Carnegie Inquiry into Poverty and Development in Southern Africa* (April 1984): 9. In the early 1980s the rand was worth around one U.S. dollar, although rampant inflation makes it difficult to provide precise comparisons.

6. Christabel Gurney, "'A Great Cause': The Origins of the Anti-Apartheid Movement, June 1959-March 1960," *Journal of Southern African Studies* 26, no. 1 (2000): 123–44.

7. Photograph of "Boycott Apartheid 89'"campaign protest, outside Bottom's Up Off-license, Bristol, England. Anti-Apartheid Movement Archive, Bodleian Library, MSS AAM 2426, pic8907, www.aamarchives.org (accessed September 2, 2021).

8. Augustus Barnett wine list, March 1972, Wine Lists, LGL, COL/LIB/PB29/9.

9. Cape Province Wines list, September 1982, André Simon Papers, LGL, AS Pam 5105.

10. Tasting Notebook, South Africa 1977, Jancis Robinson Papers, Shields Library, UC Davis Special Collections, D-612, Box 1, Folder 8.

11. Oz Clarke, *The Essential Wine Guide* (New York: Viking, 1984), 274.

12. Oz Clarke, *Sainsbury's Book of Wine* (London: Sainsbury's, 1987; 2nd ed. 1988), 238.

13. Jancis Robinson to Marvin Shanken, fax, November 8, 1995, Robinson Papers, UC Davis Special Collections, D-612, Box 1, Folder 2.

14. *The Hardy Tradition: Tracing the Growth and Development of a Great Wine-Making Family through Its First Hundred Years* (Adelaide: Thomas Hardy & Sons Limited, 1953), 2. A corroboree ground is a space for Aboriginal meeting and festivities.

15. M. J. O'Reilly, "Our Flag," in *New Zealand Tablet,* October 14, 1925.

16. "Public Service Vacancies," *Evening Star* (Wellington), June 26, 1947.

17. Paul Christoffel, "Prohibition and the Myth of 1919," *New Zealand Journal of History* 42, no. 2 (2008): 154–75.

18. Digitized and available on Papers Past, https://paperspast.natlib.govt.nz /periodicals/white-ribbon (accessed September 2, 2021).

19. "Waihirere Wine in the Making," *Gisborne Herald,* March 13, 1948, 8.

20. A. A. Corban and Sons, *Father to Son Tradition in Wine Making* (Henderson, New Zealand: Mt. Lebanon Vineyards, n.d. [c. 1960]).

21. Ibid., 15.

22. New Zealand, U.S. Embassy, *New Zealand Update* [Washington, DC]: New Zealand Embassy, November–December 1979.

23. Australian Wine Research Institute, *Sixteenth Annual Report for Year 1969–1970* (Urrbrae, South Australia, September 1970). In Johnson Mss, UCD, D-599, Box 5, Folder 9.

24. Publications of the Australian Wine Research Institute, list, www.awri .com.au/wp-content/uploads/awri_staff_pubs.pdf (accessed September 2, 2021).

25. Jessica T. Duong, "The Role of Science and Technology on the New Zealand Wine Industry: Profiling Dr. Richard E. Smart's Impact, 1982–1990," unpublished manuscript, 2018.

26. Penfolds Royal Reserve Hock etiquette, n.d. [1960s?], "Wine Literature of the World," permanent exhibition, State Library of South Australia, Adelaide. See also the CLN Morse Wine Labels digital collection, for example Dry Hunter Red 1974.

27. "Pack Sizes," European Commission informational guide, https://ec.europa.eu/growth/single-market/goods/building-blocks/legal-metrology/pack-sizes_en (accessed September 2, 2021).

28. Penfold's Royal Reserve Hock etiquette, n.d. [1960s?], "Wine Literature of the World," State Library of South Australia.

29. "Bids and Deals," *Financial Times,* May 21, 1976.

30. Kenyon, Brand & Riggs, illustration of Waihirere wine bottle, photographed 1968 by K E Niven & Co of Wellington. K E Niven and Co Collection, Alexander Turnbull Library, Wellington, New Zealand, 1/2–221047-F.

31. "Quality Schemes Explained," European Commission, https://ec.europa.eu/info/food-farming-fisheries/food-safety-and-quality/certification/quality-labels/quality-schemes-explained_en (accessed September 2, 2021).

32. John Burgoyne, "South African and Australian Wines," in *How to Choose and Enjoy Wine,* ed. Augustus Muir (London: Odhams Press, 1953), 97.

33. "John Harvey Wins Bristol Cream Suit," *Financial Times,* December 2, 1971, 17.

34. "Wine Concern's Undertaking on 'Sherry,'" *Financial Times,* December 8, 1971, 15.

35. Price list, 408 Beverages, Adelaide, April 1970. Johnson Mss, UCD, D-599, Box 5, Folder 9.

36. Mike Coomer, of Swift and Moore, "Aussie Plonk," letter to the editor of *The Bulletin,* November 28, 1978.

37. Julie McIntyre and John Germov, "'Who Wants to Be a Millionaire?' I Do: Postwar Australian Wine, Gendered Culture, and Class," *Journal of Australian Studie* 42, no. 1 (2018): 65–84; 81–82.

38. Australian Wine Center price list, June 1969. In Johnson Mss, UCD, D-599, Box 5, Folder 9.

39. Australian Wine and Brandy Corporation Act, 1980, Part VIB, Division 2, Sections 40C through 40F, www.legislation.gov.au/Details/C2008C00346 (accessed September 2, 2021).

40. Hugh Laracy, "Saint-Making: The Case of Pierre Chanel of Futuna," *New Zealand Journal of History* 34, no. 1 (2000): 148.

41. James Halliday, "Geographical Indications," n.d., www.winecompanion.com.au/resources/australian-wine-industry/geographical-indications (accessed September 2, 2021).

42. Graham Knox, *Estate Wines of South Africa,* 2nd ed (Cape Town and Johannesburg: David Phillip, 1982), 17–21.

CHAPTER 19. ALL BAR ONE

1. Windrush wine catalog, October 1992, LGL, COL/LIB/PB29.

2. All data from FAOStat.org. My calculations are based on the top twenty importing countries, so some margin of error is needed to allow for much smaller importers' effect on the overall totals.

3. FAOStat.org.

4. Food and Agriculture Organization of the United Nations. *Agribusiness Handbook: Grapes, Wine* (Rome: United Nations, 2009), table 3, 18.

5. Edmund Crooks, *Alcohol Consumption and Taxation* (London: Institute for Fiscal Studies, 1989), 19.

6. Cooperative wine list, n.d. [late 1980s], LGL, COL/LIB/PB29/26.

7. John Burnett, *Liquid Pleasures: A Social History of Drinks in Modern Britain* (London: Routledge, 1999), 155.

8. Kym Anderson, "Wine's New World," *Foreign Policy*, no. 136 (June 5, 2003): 48.

9. Asa Briggs, *Wine for Sale: Victoria Wine and the Liquor Trade, 1860–1984* (Chicago: University of Chicago Press, 1985), 185.

10. On supermarkets and drinking, see Sarah L. Holloway, Mark Jayne, and Gill Valentine, " 'Sainsbury's Is My Local': English Alcohol Policy, Domestic Drinking Practices and the Meaning of Home," *Transactions of the Institute of British Geographers* 33, no. 4 (October 2008): 532–47; Dawn Nell et al., "Investigating Shopper Narratives of the Supermarket in Early Post-War England, 1945–1975," *Oral History* 37, no. 1 (Spring 2009): 61–73.

11. Berry Bros. & Rudd wine list, Autumn 1983, 5. LGL COL/LIB/PB28/1.

12. On British supermarkets as powerful negotiators see Robert Gwynne, "U.K. Retail Concentration, Chilean Wine Producers and Value Chains," *Geographical Journal* 174, no. 2 (June 2008): 97–108.

13. She continued, in a sentiment that will be understood by all academics: "and as I am a university teaching officer I simply do not have the time to spend on such a venture." Dr R. H. Lloyd to Mr Shepherd, February 5, 1988, Wine Account, Murray Edwards College, Cambridge, NHAR/2/2/18.

14. Draft typescript, n.d. [c. 1970], Hugh Johnson Papers, UC Davis Special Collections, D-599, Box 5, Folder 9.

15. John Avery MW, 2003–4 interview, *In Vino Veritas: Extracts from an Oral History of the U.K. Wine Trade* (London: British Library National Life Story Collection, 2005), disc 2, track 18.

16. A Penfolds Gewurztraminer, in keeping with the sweet-white trend of the time. Wine Account, February 1985, Murray Edwards College, Cambridge, NHAR/2/2/18.

17. Anthony Berry, "Thespian Royalty and Rationing: The Wine Trade in 1945," *Number Three* (Autumn 1990), reprinted on the Berry Brothers & Rudd blog. http://bbrblog.com/2016/03/02/wine-trade-in-1945 (accessed September 2, 2021).

18. "Australian Wines," promotional flyer, n.d. [1987–88], Marks and Spencer Company Archives, HO/11/1/2/9.

19. Ibid.

20. Tessa Fallows, "Brave New World of Grape Expectations," *Marks & Spencer International News*, Christmas 1991, MSCA.

21. New Zealand Wine List, Kiwi Fruits, London, August–September 1993, LGL COL/LIB/PB28.

22. Shanthi Robertson, "Intertwined Mobilities of Education, Tourism, and Labour: The Consequences of 417 and 485 Visas in Australia," in *Unintended Consequences: The Impact of Migration Law and Policy,* ed. Dickie Marianne, Gozdecka Dorota, and Reich Sudrishti (Canberra: Australian National University Press, 2016), 53–80.

23. Alexander Reilly et al., "Working Holiday Makers in Australian Horticulture: Labour Market Effect, Exploitation, and Avenues for Reform," *Griffith Law Review* 27, no. 1 (2018): 99–130; 100. Since 2018, Australia has even extended visas for those working at vineyards, to fill a labor shortage.

24. Top Ten Programmes for 1989, TV since 1981, Broadcasters' Audience Research Board, www.barb.co.uk/resources/tv-facts/tv-since-1981/1989/top10 (accessed September 2, 2021).

25. Oddbins list, Summer 1991, LGL, COL/LIB/PB29/72.

26. Tim Atkins, quoted in Oddbins list, Winter 1992, LGL, COL/LIB/PB29/72.

27. Oddbins catalog, Summer 1992, LGL, COL/LIB/PB29/72.

28. Augustus Barnett wine list, Winter 1990, LGL, COL/LIB/PB29/9.

29. Berry Bros & Rudd wine list, October 1991, 134, LGL, COL/LIB/PB28/1.

CONCLUSION

1. Ashifa Kassam, "Gibraltar to Turn Wartime Tunnels into Wine Vaults," *The Guardian*, October 11, 2015. James Badcock, "Gibraltar War Tunnels To Become Massive Wine Cellar," *The Telegraph,* October 12, 2015.

2. Chardonnay and pinot noir are two of the grapes used to make actual champagne. Wine Committee records, Murray Edwards College, Cambridge, NHGB 5/21/1a 1998.

3. Marianne Merten, "The Solms-Delta way; or, How Not to Do Land Reform," *Daily Maverick* (Johannesburg, South Africa), August 14, 2018. I had planned a research trip to Solms-Delta that was canceled due to the pandemic that started in early 2020; they have not answered my requests for interviews, perhaps also because of the pandemic.

4. See the work of Ruth Morgan, for example *Running Out? Water in Western Australia* (Crawley: University of Western Australia Publishing, 2015).

5. Author's visit, Tyrell's, Hunter Valley, November 2016.

6. Myra Greer, "Wine with Myra Greer: Why We're the World's Biggest Mcguigan Fans," *Belfast Telegraph,* [n.d.: 2003?], added online July 4, 2008.

7. Rachel Martin, "Northern Ireland Market Is Our Biggest, Australian Winemaker," *Belfast Telegraph,* May 10, 2016.

8. Matthew Fort, "Great Tucker, Mate," *The Guardian,* July 27, 2001.

1. *An Act for Ascertaining and Establishing Uniformity of Weights and Measures,* *17 June 1824,* UK Public General Act, legislations.gov.uk.

2. The *Units of Measurement Regulations 1995,* amended 1995, section 6, legislation.gov.uk.

3. *Reports of the Imperial Economic Committee: Twenty-Third Report; Wine* (London: HMSO, 1932), 18.

BIBLIOGRAPHY

This bibliography is divided into the following three sections: Archives and Manuscripts, Printed Primary Sources, Secondary Sources.

ARCHIVES AND MANUSCRIPTS

Australia

State Library of New South Wales, Sydney
MLMSS 8915 Dalwood Vineyard Papers.
MLMSS 8051 Dalwood Vineyard Papers.

State Library of South Australia, Adelaide
PRG 1279 Jack Kilgour Papers.
PRG 1453 Lloyd Williams Evans Papers.
RG 309/1/2 R. H. M. Martin Papers.

Canada

Archives Canada, Ottawa
M-1406 R. B. Bennett Papers.
M-1426 R. B. Bennett Papers.
RG17 Agriculture Department Correspondence for 1881.

Digital Collections

Africa through a Lens, CO 1069/219, National Archives U.K. Digital Photograph Collection.
Anti-Apartheid Movement Archive, Bodleian Library.

Applications for Trade Marks, digitized, National Archives of Australia.
Australian National Maritime Museum.
Bombsight: Mapping the WW2 Bomb Census, bombsight.org.
British Cartoon Archive, University of Kent, cartoons.ac.uk.
Broadcasters' Audience Research Board, www.barb.co.uk.
Buttolph Collection of Menus, New York Public Library Digital Collections.
CLN Morse Wine Labels digital collection, Flicker.
C. Krishna Gairola Indian and Asian Art and Architecture Slides, University of Washington Libraries, Special Collections.
Digital collection, prints and posters, London Transport Museum.
John and Charles Bell Heritage Trust Collection, University of Cape Town Libraries.
MacDonald Family Papers, Capricornia CQ University Collection.
Menus: The Art of Dining, University of Nevada Las Vegas Digital Collections.
Monash Collections Online.
Old Bailey Proceedings Online, www.oldbaileyonline.org.
Trove Digital Collections, Australia.
UCL Legacies of Slavery-ownership Database, www.ucl.ac.uk/lbs.
"Wine Literature of the World" permanent and online exhibition, State Library of South Australia, Adelaide.

United Kingdom

Cambridge University Library, Cambridge
MS Add.9813   Francis Meynell Papers.
Royal Commonwealth Cobham Photograph Collection, RCS/Cobham/RCS.
Society Library   Cob.18.121–12; Fisher Photograph Collection, RCS/
                     GBR/0115/Fisher; Photographs of the Dalwood Vine-
                     yards, near Branxton, New South Wales, Australia, 1886,
                     RCS/Y3086B.

Churchill College Archive, Cambridge
Churchill/Amel 1/5/13 Leo Amery Papers.

King's College Archive, Cambridge
KCAR/5/6/11/2 Senior Wine A/C Book, January 1920–64.
KCAR/5/6/11/3 Junior Wine A/C Book, 2 vols.
KCAR/5/6/11/4 Wine Supply Stock List, Senior Account, 1913–51.

London Guildhall Library, London
Andre Simon / Masters of Wine Collection.
Wine lists of British importers and wine merchants, 1930s through 2008. Including: Army and Navy Stores, Arriba Kettle and Co., Arthur and Co., Atkinson Bald-

win and Co., Augustus Barnett, Australian Wine Center, Berry Bros. and Rudd, Community Wine Co., The Co-Operative, Kiwi Fruit New Zealand Wine List, Oddbins, Sainsbury's, Waitrose, Windrush, Wines of Australia.

London Metropolitan Archives, London (LMA)
Matthew Clark and Sons Papers
CLC/B/158/MS38342 Advertising and Sales Records, 1880s through 1920s.
CLC/B/158/MS38343 New Zealand Sales Book, 1930s.
CLC/B/158/MS38347 Auction Broadsheets, 1820s.
CLC/B/227–143, P. B. Burgoyne Papers, Correspondence, 1880s.
Victoria Wine Company Papers
LMA/4434/V/01/001 Director's Minute Book, 1924–33.
LMA/4434/V/01/002 Director's Minute Book, 1933–53.
LMA/4434/V/01/022 Shareholders Minute Book, 1924–51.
LMA/4434/V/01/024 List of Members, 1922 through 1930s.
LMA/4434/V/01/038 Contract Book, 1882–1933.
LMA/4453/K/07/001 Whitbread and Company, Sales Book, 1855–66.
LMA/4453/K/08/001 Whitbread Brewers, Tasting Book, 1940s.
LMA/MS29,451 Pownall Papers, Correspondence Copybook, 1895–96.

Marks and Spencer Company Archives, Leeds
Wine labels and etiquettes, 1970s through 2010s.

Murray Edwards College, Cambridge
NHAR/2/2/3 Wine Stocks [1990s].
NHAR/2/2/18 Wine Acc. [1969–c. 1991].
NHGB/5/21/1 Wine Account and Wine Committee [c. 1990–2004].
NHGB/5/21/2 Wine Committee [mid-2000s].

Trinity Hall, Cambridge
THAR/5/4/1/2 Wine Cellar Accounts 1874–89.
THAR/5/4/7/1 Steward's Papers.
THCS/17/5/2/1 [Misc Menus].
THHR/1/2/BER Anthony Berry Papers.

United Kingdom Parliamentary Papers
Board of Trade. *Production and Consumption of Alcoholic Beverages (Wine, Beer and Spirits) in the British Colonies (Australasia, Canada, and the Cape).* 1900, Cd 72.
Committees of Inquiry on Administration of Government and Finances at Cape of Good Hope. *Documents Referred to in the Reports of the Commissioners,* HC 1826–27, 406.
Committee on New Zealand. *Report,* May 23, 1844, HC 1844, 556.

Committee on Trade of Cape of Good Hope. *Report of the Commissioners of Inquiry upon the Trade of the Cape of Good Hope; the Navigation of the Coast, and the Improvement of the Harbours of That Colony.* HC 1829, 300.

Select Committee on the Affairs of the East India Company. *Report from the Select Committee on the Affairs of the East India Company; with Minutes of Evidence in Six Parts, and an Appendix and Index to Each,* HC 1831–32, 734.

Select Committee on Wine Duties. *Supplementary Appendix to the Report from the Select Committee on Wine Duties, 1879,* HC 1878–79, 278.

United Kingdom, House of Commons. *Account of Value of Imports from Cape of Good Hope, 1812–16.* 1817, 225.

———. *Account of the Quantity of Foreign Wine Imported, Exported, and Retained for Home Consumption.* 1851, 427.

———. *Accounts of the Quantities of the Principal Articles Imported into, and Exported from, the United Kingdom, the British Settlements in Australia, the United States of America, the Canadian Possessions, the British West Indies, and Brazil; &c.* 1856, 351.

———. *Correspondence Respecting the Increase in the Wine Duties.* May 1899, C 9322.

———. *Malta: Annual report for 1895.* 1896, C 172.

———. *Malta: Annual Report for 1896.* 1897, C 8279–20.

———. *Malta: Correspondence Respecting the Taxation and Expenditure of Malta.* 1878, C 2032.

———. *Papers Relating to the Administration and Finances of Cyprus.* 1883, C 3661.

———. *Papers Relative to Aboriginal Inhabitants of Cape of Good Hope. Part I. Hottentots and Bosjesmen; Caffres; Griquas.* 1835, 50.

———. *Report on the Civil Establishments of Malta.* 1880, C 2684.

———. *Reports to Secretary of State on Past and Present State of H.M. Colonial Possessions, 1869 (Part II. N. American Colonies; African Settlements and St. Helena; Australia and New Zealand; Mediterranean Possessions; Heligoland and Falkland Islands).* 1871, 415.

———. *Representations from Cape of Good Hope to H.M. Government Respecting Duties on Cape Wine.* 1831, 103.

———. *Spirits and Wine. Returns of the Quantities of British Spirits Used for Home Consumption in the United Kingdom.* 1862, 168.

———. *Statistical Abstract for the Several Colonial and Other Possessions of the United Kingdom in Each Year from 1885 to 1899.* 1900, Cd 307.

———. *Trade and Navigation. For the Month Ended 31st January 1890.* 1890, C 14-I-XI.

University of London Senate House Library, London
ICS79/1/1–15 Tallents Papers, Origin of the Empire Marketing Board.
ICS79/38/1–20 Tallents Papers, Wine.

Westminster City Archives, London
Whiteley's Department Store Papers

Acc 726/118 Newspaper clippings 1910 through 1930s.
Acc 726/119 Fine wine, spirits, and liqueurs price lists 1930–34.
Acc 726/120 Fine wine, spirits, and liqueurs price list 1931.
Acc 726/121 Autumn Sale 1933.
Acc 726/122 Whiteley's Sale of Wines and Spirits c. 1935.
Acc 726/123 Whiteley's Christmas Wine List 1934.
Acc. 726/124 Wine List c.1935.
Acc 726/125 Silver Jubilee Wine List 1935.
Acc 1993/1 Cash Book, White Family, 1838.
Acc 2108/1 BRA No 2749 Wills of Hensleigh Wedgwood.

United States

National Library of Medicine, National Institute of Health, Bethesda, MD
MS C 122, J. L. W. Thudichum Papers.

Schlesinger Library, Radcliffe Institute, Harvard University, Cambridge, MA
MC 689, Elizabeth David Papers, Series III and Series VI (provided as electronic copy).

Shields Library, UC Davis, Davis, CA
D-599, Hugh Johnson Papers.
D-612, Jancis Robinson Papers.

Watkinson Library, Trinity College, Hartford, CT
First World War poster collection.

PRINTED PRIMARY SOURCES

Andrews, E. Benj. "The Combination of Capital." *International Journal of Ethics* 4, no. 3 (April 1894): 321–34.
Annual Report of the Australian Wine Board, Year . . . : Together with Statement . . . Regarding the Operation of the Wine Overseas Marketing Act. Canberra: Government Printer, 1936–37.
Austen, Jane. *Sense and Sensibility.* London: Thomas Egerton, 1811.
Bagnall, A. Gordon. *Wines of South Africa: An Account of Their History, Their Production and Their Nature, Illustrated with Wood-Engravings by Roman Waher.* Paarl: KWV, 1961.
Barber, Mary. *Poems on several occasions.* London: C. Rivington, 1734.
Barrington, George. *A voyage to New South Wales; with a description of the country; the manners, customs, religion, &c. of the natives, in the vicinity of Botany Bay.* Philadelphia: Thomas Dobson, 1796.

Biddulph, Robert. "Cyprus." *Proceedings of the Royal Geographic Society* II, no. 12, (December 1889): 705–19.

Bragato, Romeo. *Report on the Prospects of Viticulture In New Zealand: Together with Instructions for Planting and Pruning.* Wellington: S. Costall, Government Printer, 1895.

Brown, John Crombie. *Water Supply of South Africa and Facilities for the Storage of It.* Edinburgh: Oliver and Boyd, 1877.

Brunfaut, Jules, ed. *L'Exposition Universelle de 1878 illustrée.* Vols. 173–74. Paris: n.p., December 1878.

Bunbury, Charles J. F. *Journal of a Residence at the Cape of Good Hope, with Excursions into the Interior, and Notes on the Natural History, and the Native Tribes.* London: John Murray, 1848.

Burgoyne, A. H. "Colonial Vine Culture." *Journal of the Royal Society of Arts* 60, no. 3105 (May 1912): 671–86.

Buring, Leo. *Australian Wines: 150th Anniversary of the Wine Industry of Australia.* Sydney: Federal Viticultural Council of Australia, 1938.

Busby, James. *Authentic Information Relative to New South Wales and New Zealand.* London: Joseph Cross, 1832.

———. *A Journal of a Tour through Some of the Vineyards of Spain and France.* Sydney: Stephens and Stokes, 1833.

———. *The Rebellions of the Maories Traced to Their True Origin: In Two Letters to the Right Honourable Edward Cardwell . . .* London: Strangeways & Walden, 1865.

———. *Report on the Vines, Introduced into the Colony of New South Wales, in the Year 1832: With a Catalogue of the Several Varieties Growing in the Botanical Garden, in Sydney.* Sydney: William Jones, 1834.

———. *A Treatise on the Culture of the Vine and the Art of Making Wine.* [Sydney?]: R. Howe, Government Printer, 1825.

Calcutta International Exhibition, 1883–84: Report of the Royal Commission for Victoria, at the Calcutta International Exhibition, 1883–84. Melbourne: John Ferres, Government Printer, 1884.

"Canada Vine Growers' Association." *Canadian Journal of Medical Science* (October 1878).

Campbell, John. *Travels in South Africa: Undertaken at the Request of the Missionary Society.* London: Black and Parry, 1815.

Cape of Good Hope, Department of Prime Minister. *Report of Committee Nominated by the Western Province Board of Horticulture to Inquire into the Wine and Brandy Industry of the Cape Colony, 1905.* Cape Town: Government Printers, 1905. Repr., Delhi: Facsimile Publisher, 2019.

Chaigneau, William. *The History of Jack Connor.* 2 vols. London: William Johnston, 1753.

Chambers, Trant. *A Land of Promise: A Brief and Authentic Account of the Condition and Resources of Western Australia.* Fremantle: J. B. Cant & Co., January 1, 1897.

Chaptal, Jean-Antoine. *Traité théorique et pratique sur la culture de la vigne*. Paris: Delalain, 1801.

Cherrington, Ernest H. "World-Wide Progress toward Prohibition Legislation." *Annals of the American Academy of Political and Social Science* 109 (1923): 208–24.

Christian, Charles. *Cyprus and Its Possibilities*. London: Royal Colonial Institute, 1897.

Clarke, Oz. *The Essential Wine Guide*. New York: Viking, 1984.

———. *Oz Clarke's Wine Factfinder and Taste Guide*. London: Webster's and Mitchell Beazley, 1985.

———. *Sainsbury's Book of Wine*. London: Sainsbury's, 1987. 2nd ed. 1988.

———, ed. *Webster's Wine Price Guide: Consumer and Professional Guide*. London: Webster's and Mitchell Beazley, 1984.

Cole, Alred W. *The Cape and the Kafirs; or, Notes on Five Years' Residence in South Africa*. London: R. Bentley, 1852.

Collett, John. *A Guide for Visitors to Kashmir: Enl., Rev. and Corr. Up to Date by A. Mitra; with a Route Map of Kashmir*. Calcutta: W. Newman, 1898.

Collins, David. *An Account of the English Colony in New South Wales, from Its First Settlement in January 1788, to August 1801: With Remarks on the Dispositions, Customs, Manners, &C., of the Native Inhabitants of That Country*. 2nd ed. London: T. Cadell and W. Davies, 1804.

Cooper, Michael. *The Wines and Vineyards of New Zealand*. London: Hodder and Stoughton, 1994.

Corban, A. A., and Sons. *Father to Son Tradition in Wine Making*. Henderson, New Zealand: Mt. Lebanon Vineyards, n.d. [c. 1960].

Crawford, J. G. "Some Aspects of the Food Front." *Australian Quarterly* 14, no. 3 (September 1942): 18–32.

Crosby, A. ed. *Lovell's Gazeteer of British North America*. Montreal: John Lovell, 1873.

Customs Tariffs of the United Kingdom from 1800 to 1897: With Some Notes upon the History of the More Important Branches of Receipt from the Year 1660. London: Printed for Her Majesty's Stationery Office by Darling & Son, 1897.

David, Elizabeth. *An Omelette and a Glass of Wine*. London: Robert Hale, 1984.

Davies, John. *The Innkeeper's and Butler's Guide; or, A Directory for Making and Managing British Wines: With Directions for the Managing, Colouring and Flavouring of Foreign Wines and Spirits, and, for Making British Compounds, Peppermint, Aniseed, Shrub, &c. . . .* 13th ed., rev. and corrected. Leeds: Davies, 1810.

De Bosdari, C. *Wines of the Cape*. Cape Town: A. A. Balkema, 1955.

de Castella, François. *Handbook on Viticulture for Victoria*. Melbourne: Government Printer, 1891.

de Castella, Hubert. *John Bull's Vineyard: Australian Sketches*. Melbourne: Sands and McDougall, 1886.

———. *Notes d'un Vigneron Australien*. Melbourne: George Robertson, 1882.

Delavan, Edward Cornelius. *Temperance of Wine Countries: A Letter.* Manchester: United Kingdom Alliance, 1860.

Department of Agriculture, Cape of Good Hope. *Agricultural Miscellanea: Being Extracts from Volumes I to V of the "Agricultural Journal."* Cape Town: W. A. Richards and Sons, Government Printers, 1897.

Department of Industries. "First Official Report to the Commissioner of Agriculture." *Sessional Papers of the Legislature of Ontario,* no. 3, A, 1883.

Department of Prime Minister, Cape of Good Hope (South Africa). *Report of Committee Nominated by the Western Province Board of Horticulture to Inquire into the Wine and Brandy Industry of the Cape Colony, 1905.* Cape Town: Cape Times, 1905.

Descriptive Catalogue of the Collection of Products and Manufactures Contributed by the Colony of Western Australia to the International Exhibition of 1862: With Remarks on Some of the Principal Objects Exhibited. January 1, 1862.

Downing, W. H. *Digger Dialects: A Collection of Slang Phrases Used by the Australian Soldiers on Active Service.* Melbourne and Sydney: Lothian, 1919.

Druitt, Robert. *Report on the Cheap Wines from France, Italy, Austria, Greece, and Hungary; Their Quality, Wholesomeness, and Price, and Their Use in Diet and Medicine: With Short Notes of a Lecture to Ladies on Wine, and Remarks on Acidity.* London: Henry Renshaw, 1865.

Dunlop, John. *On the Wine System of Great Britain.* Greenock, Scotland: R. B. Lusk, 1831.

———. *The Philosophy of Artificial and Compulsory Drinking Usage in Great Britain and Ireland.* London: Holston and Stoneman, 1839.

Elder, John Rawson, ed. *The Letters and Journals of Samuel Marsden, 1765–1838.* Dunedin, New Zealand: Coulls, Somerville Wilkie, 1932.

Elliott, Ebenezer. *Corn Law Rhymes.* Sheffield, Yorkshire: Mechanics' Anti-Bread-Tax Society, 1831.

Entertaining with Wines of the Cape: Choosing, Cellaring, Serving, Cooking, Recipes. Die Ko-operatiewe Wijnbouwers Vereniging van Zuid-Afrika Beperkt. Paarl, Cape, Republic of South Africa. First published 1959. 4th ed. 1971.

Eyriès, Jean-Baptiste-Benoît, and Alfred Jacobs. *Histoire générale des voyages: Publié sous la direction du contre-amiral Dumont D'Urville.* Vol. 4, *Voyage en Asie et en Afrique.* Paris: Furne, 1859.

Fallon, J. T. "Australian Vines and Wines." *Journal of the Society of Arts* 22, no. 1098 (December 1873): 37–56.

———. *The "Murray Valley Vineyard," Albury, New South Wales, and "Australian Vines and Wines."* Melbourne: n.p., 1874.

Fenning, D., and J. Collyer. *A New System of Geography; or, A General Description of the World.* London: S. Crowder et al., 1766.

Foster, Alfred Edye Manning [pseud. Diner-Out]. *Through the Wine List.* London: Bles, 1924.

Gardiner, Grace, and F. A. Steel. *The Complete Indian Housekeeper and Cook: Giving the Duties of Mistress and Servants, the General Management of the House and*

Practical Recipes for Cooking in All Its Branches. 3rd ed. Edinburgh: Edinburgh Press, 1893.

Glasse, Hannah. *The compleat confectioner: or, the whole art of confectionary made plain and easy. Shewing, The various Methods of preserving and candying, both . . .* London: Printed and sold at Mrs. Ashburner's China Shop . . ., 1760.

The Hardy Tradition: Tracing the Growth and Development of a Great Wine-Making Family through Its First Hundred Years. Adelaide: Thomas Hardy & Sons Limited, 1953.

Hawker, C. E. *Chats about Wine.* London: Daly, 1907.

Henry, Augustine. "Vine Cultivation in the Gironde." *Bulletin of Miscellaneous Information (Royal Botanic Gardens, Kew)* 33 (1889): 227–30.

Hooker, W. Jackson. "The Late Mr Cunningham." *Companion to the Botanical Magazine: Being a Journal, Containing Such Interesting Botanical Information As Does Not Come Within the Prescribed Limits of the Magazine; with Occasional Figures.* London: Printed by E. Conchman . . . for the proprietor, S. Curtis, 1835–36.

"India and Our Colonial Empire." *Westminster Review* 113–14 (July 1880): 95.

International Exhibition, Sydney, 1880: Official Catalogue of Exhibits. Melbourne, January 1, 1880.

International Health Exhibition, 1884: Official Catalogue. 2nd ed. London, 1884.

Johnson, Hugh. *Wine: A Life Uncorked.* 2nd ed. London: Phoenix, 2006.

Johnson, Hugh, and Jancis Robinson. *The World Atlas of Wine.* 7th ed. London: Mitchell Beazley, 2013.

Jullien, André. *Topographie de tous les vignobles connus.* Paris: Madame Huzard and L. Colas, 1816.

Keene, H. G. *Peepful Leaves : Poems Written in India.* London: W. H. Allen, 1879.

Kelly, A. C. *The Vine in Australia.* Sydney: Sands and Kelly, 1861.

Laffer, H. E. "Empire Wines." *Journal of the Royal Society of Arts* 85, no. 4385 (December 4, 1936): 78-96.

———. "Report of the Lecturer on Viticulture and Fruit Culture, Etc." *South Australia: Report of the Department of Agriculture for the Year Ended June 30th, 1911.* Adelaide: R. E. E. Rogers, Government Printer, 1911.

———. *The Wine Industry of Australia.* Adelaide: Australian Wine Board, 1949.

Landor, Edward Wilson. *The Bushman: Life in a New Country.* First published 1847. London: Richard Bentley; Gutenberg online edition, December 2004.

Lang, R. Hamilton. *Report (with Three Woodcuts) upon the Results of the Cyprus Representation at the Colonial & Indian Exhibition of 1886.* London: s.n., January 1, 1886.

LaTrobe, C. I. *Journal of a Visit to South Africa, in 1815, and 1816: With Some Account of the Missionary Settlements of the United Brethren, Near the Cape of Good Hope.* Cape of Good Hope: L. B. Seeley, and R. Ackermann, 1818.

Mace, Brice M., and T. Ritchie Adam. "Imperial Preference in the British Empire." *Annals of the American Academy of Political and Social Science* 168 (1933): 226–34.

MacQuitty, Jane. *Jane MacQuitty's Pocket Guide to Australian and New Zealand Wines*. London: Mitchell Beazley, 1990.

Marsden, John Buxton. *Memoirs of the Life And Labors of the Rev. Samuel Marsden: Of Paramatta, Senior Chaplain of New South Wales; and of His Early Connection with the Missions to New Zealand and Tahiti*. London: Religious Tract Society, 1838.

Maxwell, Herbert. *Half-a-Century of Successful Trade: Being a Sketch of the Rise and Development of the Business of W & A Gilbey, 1857–1907*. London: W. & A. Gilbey, 1907.

Mouillefert, P. *Translation of a Report on the Vineyards of Cyprus*. London: Foreign and Commonwealth Office Collection, 1893.

Muir, Augustus, ed. *How to Choose and Enjoy Wine*. London: Odhams Press, 1953.

New South Wales Bureau of Statistics and Economics. *Official Year Book of New South Wales*. Sydney: W. A. Gullick, 1887.

New Zealand Department of Agriculture. *Phylloxera and Other Diseases of the Grape-Vine: Correspondence and Extracts Reprinted for Public Information*. Wellington: G. Didsbury, Government Printer, 1891.

New Zealand, U.S. Embassy. *New Zealand Update* [Washington, DC]: New Zealand Embassy, November–December 1979.

Official Catalogue of Exhibits in South Australian Court, Colonial and Indian Exhibition. Adelaide: Government Printer, 1886.

Official Report of the Calcutta International Exhibition, 1883–1884. Vol. 1. Calcutta: Bengal Secretariat Press, 1885.

Ovendish, John. *A Voyage to Suratt, in the Year, 1689: Giving a Large Account of That City and Its Inhabitants, and the English Factory There*. London: Jacob Tonson, 1696.

Papers Respecting the Phylloxera Vastatrix or New Vine Scourge / Published by the Department of Agriculture for the Information of the Public Generally. Melbourne: John Ferres, Government Printer, 1873.

Perold, A. I. *Some Viticultural and Oenological Experiments Conducted at the Paarl Viticultural Experiment Station during 1915–1916*. Ed. Peter F. May. St Albans: Inform & Enlighten, 2011.

Perronet, Thomas. *A Catechism on the Corn Laws, with a List of Fallacies and the Answers*. 18th ed. London: Westminster Review, 1834.

Philip, Arthur and John Stockdale, eds. *The voyage of Governor Phillip to Botany Bay; with an account of the establishment of the colonies of Port Jackson & Norfolk Island; compiled from authentic papers, which have been obtained from the several Departments. To which are added, the journals of Lieuts. Shortland, Watts, Ball, & Capt. Marshall, with an account of their new discoveries*. London: John Stockdale, 1789.

"Phylloxera and American Vines," *Argus Annual and South African Gazeteer* (Cape Town: Argus Printing and Publishing, 1895): 298.

"Phylloxera in South Africa." *Bulletin of Miscellaneous Information (Royal Gardens, Kew)* 1889, no. 33 (January 1, 1889): 230–35.

Pym, Barbara. *Some Tame Gazelle* (1950). In *The Barbara Pym Collection,* vol. 1, *A Glass of Blessings, Some Tame Gazelle, and Jane and Prudence.* New York: Open Road Media, 2018.

Ramsden, Eric. *James Busby: The Prophet of Australian Viticulture.* Sydney: Ramsden, 1940.

Redding, Cyrus. *History and Description of Modern Wines.* 2nd ed. London: G. Bell, 1836; 3rd ed., London: Henry G. Bohn, 1860.

Report on the Statistics of New Zealand, 1890; with a Map of the Colony and Appendices. Wellington: G. Didsbury, Government Printer, 1891.

Report on the Vital Statistics of the Union of South Africa, 1926. Pretoria: Government Printers, Union of South Africa, 1929.

Reports of the Imperial Economic Committee, Twenty-third Report: Wine. London: HMSO, 1932,

Riddell, R. *Indian Domestic Economy and Receipt Book : Comprising Numerous Directions for Plain Wholesome Cookery, Both Oriental and English, with Much Miscellaneous Matter, Answering All General Purposes of Reference Connected with Household Affairs Likely to Be Immediately Required by Families, Messes, and Private Individuals, Residing at the Presidencies or Out-Stations.* Madras: Printed by D. P. L. C. Connor, 1853.

Roberts, W. H. *The British Wine-Maker and Domestic Brewer; a Complete Practical and Easy Treatise on the Art of Making and Managing Every Description of British Wines . . .* 5th ed. Edinburgh: A. & C. Black; London: Whittaker, 3rd ed., rev., 1836; and 5th ed., rev., 1849.

Rowntree, B. Seebohm. *Poverty: A Study of Town Life.* London: Macmillan, 1908.

Sabin, A. *Wine and Spirit Merchants' Accounts.* London: Gee, 1904.

Saintsbury, George. *Notes on a Cellar-Book.* London: MacMillan, 1920.

Salmon, Thomas. *Modern history; or, the present state of all nations. Describing their respective situations, persons, habits, Buildings, Manners, Laws and Customs.* London: Thomas Wotton, 1735.

Sayers, Dorothy. *The Unpleasantness at the Bellona Club.* London: Ernest Benn, 1928.

Scott, Dick. *Winemakers of New Zealand.* Auckland: Southern Cross Books, 1964.

Semler, Janet. "The Australian Wine Industry." *Australian Quarterly* 35, no. 4 (December 1, 1963): 28–35.

Shaw, Thomas George. *Wine, the Vine, and the Cellar.* London: Longman, Green, Longman, Roberts & Green, 1863,

Sherrin, Richard Arundell Augur [1832–93], Thomson W. Leys, and J. H. Wallace. *Early History of New Zealand: From Earliest Times to 1840.* Auckland: H. Brett, 1890.

Simon, André L. *Drink.* New York: Horizon Press, 1953.

———. *The History of the Wine Trade in England.* Vol. 2, *The Progress of the Wine Trade in England during the Fifteenth and the Sixteenth Centuries.* London: Wyman and Sons, 1907.

————. *The Noble Grapes and the Great Wines of France*. New York: McGraw Hill, n.d.

————, ed. *South Africa*. "Wines of the World" Pocket Library. London: Wine and Food Society, 1950.

————. *The Wines, Vineyards, and Vignerons of Australia*. London: Paul Hamlyn, 1967.

Spons' Household Manual: a Treasury of Domestic Receipts and Guide for Home Management. London and New York: C. and F. N. Spon, 1887.

Statistical Report on the Population of the Dominion of New Zealand for the Year 1907. Vol. 2. Wellington: John Mackay, Government Printer, 1908.

Sutherland, George. *The South Australian Vinegrower's Manual: A Practical Guide to the Art of Viticulture in South Australia; Prepared under Instructions from the Government of South Australia, and with the Co-operation of Practical Vinegrowers of the Province*. Adelaide: C. Bristow, Government Printer, 1892.

Theal, George McCall. *Chronicles of Cape Commanders; or, An Abstract of Original Manuscripts in the Archives of the Cape Colony*. Cape Town: W.A. Richards, Government Printers, 1882.

————, ed. *Records of the Cape Colony from May 1801 to February 1803, Copied for the Cape Government, from the Manuscript Documents in the Public Record Office, London*. Vol. 4. London: Printed for the Government of the Cape Colony, 1899.

Thomson, James. *Illustrated Handbook of Victoria, Australia*. Melbourne: J. Ferres, Government Printer, 1886.

Thudichum, J. L. W. "Report on Wines from the Colony of Victoria, Australia." *Journal of Society of Arts* 21, no. 1094 (November 7, 1873): 921–40.

Todd, William John. *A Handbook of Wine: How to Buy, Serve, Store, and Drink It*. London: Jonathan Cape, 1922.

Union of South Africa Annual Statements of Trade and Shipping. Cape Town: Government Printer, annual 1906–61.

Urbanus, Sylvanus. *The Gentleman's Magazine and Historical Chronicle*. Vol. 8. London: Edw. Cave, July 1738.

Vogel, Julius, ed. *Land and Farming in New Zealand: Information Respecting the Mode of Acquiring Land in New Zealand; with Particulars as to Farming, Wages, Prices of Provisions, Etc, in That Colony; Also the Land Acts of 1877; with Maps*. London: Waterlow and Sons, 1879.

von Dadelszen, E.J., ed. *The New Zealand Official Handbook, 1892*. Wellington: Registrar General, 1892.

Wakefield, Edward Jerningham, and John Ward. *The British Colonization of New Zealand: Being an Account of the Principles, Objects, and Plans of the New Zealand Association, Together with Particulars Concerning the Position, Extent, Soil And Climate, Natural Productions, and Native Inhabitants of New Zealand*. London: John W. Parker, 1837.

Walker, John. *The Universal Gazeteer*. London: Ogilvy and Son, 1798.

Watt, George. *The Commercial Products of India: Being an Abridgement of "The Dictionary of the Economic Products of India."* London: J. Murray, 1908.

Wheeler, Daniel. *Extracts from the Letters and Journal of Daniel Wheeler, while Engaged in a Religious Visit to the Inhabitants of Some of the Islands of the Pacific Ocean, Van Dieman's Land, New South Wales, and New Zealand, Accompanied by His Son, Charles Wheeler.* Philadelphia: Joseph Rakestraw, 1840.

Wilkinson, George Blakiston. *South Australia: Its Advantages and Its Resources.* London: J. Murray, 1848.

Wilkinson, W. Percy. *The Nomenclature of Australian Wines: In Relation to Historical Commercial Usage of European Wine Names, International Conventions for the Protection of Industrial Property, and Recent European Commercial Treaties.* Melbourne: Thomas Urquhart, 1919.

———. "The Nomenclature of Australian Wines." In *Harper's Manual.* London: Harper, 1920.

Williams, William, D.C.L., Archdeacon of Waiapu. *A Dictionary of the New Zealand Language, and a Concise Grammar, to Which Is Added a Selection of Colloquial Sentences.* 2nd ed. London: Williams and Norgate, 1852.

Wine Australia. *Directions to 2025: An Industry Strategy for Sustainable Success.* Adelaide: Wine Australia, 2007.

"Wine-Growing in British Colonies." Eighth Ordinary General Meeting, Royal Colonial Institute, June 12, 1888. *Proceedings of the Royal Colonial Institute* (London) 19 (1887–88): 295–330.

Wine, in Relation to Temperance, Trade and Revenue. London: Foreign and Commonwealth Office, 1854.

Wood, Sir Henry Trueman. "The Royal Society of the Arts. IV. The Society and the Colonies (1754–1847)." *Journal of the Royal Society of Arts* 59, no. 3071 (September 29, 1911): 1030–43.

SECONDARY SOURCES

"An Act Respecting the Canada Vine Growers' Association, May 22, 1868." *Statutes of Canada*, 1868, Part Second. Ottawa: Malcolm Cameron, 1868.

Advisory Committee to the Department of Overseas Trade (Development and Intelligence). "Maritime and Colonial Exhibition in Antwerp, 1930: Lack of Participation by Dominions and Colonies." Board of Trade and Foreign Office, BT 90/25/10, National Archives, Kew. Consulted online.

Anderson, Kym. "Wine's New World." *Foreign Policy*, no. 136 (June 5, 2003): 46–54.

Anderson, Kym, with Nanda R. Aryal. *Growth and Cycles in the Australian Wine Industry: A Statistical Compendium, 1843 to 2013.* Adelaide: University of Adelaide Press, 2015.

Anderson, Kym, and Vicente Pinilla, eds. *Wine Globalization: A New Comparative History.* Adelaide: University of Adelaide Press, 2018.

Antić, Ljubomir. "The Press as a Secondary Source for Research on Emigration from Dalmatia up to the First World War." *SEER: Journal for Labour and Social Affairs in Eastern Europe* 4, no. 4 (2002): 25–35.

Asmal, Louise. "The Campaign against South African Goods." *Fortnight*, no. 235 (1986): 13–14.

Atkins, Peter J., Peter Lummel, and Derek J. Oddy, eds. *Food and the City in Europe since 1800*. Aldershot: Ashgate, 2007.

Australian Dictionary of Biography. Canberra: National Centre of Biography, Australian National University.

"Australian English in the Twentieth Century." Oxford English Dictionary Blog, https://public.oed.com/blog/australian-english-in-the-twentieth-century (accessed July 21, 2021).

Australian Human Rights Commission, *Bringing Them Home: Report of the National Inquiry into the Separation of Aboriginal and Torres Strait Islander Children from Their Families*. Sydney, April 1997.

Banks, Fay. *Wine Drinking in Oxford, 1640–1850: A Story Revealed by Tavern, Inn, College and Other Bottles; with a Catalogue of Bottles and Seals from the Collection in the Ashmolean Museum*. British Archaelogical Reports (BAR) British Series 257. Oxford: Archaeopress, 1997.

Banks, Glenn, and John Overton. "Old World, New World, Third World? Reconceptualizing the Worlds of Wine." *Journal of Wine Research* 21, no. 1 (March 2010): 57–75.

Barnes, Felicity. "Bringing Another Empire Alive? The Empire Marketing Board and the Construction of Dominion Identity, 1926–33." *Journal Of Imperial and Commonwealth History* 42, no. 1 (2014): 61–85.

Barrington, A. and J. Stone. *Cohabitation Trends and Patterns in the U.K.* Southampton: ESRC Centre for Population Change, 2015.

Bassett, Judith. "Colonial Justice: the Treatment of Dalmatians in New Zealand During the First World War." *New Zealand Journal of History* 33, no. 2 (1999): 155–79.

Batsaki, Yota, Sarah Burke Cahalan, and Anatole Tchikine, eds. *The Botany of Empire in the Long Eighteenth Century*. Washington, DC: Dumbarton Oaks Research Library and Collection, 2016.

Beck, Roger. *The History of South Africa*. Westport, CT: Greenwood Press, 2000.

Belich, James. *Making Peoples: A History of the New Zealanders from Polynesian Settlement to the End of the Nineteenth Century*. Honolulu: University of Hawai'i Press, 1996.

———. *Paradise Reforged: A History of the New Zealanders from the 1880s to the Year 2000*. Honolulu: University of Hawai'i Press, 2001.

———. *Replenishing the Earth: The Settler Revolution and the Rise of the Anglo-World, 1783–1939*. Oxford: Oxford University Press, 2009.

———. "Response: A Cultural History of Economics?" *Victorian Studies* 53, no. 1 (Autumn 2010): 116–21.

Bell, Charles Davidson. *Jan van Riebeeck Arrives in Table Bay in April 1652*. Painting, n.d. [c. 1840–88], https://commons.wikimedia.org/wiki/File:Charles_Bell_-_Jan_van_Riebeeck_se_aankoms_aan_die_Kaap.jpg (accessed September 1, 2021).

———. "Stellenbosch Wine Waggon [*sic*]—Table Mountain in the Background,"1830s, watercolor, University of Cape Town Libraries, BC686: John and Charles Bell Heritage Trust Collection, https://digitalcollections.lib.uct.ac.za/collection/islandora-26368 (accessed September 2, 2021).

Bell, George. "The London Market for Australian Wines, 1851–1901: A South Australian Perspective." *Journal of Wine Research* 5 (1994): 19–40.

———. "The South Australian Wine Industry, 1858–1876." *Journal of Wine Research* 4, no. 3 (September 1993): 147–64.

Benedict, Carol. *Golden Silk Smoke: A History of Tobacco in China, 1550–2010*. Berkeley: University of California Press, 2011.

Berg, Maxine. "From Imitation to Invention: Creating Commodities in Eighteenth-Century Britain." *Economic History Review*, n.s., 55, no. 1 (February 1, 2002): 1–30.

Berger, Irish. *South Africa in World History*. Oxford: Oxford University Press, 2009.

Bickham, Troy. "Eating the Empire: Intersections of Food, Cookery and Imperialism in Eighteenth-Century Britain." *Past and Present* 198, no. 1 (February 2008): 71–109.

Bijsterbosch, David, and Johan Fourie. "Coffee, Slavery and a Tax Loophole: Explaining the Cape Colony's Trading Boom, 1834–1841." *South African Historical Journal* 72, no. 1 (2020): 125–47.

Bishop, Geoffrey C. "The First Fine Drop: Grape-Growing and Wine-Making in the Adelaide Hills, 1839–1937." *Australian Garden History* 13, no. 5 (2002): 4–6.

Brady, Maggie. *First Taste: How Indigenous Australians Learned about Grog*. 6 vols. Deakin, Australia: Alcohol Education & Rehabilitation Foundation, 2008.

———. *Teaching "Proper" Drinking? Clubs and Pubs in Indigenous Australia*. Canberra: Australian National University Press, 2017.

Brennan, Thomas. *Burgundy to Champagne: The Wine Trade in Early Modern France*. Baltimore: Johns Hopkins University Press, 1997.

Briggs, Asa. *Marks and Spencer, 1884–1984: A Centenary History*. London: Octopus Books, 1984.

———. *Wine for Sale: Victoria Wine and the Liquor Trade, 1860–1984*. Chicago: University of Chicago Press, 1985.

British Broadcasting Corporation, featuring Oz Clarke and Jilly Goolding. *Food and Drink*. Broadcast on BBC, April 5, 1994. Available at www.youtube.com /watch?v=6dM-Nxp0CQY (accessed September 2, 2021).

Brooking, Tom. ""Yeotopia" Found . . . But? The Yeoman Ideal That Underpinned New Zealand Agricultural Practice into the Early Twenty-First Century, with American and Australian Comparisons." *Agricultural History* 93, no. 1 (2019): 68–101.

Broomfield, Andrea. *Food and Cooking in Victorian England*. Westport, CT: Praeger, 2007.

Brown, Karen. "Agriculture in the Natural World: Progressivism, Conservation, and the State: The Case of the Cape Colony in the Late 19th and Early 20th Centuries." *Kronos* 29 (2003): 109–38.

———. "Political Entomology: The Insectile Challenge to Agricultural Development in the Cape Colony, 1895–1910." *Journal of Southern African Studies* 29, no. 2 (June 2003): 529–49.

Buettner, Elizabeth. "'Going for an Indian': South Asian Restaurants and the Limits of Multiculturalism in Britain." *Journal of Modern History* 80, no. 4 (December 1, 2008): 865–901.

Burnett, John. *Liquid Pleasures: A Social History of Drinks in Modern Britain.* London: Routledge, 1999.

Campbell, Gwynn, and Nathalie Guibert, eds. *Wine, Society, and Globalisation: Multidisciplinary Perspectives on the Wine Industry.* Basingstoke: Palgrave, 2007.

"Canada Enters the War." Canadian War Museum, www.warmuseum.ca /firstworldwar/history/going-to-war/canada-enters-the-war/canada-at-war (accessed September 1, 2021).

Cassi, Lorenzo, Andrea Morrison, and Anne L. J. Ter Wal. "The Evolution of Trade and Scientific Collaboration Networks in the Global Wine Sector: A Longitudinal Study Using Network Analysis." *Economic Geography* 88, no. 3 (July 1, 2012): 311–34.

Chatterjee, Partha. *Nationalist Thought and the Colonial World.* London: United Nations University, 1986.

Cheang, Sarah. "Selling China: Class, Gender, and Orientalism at the Department Store." *Journal of Design History* 20, no. 1 (Spring 2007): 1–16.

Chetty, Suryakanthie. "Imagining National Unity: South African Propaganda Efforts during the Second World War." *Kronos* 38 (November 2012): 106–30.

Christoffel, Paul. "Prohibition and the Myth of 1919." *New Zealand Journal of History* 42, no. 2 (2008): 154–75.

Christopher, A. J. "The Union of South Africa Censuses, 1911–1960: An Incomplete Record." *Historia* 56, no. 2 (2011): 1–18.

Clarence-Smith, William Gervase. *Cocoa and Chocolate, 1765–1914.* New York: Routledge, 2000.

Clarence-Smith, William Gervase, and Steven Topik, eds. *The Global Coffee Economy in Africa, Asia, and Latin America, 1500–1989.* Cambridge: Cambridge University Press, 2003.

Collingham, Lizzie. *The Hungry Empire: How Britain's Quest for Food Shaped the Modern World.* Basic Books, 2017.

Constantine, Stephen. "'Bringing the Empire Alive': The Empire Marketing Board and Imperial Propaganda, 1926–1933." In *Imperialism and Popular Culture,* ed. John M. Mackenzie, 192–231. Manchester: Manchester University Press, 1986.

Costello, Moya, Robert Smith, and Leonie Lane. "Australian Wine Labels: *Terroir* without Terror." *Gastronomica* 18, no. 3 (2018): 54–65.

Cozens, Erin Ford. "'With a Pretty Little Garden at the Back': Domesticity and the Construction of 'Civilized' Colonial Spaces in Nineteenth-Century Aotearoa/ New Zealand." *Journal of World History* 25, no. 4 (2014): 515–34.

Crooks, Edmund. *Alcohol Consumption and Taxation*. London: Institute for Fiscal Studies, 1989.

Cross, Kolleen M. "The Evolution of Colonial Agriculture: The Creation of the Algerian 'Vignoble,' 1870–1892." *Proceedings of the Meeting of the French Colonial Historical Society* 16 (1992): 57–72.

Crowley Mark J., and Sandra Trudgen Dawson, eds. *Home Fronts: Britain and the Empire at War, 1939–45*. Woodbridge, Suffolk: Boydell & Brewer, 2017.

Cullen, Louis M. *The Irish Brandy Houses of Eighteenth-Century France*. Dublin: Lilliput, 2000.

Curtin, Philip D. "Location in History: Argentina and South Africa in the Nineteenth Century." *Journal of World History* 10, no. 1 (1999): 41–92.

Dalziel, Raewyn. "Southern Islands: New Zealand and Polynesia." In *The Oxford History of the British Empire*, vol. 3, *The Nineteenth Century*, 573–96. Oxford: Oxford University Press, 1999.

De Vries, Jan. "The Industrial Revolution and the Industrious Revolution." *Journal of Economic History* 54, no. 2 (1994): 249–70.

Diski, Jenny. "Flowery, Rustic, Tippy, Smokey." Review of *Green Gold: The Empire of Tea*, by Alan Macfarlane and Iris Macfarlane. *London Review of Books* 25, no. 12, June 19, 2003, 11–12.

"Distillation Act 25 Vic., No. 147." *Victoria Government Gazette*, November 27, 1868.

Donington, Katie, Ryan Hanley, and Jessica Moody, eds. *Britain's History and Memory of Transatlantic Slavery: Local Nuances of a "National Sin."* Liverpool: Liverpool University Press, 2016.

Dooling, Wayne. *Slavery, Emancipation, and Colonial Rule in South Africa*. Athens: Ohio University Press, 2007.

Drake-Brockman, Jane, and Patrick Messerlin, eds.. *Potential Benefits of an Australia-EU Free Trade Agreement: Key Issues and Options*. Adelaide: University of Adelaide Press, 2018.

Driscoll, W. P. "Fallon, James Thomas (1823–1886)," *Australian Dictionary of Biography*, National Centre of Biography, Australian National University, https://adb.anu.edu.au/biography/fallon-james-thomas-3496/text5365 (published first in hardcopy, 1972) (accessed September 3, 2021).

Driver, Elizabeth, ed. *Culinary Landmarks: A Bibliography of Canadian Cookbooks, 1825–1949*. Toronto: University of Toronto Press, 2008.

Dubow, Saul. *Commonwealth of Knowledge: Science, Sensibility, and White South Africa, 1820–2000*. Oxford: Oxford University Press, 2006.

Duncan, Robert. *Pubs and Pa-triots: The Drink Crisis in Britain during World War One*. Liverpool: Liverpool University Press, 2013.

Dunstan, David. *Better Than Pommard! A History of Wine in Victoria*. Kew, Victoria: Australian Scholarly Publishing, 1994.

Duong, Jessica T. "The Role of Science and Technology on the New Zealand Wine Industry: Profiling Dr. Richard E. Smart's Impact, 1982–1990." Unpublished manuscript, 2018.

Durbach, Nadja. *Many Mouths: The Politics of Food in Britain from the Workhouse to the Welfare State*. Cambridge: Cambridge University Press, 2020.

Dutton, Jacqueline. "Imperial Eyes on the Pacific Prize: French Visions of a Perfect Penal Colony in the South Seas." In *Discovery and Empire: The French in the South Seas*, ed. John West-Sooby, 245–82. Adelaide: University of Adelaide Press, 2013.

Elijah, Annmarie, et al., eds. *Australia, the European Union and the New Trade Agenda*. Canberra: Australian National University Press, 2017.

Ewert, Joachim. "A Force for Good? Markets, Cellars and Labour in the South African Wine Industry after Apartheid." *Review of African Political Economy* 39, no. 132 (June 1, 2012): 225–42.

Ewert, Joachim, and Andries du Toit. "A Deepening Divide in the Countryside: Restructuring and Rural Livelihoods in the South African Wine Industry." *Journal of Southern African Studies* 31, no. 2 (June 1, 2005): 315–32.

Food and Agriculture Organization of the United Nations. *Agribusiness Handbook: Grapes, Wine*. Rome: United Nations, 2009.

Fourie, Johan. "The Remarkable Wealth of the Dutch Cape Colony: Measurements from Eighteenth-Century Probate Inventories." *Economic History Review* 66, no. 2 (May 2013): 419–48.

Fourie, Johan, and Dieter von Fintel. "Settler Skills and Colonial Development: The Huguenot Wine-Makers in Eighteenth-Century Dutch South Africa." *Economic History Review* 67, no. 4 (November 2014): 932–63.

Gangjee, Dev, ed. *Research Handbook on Intellectual Property and Geographical Indications*. Cheltenham, Gloucestershire: Edward Elgar, 2016.

Gately, Iain. *Drink: A Cultural History of Alcohol*. New York: Gotham, 2008.

Gentilcore, R. Louis, and C. Grant Head, eds. *Ontario's History in Maps*. Toronto: University of Toronto Press, 1984.

Geraci, Vincent. "Fermenting a Twenty-First Century California Wine Industry." *Agricultural History* 78, no. 4 (Autumn 2004): 438–65.

Gerling, Chris. "Conversion Factors: From Vineyard to Bottle." *Cornell Viticulture and Enology Newsletter* 8 (December 2011): n.p.

Giliomee, Hermann. "Western Cape Farmers and the Beginnings of Afrikaner Nationalism 1870–1915." *Journal of Southern African Studies* 14, no. 1 (1987): 38–63.

Glanville, Philippa, and Sophie Lee, eds. *The Art of Drinking*. London: V & A Publications, 2007.

Grant, Peter Warden. *Considerations on the State of the Colonial Currency and Foreign Exchanges at the Cape of Good Hope: Comprehending Also Some Statements Relative to the Population, Agriculture, Commerce, and Statistics of the Colony*. Cape Town: W. Bridekirk, Jr., 1825.

Groenewald, Gerald. "An Early Modern Entrepreneur: Hendrik Oostwald Eksteen and the Creation of Wealth in Dutch Colonial Cape Town, 1702–1741." *Kronos* 35 (November 2009): 6–31.

Guelke, Leonard. "The Anatomy of a Colonial Settler Population: Cape Colony 1657–1750." *International Journal of African Historical Studies* 21, no. 3 (1988): 453–73.

Gurney, Christabel. "'A Great Cause': The Origins of the Anti-Apartheid Movement, June 1959-March 1960." *Journal of Southern African Studies* 26, no. 1 (2000): 123–44.

Gurney, Peter. *The Making of Consumer Culture in Modern Britain.* London: Bloomsbury Academic, 2017.

———. "The Middle-Class Embrace: Language, Representation, and the Contest over Co-operative Forms in Britain, c. 1860–1914." *Victorian Studies* 37, no. 2 (1994): 253–86.

Gutzke, David. *Women Drinking Out in Britain since the Early Twentieth Century.* Manchester: Manchester University Press, 2013.

Guy, Kolleen M. *When Champagne Became French: Wine and the Making of a National Identity.* Baltimore: Johns Hopkins University Press, 2003.

Gwynne, Robert N. "U.K. Retail Concentration, Chilean Wine Producers and Value Chains." *Geographical Journal* 174, no. 2 (June 2008): 97–108.

Haines, Robin. "Indigent Misfits or Shrewd Operators? Government-Assisted Emigrants from the United Kingdom to Australia, 1831–1860." *Population Studies* 48, no. 2 (1994): 223–47.

Hall, Catherine, and Sonya Rose, eds. *At Home with the Empire: Metropolitan Culture and the Imperial World.* Cambridge: Cambridge University Press, 2007.

Hall, Martin, Yvonne Brink, and Antonia Malan. "Onrust 87/1: An Early Colonial Farm Complex in the Western Cape." *South African Archaeological Bulletin* 43, no. 148 (December 1, 1988): 91–99.

Hames, Gina. *Alcohol in World History.* London: Routledge, 2012.

Hancock, David. *Oceans of Wine: Madeira and the Emergence of American Trade and Taste.* New Haven, CT: Yale University Press, 2009.

Hannickel, Erica. *Empire of Vines: Wine Culture in America.* Philadelphia: University of Pennsylvania Press, 2013.

———. "A Fortune in Fruit: Nicholas Longworth and Grape Speculation in Antebellum Ohio." *American Studies* 51, nos. 1–2 (Spring–Summer 2010): 89–108.

Harding, Robert Graham. "The British Market for Champagne, 1800–1914." MPhil thesis, University of Cambridge, 2014.

———. "The Establishment of Champagne in Britain, 1860–1914." PhD diss., University of Oxford, 2018.

Harrison, Brian Howard. *Drink and the Victorians: The Temperance Question in England, 1815–1872.* 2nd ed. Keele, Staffordshire: Keele University Press, 1994.

Hemming, Richard. "Planting Density." In "Wine by the Numbers, Part One," September 15, 2016, at the Jancis Robinson website, www.jancisrobinson.com /articles/wine-by-numbers-part-one?layout=pdf (accessed July 23, 2021).

———. "Wine by the Numbers: Part One." Jancis Robinson website, September 15, 2016, jancisrobinson.com.

Hilton, Matthew. *Smoking in British Popular Culture, 1800–2000.* Manchester: Manchester University Press, 2000.

Hofmeester, Karin, and Pim De Zwart, eds. *Colonialism, Institutional Change, and Shifts in Global Labour Relations.* Amsterdam: Amsterdam University Press, 2018. Available at doi 10.5117/9789462984363 (accessed September 2, 2021).

Holloway, Sarah L., Mark Jayne, and Gill Valentine. "'Sainsbury's Is My Local': English Alcohol Policy, Domestic Drinking Practices and the Meaning of Home." *Transactions of the Institute of British Geographers* 33, no. 4 (October 2008): 532–47.

Hopkins, A. G., ed. *Globalization in World History.* London: Pimlico, 2002.

Hori, Motoko. "The Price and Quality of Wine and Conspicuous Consumption in England, 1646–1759." *English Historical Review* 123, no. 505 (December 2008): 1457–69.

Hyslop, Jonathan. "'Undesirable inhabitant of the union . . . supplying liquor to natives': D. F. Malan and the Deportation of South Africa's British and Irish Lumpen Proletarians, 1924–1933." *Kronos* 40, no. 1 (2014): 178–97.

In Vino Veritas: Extracts from an Oral History of the U.K. Wine Trade. London: British Library National Life Story Collection, 2005.

Inglis, David, and Anna-Mari Almila, eds. *The Globalization of Wine.* London: Bloomsbury Academic, 2019.

Jacobs, Julius. "California's Pioneer Wine Families." *California Historical Quarterly* 54, no. 2 (Summer 1975): 139–74.

Jeffreys, Henry. *Empire of Booze: British History through the Bottom of a Glass.* London: Unbound, 2016.

Jennings, Paul. *A History of Drink and the English, 1500–2000.* New York: Routledge, 2016.

Johnson, Hugh. *Vintage: The Story of Wine.* London: Mitchell Beardsley, 1989.

Jones, Martin J. "Dalmatian Settlement and Identity in New Zealand: The Devcich Farm, Kauaeranga Valley, near Thames." *Australasian Historical Archaeology* 30 (2012): 24–33.

Keegan, Timothy. *South Africa and the Origins of the Racial Order.* Cape Town: David Philip, 1996.

Kelly's London Post Office Directory, Part Two: Street Index. London: Kelly, 1895.

Kennelly, James J. "The 'Dawn of the Practical': Horace Plunkett and the Cooperative Movement." *New Hibernia Review / Iris Éireannach Nua* 12, no. 1 (2008): 62–81.

Kirkby, Diane Erica. "Drinking 'The Good Life': Australia, c.1880–1980." In *Alcohol: A Social and Cultural History,* ed. Mack P. Holt, 203–24. Oxford: Berg, 2007.

Knox, Graham. *Estate Wines of South Africa.* 2nd ed. Cape Town and Johannesburg: David Phillip, 1982.

Lambert, W. R. *Drink and Sobriety in Victorian Wales, c. 1820–1895.* Cardiff: University of Wales Press, 1983.

Laracy, Hugh. "Saint-Making: The Case of Pierre Chanel of Futuna." *New Zealand Journal of History* 34, no. 1 (2000): 145–61.

Laudan, Rachel. *Cuisine and Empire: Cooking in World History*. Berkeley: University of California Press, 2013.

Leacy, F. H., ed. *Historical Statistics of Canada*. 2nd ed. Ottawa: Statistics Canada, 1983.

Lee, J. M. "The Dissolution of the Empire Marketing Board, 1933: Reflections on a Diary." *Journal of Imperial and Commonwealth History* 1, no. 1 (1972): 49–57.

Lenta, Margaret. "Degrees of Freedom: Lady Anne Barnard's Cape Diaries." *English in Africa* 19, no. 2 (October 1992): 55–68.

Lester, Alan. *Imperial Networks: Creating Identities in Nineteenth-Century South Africa and Britain*. London: Routledge, 2001.

Light, Roy, and Susan Heenan. "Controlling Supply: The Concept of 'Need' in Liquor Licensing." Final report for Alcohol Research Development Grant, Bristol, 1999. Available at www.researchgate.net/publication/265990013_Controlling_Supply_The_Concept_of_'Need'_in_Liquor_Licensing (accessed September 2, 2021).

Lobell, Steven E. "Second Image Reversed Politics: Britain's Choice of Freer Trade or Imperial Preferences, 1903–1906, 1917–1923, 1930–1932." *International Studies Quarterly* 43, no. 4 (1999): 671–93.

Ludington, Charles. *The Politics of Wine in Britain: A New Cultural History*. Basingstoke: Palgrave, 2013.

Lukacs, Paul. *Inventing Wine: A New History of One of the World's Most Ancient Pleasures*. New York: Norton, 2012.

Mabbett, Jason. "The Dalmatian Influence on the New Zealand Wine Industry." *Journal of Wine Research* 9, no. 1 (April 1998): 15–25.

Macgregor, Paul. "Lowe Kong Meng and Chinese Engagement in the International Trade of Colonial Victoria." *Provenance: The Journal of Public Record Office Victoria* 11 (2012): 26–43.

MacNalty, Arthur. "Sir Victor Horsley: His Life and Work." *British Medical Journal* 5024, no. 1 (April 20, 1957): 910–16.

Mager, Anne Kelk. "The First Decade of 'European Beer' in Apartheid South Africa: The State, the Brewers and the Drinking Public, 1962–72." *Journal of African History* 40, no. 3 (January 1, 1999): 367–88.

———. "'One Beer, One Goal, One Nation, One Soul': South African Breweries, Heritage, Masculinity and Nationalism, 1960–1999." *Past and Present* 188, no. 1 (2005): 163–94.

Martin, Laura C. *Tea: The Drink That Changed the World*. Rutland, VT: Tuttle, 2007.

Martínez-Carrión, José Miguel, and Francisco Medina-Albaladejo. "Change and Development in the Spanish Wine Sector." *Journal of Wine Research* 21, no. 1 (March 2010): 77–95.

Maynard, Kristen, Sarah Wright, and Shirleyanne Brown. "Ruru Parirao: Mäori and Alcohol; The Importance of Destabilising Negative Stereotypes and the Implications for Policy and Practice." *MAI Journal* 2, no. 2 (2012): 78–90.

McDonald, John, and Eric Richards. "The Great Emigration of 1841: Recruitment for New South Wales in British Emigration Fields." *Population Studies* 51, no. 3 (1997): 337-55.

McIntyre, Julie. "Camden to London and Paris: The Role of the Macarthur Family in the Early New South Wales Wine Industry." *History Compass* 5, no. 2 (2007): 427–38.

———. *First Vintage: Wine in Colonial New South* Wales. Sydney: University of New South Wales Press, 2012.

———. "Resisting Ages-Old Fixity as a Factor in Wine Quality: Colonial Wine Tours and Australia's Early Wine Industry." *Locale* 1 (2011): 42–64.

McIntyre, Julie, and John Germov. *Hunter Wine: A History.* Sydney: NewSouth: 2018.

———. "'Who Wants to Be a Millionaire?' I Do: Postwar Australian Wine, Gendered Culture, and Class." *Journal of Australian Studies* 42, no. 1 (2018): 65–82.

Mercer, Helen. "Retailer-Supplier Relationships before and after the Resale Prices Act, 1964: A Turning Point in British Economic History?" *Enterprise and Society* 15, no. 1 (March 2014): 132–65.

Merrington, Peter. "Cape Dutch Tongaat: A Case Study in 'Heritage.'" *Journal of Southern African Studies* 32, no. 4 (December 1, 2006): 683–99.

Millon, Marc. *Wine: A Global History.* London: Reaktion, 2013.

Ministry of Information, U.K. *Food from the Empire.* 1940. Short film, available on Colonial Film website, www.colonialfilm.org.uk (accessed July 21, 2021).

Mintz, Sidney. *Sweetness and Power: The Place of Sugar in Modern History.* 2nd ed. New York: Penguin, 1986.

Monty Python, "Australian Table Wines." In *The Monty Python Instant Record Collection.* London: Charisma, 1977. Available at www.youtube.com/watch?v= Cozwo88w44Q (accessed September 2, 2021).

Morgan, Ruth. *Running Out? Water in Western Australia.* Crawley: University of Western Australia Publishing, 2015.

Morrison, Andrea, and Roberta Rabellotti. "Gradual Catch Up and Enduring Leadership in the Global Wine Industry." *American Association of Wine Economists Working Paper* 148 (February 2014): 1–34.

Mougel, Nadège. "World War I Casualties." *Repères.* Part of a series created by a multidisciplinary grant project. Scy-Chazelles: Centre européen Robert Schuman, 2011.

Narayanan, Divya. "Cultures of Food and Gastronomy in Mughal and Post-Mughal India." PhD diss., University of Heidelberg, 2015.

Nasson, Bill. "Bitter Harvest: Farm Schooling for Black South Africans." *Second Carnegie Inquiry into Poverty and Development in Southern Africa, Conference Papers* 97 (April 1984): 1–46.

National Nutrient Database for Standard Reference. April 2018. United States Department of Agriculture Agricultural Research Service, ndb.nal.usda.gov.

Nell, Dawn, ed al. "Investigating Shopper Narratives of the Supermarket in Early Post-War England, 1945–1975." *Oral History* 37, no. 1 (Spring 2009): 61–73.

Nelson, Valerie, Adrienne Martin, and Joachim Ewert. "The Impacts of Codes of Practice on Worker Livelihoods: Empirical Evidence from the South African Wine and Kenyan Cut Flower Industries." *Journal of Corporate Citizenship*, no. 28 (2007): 61–72.

Neswald, Elizabeth, David F. Smith, and Ulrike Thoms, eds. *Setting Nutritional Standards: Theory, Policies, Practices.* Woodbridge, Suffolk: Boydell & Brewer, 2017.

Neumark, S. Daniel. *Economic Influences on the South African Frontier, 1652–1836.* Stanford, CA: Stanford University Press, 1957.

Nossiter, Jonathan, dir. *Mondovino.* Screenplay by Jonathan Nossiter. New York: Velocity/THINKFilm, 2004.

Nugent, Paul. "Do Nations Have Stomachs? Food, Drink, and Imagined Community in Africa." *Africa Spectrum* 45, no. 3 (January 1, 2010): 87–113.

———. "The Temperance Movement and Wine Farmers at the Cape: Collective Action, Racial Discourse, and Legislative Reform, c. 1890–1965." *Journal of African History* 52, no. 3 (January 1, 2011): 341–63.

Nützenadel, Alexander, and Frank Trentmann, eds. *Food and Globalization: Consumption, Markets, and Politics in the Modern World.* New York: Berg, 2008.

Nye, John. *War, Wine, and Taxes: The Political Economy of Anglo-French Trade, 1689–1900.* Princeton, NJ: Princeton University Press, 2007.

Olsen, Janeen E., Liz Thach And, and Linda Nowak. "Wine for My Generation: Exploring How US Wine Consumers Are Socialized to Wine." *Journal of Wine Research* 18, no. 1 (2007): 1–18.

Osso, Giulio. "Rare Portrait of Simon Van Der Stel Highlight of the National Antiques Faire," n.d. [2012], Wine.co.za, https://services.wine.co.za/pdf-view .aspx?PDFID=2505 (accessed September 1, 2021).

Overy, Richard. *The Morbid Age: Britain between the Wars.* London: Allen Lane, 2009.

Parezo, Nancy J., and Don D. Fowler. *Anthropology Goes to the Fair: The 1904 Louisiana Purchase Exposition.* Lincoln: University of Nebraska Press, 2007.

Petersen, Christian. *Bread and the British Economy, c. 1770–1870.* Ed. Andrew Jenkins. Aldershot: Scolar Press, 1995.

Phillips, Rod. *Alcohol: A History.* Chapel Hill: University of North Carolina Press, 2014.

———. *French Wine: A History.* Berkeley: University of California Press, 2016.

———. *A Short History of Wine.* London: Allen Lane, 2000.

Pilcher, Jeffrey. *Food in World History.* New York: Routledge, 2006.

Pinilla, Vicente. "Wine Historical Statistics: A Quantitative Approach to its Consumption, Production and Trade, 1840–1938." *American Association of Wine Economists Working Paper* 167 (August 2014): 1–57.

Pinney, Thomas. *A History of Wine in America.* Vols. 1 and 2. Berkeley: University of California Press, 2005.

Pourgouris, Marinos. *The Cyprus Frenzy of 1878 and the British Press.* London: Lexington, 2019.

Porter, Bernard. *The Absentminded Imperialists.* Oxford: Oxford University Press, 2004.

Pratten, J. D., and J.-B. Carlier. "Women and Wine in the U.K.: A Business Opportunity for Bars." *Journal of Food Products Marketing* 18, no. 2 (2012): 126–38.

Prendergast, Mark. *Uncommon Grounds: The History of Coffee and How It Transformed Our World.* New York: Basic Books, 2010.

"Preserved in Time: 13,000 Crosse & Blackwell .Containers Discovered at Crossrail Site." January 9, 2017. Museum of London Archaeology, mola.org.uk.

Quigley, Killian. "Indolence and Illness: Scurvy, the Irish, and Early Australia." *Eighteenth-Century Life* 41, no. 2 (2017): 139–53.

Rappaport, Ericka. *A Thirst for Empire: How Tea Shaped the Modern World.* Princeton, NJ: Princeton University Press, 2017.

Rayner, Mary. "Wine and Slaves: The Failure of an Export Economy and the Ending of Slavery in the Cape Colony, South Africa, 1806–1834." PhD diss., Duke University, 1986.

Razdan, Vinayak. "Wine of Kashmir." www.searchkashmir.org (accessed September 1, 2021).

Regan-Lefebvre, Jennifer. "From Colonial Wine to New World: British Wine Drinking, c. 1900–1990." *Global Food History* 5, nos. 1–2 (2019): 67–83.

———. "John Bull's Other Vineyard: Selling Australian Wine in Nineteenth-Century Britain." *Journal of Imperial and Commonwealth History* 45, no. 2 (April 2017): 259–83.

———, ed. *For the Liberty of Ireland at Home and Abroad: The Autobiography of J. F. X. O'Brien.* Classics in Irish History Series. Dublin: University College Dublin Press, 2010.

——— [as Jennifer M. Regan]. "'We could be of service to other suffering people': Representations of India in the Irish Nationalist Press, 1857–1887." *Victorian Periodicals Review* 41, no. 1 (Spring 2008): 61–77.

Reilly, Alexander, et al. "Working Holiday Makers in Australian Horticulture: Labour Market Effect, Exploitation, and Avenues for Reform." *Griffith Law Review* 27, no. 1 (2018): 99–130.

Rickard, Bradley. "The Economics of Introducing Wine into Grocery Stores." *Contemporary Economic Policy* 30, no. 3 (July 2012): 382–98.

Robbins, Bruce. "Commodity Histories." *PMLA* 120, no. 2 (March 2005): 455–63.

Roberts, Daniel Sanjiv. "'Merely Birds of Passage': Lady Hariot Dufferin's Travel Writings and Medical Work in India, 1884–1888." *Women's History Review* 15, no. 3 (2006): 443–57.

Robertson, Shanthi. "Intertwined Mobilities of Education, Tourism, and Labour: The Consequences of 417 and 485 Visas in Australia." In *Unintended Consequences: The Impact of Migration Law and Policy,* ed. Dickie Marianne, Gozdecka Dorota, and Reich Sudrishti, 53–80. Canberra: Australian National University Press, 2016.

Robinson, Jancis. *The Oxford Companion to Wine.* 2nd ed. Oxford: Oxford University Press, 2006.

Robinson, Jancis, Julia Harding, and José Vouillamoz. *Wine Grapes.* London: Allen Lane, 2012.

Romero, Patricia W. "Encounter at the Cape: French Huguenots, the Khoi, and Other People of Color." *Journal of Colonialism and Colonial History* 5, no. 1 (2004).

Ross, Robert. "The Rise of the Cape Gentry." *Journal of Southern African Studies* 9, no. 2 (April 1, 1983): 193–217.

Ryan, Chris. "Trends Past and Present in the Package Holiday Industry." *Service Industries Journal* 9, no. 1 (1989): 61–78.

Said, Edward. *Culture and Imperialism*. New York: Vintage, 1994.

Schneer, Jonathan. *London 1900: The Imperial Metropolis*. New Haven, CT: Yale University Press, 1999.

Scholliers, Peter, ed. *Food, Drink, and Identity: Cooking, Eating, and Drinking in Europe since the Middle Ages*. Oxford: Berg, 2001.

Scully, Pamela. *Liberating the Family? Gender and British Slave Emancipation in the Rural Western Cape, South Africa, 1823–1853*. Cape Town: David Philip, 1997.

Shiman, Lilian Lewis. *Crusade against Drink in Victorian England*. New York: St. Martin's Press, 1988.

Simmons, Alexy. "Postcard from Te Awamutu: Eating and Drinking with the Troops on the New Zealand War Front." In *Table Settings: The Material Culture and Social Context of Dining, a.d. 1700–1900*, ed. Symonds James, 163–82. Oxford; Oakville: Oxbow Books, 2010.

Simpson, James. *Creating Wine: The Emergence of a World Industry, 1840–1914*. Princeton, NJ: Princeton University Press, 2011.

Stewart, Keith. *Chancers and Visionaries: A History of Wine in New Zealand*. Auckland: Godwit, 2010.

Stone, Marjorie. "Lyric Tipplers: Elizabeth Barrett Browning's 'Wine of Cyprus,' Emily Dickinson's 'I Taste a Liquor,' and the Transatlantic Anacreontic Tradition." *Victorian Poetry* 54, no. 2 (Summer 2016): 123–54.

Stuer, Anny P. L. "The French in Australia, with Special Emphasis on the Period 1788–1947." PhD diss., Australian National University, 1979.

Talbot, John M. "On the Abandonment of Coffee Plantations in Jamaica after Emancipation." *Journal of Imperial and Commonwealth History* 43, no. 1 (2015): 33–57.

Te Ara: The Encyclopedia of New Zealand. Auckland, New Zealand: Minister for Culture and Heritage. Available at https://teara.govt.nz.

Thompson, Andrew, and Gary Magee. *Empire and Globalisation: Networks of People, Goods, and Capital in the British World, c. 1850–1914*. Cambridge: Cambridge University Press, 2010.

———. "A Soft Touch? British Industry, Empire Markets, and the Self-Governing Dominions, c. 1870–1914." *Economic History Review*, n.s., 56, no. 4 (November 1, 2003): 689–717.

Todd, Selina. "Class Conflict and the Myth of Cultural 'Inclusion' in Modern Manchester." In *Culture in Manchester: Institutions and Urban Change since 1850*, ed. Mike Savage and Janet Wolff, 194–216. Manchester: Manchester University Press, 2013.

Trentmann, Frank. *Empire of Things: How We Became a World of Consumers, from the Fifteenth Century to the Twenty-First*. New York: HarperCollins, 2016.
—————. *Free Trade Nation*. Oxford: Oxford University Press, 2009.
Tuckwell, Charles. "Combatting Australia's founding myth: the motives behind the British Settlement of Australia." Senior thesis, Trinity College, Hartford, CT, 2018.
Turner, John. "State Purchase of the Liquor Trade in the First World War." *Historical Journal* 23, no. 3 (September 1980): 589–615.
United Nations Food and Agriculture Organization Database. FAOStat.org.
Valenze, Deborah. *Milk: A Local and Global History*. New Haven, CT: Yale University Press, 2011.
Varriano, John. *Wine: A Cultural History*. London: Reaktion, 2011.
Victoria Bureau of Statistics. *Victorian Year-Book*. Melbourne: Government Printer, 1883, 1888, 1889.
Vidal, Michel. *Histoire de la vigne et des vins dans le monde, XIX-XXe siècle*. Bordeaux: Editions Féret, 2001.
Viljoen, Russel. "Aboriginal Khoikhoi Servants and Their Masters in Colonial Swellendam, South Africa, 1745–1795." *Agricultural History* 75, no. 1 (2001): 28–51.
Waihirere District Council. "Te Kauwhata & District." *Built Heritage Assessment Historic Overview*, November 2017. Available at https://wdcsitefinity.blob.core .windows.net/sitefinity-storage/docs/default-source/your-council/plans-policies -and-bylaws/plans/district-plan-review/section-32-reports/historic-heritage/appen-dix-10-4---s32-historic-overview-of-waikato-district.pdf?sfvrsn=e22480c9_2. (accessed September 1, 2021).
Walker, Julian. "Slang Terms at the Front." BL.uk, January 29, 2014, www.bl.uk /world-war-one/articles/slang-terms-at-the-front (accessed September 1, 2021).
Wallace, Frederick William, ed. *Canadian Ports and Shipping Directory*. Gardendale, Quebec: National Business Publications, 1936.
Walton, John K. "Another Face of 'Mass Tourism': San Sebastián and Spanish Beach Resorts under Franco, 1936–1975." *Urban History* 40, no. 3 (2013): 483–506.
Warde, Aland, and Lydia Martens. *Eating Out: Social Differentiation, Consumption, and Pleasure*. Cambridge: Cambridge University Press, 2000.
Weaver, Robert J. "Some Observations on Grape Growing in the Republic of South Africa." *Economic Botany* 30, no. 1 (January 1, 1976): 81–93.
Wilson, George B. *Alcohol and the Nation*. London: Nicholson and Watson, 1940.
The Wine Institute. *Per Capita Wine Consumption Data*, www.wineinstitute.org.
Wohl, Anthony S. *Endangered Lives: Public Health in Victorian Britain*. Cambridge, MA: Harvard University Press, 1983.
Woolacott, Angela. "A Radical's Career: Responsible Government, Settler Colonialism and Indigenous Dispossession." *Journal of Colonialism and Colonial History* 16, no. 2 (Summer) 2015: [n.p., online only].
Worden, Nigel. "The Changing Politics of Slave Heritage in the Western Cape, South Africa." *Journal of African History* 50, no. 1 (January 1, 2009): 23–40.
—————. *Slavery in Dutch South Africa*. Cambridge: Cambridge University Press, 1985.

————. "Strangers Ashore: Sailor Identity and Social Conflict in Mid-18th Century Cape Town." *Kronos* 33 (November 2007): 72–83.

Worger, William H. "Gods, Warriors, or Kings? Images of the Land in South Africa and New Zealand." *New Zealand Journal of History* 31, no. 1 (1997): 169–88.

Yeomans, Henry. *Alcohol and Moral Regulation: Public Attitudes, Spirited Measures, and Victorian Hangovers.* Bristol: Bristol University Press, 2014.

Young, Gordon. "Early German Settlements in South Australia." *Australian Journal of Historical Archaeology* 3 (1985): 43–55.

Young, Paul. *Globalization and the Great Exhibition: The Victorian New World Order.* Palgrave Studies in Nineteenth-Century Writing and Culture. Basingstoke; New York: Palgrave Macmillan, 2009.

INDEX

Fourie, Johan, 38
free trade, 65, 88, 175, 179, 217
French wine expertise, 45, 49. *See also* huguenots

gamay, 51
geographic indications, 12, 230. *See also* copyright
geography of wine, 50
German migrants, 45, 75, 78, 111, 196–97
Germany, wines from, 162, 199–201, 216, 233
German-style wine. *See* hock
Gibraltar, 239
Gilbey, 96
Giliomee, Hermann, 124
gin, 25, 199–200
Glasgow, 187
gouais, 107, 142–43
grape varieties, choice of, 51, 78, 106–8, 119
grape varieties and varietal wines. *See* individual grapes
Greco-Roman ideas, 2, 42
grenache, 51, 108, 142
Guy, Kolleen, 25

hanepoot. *See* muscat
Hardy, Thomas, 83, 107, 116, 127–28, 223, 227
Harvest Burgundy, 212–13
health, wine and, 36, 79, 92–93, 98, 131, 187
Hermitage, 50–51, 78, 106–8, 130, 229
Hobsbawm, Eric, 201
hock, German-style wine, 35, 75–76, 78, 108, 140, 143, 164
huguenots, 33–34
Hungarian wine, 181, 214, 237
Hunter Valley, 1–2, 49, 114–16, 242

Idle, Eric, 219
Imperial Economic Conference of 1932, 176, 179
India: wine imports, 138, 140–42; wine production, 137, 143
industrial revolution, 25–27
Ireland and the Irish, 26, 101, 111–12, 172, 242
irrigation, 104, 123

Jacob's Creek, 2–3, 236, 240
Johnson, Hugh, 20, 216–17, 235, 248n1

Kashmir, 137
Kelly, Alexander, 107, 109, 112
Khoikhoi people, 31–32, 39, 80
King's College, Cambridge, 162, 198–202
Kohler, C. W., 172–73, 175
KWV, 173, 177–78, 198, 230

labor shortages: in Australia, 45, 101, 103, 111, 197, 288n23; in the Cape, 86, 109, 170; in New Zealand, 195
lambruscat, 107
licensing laws, 93, 97, 125, 149–50, 213; wartime, 161, 164–65, 194–95
liebfraumilch, 215
Liverpool, 46, 65–66, 74
London Missionary Society, 75
Low, David, 194, 198
Ludington, Charles, 28, 64, 68, 71
Lukacs, Paul, 21

MacArthur, John, 48
Madeira, 75, 107–8, 162
Malta, 149–50, 208
Mandela, Nelson, 231
Maori society, 52–58
marists, 56–57, 230
Marks and Spencer, 214–16, 227, 233, 235–36
Marsden, Samuel, 53–54
mataro, 107, 142
Mauritius, 144, 174
McGuigan's, 242
McIntyre, Julie, 46–47, 85
medals and prizes for wines, 76, 183, 32, 125, 131, 143
medicine. *See* health
migration, imperial, 27, 45, 111, 216. *See also* convicts, enslaved people
Milner, Alfred, 122
Minogue, Kylie, 236
missionaries, 23, 53–54, 78. *See also* Church Mission Society, Marists
Montpellier, 50–51, 219
Monty Python, 6, 219
Moody, Jessica, 46

Mouillefert, M. P., 120–21
mourvèdre, 108, 143
Mughal empire, 136–37
Murphy, Hazel, 12
Murray Edwards College (New Hall), 235, 240
muscat grapes, 37, 51, 78

Nasson, Bill, 221
New Hall. See Murray Edwards
Newcastle, Australia, 114, 141

Oddbins, 24, 214, 233, 237
oidium, 118, 124
Old World, definition, 11
overproduction of wine, 170–71, 197–98

parliament (London/Westminster), debates and enquiries, 67–69, 88, 138, 149, 208–9
Parramatta, 44
Penfold's Grange, 108, 113
Penfolds, 128, 211
Phillips, Rod, 30
phylloxera, 118–23, 143
pinot grapes, 51, 106–7, 225, 240
pinotage, 222
plonk, 165–67
port-style wines, 64, 78, 91–93, 143, 152, 162, 169, 172–74, 177, 180, 198, 201–2, 210
Portugal, 43, 64, 89, 160
Pownall, W., 127–28
prisoner of war camps, 67, 97
pruning, 33, 45, 106, 110, 226
public transportation, 114, 188
Punch, 182, 200, 211–12
punches, 7–8, 211
Pym, Barbara, 210

quality, discussions of colonial wine, 32–35, 76–77, 89–96, 171, 212, 219

rationing, 194–95, 210
Rayner, Mary, 38
retail price management, 212–23
Rhône, 50, 78, 107, 119. See also Hermitage
riesling, 107, 162, 215, 226–7. See also hock
Riley, C. V., 121

Robinson, Jancis, 164, 222–23
Roseworthy Agricultural College, 123, 226
Royal Air Force, 192, 199
rugby, 208, 243
Rutherglen, 130, 144

sailors, 35, 43–44, 81
Sainsbury's, 222
Saintsbury Club, 198–99
San peoples, 77
sausage-making, 152
sauvignon blanc, 107, 231
screw-caps, 242
scurvy, 43–44
semillon, 37, 51
Seppelt family, 111, 113, 116, 128, 211
sherry-style wines, 169, 177, 201–2, 207, 209, 212, 228
shipwrecks, 43, 163
shiraz, 51, 107–8, 185, 226. See also Hermitage
six o'clock swill, 224
slavery, importance to winemaking, 38–39, 79–80, 240. See also enslaved people
Smart, Richard, 226
social class, and wine consumption, 4, 27–28, 36, 69–70, 82, 97–99, 233–34
Society of Arts, London, 76, 107, 122
soil: as filth, 79–80, 84, 89, 92; in promoting wine, 131–32, 187; suitability for wine, 34, 80, 57, 69, 73, 137
Solms-Delta, 240
South African Wine Farmers' Association, 209, 212
Southampton, 192, 209
Spain, 15, 50, 68, 71, 133, 228
Spanish-style wine. See sherry
sparkling wine, 162, 184, 198–99, 202, 240
spirits. See individual beverages
St. Helena, 39, 67
steen. See chenin blanc
Stellenbosch, 113, 124, 192, 201–2, 221
Stolen Generation, 219, 233
sulphur, 114, 119, 124
supermarkets and food halls, 183–84, 213–14, 234
sweet wines, 145, 152, 187, 189, 214–25, 233

Sydney, 41, 44, 51, 83, 164
syrah. *See* shiraz

Tallents, Stephen, 190–91, 202–3
tariffs, import: Australian, 100, 104; British, 64–70, 95–101, 133–34, 177, 209, 217; European, 218; New Zealand, 109
Te Kauwhata, 125, 224–25
tea, 18, 21, 28, 79, 136
television, 12, 222, 236; wine advertising on, 207, 212
temperance and abstinence, 81–82, 97–99, 160–61,191; in New Zealand, 164–65, 224
terra nullius, 24, 42
Thudichum, Johann L. W., 91–92, 101–2, 122–23
Tintara, 129, 184, 187
Tokay, 106, 108, 143, 181
tot system. *See* dop system
tourism, 131, 143, 149, 242
trains. *See* public transportation
Trinity Hall, 201
Tuckwell, Charles, 41
Turing, Alan, 201

United States, in wine history, 11, 13, 16–17, 249n14
urbanization, 26, 88, 93, 241

Van der Stel, Simon, 29–34
Van Riebeeck, 31–32
Verdeilho, 107
Victoria Wine Company, 179, 186, 234
VOC, 29, 31–32

Waerenga Wines, 190*fig*9
wages, 11, 114, 149. *See also* dop system
wagons. *See* carts
Westminster. *See* parliament
whisk[e]y, 81, 90, 162, 199–200
Whiteley's, 162–63, 184–86, 212
Wine Australia, 14
wine bands. *See* geography of wine
wine, naming conventions, 35, 75, 130, 142, 185
women, as wine consumers, 7, 182–83, 211, 235
wood. *See* barrels and casks
Wyndham, family, 1–2, 84, 115, 141

Yugoslavian wine, 215–16, 227

Founded in 1893,
UNIVERSITY OF CALIFORNIA PRESS
publishes bold, progressive books and journals
on topics in the arts, humanities, social sciences,
and natural sciences—with a focus on social
justice issues—that inspire thought and action
among readers worldwide.

The UC PRESS FOUNDATION
raises funds to uphold the press's vital role
as an independent, nonprofit publisher, and
receives philanthropic support from a wide
range of individuals and institutions—and from
committed readers like you. To learn more, visit
ucpress.edu/supportus.